Bayesian Methods in Finance

THE FRANK J. FABOZZI SERIES

Fixed Income Securities, Second Edition by Frank J. Fabozzi
Focus on Value: A Corporate and Investor Guide to Wealth Creation by James L. Grand and James A. Abater
Handbook of Global Fixed Income Calculations by Dragomir Krgin
Managing a Corporate Bond Portfolio by Leland E. Crabbe and Frank J. Fabozzi
Real Options and Option-Embedded Securities by William T. Moore
Capital Budgeting: Theory and Practice by Pamela P. Peterson and Frank J. Fabozzi
The Exchange-Traded Funds Manual by Gary L. Gastineau
Professional Perspectives on Fixed Income Portfolio Management, Volume 3 edited by Frank J. Fabozzi
Investing in Emerging Fixed Income Markets edited by Frank J. Fabozzi and Efstathia Pilarinu
Handbook of Alternative Assests by Mark J. P. Anson
The Exchange-Trade Funds Manual by Gary L. Gastineau
The Global Money Markets by Frank J. Fabozzi, Steven V. Mann, and Moorad Choudhry
The Handbook of Financial Instruments edited by Frank J. Fabozzi
Collateralized Debt Obligations: Structures and Analysis by Laurie S. Goodman and Frank J. Fabozzi
Interest Rate, Term Structure, and Valuation Modeling edited by Frank J. Fabozzi
Investment Performance Measurement by Bruce J. Feibel
The Handbook of Equity Style Management edited by T. Daniel Coggin and Frank J. Fabozzi
The Theory and Practice of Investment Management edited by Frank J. Fabozzi and Harry M. Markowitz
Foundations of Economics Value Added: Second Edition by James L. Grant
Financial Management and Analysis: Second Edition by Frank J. Fabozzi and Pamela P. Peterson
Measuring and Controlling Interest Rate and Credit Risk: Second Edition by Frank J. Fabozzi, Steven V. Mann, and Moorad Choudhry
Professional Perspectives on Fixed Income Portfolio Management, Volume 4 edited by Frank J. Fabozzi
The Handbook of European Fixed Income Securities edited by Frank J. Fabozzi and Moorad Choudhry
The Handbook of European Structured Financial Products edited by Frank J. Fabozzi and Moorad Choudhry
The Mathematics of Financial Modeling and Investment Management by Sergio M. Focardi and Frank J. Fabozzi
Short Selling: Strategies, Risk and Rewards edited by Frank J. Fabozzi
The Real Estate Investment Handbook by G. Timothy Haight and Daniel Singer
Market Neutral: Strategies edited by Bruce I. Jacobs and Kenneth N. Levy
Securities Finance: Securities Lending and Repurchase Agreements edited by Frank J. Fabozzi and Steven V. Mann
Fat-Tailed and Skewed Asset Return Distributions by Svetlozar T. Rachev, Christian Menn, and Frank J. Fabozzi
Financial Modeling of the Equity Market: From CAPM to Cointegration by Frank J. Fabozzi, Sergio M. Focardi, and Petter N. Kolm
Advanced Bond Portfolio management: Best Practices in Modeling and Strategies edited by Frank J. Fabozzi, Lionel Martellini, and Philippe Priaulet
Analysis of Financial Statements, Second Edition by Pamela P. Peterson and Frank J. Fabozzi
Collateralized Debt Obligations: Structures and Analysis, Second Edition by Douglas J. Lucas, Laurie S. Goodman, and Frank J. Fabozzi
Handbook of Alternative Assets, Second Edition by Mark J. P. Anson
Introduction to Structured Finance by Frank J. Fabozzi, Henry A. Davis, and Moorad Choudhry
Financial Econometrics by Svetlozar T. Rachev, Stefan Mittnik, Frank J. Fabozzi, Sergio M. Focardi, and Teo Jasic
Developments in Collateralized Debt Obligations: New Products and Insights by Douglas J. Lucas, Laurie S. Goodman, Frank J. Fabozzi, and Rebecca J. Manning
Robust Portfolio Optimization and Management by Frank J. Fabozzi, Peter N. Kolm, Dessislava A. Pachamanova, and Sergio M. Focardi
Advanced Stochastic Models, Risk Assesment, and Portfolio Optimizations by Svetlozar T. Rachev, Stogan V. Stoyanov, and Frank J. Fabozzi
How to Select Investment Managers and Evalute Performance by G. Timothy Haight, Stephen O. Morrell, and Glenn E. Ross
Bayesian Methods in Finance by Svetlozar T. Rachev, John S. J. Hsu, Biliana S. Bagasheva, and Frank J. Fabozzi

Bayesian Methods in Finance

SVETLOZAR T. RACHEV
JOHN S. J. HSU
BILIANA S. BAGASHEVA
FRANK J. FABOZZI

WILEY

John Wiley & Sons, Inc.

Published by John Wiley & Sons, Inc., Hoboken, New Jersey.
Published simultaneously in Canada.

For general information on our other products and services or for technical support, please contact our Customer Care Department within the United States at (800) 762-2974, outside the United States at (317) 572-3993, or fax (317) 572-4002.

Wiley also publishes its books in a variety of electronic formats. Some content that appears in print may not be available in electronic books. For more information about Wiley products, visit our Web site at www.wiley.com.

ISBN: 978-0-471-92083-0

Printed in the United States of America.

10 9 8 7 6 5 4 3 2 1

S.T.R.
To Iliana and Zoya

J.S.J.H.
To Serene, Justin, and Andrew

B.S.B.
To my mother, Gökhan, and my other loved ones

F.J.F.
To my wife Donna and my children Francesco,
Patricia, and Karly

Contents

Preface

This book provides the fundamentals of Bayesian methods and their applications to students in finance and practitioners in the financial services sector. Our objective is to explain the concepts and techniques that can be applied in real-world Bayesian applications to financial problems. While statistical modeling has been used in finance for the last four or five decades, recent years have seen an impressive growth in the variety of models and modeling techniques used in finance, particularly in portfolio management and risk management. As part of this trend, Bayesian methods are enjoying a rediscovery by academics and practitioners alike and growing in popularity. The choice of topics in this book reflects the current major developments of Bayesian applications to risk management and portfolio management.

Three fundamental factors are behind the increased adoption of Bayesian methods by the financial community. Bayesian methods provide (1) a theoretically sound framework for combining various sources of information; (2) a robust estimation setting that incorporates explicitly estimation risk; and (3) the flexibility to handle complex and realistic models. We believe this book is the first of its kind to present and discuss Bayesian financial applications. The fundamentals of Bayesian analysis and Markov Chain Monte Carlo are covered in Chapters 2 through 5 and the applications are introduced in the remaining chapters. Each application presentation begins with the basics, works through the frequentist perspective, followed by the Bayesian treatment.

The applications include:

- The Bayesian approach to mean-variance portfolio selection and its advantages over the frequentist approach (Chapters 6 and 7).
- A general framework for reflecting degrees of belief in an asset pricing model when selecting the optimal portfolio (Chapters 6 and 7).
- Bayesian methods to portfolio selection within the context of the Black-Litterman model and extensions to it (Chapter 8).
- Computing measures of market efficiency and the way predictability influences optimal portfolio selection (Chapter 9).

- Volatility modeling (ARCH-type and SV models) focusing on the various numerical methods available for Bayesian estimation (Chapters 10, 11, and 12).
- Advanced techniques for model selection, notably in the setting of nonnormality of stock returns (Chapter 13).
- Multifactor models of stock returns, including risk attribution in both an analytical and a numerical setting (Chapter 14).

ACKNOWLEDGMENTS

We thank several individuals for their assistance in various aspects of this project. Thomas Leonard provided us with guidance on several theoretical issues that we encountered. Doug Steigerwald of the University of California–Santa Barbara directed us in the preparation of the discussion on the efficient methods of moments in Chapter 10.

Svetlozar Rachev gratefully acknowledges research support by grants from Division of Mathematical, Life and Physical Sciences, College of Letters and Science, University of California–Santa Barbara; the Deutschen Forschungsgemeinschaft; and the Deutscher Akademischer Austausch Dienst. Biliana Bagasheva gratefully acknowledges the support of the Fulbright Program at the Institute of International Education and the Department of Statistics and Applied Probability, University of California–Santa Barbara. Lastly, Frank Fabozzi gratefully acknowledges the support of Yale's International Center for Finance.

Svetlozar T. Rachev
John S. J. Hsu
Biliana S. Bagasheva
Frank J. Fabozzi

About the Authors

Svetlozar (Zari) T. Rachev completed his Ph.D. degree in 1979 from Moscow State (Lomonosov) University and his doctor of science degree in 1986 from Steklov Mathematical Institute in Moscow. Currently, he is chair-professor in statistics, econometrics and mathematical finance at the University of Karlsruhe in the School of Economics and Business Engineering. He is also Professor Emeritus at the University of California–Santa Barbara in the Department of Statistics and Applied Probability. He has published seven monographs, eight handbooks, and special-edited volumes, and over 250 research articles. His recently coauthored books published by John Wiley & Sons in mathematical finance and financial econometrics include *Financial Econometrics: From Basics to Advanced Modeling Techniques* (2007); *Operational Risk: A Guide to Basel II Capital Requirements, Models, and Analysis* (2007); and *Advanced Stochastic Models, Risk Assessment and Portfolio Optimization: The Ideal Risk, Uncertainty, and Performance Measures* (2008). Professor Rachev is cofounder of Bravo Risk Management Group specializing in financial risk-management software. Bravo Group was recently acquired by FinAnalytica, for which he currently serves as chief-scientist.

John S. J. Hsu is professor of statistics and applied probability at the University of California, Santa Barbara. He is also a faculty member in the University's Center for Research in Financial Mathematics and Statistics. He obtained his Ph.D. in statistics with a minor in business from the University of Wisconsin–Madison in 1990. Professor Hsu has published numerous papers and coauthored a Cambridge University Press advanced series text, *Bayesian Methods: An Analysis for Statisticians and Interdisciplinary Researchers* (1999), with Thomas Leonard.

Biliana S. Bagasheva completed her Ph.D. in Statistics at the University of California–Santa Barbara. Her research interests include risk management, portfolio construction, Bayesian methods, and financial econometrics. Currently, Biliana is a consultant in London.

Frank J. Fabozzi is Professor in the Practice of Finance in the School of Management at Yale University. Prior to joining the Yale faculty, he was a visiting professor of finance in the Sloan School at MIT. He is a Fellow of the International Center for Finance at Yale University and on the Advisory Council for the Department of Operations Research and

Financial Engineering at Princeton University. Professor Fabozzi is the editor of the *Journal of Portfolio Management*. His recently coauthored books published by John Wiley & Sons in mathematical finance and financial econometrics include *The Mathematics of Financial Modeling and Investment Management* (2004); *Financial Modeling of the Equity Market: From CAPM to Cointegration* (2006); *Robust Portfolio Optimization and Management* (2007); and *Advanced Stochastic Models, Risk Assessment, and Portfolio Optimization: The Ideal Risk, Uncertainty and Performance Measures* (2008). He earned a doctorate in economics from the City University of New York in 1972. In 2002, he was inducted into the Fixed Income Analysts Society's Hall of Fame and is the 2007 recipient of the C. Stewart Sheppard Award given by the CFA Institute. He earned the designation of Chartered Financial Analyst and Certified Public Accountant. He has authored and edited numerous books in finance.

Bayesian Methods in Finance

CHAPTER 1

Introduction

Quantitative financial models describe in mathematical terms the relationships between financial random variables through time and/or across assets. The fundamental assumption is that the model relationship is valid independent of the time period or the asset class under consideration. Financial data contain both meaningful information and random noise. An adequate financial model not only extracts optimally the relevant information from the historical data but also performs well when tested with new data. The uncertainty brought about by the presence of data noise makes imperative the use of statistical analysis as part of the process of financial model building, model evaluation, and model testing.

Statistical analysis is employed from the vantage point of either of the two main statistical philosophical traditions—"frequentist" and "Bayesian." An important difference between the two lies with the interpretation of the concept of probability. As the name suggests, advocates of frequentist statistics adopt a *frequentist* interpretation: The probability of an event is the limit of its long-run relative frequency (i.e., the frequency with which it occurs as the amount of data increases without bound). Strict adherence to this interpretation is not always possible in practice. When studying rare events, for instance, large samples of data may not be available and in such cases proponents of frequentist statistics resort to theoretical results. The Bayesian view of the world is based on the *subjectivist* interpretation of probability: Probability is subjective, a degree of belief that is updated as information or data are acquired.[1]

[1]The concept of subjective probability is derived from arguments for rationality of the preferences of agents. It originated in the 1930s with the (independent) works of Bruno de Finetti and Frank Ramsey, and was further developed by Leonard Savage and Dennis Lindley. The subjective probability interpretation can be traced back to the Scottish philosopher and economist David Hume, who also had philosophical influence over Harry Markowitz (by Markowitz's own words in his autobiography

Closely related to the concept of probability is that of uncertainty. Proponents of the frequentist approach consider the source of uncertainty to be the randomness inherent in realizations of a random variable. The probability distributions of variables are not subject to uncertainty. In contrast, Bayesian statistics treats probability distributions as uncertain and subject to modification as new information becomes available. Uncertainty is implicitly incorporated by probability updating. The probability beliefs based on the existing knowledge base take the form of the *prior probability*. The *posterior probability* represents the updated beliefs.

Since the beginning of last century, when quantitative methods and models became a mainstream tool to aid in understanding financial markets and formulating investment strategies, the framework applied in finance has been the frequentist approach. The term "frequentist" usually refers to the Fisherian philosophical approach named after Sir Ronald Fisher. Strictly speaking, "Fisherian" has a broader meaning as it includes not only frequentist statistical concepts such as unbiased estimators, hypothesis tests, and confidence intervals, but also the maximum likelihood estimation framework pioneered by Fisher. Only in the last two decades has Bayesian statistics started to gain greater acceptance in financial modeling, despite its introduction about 250 years ago by Thomas Bayes, a British minister and mathematician. It has been the advancements of computing power and the development of new computational methods that has fostered the growing use of Bayesian statistics in finance.

On the applicability of the Bayesian conceptual framework, consider an excerpt from the speech of former chairman of the Board of Governors of the Federal Reserve System, Alan Greenspan:

> *The Federal Reserve's experiences over the past two decades make it clear that uncertainty is not just a pervasive feature of the monetary policy landscape; it is the defining characteristic of that landscape. The term "uncertainty" is meant here to encompass both "Knightian uncertainty," in which the probability distribution of outcomes is unknown, and "risk," in which uncertainty of outcomes is delimited by a known probability distribution. [...] This conceptual framework emphasizes understanding as much as possible the many sources of risk and uncertainty that policymakers face, quantifying those risks when possible, and assessing the costs associated with each of the risks. In essence, the risk management*

published in *Les Prix Nobel* (1991)). Holton (2004) provides a historical background of the development of the concepts of risk and uncertainty.

> *approach to monetary policymaking is an application of Bayesian [decision-making].*[2]

The three steps of Bayesian decision making that Alan Greenspan outlines are:

1. Formulating the prior probabilities to reflect existing information.
2. Constructing the quantitative model, taking care to incorporate the uncertainty intrinsic in model assumptions.
3. Selecting and evaluating a utility function describing how uncertainty affects alternative model decisions.

While these steps constitute the rigorous approach to Bayesian decision-making, applications of Bayesian methods to financial modeling often only involve the first two steps or even only the second step. This tendency is a reflection of the pragmatic Bayesian approach that researchers of empirical finance often favor and it is the approach that we adopt in this book.

The aim of the book is to provide an overview of the theory of Bayesian methods and explain their applications to financial modeling. While the principles and concepts explained in the book can be used in financial modeling and decision making in general, our focus will be on portfolio management and market risk management since these are the areas in finance where Bayesian methods have had the greatest penetration to date.[3]

A FEW NOTES ON NOTATION

Throughout the book, we follow the convention of denoting vectors and matrices in boldface.

We make extensive use of the proportionality symbol, '$\propto$', to denote the cases where terms constant with respect to the random variable of interest have been dropped from that variable's density function. To illustrate, suppose that the random variable, $\mathbf{X}$, has a density function

$$p(x) = 2x. \tag{1.1}$$

[2]Alan Greenspan made these remarks at the Meetings of the American Statistical Association in San Diego, California, January 3, 2004.

[3]Bayesian methods have been applied in corporate finance, particularly in capital budgeting. An area of Bayesian methods with potentially important financial applications is Bayesian networks. Bayesian networks have been applied in operational risk modeling. See, for example, Alexander (2000) and Neil, Fenton, and Tailor (2005).

Then, we can write

$$p(x) \propto x. \tag{1.2}$$

Now suppose that we take the logarithm of both sides of (1.2). Since the logarithm of a product of two terms is equivalent to the sum of the logarithms of those terms, we obtain

$$\log(p(x)) = \text{const} + \log(x), \tag{1.3}$$

where *const* = log(2) in this case. Notice that it would not be precise to write $\log(p(x)) \propto \log(x)$. We come across the transformation in (1.3) in Chapters 10 through 14, in particular.

OVERVIEW

The book is organized as follows. In Chapters 2 through 5, we provide an overview of the theory of Bayesian methods. The depth and scope of that overview are subordinated to the methodological requirements of the Bayesian applications discussed in later chapters and, therefore, in certain instances lacks the theoretical rigor that one would expect to find in a purely statistical discussion of the topic.

In Chapters 6 and 7, we discuss the Bayesian approach to mean-variance portfolio selection and its advantages over the frequentist approach. We introduce a general framework for reflecting degrees of belief in an asset pricing model when selecting the optimal portfolio. We close Chapter 7 with a description of Bayesian model averaging, which allows the decision maker to combine conclusions based on several competing quantitative models.

Chapter 8 discusses an emblematic application of Bayesian methods to portfolio selection—the Black-Litterman model. We then show how the Black-Litterman framework can be extended to active portfolio selection and how trading strategies can be incorporated into it.

The focus of Chapter 9 is market efficiency and predictability. We analyze and illustrate the computation of measures of market inefficiency. Then, we go on to describe the way predictability influences optimal portfolio selection. We base that discussion on a Bayesian *vector autoregressive* (VAR) framework.

Chapters 10, 11, and 12 deal with volatility modeling. We devote Chapter 10 to an overview of volatility modeling. We introduce the two types of volatility models—*autoregressive conditionally heteroskedastic* (ARCH)-type models and *stochastic volatility* (SV) models—and discuss some of their important characteristics, along with issues of estimation within the boundaries of frequentist statistics. Chapters 11 and 12 cover, respectively, ARCH-type and SV Bayesian model estimation. Our focus is on the various numerical methods that could be used in Bayesian estimation.

In Chapter 13, we deal with advanced techniques for model selection, notably, recognizing nonnormality of stock returns. We first investigate an approach in which higher moments of the return distribution are explicitly included in the investor's utility function. We then go on to discuss an extension of the Black-Litterman framework that, in particular, employs minimization of the conditional *value-at-risk* (CVaR). In Appendix A of that chapter, we present an overview of risk measures that are alternatives to the standard deviation, such as *value-at-risk* (VaR) and CVaR.

Chapter 14 is devoted to multifactor models of stock returns. We discuss risk attribution in both an analytical and a numerical setting and examine how the multifactor framework provides a natural setting for a coherent portfolio selection and risk management approach.

CHAPTER 2

The Bayesian Paradigm

Likelihood Function and Bayes' Theorem

One of the basic mechanisms of learning is assimilating the information arriving from the external environment and then updating the existing knowledge base with that information. This mechanism lies at the heart of the Bayesian framework. A Bayesian decision maker learns by revising beliefs in light of the new data that become available. From the Bayesian point of view, probabilities are interpreted as degrees of belief. Therefore, the Bayesian learning process consists of revising of probabilities.[1] Bayes' theorem provides the formal means of putting that mechanism into action; it is a simple expression combining the knowledge about the distribution of the model parameters and the information about the parameters contained in the data.

In this chapter, we present some of the basic principles of Bayesian analysis.

THE LIKELIHOOD FUNCTION

Suppose we are interested in analyzing the returns on a given stock and have available a historical record of returns. Any analysis of these returns, beyond a very basic one, would require that we make an educated guess about (propose) a process that might have generated these return data. Assume that we have decided on some statistical distribution and denote it by

$$p\left(y \mid \theta\right), \tag{2.1}$$

[1]Contrast this with the way probability is interpreted in the classical (frequentist) statistical theory—as the relative frequency of occurrence of an event in the limit, as the number of observations goes to infinity.

where y is a realization of the random variable Y (stock return) and θ is a parameter specific to the distribution, p. Assuming that the distribution we proposed is the one that generated the observed data, we draw a conclusion about the value of θ. Obviously, central to that goal is our ability to summarize the information contained in the data. The likelihood function is a statistical construct with this precise role. Denote the n observed stock returns by $y_1, y_2, \ldots, y_n$. The joint density function of Y, for a given value of θ, is[2]

$$f(y_1, y_2, \ldots, y_n \mid \theta).$$

We can observe that the function above can also be treated as a function of the unknown parameter, θ, given the observed stock returns. That function of θ is called *the likelihood function*. We write it as

$$L(\theta \mid y_1, y_2, \ldots, y_n) = f(y_1, y_2, \ldots, y_n \mid \theta). \tag{2.2}$$

Suppose we have determined from the data two competing values of θ, θ_1 and θ_2, and want to determine which one is more likely to be the true value (at least, which one is closer to the true value). The likelihood function helps us make that decision. Assuming that our data were indeed generated by the distribution in (2.1), θ_1 is more likely than θ_2 to be the true parameter value whenever $L(y_1, y_2, \ldots, y_n \mid \theta_1) > L(y_1, y_2, \ldots, y_n \mid \theta_2)$. This observation provides the intuition behind the method most often employed in "classical" statistical inference to estimate θ from the data alone—*the method of maximum likelihood*. The value of θ most likely to have yielded the observed sample of stock return data, $y_1, y_2, \ldots, y_n$, is *the maximum likelihood estimate*, $\widehat{\theta}$, obtained from maximizing the likelihood function in (2.2).

To illustrate the concept of a likelihood function, we briefly discuss two examples—one based on the Poisson distribution (a discrete distribution) and another based on the normal distribution (one of the most commonly employed continuous distributions).

The Poisson Distribution Likelihood Function

The Poisson distribution is often used to describe the random number of events occurring within a certain period of time. It has a single parameter,

---

[2]By using the term "density function," we implicitly assume that the distribution chosen for the stock return is continuous, which is invariably the case in financial modeling.

θ, indicating the rate of occurrence of the random event, that is, how many events happen on average per unit of time. The probability distribution of a Poisson random variable, X, is described by the following expression:[3]

$$p\left(X = k\right) = \frac{\theta^k}{k!}e^{-\theta}, \qquad k = 0, 1, 2, \ldots. \tag{2.3}$$

Suppose we are interested to examine the annual number of defaults of North American corporate bond issuers and we have gathered a sample of data for the period from 1986 through 2005. Assume that these corporate defaults occur according to a Poisson distribution. Denoting the 20 observations by $x_1, x_2, \ldots, x_{20}$, we write the likelihood function for the Poisson parameter θ(the average rate of defaults) as[4]

$$\begin{aligned} L\left(\theta \mid x_1, x_2, \ldots, x_{20}\right) &= \prod_{i=1}^{20} p(X = x_i \mid \theta) = \prod_{i=1}^{20} \frac{\theta^{x_i}}{x_i!}e^{-\theta} \\ &= \frac{\theta^{\sum_{i=1}^{20} x_i}}{\prod_{i=1}^{20} x_i!}e^{-20\theta}. \end{aligned} \tag{2.4}$$

As we see in later chapters, it is often customary to retain in the expressions for the likelihood function and the probability distributions only the terms that contain the unknown parameter(s); that is, we get rid of the terms that are constant with respect to the parameter(s). Thus, (2.4) could be written as

$$L\left(\theta \mid x_1, x_2, \ldots, x_{20}\right) \propto \theta^{\sum_{i=1}^{20} x_i} e^{-20\theta}, \tag{2.5}$$

where $\propto$ denotes "proportional to." Clearly, for a given sample of data, the expressions in (2.4) and (2.5) are proportional to each other and therefore contain the same information about θ. Maximizing either of them with

[3]The Poisson distribution is employed in the context of finance (most often, but not exclusively, in the areas of credit risk and operational risk) as the distribution of a stochastic process, called *the Poisson process*, which governs the occurrences of random events.

[4]In this example, we assume, perhaps unrealistically, that θ stays constant through time and that the annual number of defaults in a given year is independent from the number of defaults in any other year within the 20-year period. The independence assumption means that each observation of the number of annual defaults is regarded as a realization from a Poisson distribution with the same average rate of defaults, θ; this allows us to represent the likelihood function as the product of the mass function at each observation.

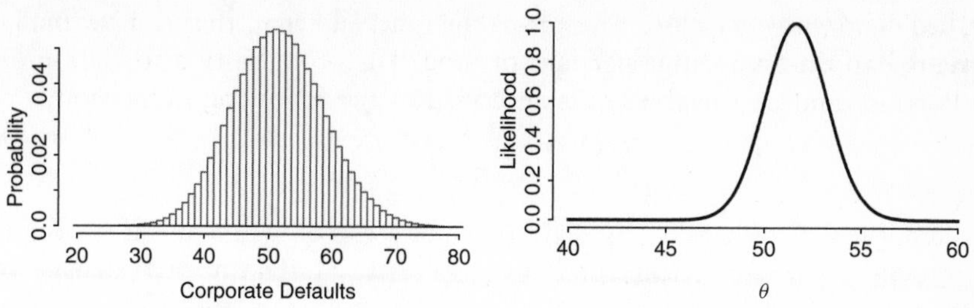

EXHIBIT 2.1 The poisson distribution function and likelihood function
Note: The graph on the left-hand side represents the plot of the distribution function of the Poisson random variable evaluated at the maximum-likelihood estimate, $\widehat{\theta} = 51.6$. The graph on the right-hand side represents the plot of the likelihood function for the parameter of the Poisson distribution.

respect to θ, we obtain that the maximum likelihood estimator of the Poisson parameter, θ, is the sample mean, $\overline{x}$:

$$\widehat{\theta} = \overline{x} = \frac{\sum_{i=1}^{20} x_i}{20}.$$

For the 20 observations of annual corporate defaults, we get a sample mean of 51.6. The Poisson probability distribution function (evaluated at θ equal to its maximum-likelihood estimate, $\widehat{\theta} = 51.6$) and the likelihood function for θ can be visualized, respectively, in the left-hand-side and right-hand-side plots in Exhibit 2.1.

The Normal Distribution Likelihood Function

The normal distribution (also called the *Gaussian distribution*) has been the predominant distribution of choice in finance because of the relative ease of dealing with it and the availability of attractive theoretical results resting on it.[5] It is certainly one of the most important distributions in statistics. Two parameters describe the normal distribution—the location parameter, μ, which is also its mean, and the scale (dispersion) parameter, σ, also

[5] For example, in an introductory course in statistics students are told of the Central Limit Theorem, which asserts that (under some conditions) the sum of independent random variables has a normal distribution as the terms of the sum become infinitely many.

called *standard deviation*. The probability density function of a normally distributed random variable Y is expressed as

$$f(y) = \frac{1}{\sqrt{2\pi}\sigma} e^{-\frac{(y-\mu)^2}{2\sigma^2}}, \tag{2.6}$$

where y and μ could take any real value and σ can only take positive values. We denote the distribution of Y by $Y \sim N(\mu, \sigma)$. The normal density is symmetric around the mean, μ, and its plot resembles a bell.

Suppose we have gathered daily dollar return data on the MSCI-Germany Index for the period January 2, 1998, through December 31, 2003 (a total of 1,548 returns), and we assume that the daily return is normally distributed. Then, given the realized index returns (denoted by y_1, $y_2, \ldots, y_{1548}$), the likelihood function for the parameters μ and σ is written in the following way:

$$\begin{aligned} L(\mu, \sigma \mid y_1, y_2, \ldots, y_{1548}) &= \prod_{i=1}^{1548} f(y_i) \\ &= \left(\frac{1}{\sqrt{2\pi}\sigma}\right)^{1548} e^{-\sum_{i=1}^{1548} \frac{(y_i-\mu)^2}{\sigma^2}} \\ &\propto \sigma^{-1548} e^{-\sum_{i=1}^{1548} \frac{(y_i-\mu)^2}{\sigma^2}}. \end{aligned} \tag{2.7}$$

We again implicitly assume that the MSCI-Germany index returns are independently and identically distributed (i.i.d.), that is, each daily return is a realization from a normal distribution with the same mean and standard deviation.

In the case of the normal distribution, since the likelihood is a function of two arguments, we can visualize it with a three-dimensional surface as in Exhibit 2.2. It is also useful to plot the so-called contours of the likelihood, which we obtain by "slicing" the shape in Exhibit 2.2 horizontally at various levels of the likelihood. Each contour corresponds to a pair of parameter values (and the respective likelihood value). In Exhibit 2.3, for example, we could observe that the pair $(\mu, \sigma) = (-0.23e-3, 0.31e-3)$, with a likelihood value of 0.6, is more likely than the pair $(\mu, \sigma) = (0.096e-3, 0.33e-3)$, with a likelihood value of 0.1, since the corresponding likelihood is larger.

THE BAYES' THEOREM

Bayes' theorem is the cornerstone of the Bayesian framework. Formally, it is a result from introductory probability theory, linking the unconditional

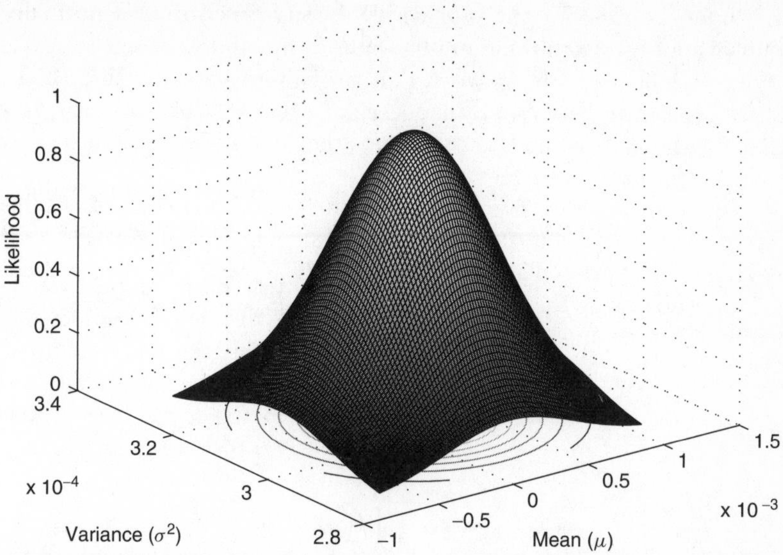

EXHIBIT 2.2 The likelihood function for the parameters of the normal distribution

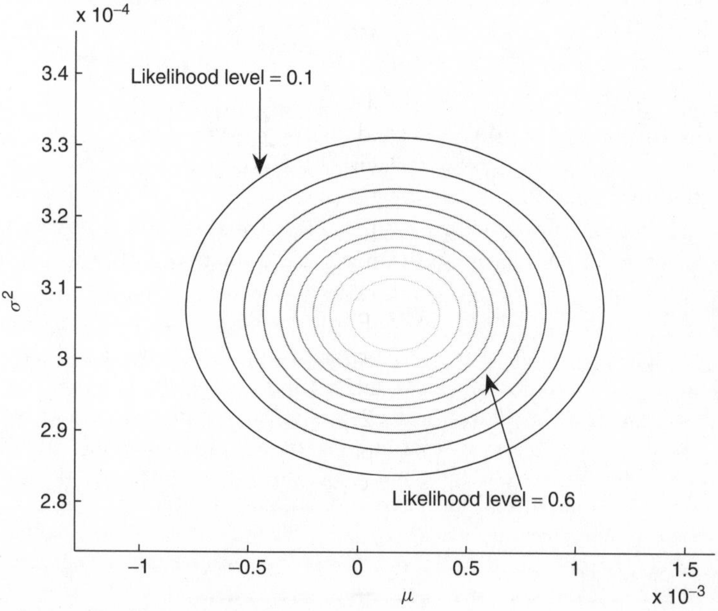

EXHIBIT 2.3 The likelihood function for the parameters of the normal distribution: contour plot

distribution of a random variable with its conditional distribution. For Bayesian proponents, it is the representation of the philosophical principle underlying the Bayesian framework that probability is a measure of the degree of belief one has about an uncertain event.[6] Bayes' theorem is a rule that can be used to update the beliefs that one holds in light of new information (for example, observed data).

We first consider the discrete version of Bayes' theorem. Denote the evidence prior to observing the data by E and suppose that a researcher's belief in it can be expressed as the probability $P(E)$. The Bayes' theorem tells us that, after observing the data, D, the belief in E is adjusted according to the following expression:

$$P(E \mid D) = \frac{P(D \mid E) \times P(E)}{P(D)}, \tag{2.8}$$

where:

1. $P(D \mid E)$ is the conditional probability of the data given that the prior evidence, E, is true.
2. $P(D)$ is the unconditional (marginal) probability of the data, $P(D) > 0$; that is, the probability of D irrespective of E, also expressed as

$$P(D) = P(D \mid E) \times P(E) + P(D \mid E^c) \times P(E^c),$$

where the subscript c denotes a complementary event.[7]

The probability of E before seeing the data, $P(E)$, is called the *prior probability*, whereas the updated probability, $P(E \mid D)$, is called the *posterior probability*.[8] Notice that the magnitude of the adjustment of the prior

---

[6]Even among Bayesians there are those who do not entirely agree with the subjective flavor this probability interpretation carries and attempt to "objectify" probability and the inference process (in the sense of espousing the requirement that if two individuals possess the same evidence regarding a source of uncertainty, they should make the same inference about it). Representatives of this school of Bayesian thought are, among others, Harold Jeffreys, José Bernardo, and James Berger.
[7]The complement (complementary event) of E, E^c, includes all possible outcomes that could occur if E is not realized. The probabilities of an event and its complement always sum up to 1: $P(E) + P(E^c) = 1$.
[8]The expression in (2.6) is easily generalized to the case when a researcher updates beliefs about one of many mutually exclusive events (such that two or more of them occur at the same time). Denote these events by $E_1, E_2, \ldots, E_K$. The events are such

probability, $P(E)$, after observing the data is given by the ratio $P(D \mid E)/P(D)$. The conditional probability, $P(D \mid E)$, when considered as a function of E is in fact the likelihood function, as will become clear further below.

As an illustration, consider a manager in an event-driven hedge fund. The manager is testing a strategy that involves identifying potential acquisition targets and examines the effectiveness of various company screens, in particular the ratio of stock price to free cash flow per share (PFCF). Let us define the following events:

D = Company X's PFCF has been more than three times lower than the sector average for the past three years.
E = Company X becomes an acquisition target in the course of a given year.

Independently of the screen, the manager assesses the probability of company X being targeted at 40%. That is, denoting by E^c the event that X does not become a target in the course of the year, we have

$$P(E) = 0.4$$

and

$$P(E^c) = 0.6.$$

Suppose further that the manager's analysis suggests that the probability a target company's PFCF has been more than three times lower than the sector average for the past three years is 75% while the probability that a nontarget company has been having that low of a PFCF for the past three years is 35%:

$$P(D \mid E) = 0.75$$

and

$$P(D \mid E^c) = 0.35.$$

---

that their probabilities sum up to 1: $P(E_1) + \cdots + P(E_K) = 1$. Bayes' theorem then takes the form

$$P(E_k \mid D) = \frac{P(D \mid E_k) \times P(E_k)}{P(D \mid E_1) \times P(E_1) + P(D \mid E_2) \times P(E_2) + \cdots + P(D \mid E_K) \times P(E_K)}$$

for $k = 1, \ldots, K$ and $P(D) > 0$.

If a bidder does appear on the scene, what is the chance that the targeted company had been detected by the manager's screen? To answer this question, the manager needs to update the prior probability $P(E)$ and compute the posterior probability $P(E \mid D)$. Applying (2.8), we obtain

$$\begin{aligned} P(E \mid D) &= \frac{0.75 \times 0.4}{0.75 \times 0.4 + 0.35 \times 0.6} \\ &\approx 0.59. \end{aligned} \tag{2.9}$$

After taking into account the company's persistently low PFCF, the probability of a takeover increases from 40% to 59%.

In financial applications, the continuous version of the Bayes' theorem (as follows later) is predominantly used. Nevertheless, the discrete form has some important uses, two of which we briefly outline now.

Bayes' Theorem and Model Selection

The usual approach to modeling of a financial phenomenon is to specify the analytical and distributional properties of a process that one thinks generated the observed data and treat this process as if it were the true one. Clearly, in doing so, one introduces a certain amount of error into the estimation process. Accounting for model risk might be no less important than accounting for (within-model) parameter uncertainty, although it seems to preoccupy researchers less often.

One usually entertains a small number of models as plausible ones. The idea of applying the Bayes' theorem to model selection is to combine the information derived from the data with the prior beliefs one has about the degree of model validity. One can then select the single "best" model with the highest posterior probability and rely on the inference provided by it or one can weigh the inference of each model by its posterior probability and obtain an "averaged-out" conclusion. In Chapter 6, we discuss in detail Bayesian model selection and averaging.

Bayes' Theorem and Classification

Classification refers to assigning an object, based on its characteristics, into one out of several categories. It is most often applied in the area of credit and insurance risk, when a creditor (an insurer) attempts to determine the creditworthiness (riskiness) of a potential borrower (policyholder). Classification is a statistical problem because of the existence of information asymmetry—the creditor's (insurer's) aim is to determine with very high probability the unknown status of the borrower (policyholder). For example, suppose that a bank would like to rate a borrower into one of three categories: low risk (L), medium risk (M), and high risk (H). It collects data on the borrower's characteristics such as the current ratio, the debt-to-equity ratio, the interest coverage ratio, and the return on capital. Denote these observed data by the four-dimensional vector y. The dynamics of y depends on the borrower's category and is described by one of three (multivariate) distributions,

$$f(y \mid C = L),$$
$$f(y \mid C = M),$$

or

$$f(y \mid C = H),$$

where C is a random variable describing the category. Let the bank's belief about the borrower's category be π_i, where

$$\pi_1 = \pi(C = L),$$
$$\pi_2 = \pi(C = M),$$

and

$$\pi_3 = \pi(C = H).$$

The discrete version of Bayes' theorem can be employed to evaluate the posterior (updated) probability, $\pi(C = i \mid y)$, $i = L, M, H$, that the borrower belongs to each of the three categories.[9]

Let us now take our first steps in illustrating how Bayes' theorem helps in making inferences about an unknown distribution parameter.

Bayesian Inference for the Binomial Probability

Suppose we are interested in analyzing the dynamic properties of the intraday price changes for a stock. In particular, we want to evaluate the probability of consecutive trade-by-trade price increases. In an oversimplified scenario, this problem could be formalized as a binomial experiment.

---

[9] See the appendix to Chapter 3 for details on the logistic regression, one of the most commonly used econometric models in credit-risk analysis.

The binomial experiment is a setting in which the source of randomness is a binary one (only takes on two alternative modes/states) and the probability of both states is constant throughout.[10] The binomial random variable is the number of occurrences of the state of interest. In our illustration, the two states are "the consecutive trade-by-trade price change is an increase" and "the consecutive trade-by-trade price change is a decrease or null." The random variable is the number of consecutive price increases. Denote it by X. Denote the probability of a consecutive increase by θ. Our goal is to draw a conclusion about the unknown probability, θ.

As an illustration, we consider the transaction data for the AT&T stock during the two-month period from January 4, 1993, through February 26, 1993 (a total of 55,668 price records). The diagram in Exhibit 2.4 shows how we define the binomial random variable given six price observations, $P_1, \ldots, P_6$. (Notice that the realizations of the random variable are one less than the number of price records.) A consecutive price increase is "encoded" as $A = 2$ and its probability is $\theta = P(A = 2)$; all other realizations of A ($A = -2, -1, 0$ or 1) have a probability of $1 - \theta$. We say that the number of

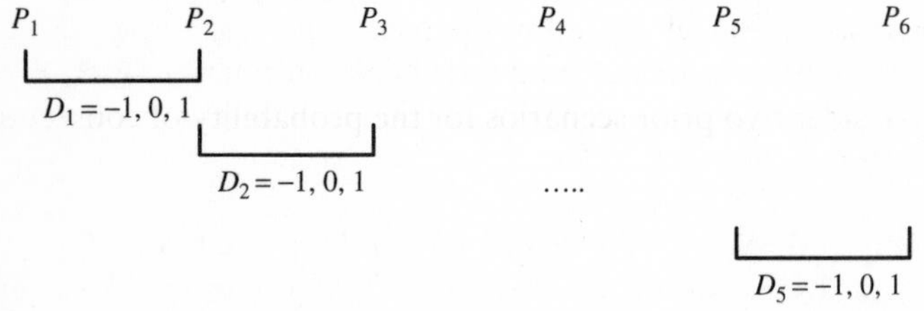

where

$$D_i = -1 \quad \text{if } P_{i+1} < P_i$$
$$D_i = 0 \quad \text{if } P_{i+1} = P_i$$
$$D_i = 1 \quad \text{if } P_{i+1} > P_i$$

$$A_1 = D_1 + D_2$$
$$A_2 = D_2 + D_3$$
$$\ldots$$
$$A_4 = D_4 + D_5$$

Note: X = number of occurences of $A = 2$ within the sample period

EXHIBIT 2.4 The number of consecutive trade-by-trade price increases

[10]The binomial experiment is formally characterized by these and a few additional requirements. As a reference, see any introductory statistics text.

consecutive price increases, X, is distributed as a binomial random variable with parameter θ. The probability mass function of X is represented by the expression

$$P(X = x \mid \theta) = \binom{n}{x} \theta^x (1-\theta)^{n-x},$$
$$x = 0, 1, 2, \ldots, n, \tag{2.10}$$

where n is the sample size (the number of trade-by-trade price changes; a price change could be zero) and $\binom{n}{x} = \frac{n!}{x!(n-x)!}$. During the sample period, there are $X = 176$ trade-by-trade consecutive price increases. This information is embodied in the likelihood function for θ:

$$L\big(\theta \mid X = 176\big) = \theta^{176}(1-\theta)^{55667-176}. \tag{2.11}$$

We would like to combine that information with our prior belief about what the probability of a consecutive price increase is. Before we do that, we recall the notational convention we stick to throughout the book. We denote the prior distribution of an unknown parameter θ by $\pi(\theta)$, the posterior distribution of θ by $\pi(\theta|\text{data})$, and the likelihood function by $L(\theta \mid \text{data})$.

We consider two prior scenarios for the probability of consecutive price increases, θ:

1. We do not have any particular belief about the probability θ. Then, the prior distribution could be represented by a uniform distribution on the interval [0, 1]. Note that this prior assumption implies an expected value for θ of 0.5. The density function of θ is given by

$$\pi(\theta) = 1, \qquad 0 \le \theta \le 1.$$

2. Our intuition suggests that the probability of a consecutive price increase is around 2%. A possible choice of a prior distribution for θ is the beta distribution.[11] The density function of θ is then written as

$$\pi(\theta \mid \alpha, \beta) = \frac{1}{B(\alpha, \beta)} \theta^{\alpha-1}(1-\theta)^{\beta-1}, \qquad 0 \le \theta \le 1, \tag{2.12}$$

[11]The beta distribution is the conjugate distribution for the parameter, θ, of the binomial distribution. See Chapter 3 for more details on conjugate prior distributions.

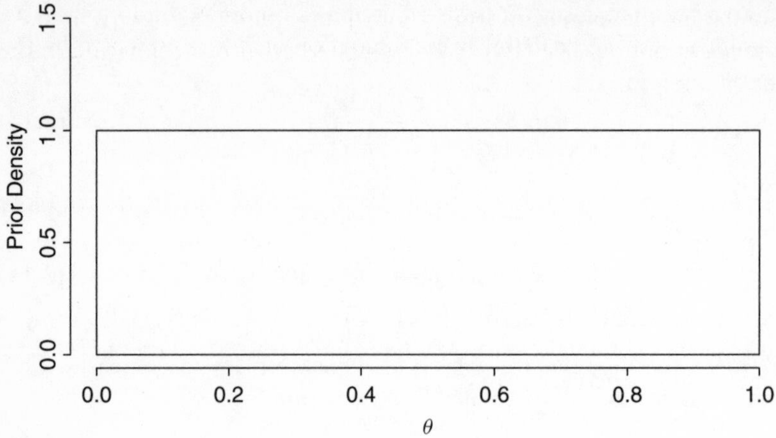

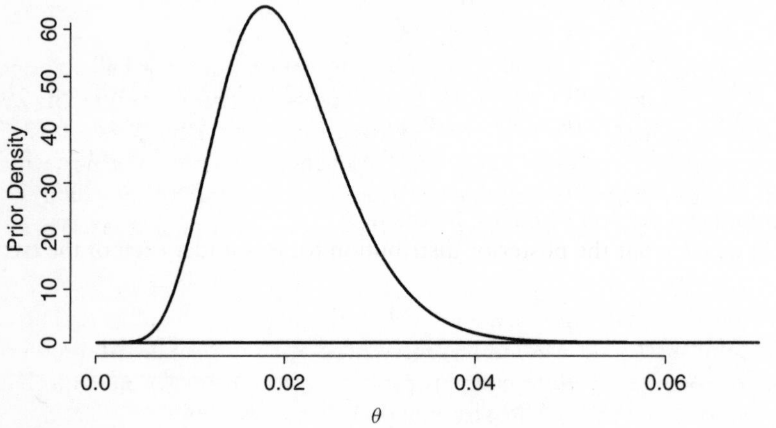

EXHIBIT 2.5 Density curves of the two prior distributions for the binomial parameter, θ

Note: The density curve on the left-hand side is the uniform density, while the one on the right-hand side is the beta density.

where $\alpha > 0$ and $\beta > 0$ are the parameters of the beta distribution and $B(\alpha, \beta)$ is the so-called *beta function*. We set the parameters α and β to 1.6 and 78.4, respectively, and we postpone the discussion of prior specification until the next chapter.

Exhibit 2.5 presents the plots of the two prior densities. Notice that under the uniform prior, all values of θ are equally likely, while under the beta prior, we assert higher prior probability for some values and lower prior probability for others.

Combining the sample information with the prior beliefs, we obtain θ's posterior distribution. We rewrite Bayes' theorem with the notation in the current discussion:

$$p(\theta \mid x) = \frac{L(\theta \mid x)\pi(\theta)}{f(x)}, \tag{2.13}$$

where $f(x)$ is the unconditional (marginal) distribution of the random variable X, given by

$$f(x) = \int L(\theta \mid x)\pi(x)\, d\theta. \tag{2.14}$$

Since $f(x)$ is obtained by averaging over all possible values of θ, it does not depend on θ. Therefore, we can rewrite (2.8) as

$$\pi(\theta \mid x) \propto L(\theta \mid x)\pi(\theta). \tag{2.15}$$

The expression in (2.15) provides us with the posterior density of θ up to some unknown constant. However, in certain cases we would still be able to recognize the posterior distribution as a known distribution, as we see shortly.[12] Since both assumed prior distributions of θ are continuous, the posterior density is also continuous and (2.13) and (2.15), in fact, represent the *continuous version of Bayes' theorem.*

Let us see what the posterior distribution for θ is under each of the two prior scenarios.

1. The posterior of θ under the uniform prior scenario is written as

$$\begin{aligned} \pi(\theta \mid x) &\propto L(\theta \mid x) \times 1 \\ &\propto \theta^{176}(1-\theta)^{55667-176} \\ &= \theta^{177-1}(1-\theta)^{55492-1}, \end{aligned} \tag{2.16}$$

where the first $\propto$ refers to omitting the marginal data distribution term in (2.14), while the second $\propto$ refers to omitting the constant term from the likelihood function.

The expression $\theta^{177-1}(1 - \theta)^{55492-1}$ above resembles the density function of the beta distribution in (2.12). The missing part is the term $B(177, 55492)$, which is a constant with respect to θ. We call $\theta^{\alpha-1}$

[12] When the posterior distribution is not recognizable as a known distribution, inference about θ is accomplished with the help of numerical methods, the foundations of which we discuss in Chapter 3.

$(1 - \theta)^{\beta-1}$ the kernel of a beta distribution with parameters α and β. Obtaining it is sufficient to identify uniquely the posterior of θ as a beta distribution with parameters $\alpha = 177$ and $\beta = 55492$.

2. The beta distribution is the conjugate prior distribution for the binomial parameter θ. This means that the posterior distribution of θ is also a beta distribution (of course, with updated parameters):

$$\begin{aligned}\pi(\theta \mid x) &\propto L(\theta \mid x)\pi(\theta)\\ &\propto \theta^{176}(1-\theta)^{55667-176}\theta^{1.6-1}(1-\theta)^{78.4-1}\\ &= \theta^{177.6-1}(1-\theta)^{55569.4-1},\end{aligned} \tag{2.17}$$

where again we omit any constants with respect to θ. As expected, we recognize the expression in the last line above as the kernel of a beta distribution with parameters $\alpha = 177.6$ and $\beta = 55569.4$.

Finally, we might want to obtain a single number as an estimate of θ. In the classical (frequentist) setting, the usual estimator of θ is the maximum likelihood estimator (the value maximizing the likelihood function in (2.11)), which happens to be the sample proportion $\widehat{\theta}$:

$$\widehat{\theta} = \frac{176}{55667} = 0.00316 \tag{2.18}$$

or 0.316%.

In the Bayesian setting, one possible estimate of θ is the *posterior mean*, that is, the mean of θ's posterior distribution. Since the mean of the beta distribution is given by $\alpha/(\alpha + \beta)$, the posterior mean of θ(the expected probability of consecutive trade-by-trade increase in the price of the AT&T stock) under the uniform prior scenario is

$$\widetilde{\theta}_U = \frac{177}{177 + 55492} = 0.00318$$

or 0.318%, while the posterior mean of θ under the beta prior scenario is

$$\widetilde{\theta}_B = \frac{177.6}{177.6 + 55569.4} = 0.00319$$

or 0.319%.

The two posterior estimates and the maximum-likelihood estimate are the same for all practical purposes. The reason is that the sample size is so large that the information contained in the data sample "swamps out" the prior information. In Chapter 3, we further illustrate and comment on the role sample size plays in posterior inference.

SUMMARY

In this chapter we laid the foundations of Bayesian analysis, emphasizing its practical rather than philosophical and methodological aspects. The objective is to employ its framework for representing the uncertainty arising in various scenarios through combining information derived from different sources—the observed data and prior beliefs. We introduced Bayes' theorem and the concepts of likelihood functions, prior distributions, and posterior distributions. In the next chapter, we discuss the nature of prior information and delve deeper into Bayesian inference.

CHAPTER 3

Prior and Posterior Information, Predictive Inference

In this chapter, we focus on the essentials of Bayesian inference. Formalizing the practitioner's knowledge and intuition into prior distributions is a key part of the inferential process. Especially when the data records are not abundant, the choice of prior distributions can influence greatly posterior conclusions. After presenting an overview of some approaches to prior specification, we focus on the elements of posterior analysis. Posterior and predictive results can be summarized in a few numbers, as in the classical statistical approach, but one could also easily examine and draw conclusions about all other aspects of the posterior and predictive distributions of the (functions of the) parameters.

PRIOR INFORMATION

In the previous chapter, we explained why the prior distribution for the model parameters is an integral component of the Bayesian inference process. The updated (posterior) beliefs are the result of the trade-off between the prior and data distributions. For ease of exposition, we rewrite below the continuous form of Bayes' theorem given in (2.15) in Chapter 2:

$$p(\theta \mid \boldsymbol{y}) \propto L(\theta \mid \boldsymbol{y})\pi(\theta), \tag{3.1}$$

where:
θ = unknown parameter whose inference we are interested in.
$\boldsymbol{y}$ = a vector (or a matrix) of recorded observations.
$\pi(\theta)$ = prior distribution of θ depending on one or more parameters, called *hyperparameters*.
$L(\theta|\boldsymbol{y})$ = likelihood function for θ.
$p(\theta|\boldsymbol{y})$ = posterior (updated) distribution of θ.

Two factors determine the degree of posterior trade-off—the strength of the prior information and the amount of data available. Generally, unless the prior is very informative (in a sense that will become clear), the more observations, the greater the influence of the data on the posterior distribution. On the contrary, when very few data records are available, the prior distribution plays a predominant role in the updated beliefs.

How to translate the prior information about a parameter into the analytical (distributional) form, $\pi(\theta)$, and how sensitive the posterior inference is to the choice of prior have been questions of considerable interest in the Bayesian literature.[1] There is, unfortunately, no "best" way to specify the prior distribution and translating subjective views into prior values for the distribution parameters could be a difficult undertaking.

Before we review some commonly used approaches to prior elicitation, we make the following notational and conceptual note. It is often convenient to represent the posterior distribution, $p(\theta \mid y)$, in a logarithmic form. Then, it is easy to see that the expression in (3.1) is transformed according to

$$\log(p(\theta \mid y)) = \text{const} + \log(L(\theta \mid y)) + \log(\pi(\theta)),$$

where const is the logarithm of the constant of proportionality.

Informative Prior Elicitation

Prior beliefs are informative when they modify substantially the information contained in the data sample so that the conclusions we draw about the model parameters based on the posterior distribution and on the data distribution alone differ. The most commonly used approach to representing informative prior beliefs is to select a distribution for the unknown parameter and specify the hyperparameters so as to reflect these beliefs.

Informative Prior Elicitation for Location and Scale Parameters Usually, when we think about the average value that a random variable takes, we have the typical value in mind. Therefore, we hold beliefs about the median of the distribution rather than its mean.[2] This distinction does not

[1]See Chapter 3 in Berger (1985), Chapter 3 in Leonard and Hsu (1999), Berger (1990, 2006), and Garthwaite, Kadane, and O'Hagan (2005), among others.

[2]The median is a measure of the center of a distribution alternative to the mean, defined as the value of the random variable, which divides the probability mass in halves. The median is the typical value the random variable takes. It is a more robust measure than the mean as it is not affected by the presence of extreme observations and, unless the distribution is symmetric, is not equal to the mean.

matter in the case of symmetric distributions, since then the mean and the median coincide. However, when the distribution we selected is not symmetric, care must be taken to ensure that the prior parameter values reflect our beliefs. Formulating beliefs about the spread of the distribution is less intuitive. The easiest way is to do so is to ask ourselves questions such as: Which value of the random variable do a quarter of the observations fall below/above? Denoting the random variable by X, the answers to these questions give us the following probability statements:

$$P(X < x_{0.25}) = 0.25$$

and

$$P(X > x_{0.75}) = 0.25,$$

where $x_{0.25}$ and $x_{0.75}$ are the values we have subjectively determined and are referred to as the first and third quartiles of the distribution, respectively. Other similar probability statements can be formulated, depending on the prior beliefs.

As an example, suppose that we model the behavior of the monthly returns on some financial asset and the normal distribution, $N(\mu, \sigma^2)$ (along with the assumption that the returns are independently and identically distributed), describes their dynamics well. Assume for now that the variance is known, $\sigma^2 = \sigma^{2*}$, and thus we only need to specify a prior distribution for the unknown mean parameter, μ. We believe that a symmetric distribution is an appropriate choice and go for the simplicity of a normal prior:

$$\mu \sim N(\eta, \tau^2), \tag{3.2}$$

where η is the prior mean and τ^2 is the prior variance of μ; to fully specify μ's prior, we need to (subjectively) determine their values. We believe that the typical monthly return is around 1%, suggesting that the median of μ's distribution is 1%. Therefore, we set η to 1%. Further, suppose we (subjectively) estimate that there is about a 25% chance that the average monthly return is less than 0.5% (i.e., $\mu_{0.25} = 0.5\%$). Then, using the tabulated cumulative probability values of the standard normal distribution, we find that the implied variance, τ^2, is approximately equal to 0.74^2.[3] Our choice for the prior distribution of μ is thus $\pi(\mu) = N(1, 0.74^2)$.

[3] A random variable, $X \sim N(\mu, \sigma^2)$, is transformed into a standard normal random variable, $Z \sim N(0, 1)$, by subtracting the mean and dividing by its standard deviation:

$$Z = \frac{X - \mu}{\sigma}.$$

Informative Prior Elicitation for the Binomial Probability Let us return to our discussion on Bayesian inference for the binomial probability parameter, θ, in Chapter 2. One of the prior assumptions we made there was that θ is distributed with a beta distribution with parameters $\alpha = 1.6$ and $\beta = 78.4$. We determined these prior values so as to match our prior beliefs that on average around 2% of the consecutive trade-by-trade price changes are increases and that there is around a 30% chance that the proportion of the consecutive price increases is less than 1%, that is[4]

$$\frac{\alpha}{\alpha+\beta} = 0.02$$

and

$$P(\theta < 0.01) = 0.3,$$

where $\frac{\alpha}{\alpha+\beta}$ is the expression for the mean of a beta-distributed random variable. Since there are two unknown hyperparameters (α and β), the two expressions above uniquely determine their values.

Noninformative Prior Distributions

In many cases, our prior beliefs are vague and thus difficult to translate into an informative prior. We therefore want to reflect our uncertainty about the model parameter(s) without substantially influencing the posterior parameter inference. The so-called *noninformative priors*, also called *vague* or *diffuse* priors, are employed to that end.

Most often, the noninformative prior is chosen to be either a uniform (flat) density defined on the support of the parameter or the Jeffreys' prior.[5] The noninformative distribution for a location parameter, μ, is given by a uniform distribution on its support ($(-\infty, \infty)$), that is,[6]

$$\pi(\mu) \propto 1. \tag{3.3}$$

[4]Notice that this choice of hyperparameter values implies that the probability of the proportion of consecutive price increases being greater than 5% is around 5%. If this contradicts substantially our prior beliefs, we might want to reconsider the choice of the beta distribution as a prior distribution. In general, once we have selected a certain distribution to represent our beliefs, we lose some flexibility in reflecting the beliefs as accurately as possible.

[5]Reference priors are another class of noninformative priors developed by Berger and Bernardo (1992); see also Bernardo and Smith (1994). Their derivation is somewhat involved and applications in the field of finance are rare. One exception is Aguilar and West (2000).

[6]Suppose a density has the form $f(x - \mu)$. The parameter μ is called the *location parameter* if it only appears within the expression $(x - \mu)$. The density, f, is then called a location density. For example, the normal density, $N(\mu, \sigma^{2*})$, is a location density when σ^{2*} is fixed.

The noninformative distribution for a scale parameter, σ (defined on the interval $(0, \infty)$) is[7]

$$\pi(\sigma) \propto \frac{1}{\sigma}. \tag{3.4}$$

Notice that the prior densities in both (3.3) and (3.4) are not proper densities, in the sense that they do not integrate to one:

$$\int_{-\infty}^{\infty} 1 \, \mathrm{d}\mu = \infty$$

and

$$\int_{0}^{\infty} \frac{1}{\sigma} \, \mathrm{d}\sigma = \infty.$$

Even though the resulting posterior densities are usually proper, care must be taken to ensure that this is indeed the case. In Chapter 11, for example, we see that an improper prior for the degrees-of-freedom parameter, ν, of the Student's *t*-distribution leads to an improper posterior. To avoid impropriety of the posterior distributions, one could employ proper prior distributions but make them noninformative, as we discuss further on.

When one is interested in the joint posterior inferences for μ and σ, these two parameters are often assumed independent, giving the joint prior distribution

$$\pi(\mu, \sigma) \propto \frac{1}{\sigma}. \tag{3.5}$$

The prior in (3.5) is often referred to as the *Jeffreys' prior*.[8]

Prior ignorance could also be represented by a (proper) standard distribution with a very large dispersion—the so-called flat or diffuse proper

---

[7]Suppose a density has the form $\frac{1}{\sigma}f(\frac{x}{\sigma})$. The parameter σ is the *scale parameter*. For example, the normal density, $N(\mu^*, \sigma^2)$, is a scale density when the mean is fixed at some μ^*.

[8]See Jeffreys (1961). In general, Jeffreys' prior of a parameter (vector), $\boldsymbol{\theta}$, is given by

$$\pi(\boldsymbol{\theta}) = |I(\boldsymbol{\theta})|^{1/2},$$

where $I(\boldsymbol{\theta})$ is the so-called Fisher's information matrix for $\boldsymbol{\theta}$, given by

$$I(\boldsymbol{\theta}) = -E\left(\frac{\partial^2 \log f(\boldsymbol{x} \mid \boldsymbol{\theta})}{\partial \boldsymbol{\theta} \partial \boldsymbol{\theta}'}\right),$$

prior distribution. Let us turn again to the example for the monthly returns for some financial asset we considered earlier and suppose that we do not have particular prior information about the range of typical values the mean monthly return could take. To reflect this ignorance, we might center the normal distribution of μ around 0 (a neutral value, so to speak) and fix the standard deviation, τ, at a large value such as 10^6, that is, $\pi(\mu) = N(0, (10^6)^2)$.

The prior of μ could take alternative distributional forms. For instance, a symmetric Student's *t*-distribution could be asserted. A standard Student's *t*-distribution has a single parameter, the degrees of freedom, ν, which one can use to regulate the heaviness of the prior's tails—the lower ν is, the flatter the prior distribution. Asserting a scaled Student's *t*-distribution with a scale parameter, σ, provides additional flexibility in specifying the prior of μ.[9] It can be argued that eliciting heavy-tailed prior distributions (with tails heavier than the tails of the data distribution), increases the posterior's robustness, that is, lowers the sensitivity of the posterior to the prior specification.

Conjugate Prior Distributions

In many situations, the choice of a prior distribution is governed by the desire to obtain analytically tractable and convenient posterior distribution. Thus, if one assumes that the data have been generated by a certain class of distributions, employing the class of the so-called "conjugate prior distributions" guarantees that the posterior distribution is of the same class as the prior distribution.[10] Although the prior and posterior distributions have the same form, their parameters differ—the parameters of the posterior distribution reflects the trade-off between prior and sample information. We now consider the case of the normal data distribution, since it is central to our discussions of financial applications. Any other conjugate scenarios we come across is discussed in the respective chapters.

If the data, x, are assumed to come from a normal distribution, the conjugate priors for the normal mean, μ, and variance, σ^2, are, respectively,

---

and the expectation is with respect to the random variable $\boldsymbol{X}$, whose density function is $f(\boldsymbol{x} \mid \boldsymbol{\theta})$. Notice that applying the expression for $\pi(\boldsymbol{\theta})$ to, for example, the normal distribution, one obtains the joint prior $\pi(\mu, \sigma) \propto 1/\sigma^2$, instead of the one in (3.5). Nevertheless, Jeffreys advocated the use of (3.5) since he assumed independence of the location and scale parameters.

[9] The Student's *t*-distribution has heavier tails than the normal distribution. For values of ν less than 2, its variance is not defined. See the appendix to this chapter for the definition of the Student's *t*-distribution.

[10] Technically speaking, for the parameters of all distributions belonging to the exponential family there are conjugate prior distributions.

a normal distribution and an inverted χ^2 distribution (see (3.28)),[11]

$$\pi(\mu \mid \sigma^2) = \mathrm{N}\left(\eta, \frac{\sigma^2}{T}\right)$$

and

$$\pi(\sigma^2) = \mathrm{Inv} - \chi^2(\nu_0, c_0^2), \tag{3.6}$$

where $\mathrm{Inv} - \chi^2(\nu, c^2)$ denotes the inverted χ^2 distribution with ν_0 degrees of freedom and a scale parameter c_0^2.[12] The prior parameters (hyperparameters) that need to be (subjectively) specified in advance are η, T, ν_0, and c_0^2. The parameter T plays the role of a discount factor, reflecting the degree of uncertainty about the distribution of μ. Usually, T is greater than one since one naturally holds less uncertainty about the distribution of the mean, μ, (with variance σ^2/T) than the data, $\boldsymbol{x}$ (with variance σ^2).

In our discussions of various financial applications in the following chapters, we see that the normal distribution is often not the most appropriate assumption for a data-generation process in view of various empirical features that financial data exhibit. Alternative distributional choices most often do not have corresponding conjugate priors and the resulting posterior distributions might not be recognizable as any known distributions. Then, numerical methods are applied to compute the posteriors. (See, for example, Chapter 4.)

In general, eliciting conjugate priors should be preceded by an analysis of whether prior beliefs would be adequately represented by them.

Empirical Bayesian Analysis

So far in this chapter, we took care to emphasize the subjective manner in which prior information is translated into a prior distribution. This involves specifying the prior hyperparameters (if an informative prior is asserted) before observing/analyzing the set of data used for model evaluation. One approach for eliciting the hyperparameters parts with this tradition—the

---

[11]Notice that μ and σ^2 are not independent in (3.6). This prior scenario is the so-called natural conjugate prior scenario. *Natural conjugate priors* are priors whose functional form is the same as the likelihood's. The joint prior density of μ and σ^2, $\pi(\mu, \sigma^2)$ can be represented as the product of a conditional and a marginal density: $\pi(\mu, \sigma^2) = \pi(\mu|\sigma^2)\pi(\sigma^2)$. If the dependence of the normal mean and variance is deemed inappropriate for the particular application, it is possible to make them independent and still benefit from the convenience of their functional forms—by eliciting a prior for μ as in (3.2).

[12]See the appendix to this chapter for details on the inverted χ^2 distribution.

so-called "empirical Bayesian approach." In it, sample information is used to compute the values of the hyperparameters. Here we provide an example with the natural conjugate prior for a normal data distribution.

Denote the sample of n observations by $\boldsymbol{x} = (x_1, x_2, \ldots, x_n)$. It can be shown that the normal likelihood function can be expressed in the following way:

$$\begin{aligned} L(\mu, \sigma^2 \mid \boldsymbol{x}) &= \left(2\pi\sigma^2\right)^{-n/2} \exp\left(-\frac{\sum_{i=1}^{n}(x_i - \mu)^2}{2\sigma^2}\right) \\ &= \left(2\pi\sigma^2\right)^{-n/2} \exp\left(-\frac{1}{2\sigma^2}\left(\nu s^2 + n(\mu - \hat{\mu})^2\right)\right), \qquad (3.7) \end{aligned}$$

where

$$\hat{\mu} = \frac{\sum_{i=1}^{n} x_i}{n}, \qquad \nu = n - 1, \qquad \text{and} \qquad s^2 = \frac{\sum_{i=1}^{n}(x_i - \hat{\mu})^2}{n-1}. \qquad (3.8)$$

The quantities $\hat{\mu}$ and s^2 are, respectively, the unbiased estimators of the mean, μ, and the variance, σ^2, of the normal distribution.[13] It is now easy to see that the likelihood in (3.7) can be viewed as the product of two distributions—a normal distribution for μ conditional on σ^2,

$$\mu \mid \sigma \sim \mathrm{N}\left(\hat{\mu}, \frac{\sigma^2}{n}\right)$$

and an inverted χ^2 distribution for σ^2,

$$\sigma^2 \sim \text{Inv-}\chi^2\left(\nu, s^2\right),$$

which become the prior distributions under the empirical Bayesian approach. We can observe that these two distributions are, of course, the same as the ones in (3.6). Their parameters are functions of the two sufficient statistics for the normal distribution, instead of subjectively elicited quantities. The sample size, n, above plays the role of the discount factor, T, in (3.6)—the more data available, the less uncertain one is about the prior distribution of μ (its prior variance decreases).

[13] An unbiased estimator of a parameter θ is a function of the data (a statistic), whose expected value is θ. The statistics $\hat{\mu}$ and s^2 are the so-called *sufficient statistics* for the normal distribution—knowing them is sufficient to uniquely determine the normal distribution which generated the data. In empirical Bayesian analysis, the hyperparameters are usually functions of the sufficient statistics of the sampling distribution.

We now turn to a discussion of the fundamentals of posterior inference. Later in this chapter, we provide an illustration of the effect various prior assumptions have on the posterior distribution.

POSTERIOR INFERENCE

The posterior distribution of a parameter (vector) θ given the observed data x is denoted as $p(\theta \mid x)$ and obtained by applying the Bayes' theorem discussed in Chapter 2 (see also (3.2)). Being a combination of the data and the prior, the posterior contains all relevant information about the unknown parameter θ. One could plot the posterior distribution, as we did in the illustration involving the binomial probability in Chapter 2, in order to visualize how the posterior probability mass is distributed.

Posterior Point Estimates

Although the benefit of being able to visualize the whole posterior distribution is unquestionable, it is often more practical to report several numerical characteristics describing the posterior, especially if reporting the results to an audience used to the classical (frequentist) statistical tradition. Commonly used for this purpose are the point estimates, such as the posterior mean, the posterior median, and the posterior standard deviation.[14] When the posterior is available in closed form, these numerical summaries can also be expressed in closed form. For example, we computed analytically the posterior mean of the binomial probability, θ, in Chapter 2. The posterior parameters in the natural conjugate prior scenario with a normal sampling density (see (3.6)) are also available analytically. The mean parameter, μ, of the normal distribution has a normal posterior, conditional on σ^2,

$$p\left(\mu \mid x, \sigma^2\right) = \mathrm{N}\left(\mu^*, \frac{\sigma^2}{T+n}\right). \tag{3.9}$$

[14]In decision theory, loss functions are used to assess the impact of an action. In the context of parameter inference, if θ^* is the true parameter value, the loss associated with employing the estimate $\widehat{\theta}$ instead of θ^* is represented by the loss function $L(\theta^*, \widehat{\theta})$. One approach to estimating θ is to determine the value that minimizes the expected resulting loss. In Bayesian analysis, we minimize the expected posterior loss—its expectation is computed with respect to θ's posterior distribution. It can be shown that the estimate of central tendency that minimizes the expected, posterior, squared-error loss function, $L(\theta^*, \widehat{\theta}) = (\theta^* - \widehat{\theta})^2$, is the posterior mean, while the estimate that minimizes the expected, posterior, absolute-error loss function, $L(\theta^*, \widehat{\theta}) = |\theta^* - \widehat{\theta}|$, is the posterior median. The expectation of the loss function is calculated with respect to θ's posterior distribution.

The posterior mean and variance of μ are, given, respectively, by

$$\begin{aligned} \mathrm{E}(\mu \mid \boldsymbol{x}, \sigma^2) \quad &\equiv \quad \mu^* = \hat{\mu}\frac{\frac{n}{\sigma^2}}{\frac{n}{\sigma^2}+\frac{T}{\sigma^2}} + \eta\frac{\frac{T}{\sigma^2}}{\frac{n}{\sigma^2}+\frac{T}{\sigma^2}} \\ &= \hat{\mu}\frac{n}{n+T} + \eta\frac{T}{n+T} \end{aligned} \tag{3.10}$$

where $\hat{\mu}$ is the sample mean as given in (3.8) and

$$\mathrm{var}(\mu \mid \boldsymbol{x}, \sigma^2) = \frac{\sigma^2}{T+n}. \tag{3.11}$$

In practical applications, usually the emphasis is placed on obtaining the posterior distribution of μ, not least because it is more difficult to formulate prior beliefs about the variance, σ^2 (let alone the whole covariance matrix in the multivariate setting). Often, then, the covariance matrix is estimated outside of the regression model and then fed into it, as if it were the "known" covariance matrix.[15] Nevertheless, for completeness, we provide σ^2's posterior distribution—an inverted χ^2,

$$p\left(\sigma^2 \mid \boldsymbol{x}\right) = \text{Inv-}\chi^2\left(\nu^*, c^{2^*}\right), \tag{3.12}$$

where

$$\nu^* = \nu_0 + n, \tag{3.13}$$

$$c^{2^*} = \frac{1}{\nu^*}\left(\nu_0 c_0^2 + (n-1)s^2 + \frac{Tn}{T+n}(\hat{\mu}-\eta)^2\right), \tag{3.14}$$

and s^2 is the unbiased sample estimator of the normal variance as given in (3.8). Using (3.13) and (3.14), one can now compute the posterior mean and variance of σ^2, respectively, as[16]

$$\mathrm{E}(\sigma^2 \mid \boldsymbol{x}) = \frac{\nu^*}{\nu^*-2}c^{2^*} \tag{3.15}$$

and

$$\mathrm{var}(\sigma^2 \mid \boldsymbol{x}) = \frac{2\nu^{*2}}{(\nu^*-2)^2(\nu^*-4)}\left(c^{2^*}\right)^2. \tag{3.16}$$

---

[15] One example for such an approach is the Black-Litterman model, which we discuss in Chapter 8.

[16] These are the expressions for expected value and variance of a random variable with the inverted χ^2 distribution; see the appendix for details.

When the posterior is not of known form and is computed numerically (through simulations), so are the posterior point estimates, as well as the distributions of any functions of these estimates, as we will see in Chapter 4.

Bayesian Intervals

The point estimate for the center of the posterior distribution is not too informative if the posterior uncertainty is significant. To assess the degree of uncertainty, a posterior $(1 - \alpha)$ interval $[a, b]$, called a *credible interval*, can be constructed. The probability that the unknown parameter, θ, falls between a and b is $(1 - \alpha)$,

$$P(a < \theta < b \,|\, \boldsymbol{x}) = \int_a^b p(\theta \,|\, \boldsymbol{x})\, \mathrm{d}\theta = 1 - \alpha.$$

For reasons of convenience, the interval bounds may be determined so that an equal probability, $\alpha/2$, is left in the tails of the posterior distribution. For example, a could be chosen to be the 25th quantile, while b—the 75th quantile. The interpretation of the credible interval is often mistakenly ascribed to the classical confidence interval. In the classical setting, $(1 - \alpha)$ is a coverage probability—if arbitrarily many repeated samples of data are recorded, $100(1 - \alpha)\%$ of the corresponding confidence intervals will contain θ—a much less intuitive interpretation.

The credible interval is computed either analytically, by finding the theoretical quantiles of the posterior distribution (when it is of known form), or numerically, by finding the empirical quantiles using the simulations of the posterior density (see Chapter 4).[17]

Bayesian Hypothesis Comparison

The title of this section[18] abuses the usual terminology by intentionally using "comparison" instead of "testing" in order to stress that the Bayesian

---

[17]A special type of Bayesian interval is *the highest posterior density* (HPD) *interval*. It is built so as to include the values of θ that have the highest posterior probability (the most likely values). When the posterior is symmetric and has a single peak (is unimodal), credible and HPD intervals coincide. With very skewed posterior distributions, however, the two intervals look very different. A disadvantage of HPD intervals is that they could be disjoint when the posterior has more than one peak (is multimodal). In unimodal settings, the Bayesian HPD interval obtained under the assumptions of a noninformative prior corresponds to the classical confidence interval.

[18]In this section, we emphasize a practical approach to Bayesian hypothesis testing. For a rigorous description of Bayesian hypothesis testing, see, for example, Zellner (1971).

framework affords one more than the mere binary reject/do-not-reject decision of the classical hypothesis testing framework. In the classical setting, the probability of a hypothesis (null or alternative) is either 0 or 1 (since frequentist statistics considers parameters as fixed, although unknown, quantities).

In contrast, in the Bayesian setting (where parameters are treated as random variables), the probability of a hypothesis can be computed (and is different from 0 or 1, in general), allowing for a true hypotheses comparison.[19]

Suppose one wants to compare the null hypothesis

$$H_0 : \theta \text{ is in } \Theta_0$$

with the alternative hypothesis

$$H_1 : \theta \text{ is in } \Theta_1,$$

where Θ_0 and Θ_1 are sets of possible values for the unknown parameter θ. As with point estimates and credible intervals, hypothesis comparison is entirely based on θ's posterior distribution. We compute the posterior probabilities of the null and alternative hypotheses,

$$P(\theta \text{ is in } \Theta_0 \mid \boldsymbol{x}) = \int_{\Theta_0} p(\theta \mid \boldsymbol{x})\, d\theta \tag{3.17}$$

and

$$P(\theta \text{ is in } \Theta_1 \mid \boldsymbol{x}) = \int_{\Theta_1} p(\theta \mid \boldsymbol{x})\, d\theta, \tag{3.18}$$

respectively. These posterior hypotheses probabilities naturally reflect both the prior beliefs and the data evidence about θ. An informed decision can

[19]In the classical setting, the decision to reject or not the null hypothesis is made on the basis of the realization of a test statistic—a function of the data—whose distribution is known. The p-value of the hypothesis test is the probability of obtaining a value of the statistic as extreme or more extreme than the one observed. The p-value is compared to the test's significance level, which represents the predetermined probability of rejecting the null hypothesis falsely. If the p-value is sufficiently small (smaller than the significance level), the null hypothesis is rejected. The p-value is often mistakenly given the interpretation of a posterior probability of the null hypothesis. It has been suggested that a low p-value, interpreted by many as strong evidence against the null hypothesis, could be in fact quite a misleading signal about evidence strength. See, for example, Berger (1985) and Stambaugh (1999).

now be made incorporating that knowledge. For example, the posterior probabilities could be employed in scenario-generation—a tool of great importance in risk analysis.

The Posterior Odds Ratio Although the framework outlined the previous section is generally sufficient to make an informed decision about the relevance of hypotheses, we briefly discuss a somewhat more formal approach for Bayesian hypothesis testing. That approach consists of summarizing the posterior relevance of the two hypotheses into a single number—the posterior odds ratio. The posterior odds ratio is the ratio of the weighted likelihoods for the model parameters under the null hypothesis and under the alternative hypothesis, multiplied by the prior odds. The weights are the prior parameter distributions (thus, parameter uncertainty is taken into account).[20]

Denote the a priori probability of the null hypothesis by α. Then, the prior odds are the ratio $\alpha/(1-\alpha)$. The posterior odds, denoted by PO, are simply the prior odds updated with the information contained in the data and are given by

$$\mathrm{PO} = \frac{\alpha}{1-\alpha} \times \frac{\int L(\theta \mid \boldsymbol{x}, H_0)\, \pi(\theta)\, d\theta}{\int L(\theta \mid \boldsymbol{x}, H_1)\, \pi(\theta)\, d\theta}, \tag{3.19}$$

where $L(\theta \mid \boldsymbol{x},\ H_0)$ is the likelihood function reflecting the restrictions imposed by the null hypothesis and $L(\theta \mid \boldsymbol{x},\ H_1)$ is the likelihood function under the alternative hypothesis.

When no prior evidence in favor or against the null hypothesis exists, the prior odds is usually set equal to one. A low value of the posterior odds generally indicates evidence against the null hypothesis.

BAYESIAN PREDICTIVE INFERENCE

After performing Bayesian posterior inference about the parameters of the data-generating process, one may use the process to predict the realizations of the random variable ahead in time. The purpose of such a prediction could be to test the predictive power of the model (for example, by analyzing a metric for the distance between the model's predictions and the actual realizations) as part of a backtesting procedure or to directly use it in the decision-making process.

As in the case of posterior inference, predictive inference provides more than simply a point prediction—one has available the whole predictive

[20] The posterior odds ratio bears similarity to the likelihood ratio which is at the center of most classical hypothesis tests. As its name suggests, the likelihood ratio is the ratio of the likelihoods under the null and the alternative hypotheses.

distribution (either analytically or numerically) and thus increased modeling flexibility.[21] The density of the predictive distribution is the sampling (data) distribution weighted by the posterior parameter density. By averaging out the parameter uncertainty (contained in the posterior), the predictive distribution provides a superior description of the model's predictive ability. In contrast, the classical approach to prediction involves computing point predictions or prediction intervals by plugging in the parameter estimates into the sampling density, treating those estimates as if they were the true parameter values.

Denoting the sampling and the posterior density by $f(x \mid \theta)$ and $p(\theta \mid x)$, respectively, the predictive density one step ahead is given by[22]

$$f(x_{+1} \mid x) = \int f(x_{+1} \mid \theta) p(\theta \mid x) \, d\theta, \tag{3.20}$$

where x_{+1} denotes the one-step-ahead realization. Notice that since we integrate (average) over the values of θ, the predictive distribution is independent of θ and depends only on the past realizations of the random variable X—it describes the process we assume has generated the data. The predictive density could be used to obtain a point prediction (for example, the predictive mean) or an interval prediction (similar in spirit to the Bayesian interval discussed above) or to perform a hypotheses comparison.

ILLUSTRATION: POSTERIOR TRADE-OFF AND THE NORMAL MEAN PARAMETER

Using an illustration, we show the effects prior distributions have on posterior inference. For simplicity, we look at the case of a normal data distribution with a known variance, $\sigma^2 = 1$. That is, we need to elicit a prior distribution of the mean parameter, μ, only. We investigate the following prior assumptions:

1. A noninformative, improper prior (Jeffreys' prior): $\pi(\mu) \propto 1$.
2. A noninformative, proper prior: $\pi(\mu) = N(\eta, \tau^2)$, where $\eta = 0$ and $\tau = 10^6$.
3. An informative conjugate prior with subjectively determined hyperparameters: $\pi(\mu) = N(\eta, \tau^2)$, where $\eta = 0.02$ and $\tau = 0.1$.

[21]The predictive density is usually of known (closed) form under conjugate prior assumptions.

[22]Here, we assume that θ is continuous, which is the case in most financial applications.

As mentioned earlier in the chapter, the relative strengths of the prior and the sampling distribution determine the degree of trade-off of prior and data information in the posterior. When the amount of available data is large, the sampling distribution dominates the prior in the posterior inference. (In the limit, as the number of observations grows indefinitely, only the sampling distribution plays a role in determining posterior results.[23]) To illustrate this sample-size effect, we consider the following two samples of data:

1. The monthly return on the S&P 500 stock index for the period January 1999 through December 2005 (a total of 192 returns).
2. The monthly return on the S&P 500 stock index for the period January 2005 through December 2005 (a total of 12 returns).

Let us denote the return data by the $n \times 1$ vector $\boldsymbol{r} = (r_1, r_2, \ldots, r_n)$, where $n = 192$ or $n = 12$. We assume that the sampling (data) distribution is normal, $R \sim \text{N}(\mu, \sigma^2)$. Combining the normal likelihood and the noninformative improper prior, we obtain for the posterior distribution of μ

$$
\begin{aligned}
p\left(\mu \,|\, \boldsymbol{r}, \sigma^2 = 1\right) &\propto (2\pi)^{-n/2} \exp\left(-\frac{\sum_{i=1}^{n}(r_i - \mu)^2}{2}\right) \\
&\propto \exp\left(-\frac{n(\mu - \hat{\mu})^2}{2}\right),
\end{aligned}
\tag{3.21}
$$

where $\hat{\mu}$ is the sample mean as given in (3.8). Therefore, the posterior of μ is a normal distribution with mean $\hat{\mu}$ and variance $1/n$. As expected, the data completely determine the posterior distributions for both data samples, since we assumed prior ignorance about μ.

When a normal prior for μ, $\text{N}(\eta, \tau^2)$, is asserted, the posterior can be shown to be normal as well. In the generic case, for an arbitrary data variance σ^2, we have

$$
\begin{aligned}
p\left(\mu \,|\, \boldsymbol{r}, \sigma^2\right) &= (2\pi\sigma^2)^{-n/2} \exp\left(-\frac{\sum_{i=1}^{n}(r_i - \mu)^2}{\sigma^2}\right) \\
&\quad \times (2\pi\tau^2)^{-1/2} \exp\left(-\frac{(\mu - \eta)^2}{2\tau^2}\right) \\
&\propto \exp\left(-\frac{(\mu - \mu^*)^2}{2\tau^{2*}}\right),
\end{aligned}
\tag{3.22}
$$

[23]This statement is valid only if one assumes that the data-generating process remains unchanged through time.

where the posterior mean, μ^*, is

$$\mu^* = \hat{\mu}\frac{\frac{n}{\sigma^2}}{\frac{n}{\sigma^2}+\frac{1}{\tau^2}} + \eta\frac{\frac{1}{\tau^2}}{\frac{n}{\sigma^2}+\frac{1}{\tau^2}} \tag{3.23}$$

and the posterior variance, τ^{2*}, is

$$\tau^{2*} = \frac{1}{\frac{n}{\sigma^2}+\frac{1}{\tau^2}}. \tag{3.24}$$

Notice that the posterior mean is a weighted average of the sample mean, $\hat{\mu}$, and the prior mean, η. The quantities $1/\sigma^2$ and $1/\tau^2$ have self-explanatory names: *data precision* and *prior precision*, respectively. The higher the precision, the more concentrated the distribution around its mean value.[24] Let us see how the information trade-off between the data and the prior is reflected in the values of the posterior parameters.

In the case of the noninformative, proper prior, $\tau = 10^6$. The right-most term in (3.23) is then negligibly small and the posterior mean is very close to the sample mean: $\mu^* \approx \hat{\mu}$, while the posterior variance in (3.24) is approximately equal to $1/n$ (substituting in $\sigma^2 = 1$). That is, for both data samples, the noninformative proper prior produced posteriors almost the same as in the case of the noninformative improper prior, as expected.

Consider how the posterior is affected when informativeness of the prior is increased, as in the third prior scenario. Exhibit 3.1 helps visualize the posterior trade-off for the long and short data samples, respectively. The smaller the amount of observed data, the larger the influence of the prior on the posterior (the "closer" the posterior to the prior).

SUMMARY

In this chapter, Bayesian prior and posterior inference are described. We discuss uninformative and informative priors. When a normal data density is assumed, the choice of priors is often guided by arguments of analytical tractability of the posterior distributions. Careful selection of the parameters of the prior distributions is necessary to ensure that they accurately reflect the

[24]The posterior mean is an example for the shrinkage effect that combining prior and data information has. See Chapter 6 for an extended discussion of shrinkage estimators.

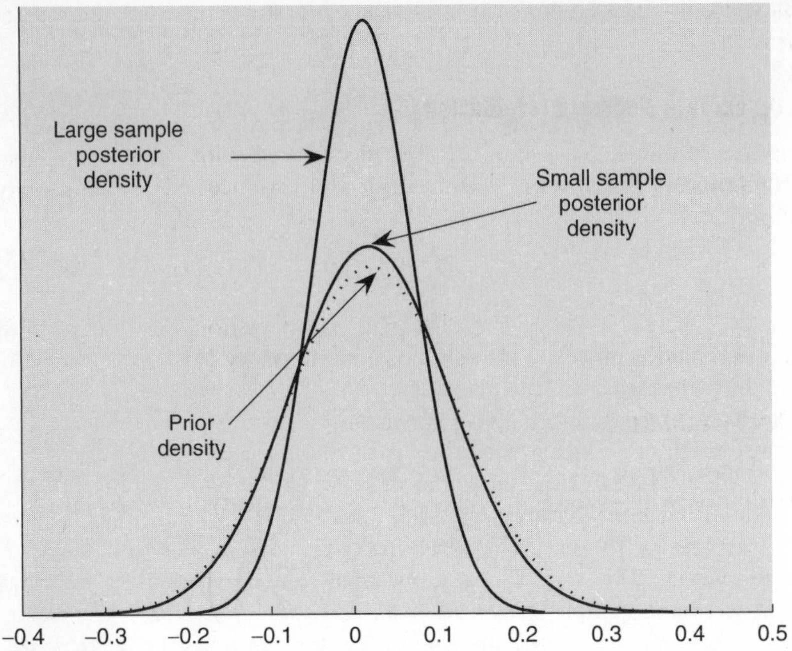

EXHIBIT 3.1 Sample size and posterior trade-off for the normal mean parameter

researcher's prior intuition. We look at both the full and empirical Bayesian approaches to prior assertion. Posterior inference is straightforward when the posteriors are analytically available.

In the next chapter, we discuss the univariate and multivariate linear regression models, which, under the assumptions of normality of the regression disturbances and conjugate priors, are straightforward extensions of this chapter's framework.

APPENDIX: DEFINITIONS OF SOME UNIVARIATE AND MULTIVARIATE STATISTICAL DISTRIBUTIONS

Here we review some statistical distributions commonly used in Bayesian financial applications. Other distributions are defined in the chapters where they are mentioned. See, for example, Chapter 13 for an overview of several heavy-tailed and asymmetric distributions that have been employed in the empirical finance literature to model asset returns.[25]

The Univariate Normal Distribution

A random variable, X, $-\infty < x < \infty$, distributed with the normal (also called *Gaussian*) distribution with mean μ and variance σ^2, has the density function

$$f(x \mid \mu, \sigma^2) = \frac{1}{\sqrt{2\pi}\,\sigma} e^{-\frac{(x-\mu)^2}{2\sigma^2}}, \tag{3.25}$$

where $-\infty < \mu < \infty$ and $\sigma > 0$. The standard deviation, σ, is the scale of the normal distribution. We denote the distribution by $N(\mu, \sigma^2)$.

The Univariate Student's *t*-Distribution

A random variable X, $-\infty < x < \infty$, distributed with the Student's t-distribution with ν degrees of freedom, has the density function

$$f(x \mid \nu, \mu, \sigma) = \frac{\Gamma(\frac{\nu+1}{2})}{\sigma\Gamma(\frac{\nu}{2})\sqrt{\nu\pi}} \left(1 + \frac{1}{\nu}\left(\frac{x-\mu}{\sigma}\right)^2\right)^{-(\nu+1)/2}, \tag{3.26}$$

where Γ is the Gamma function, $-\infty < \mu < \infty$ is the mode of X and $\sigma > 0$ is the scale parameter of X. We denote this distribution by $t(\nu, \mu, \sigma)$. The mean and variance of X are given, respectively, by

$$E(X) = \mu$$

and

$$\operatorname{var}(X) = \frac{\nu}{\nu - 2}\sigma^2. \tag{3.27}$$

The variance exists for values of ν greater than 2 and the mean—for ν greater than 1.

The Inverted χ^2 Distribution

A random variable X, $x > 0$, distributed with the inverted χ^2 distribution with ν degrees of freedom and scale parameter c, has the following density

[25] For details on the statistical properties of the distributions discussed below, see Johnson, Kotz, and Balakrishnan (1995), Anderson (2003), Kotz, Balakrishnan, and Johnson (2000), and Zellner (1971).

function,

$$f(x \mid \nu, c) = \frac{1}{\Gamma\left(\frac{\nu}{2}\right)}\left(\frac{\nu}{2}\right)^{\nu/2} c^{\nu} x^{-(\frac{\nu}{2}+1)} \exp\left(-\frac{\nu c}{2x}\right), \tag{3.28}$$

where $\nu > 0$, $c > 0$, and $x > 0$. The inverted χ^2 distribution is denoted as Inv$-\chi^2(\nu, c)$. Its kernel consists of the nonconstant part of the density function,

$$x^{-(\frac{\nu}{2}+1)} \exp\left(-\frac{\nu c}{2x}\right).$$

The inverted χ^2 distribution is a particular case of the inverted gamma distribution,

$$\text{Inv-}\chi^2(\nu, c) \equiv \text{IG}\left(\frac{\nu}{2}, \frac{\nu c}{2}\right).$$

The mean (defined for $\nu > 2$) and the variance (defined for $\nu > 4$) of X are given, respectively, by

$$\text{E}(X) = \frac{\nu}{\nu - 2}c$$

and

$$\text{var}(X) = \frac{2\nu^2}{(\nu - 2)^2(\nu - 4)}c^2. \tag{3.29}$$

The Multivariate Normal Distribution

An $n \times 1$ vector $\boldsymbol{x} = (x_1, x_2, \ldots, x_n)'$, distributed with the multivariate normal distribution, has a density

$$f(\boldsymbol{x} \mid \boldsymbol{\mu}, \boldsymbol{\Sigma}) = (2\pi)^{n/2}|\boldsymbol{\Sigma}|^{-1/2} \exp\left(-\frac{1}{2}(\boldsymbol{x} - \boldsymbol{\mu})'\boldsymbol{\Sigma}^{-1}(\boldsymbol{x} - \boldsymbol{\mu})\right), \tag{3.30}$$

where the $n \times 1$ vector of means is $\boldsymbol{\mu} = (\mu_1, \mu_2, \ldots, \mu_n)'$ and the $n \times n$ matrix $\boldsymbol{\Sigma}$ is the (positive semidefinite) covariance matrix. The diagonal elements of $\boldsymbol{\Sigma}$ are the variances of each of the components of $\boldsymbol{x}$, while the off-diagonal elements are the covariances, cov(x_i, x_j), $i \neq j$, between each two components of $\boldsymbol{x}$. Since cov(x_i, x_j) is the same as cov(x_j, x_i), $\boldsymbol{\Sigma}$ is symmetric and contains $n(n - 1)/2$ distinct elements.

The Multivariate Student's *t*-Distribution

An $n \times 1$ vector $\boldsymbol{x} = (x_1, x_2, \ldots, x_n)'$, distributed with the multivariate (scaled, non-central) Student's t-distribution, has the density

$$f(\boldsymbol{x} \mid \nu, \boldsymbol{\mu}, S) = C \times \left(\nu + (\boldsymbol{x} - \boldsymbol{\mu})'S(\boldsymbol{x} - \boldsymbol{\mu})\right)^{-(n+\nu)/2},$$

where $C = \frac{\nu^{\nu/2}\Gamma((\nu+n)/2)|S|^{1/2}}{\pi^{n/2}\Gamma(\nu/2)}$, ν is the degrees-of-freedom parameter, regulating the tail thickness, $\boldsymbol{\mu}$ is the mean vector, and S is the scale matrix. We denote the distribution by $t(\nu,\ \boldsymbol{\mu},\ S)$. The covariance matrix of $\boldsymbol{x}$ is given by

$$\boldsymbol{\Sigma} = S^{-1}\frac{\nu}{\nu - 2}. \tag{3.31}$$

The covariance matrix exists for $\nu > 2$, and the mean—for $\nu > 1$.

The Wishart Distribution

Suppose we have observed a sample of $N \times 1$ vectors, $X_1, \ldots, X_t, \ldots, X_T$. The vectors are independently distributed with multivariate normal distribution, $\mathrm{N}(\boldsymbol{\mu},\ \boldsymbol{\Sigma})$. The Wishart distribution arises in statistics as the distribution of the quantity, Q,

$$Q = \sum_{i=1}^{T}(X_t - \overline{X})(X_t - \overline{X})',$$

which is equal to T times the sample covariance matrix and $\overline{X} = \frac{1}{T}\sum_{t=1}^{T} X_t$. If Q is a positive definite matrix, its density function is given by

$$f(Q \mid T, \boldsymbol{\Sigma}) = \frac{|Q|^{\frac{1}{2}(T-N-1)}\exp\left(-\frac{1}{2}\mathrm{tr}\boldsymbol{\Sigma}^{-1}Q\right)}{2^{NT/2}\,\pi^{N(N-1)/4}\,|\boldsymbol{\Sigma}|^{T/2}\prod_{i=1}^{N}\Gamma\left((T+1-i)/2\right)}. \tag{3.32}$$

The Wishart distribution is denoted by $\mathrm{W}(T-1,\ \boldsymbol{\Sigma})$.

The Inverted Wishart Distribution

In the Bayesian framework, the inverted Wishart distribution is the conjugate prior distribution of the normal covariance matrix. Consider the positive definite matrix Q above. Denote by S its inverse, $S = Q^{-1}$. Its density is given by

$$f(S \mid \Psi, \nu) = \frac{|\boldsymbol{\Psi}|^{\nu/2}}{2^{\nu N/2}\,\pi^{N(N-1)/4}\prod_{i=1}^{N}\Gamma(\nu - i + 1)/2}\,\frac{\exp\left(-\frac{1}{2}\mathrm{tr}S^{-1}\boldsymbol{\Psi}\right)}{|S|^{(\nu+n+1)/2}}, \tag{3.33}$$

where $\boldsymbol{\Psi} = \boldsymbol{\Sigma}^{-1}$ and ν is a (scalar) degrees-of-freedom parameter, such that $\nu \geq N$. We denote the distribution above as $\mathrm{IW}(\boldsymbol{\Psi},\ \nu)$.[26]

[26]The notation $W^{-1}(\boldsymbol{\Psi},\ \nu)$ is sometimes also used.

The inverted Wishart distribution is a generalization of the inverted gamma distribution to the multivariate case. The diagonal elements of S have the inverted χ^2 distribution in (3.28).

The expectation of an inverted Wishart random variable is

$$E(S) = \boldsymbol{\Psi}\frac{1}{N - T - 1}. \tag{3.34}$$

CHAPTER 4

Bayesian Linear Regression Model

Regression analysis is one of the most common econometric tools employed in the area of investment management. Since the following chapters rely on it in the discussion of various financial applications, here we review the Bayesian approach to estimation of the univariate and multivariate regression models.

THE UNIVARIATE LINEAR REGRESSION MODEL

The univariate linear regression model attempts to explain the variability in one variable (called *the dependent variable*) with the help of one or more other variables (called *explanatory* or *independent variables*) by asserting a linear relationship between them. We write the model as

$$Y = \alpha + \beta_1 X_1 + \beta_2 X_2 + \cdots \beta_{K-1} X_{K-1} + \epsilon, \tag{4.1}$$

where: Y = dependent variable.
X_k = independent (explanatory) variables, $k = 1, \ldots, K-1$.
α = regression intercept.
β_k = regression (slope) coefficients, $k = 1, \ldots, K-1$, representing the effect a unit change in X_k, $k = 1, \ldots, K-1$, has on Y, keeping the remaining independent variables, X_j, $j \neq k$, fixed.
ϵ = regression disturbance.

The regression disturbance is the source of randomness about the linear (deterministic) relationship between the dependent and independent variables. Whereas $\alpha + \beta_1 X_1 + \cdots + \beta_{K-1} X_{K-1}$ represents the part of Y's variability explained by X_k, $k = 1, \ldots, K-1$, ϵ represents the variability in Y left unexplained.[1]

Suppose that we have n observations of the dependent and the independent variables available. These data are then described by

$$y_i = \alpha + \beta_1 x_{1,i} + \cdots + \beta_{K-1} x_{K-1,i} + \epsilon_i \qquad i = 1, \ldots, n. \tag{4.2}$$

The subscript i, $i = 1, \ldots, n$, refers to the ith observation of the respective random variable. To describe the source of randomness, ϵ, one needs to make a distributional assumption about it. For simplicity, assume that ϵ_i, $i = 1, \ldots, n$, are independently and identically distributed (i.i.d.) with the normal distribution and have zero means and (equal) variances, σ^2. Then, the dependent variable, Y, has a normal distribution as well,

$$y_i \sim \mathrm{N}(\mu_i, \sigma^2), \tag{4.3}$$

where $\mu_i = \alpha + \beta_1 x_{1,i} + \cdots + \beta_{K-1} x_{K-1,i}$. Notice that the constant-variance assumption in (4.3) is quite restrictive. We come back to this issue later in the chapter.

The expression in (4.2) is often written in the following compact form:

$$\boldsymbol{y} = \boldsymbol{X\beta} + \boldsymbol{\epsilon}, \tag{4.4}$$

where $\boldsymbol{y}$ is a $n \times 1$ vector,

$$\boldsymbol{y} = \begin{pmatrix} y_1 \\ y_2 \\ \vdots \\ y_n \end{pmatrix},$$

$\boldsymbol{\beta}$ is a $(K) \times 1$ vector,

$$\boldsymbol{\beta} = \begin{pmatrix} \alpha \\ \beta_1 \\ \vdots \\ \beta_{K-1} \end{pmatrix},$$

[1]We generally assume that the independent variables are fixed (nonstochastic). However, see Chapter 7 for an application in which we do consider them random and make distributional assumptions about them.

X is a $n \times (K)$ matrix whose first column consists of ones,

$$X = \begin{pmatrix} 1 & x_{1,1} & \cdots & x_{K-1,1} \\ 1 & x_{1,2} & \cdots & x_{K-1,2} \\ \vdots & \vdots & \vdots & \vdots \\ 1 & x_{1,n} & \cdots & x_{K-1,n} \end{pmatrix},$$

and $\boldsymbol{\epsilon}$ is a $n \times 1$ vector,

$$\boldsymbol{\epsilon} = \begin{pmatrix} \epsilon_1 \\ \epsilon_2 \\ \vdots \\ \epsilon_n \end{pmatrix}.$$

We write the normal distributional assumption for the regression disturbances in compact form as

$$\boldsymbol{\epsilon} \sim \mathrm{N}(0, \sigma^2 I_n),$$

where I_n is a $(n \times n)$ identity matrix. The parameters in (4.4) we need to estimate are $\widehat{\boldsymbol{\beta}}$ and σ^2. Assuming normally distributed disturbances, we write the likelihood function for the model parameters as

$$L(\alpha, \beta_1, \beta_2, \sigma \mid \boldsymbol{y}, \boldsymbol{X}) = (2\pi\sigma^2)^{-n/2} \times \exp\left\{ -\frac{1}{2\sigma^2} \sum_{i=1}^{n} (y_i - \alpha - \beta_1 x_{1,i} - \cdots - \beta_{K-1} x_{K-1,i})^2 \right\}.$$

Or, in vector notation, we have the likelihood function for the parameters of a multivariate normal distribution,

$$L(\boldsymbol{\beta}, \sigma \mid \boldsymbol{y}, \boldsymbol{X}) = (2\pi\sigma^2)^{-n/2} \exp\left\{ -\frac{1}{2\sigma^2} (\boldsymbol{y} - \boldsymbol{X}\boldsymbol{\beta})'(\boldsymbol{y} - \boldsymbol{X}\boldsymbol{\beta}) \right\}. \tag{4.5}$$

Bayesian Estimation of the Univariate Regression Model

In the classical setting, the regression parameters are usually estimated by maximizing the model's likelihood with respect to $\widehat{\boldsymbol{\beta}}$ and σ^2, for instance, the likelihood in (4.5) if the normal distribution is assumed. When disturbances are assumed to be normally distributed, the maximum likelihood and the *ordinary least squares* (OLS) methods produce identical parameter estimates. It can be shown that the OLS estimator of the regression coefficients vector, $\widehat{\boldsymbol{\beta}}$, is given by

$$\widehat{\boldsymbol{\beta}} = (\mathbf{X}'\mathbf{X})^{-1}\mathbf{X}\boldsymbol{y}, \tag{4.6}$$

where the prime symbol (′) denotes a matrix transpose.[2] The estimator of σ^2 is[3]

$$\widehat{\sigma}^2 = \frac{1}{n-K}(\boldsymbol{y} - \mathbf{X}\widehat{\boldsymbol{\beta}})'(\boldsymbol{y} - \mathbf{X}\widehat{\boldsymbol{\beta}}). \tag{4.7}$$

To account for the parameters' estimation risk and to incorporate prior information, regression estimation can be cast in a Bayesian setting. Our earlier discussion of prior elicitation applies with full force here. We consider two prior scenarios: a diffuse improper prior and an informative conjugate prior for the regression parameter vector, $((\boldsymbol{\beta}, \sigma^2))$.

Diffuse Improper Prior The joint diffuse improper prior for $\boldsymbol{\beta}$ and σ^2 is given by

$$\pi(\boldsymbol{\beta}, \sigma^2) \propto \frac{1}{\sigma^2}, \tag{4.8}$$

where the regression coefficients can take any real value, $-\infty < \beta_k < \infty$, for $k = 1, \ldots, K$, and the disturbance variance is positive, $\sigma^2 > 0$.

Combining the likelihood in (4.5) and the prior above, we obtain the posteriors of the model parameters as follows:

- The posterior distribution of $\boldsymbol{\beta}$ conditional on σ^2 is (multivariate) normal:[4]

$$p\left(\boldsymbol{\beta} \mid \boldsymbol{y}, \mathbf{X}, \sigma^2\right) = \mathrm{N}\left(\widehat{\boldsymbol{\beta}}, (\mathbf{X}'\mathbf{X})^{-1}\sigma^2\right), \tag{4.9}$$

  where $\widehat{\boldsymbol{\beta}}$ is the OLS estimate in (4.6) and $(\mathbf{X}'\mathbf{X})^{-1}\sigma^2$ is the covariance matrix of $\widehat{\boldsymbol{\beta}}$.

---

[2]In order for the inverse matrix in (4.6) to exist, it is necessary that $\mathbf{X}'\mathbf{X}$ be nonsingular, that is, that the $n \times K$ matrix $\mathbf{X}$ have a rank K (all its columns be linearly independent).

[3]The MLE of σ^2 is in fact

$$\widehat{\sigma}^2_{MLE} = \frac{1}{n}(\boldsymbol{y} - \mathbf{X}\widehat{\boldsymbol{\beta}})'(\boldsymbol{y} - \mathbf{X}\widehat{\boldsymbol{\beta}}).$$

However, as it is not unbiased, the estimator in (4.7) is more often employed.

[4]See the appendix to Chapter 3 for the definition of the multivariate normal distribution.

- The posterior distribution of σ^2 is inverted χ^2:

$$p\left(\sigma^2 \mid y, X\right) = \text{Inv-}\chi^2\left(n-K, \widehat{\sigma}^2\right), \tag{4.10}$$

where $\widehat{\sigma}^2$ is the estimator of σ^2 in (4.7).

It could be useful to obtain the marginal (unconditional) distribution of $\boldsymbol{\beta}$ in order to characterize it independently of σ^2 (as in practical applications, the variance is an unknown parameter).[5] It can be shown, by integrating the joint posterior distribution

$$p\left(\boldsymbol{\beta}, \sigma^2 \mid y, \mathbf{X}\right) = p\left(\boldsymbol{\beta} \mid y, \mathbf{X}, \sigma^2\right) p\left(\sigma^2 \mid y, \mathbf{X}\right)$$

with respect to σ^2, that $\boldsymbol{\beta}$'s unconditional posterior distribution is a multivariate Student's t-distribution with a kernel given by[6]

$$p\left(\boldsymbol{\beta} \mid y, \mathbf{X}\right) \propto \left((n-K) + (\boldsymbol{\beta} - \widehat{\boldsymbol{\beta}})' \frac{\mathbf{X}'\mathbf{X}}{\widehat{\sigma}^2} (\boldsymbol{\beta} - \widehat{\boldsymbol{\beta}})\right)^{-n/2}. \tag{4.11}$$

Notice that integrating σ^2 out makes $\boldsymbol{\beta}$'s distribution more heavy-tailed, duly reflecting the uncertainty about σ^2's true value. Although $\boldsymbol{\beta}$'s mean vector is unchanged, its variance increased (on average) by the term $\nu/(\nu-2)$:

$$\boldsymbol{\Sigma}_{\beta} = \widehat{\sigma}^2 (\mathbf{X}'\mathbf{X})^{-1} \frac{\nu}{\nu - 2},$$

where $\nu = n - K$ is the degrees of freedom parameter of the multivariate Student's t-distribution.

In conclusion of our discussion of the posteriors in the diffuse improper prior scenario, suppose we are interested particularly in one of the regression coefficients, say β_k. For example, β_k could be the return on a factor (size, value, momentum, etc.) in a multifactor model of stock returns. It can be shown that the standardized β_k has a Student's t-distribution with $n - K$

[5] In fact, using the numerical methods in Chapter 5, it is possible to describe the distribution of $\boldsymbol{\beta}$, even without knowing its unconditional distribution, by employing the Gibbs sampler and making inferences on the basis of samples drawn from $\boldsymbol{\beta}$'s and σ^2's posterior distributions.

[6] See the appendix to Chapter 3 for the definition of the multivariate Student's t-distribution.

degrees of freedom as its marginal posterior distribution,

$$\frac{\beta_k - \widehat{\beta}_k}{(h_{k,k})^{1/2}} \mid y, X \sim t_{n-K}, \tag{4.12}$$

where $h_{k,k}$ is the kth diagonal element of $\widehat{\sigma}^2(X'X)^{-1}$ and $\widehat{\beta}_k$ is the OLS estimate of β_k (the corresponding component of $\widehat{\boldsymbol{\beta}}$). Bayesian intervals for β_k can then be constructed analytically.

Informative Prior Under the normality assumption for the regression residuals in (4.1), one can make use of the natural conjugate framework to reflect the existing prior knowledge and to obtain convenient analytical posterior results. Thus, let us assume that the regression coefficients vector, $\boldsymbol{\beta}$, has a normal prior distribution (conditional on σ^2) and σ^2—an inverted χ^2 prior distribution:

$$\boldsymbol{\beta} \mid \sigma \sim \mathrm{N}(\boldsymbol{\beta}_0, \sigma^2 \boldsymbol{A}) \tag{4.13}$$

and

$$\sigma^2 \sim \text{Inv-}\chi^2\left(\nu_0, c_0^2\right). \tag{4.14}$$

Four parameters have to be determined a priori: $\boldsymbol{\beta}_0$, A, ν_0, and c_0^2. The scale matrix $\mathbf{A}$ is often chosen to be $\tau^{-1}(X'X)^{-1}$ in order to obtain a prior covariance the same as the covariance matrix of the OLS estimator of $\boldsymbol{\beta}$ up to a scaling constant. Varying the (scale) parameter, τ, allows one to adjust the degree of confidence one has that $\boldsymbol{\beta}$'s mean is $\boldsymbol{\beta}_0$—the smaller the value of τ, the greater the degree of uncertainty about $\boldsymbol{\beta}$.

The easiest way to assert the prior mean, $\boldsymbol{\beta}_0$, is to fix it at some default value (such as 0, depending on the estimation context), unless more specific prior information is available, or to set it equal to the OLS estimate, $\widehat{\boldsymbol{\beta}}$, obtained from running the regression (4.1) on a prior sample of data.[7]

The parameters of the inverted χ^2 distribution could be asserted using a prior sample of data as follows:

$$\nu_0 = n_0 - K$$

$$c_0^2 = \frac{1}{\nu_0}\left(y_0 - X_0\widehat{\boldsymbol{\beta}}_0\right)'\left(y_0 - X_0\widehat{\boldsymbol{\beta}}_0\right).$$

[7]Recall our earlier discussion of prior parameter assertion—the full Bayesian approach calls for specifying the hyperprior parameters independently of the data used for model estimation. In contrast, an empirical Bayesian approach would use the OLS estimate, $\widehat{\boldsymbol{\beta}}$, obtained from the data sample used for estimation.

where the subscript, 0, refers to the prior data sample. If no prior data sample is available, the inverted χ^2 hyperparameters could be specified by expressing beliefs about the prior mean and variance of σ^2, using the expressions in (3.28) in Chapter 3.

The posterior distributions for the model parameters, $\boldsymbol{\beta}$ and σ^2 have the same form as the prior distributions, however, their parameters are updated to reflect the data information, along with the prior beliefs.

- The posterior for $\boldsymbol{\beta}$ is

$$p\left(\boldsymbol{\beta} \mid y, X, \sigma^2\right) = \mathrm{N}\left(\boldsymbol{\beta}^*, \boldsymbol{\Sigma}_{\beta}\right), \tag{4.15}$$

where the posterior mean and covariance matrix of $\boldsymbol{\beta}$ are given by

$$\boldsymbol{\beta}^* = \left(A^{-1} + X'X\right)^{-1}\left(A^{-1}\boldsymbol{\beta}_0 + X'X\widehat{\boldsymbol{\beta}}\right) \tag{4.16}$$

and

$$\boldsymbol{\Sigma}_{\beta} = \sigma^2\left(A^{-1} + X'X\right)^{-1}. \tag{4.17}$$

We can observe that the posterior mean is a weighted average of the prior mean and the OLS estimator of $\boldsymbol{\beta}$, as noted earlier in the chapter as well. See Chapter 6 for more details on this shrinkage effect.

- The inverted χ^2 posterior distribution of σ^2 is

$$p\left(\sigma^2 \mid y, X\right) = \text{Inv-}\chi^2\left(\nu^*, c^{2*}\right). \tag{4.18}$$

The parameters of σ^2's posterior distribution are given by

$$\nu^* = \nu_0 + n \tag{4.19}$$

and

$$\nu^* c^{2*} = (n-K)\widehat{\sigma}^2 + (\boldsymbol{\beta}_0 - \widehat{\boldsymbol{\beta}})' H (\boldsymbol{\beta}_0 - \widehat{\boldsymbol{\beta}}) + \nu_0 c_0^2, \tag{4.20}$$

where $H = \left((X'X)^{-1} + A\right)^{-1}$

As done earlier, we can derive the marginal posterior distribution of $\boldsymbol{\beta}$ by integrating σ^2 out of the joint posterior distribution. We obtain again a multivariate Student's t-distribution, $t(t(\nu^*, \boldsymbol{\beta}^*, Q))$,

$$p\left(\boldsymbol{\beta} \mid y, X\right) \propto \left(\nu^* + (\boldsymbol{\beta} - \boldsymbol{\beta}^*)' Q (\boldsymbol{\beta} - \boldsymbol{\beta}^*)\right)^{-\nu^*/2}, \tag{4.21}$$

where $Q = \left(A^{-1} + X'X\right)/c^{2*}$.

The mean of $\boldsymbol{\beta}$ remains the same, $\boldsymbol{\beta}^*$ (as it is independent of σ^2), while its unconditional (with respect to σ^2) covariance matrix can be calculated using (3.30) in Chapter 3. The marginal posterior distribution for a single regression coefficient, β_k, can be shown to be

$$\frac{\beta_k - \beta_k^*}{(q_{k,k})^{1/2}} \,|\, \mathbf{y}, \mathbf{X} \sim t_{\nu_0+n-K}, \tag{4.22}$$

where $q_{k,k}$ is the kth diagonal element of Q^{-1} and β_k^* is the kth component of $\boldsymbol{\beta}^*$.

Prediction Suppose that we would like to predict the dependent variable, Y, p steps ahead in time and denote by the $p \times 1$ vector $\widetilde{\mathbf{y}} = (y_{T+1}, y_{T+2}, \ldots, y_{T+p})$ these future observations. We assume that the future observations of the independent variables are known and given by $\widetilde{\mathbf{X}}$. Let us use (3.20) in Chapter 3 to express the predictive density in the linear regression context,

$$p(\widetilde{\mathbf{y}} \,|\, \mathbf{y}, \widetilde{\mathbf{X}}, \mathbf{X}) = \iint p(\widetilde{\mathbf{y}} \,|\, \boldsymbol{\beta}, \sigma^2, \widetilde{\mathbf{X}}) p(\boldsymbol{\beta}, \sigma^2 \,|\, \mathbf{y}, \mathbf{X})\, \mathrm{d}\boldsymbol{\beta}, \sigma^2, \tag{4.23}$$

where $p(\boldsymbol{\beta}, \sigma^2 \,|\, \mathbf{y}, \mathbf{X})$ is the joint posterior distribution of $\boldsymbol{\beta}$ and σ^2.

It can be shown that the predictive distribution is multivariate Student's t. Under the diffuse improper prior scenario, the predictive distribution is

$$p(\widetilde{\mathbf{y}} \,|\, \mathbf{y}, \widetilde{\mathbf{X}}, \mathbf{X}) = t(n - K, \widetilde{\mathbf{X}}\widehat{\boldsymbol{\beta}}, S), \tag{4.24}$$

where $S = \widehat{\sigma}^2(I_p + \widetilde{\mathbf{X}}(\mathbf{X}'\mathbf{X})^{-1}\widetilde{\mathbf{X}}')$ and $\widehat{\boldsymbol{\beta}}$ is the posterior mean of $\boldsymbol{\beta}$ under the diffuse improper scenario. In the case of the informative prior, the predictive distribution of $\widetilde{\mathbf{y}}$ is

$$p(\widetilde{\mathbf{y}} \,|\, \mathbf{y}, \widetilde{\mathbf{X}}, \mathbf{X}) = t(\nu_0 + n, \widetilde{\mathbf{X}}\boldsymbol{\beta}^*, V), \tag{4.25}$$

where $V = c^{2*}(I_p + \widetilde{\mathbf{X}}(A^{-1} + \mathbf{X}'\mathbf{X})^{-1}\widetilde{\mathbf{X}}')$ and $\boldsymbol{\beta}^*$ is the posterior mean of $\boldsymbol{\beta}$ in (4.16).

Certainly, it is again possible to derive the distribution for the predictive distribution for a single component of $\widetilde{\mathbf{y}}$—a univariate Student's t-distribution—in the two scenarios, respectively,

$$\frac{\widetilde{y}_k - \widetilde{\mathbf{X}^k}\widehat{\beta}_k}{s_{k,k}^{1/2}} \sim t_{n-K}, \tag{4.26}$$

where $\widetilde{X^k}$ is the kth row of $\widetilde{X}$ (the observations of the independent variables pertaining to the kth future period), and $s_{k,k}$ is the kth diagonal element of the scale matrix, S, in (4.24), and

$$\frac{\widetilde{y}_k - \widetilde{X^k}\beta_k^*}{v_{k,k}^{1/2}} \sim t_{\nu_0+n-K}, \tag{4.27}$$

where $v_{k,k}$ is the kth diagonal element of the scale matrix, V, in (4.25).

The Case of Unequal Variances We mentioned earlier in the chapter that the equal-variance assumption in (4.3) might be somewhat restrictive. Two examples would help clarify what that means. First, suppose that the n observations of Y are collected through time. It is a common practice in statistical estimation to use the longest available data record, likely spanning many years. Changes in the underlying economic or financial paradigms, the way data are recorded, and so on, that might have occurred during the sample period might have caused the variance of the random variable (as well as its mean, for that matter) to shift.[8] The equal-variance assumption would then lead to variance overestimation in the low-variance period(s) and variance underestimation in the high-variance period(s). When the variance (and/or mean) shifts permanently, the so-called "structural-break" models can be employed to reflect it.[9] In Chapter 11, we discuss the so-called "regime-switching" models, in which parameters are allowed to change values according to the state of the world prevailing in a particular period in time.

Second, if our estimation problem is based on observations recorded at a particular point in time (producing a cross-sectional sample), the equal-variance assumption might be violated again. All units in our sample could potentially have different variances, so that $\text{var}(y_i) = \sigma_i^2$, instead of $\text{var}\ (y_i) = \sigma^2$ as in (4.3), for $i = 1, \ldots, n$. Estimation would then be severely hampered because this would imply a greater number of unknown parameters (variances and regression coefficients) than available data points.

In practice one would perhaps be able to identify groups of homogeneous sample units that can be assumed to have equal variances. Suppose, for instance, that the cross-sectional sample consists of small-cap and large-cap stock returns. One could then expect that the return variances (volatilities) across the two groups differ but assume that companies within each group

[8] Returns on interest rate instruments and foreign exchange are particularly likely to exhibit structural breaks.

[9] See, for example, Wang and Zivot (2000).

have equal return volatilities. More generally, one could assume some form of functional relation among the unknown variances—this would serve to reduce the number of unknown parameters to estimate. We now provide one possible way to address the variance inequality in the case when the sample observations can be divided into two homogeneous (with respect to their variances) groups or when a structural break (whose timing we know) is present in the sample.[10]

Denote the observations from the two groups by $\boldsymbol{y}_1 = (y_{1,1}, y_{1,2}, \ldots, y_{1,n_1})$ and $\boldsymbol{y}_2 = (y_{2,1}, y_{2,2}, \ldots, y_{2,n_2})$, so that $\boldsymbol{y} = (\boldsymbol{y}_1,\ \boldsymbol{y}_2)$ and $n_1 + n_2 = n$. The univariate regression setup in (4.1) is modified as

$$\begin{aligned} \boldsymbol{y}_1 &= \boldsymbol{X}_1\boldsymbol{\beta} + \boldsymbol{\epsilon}_1 \\ \boldsymbol{y}_2 &= \boldsymbol{X}_2\boldsymbol{\beta} + \boldsymbol{\epsilon}_2, \end{aligned} \tag{4.28}$$

where $\boldsymbol{X}_1$ and $\boldsymbol{X}_2$ are, respectively, $(n_1 \times K)$ and $(n_2 \times K)$ matrices of observations of the independent variables. The disturbances are assumed to be independent and distributed as

$$\begin{aligned} \boldsymbol{\epsilon}_1 &\sim \mathrm{N}(0, \sigma_1^2 I_{n_1}) \\ \boldsymbol{\epsilon}_2 &\sim \mathrm{N}(0, \sigma_2^2 I_{n_2}), \end{aligned} \tag{4.29}$$

where $\sigma_1^2 \neq \sigma_2^2$. The likelihood function for the model parameters, $\boldsymbol{\beta}$, σ_1^2, and σ_2^2 is given by

$$\begin{aligned} L\left(\boldsymbol{\beta}, \sigma_1^2, \sigma_2^2 \mid \boldsymbol{y}, \boldsymbol{X}_1, \boldsymbol{X}_2\right) \propto\ & (\sigma_1^2)^{-\frac{n_1}{2}} (\sigma_2^2)^{-\frac{n_2}{2}} \\ & \times \exp\left(-\frac{1}{2\sigma_1^2}(\boldsymbol{y}_1 - \boldsymbol{X}_1\boldsymbol{\beta})'(\boldsymbol{y}_1 - \boldsymbol{X}_1\boldsymbol{\beta}) \right. \\ & \left. -\frac{1}{2\sigma_2^2}(\boldsymbol{y}_2 - \boldsymbol{X}_2\boldsymbol{\beta})'(\boldsymbol{y}_2 - \boldsymbol{X}_2\boldsymbol{\beta})\right). \end{aligned} \tag{4.30}$$

A noninformative diffuse prior can be asserted, as in (3.5), by assuming that the parameters are independent. The prior is written, then, as

$$\pi(\boldsymbol{\beta}, \sigma_1, \sigma_2) \propto \frac{1}{\sigma_1 \sigma_2}.$$

It is straightforward to write out the joint posterior density of $\boldsymbol{\beta}$, σ_1^2, and σ_2^2, which can be integrated with respect to the two variances to obtain the marginal posterior distribution of the regression coefficients vector.

---

[10]See Chapter 4 in Zellner (1971).

Zellner (1971) shows that the marginal posterior of $\boldsymbol{\beta}$ is the product of two multivariate Student's t-densities (not a surprising result, since the likelihood in (4.30) is the product of two normal likelihoods),

$$p(\boldsymbol{\beta} \mid \mathbf{y}, \mathbf{X}_1, \mathbf{X}_2) \propto t(\nu_1, \widehat{\boldsymbol{\beta}}_1, S_1) \times t(\nu_2, \widehat{\boldsymbol{\beta}}_2, S_2),$$

where, for $i = 1, 2$, $\widehat{\boldsymbol{\beta}}_i$ is the OLS estimator of $\boldsymbol{\beta}$ in the two expressions in (4.28) viewed as separate regressions,

$$\nu_i = n_i - K, \qquad S_i = \widehat{s_i^2}(\mathbf{X}_i'\mathbf{X}_i),$$

and

$$\widehat{s_i^2} = \frac{1}{n_i - K}(\mathbf{y}_i - \mathbf{X}_i\widehat{\boldsymbol{\beta}}_i)'(\mathbf{y}_i - \mathbf{X}_i\widehat{\boldsymbol{\beta}}_i).$$

Zellner shows that the marginal posterior of $\boldsymbol{\beta}$ above can be approximated with a normal distribution (through a series of asymptotic expansions).

We conclude this discussion with a brief comment on a related violation of the univariate regression assumptions outlined earlier in the chapter. When analyzing data collected through time, it is more likely than not that the data are serially correlated. That is, the assumption that the regression disturbances are independent is violated. For example, dependence of returns through time might be caused by time-dependence of the return volatility (and/or the mean of returns). We discuss volatility modeling in Chapters 10, 11, and 12.

Illustration: The Univariate Linear Regression Model

We now illustrate the posterior and predictive inference in a univariate linear regression model. We restrict our attention to the diffuse noninformative prior and the informative prior discussed thus far in order to take advantage of their analytical convenience. In the next chapter, we show how to employ numerical computation to tackle inference when no analytical results are available.

Our data consist of the monthly returns on 25 portfolios; the companies in each portfolio are ranked according to market capitalization and book-to-market (BM) ratios. (See Chapter 9 for further details on this data set.) The returns we use for model estimation span the period from January 1995 to December 2005 (a total of 132 time periods). We extract the factors that best explain the variability of returns of the 25 portfolios using principal components analysis. (See Chapter 14 for more details on multifactor models.) The first five factors explain around 95% of the variability and we use their returns as the independent variables in our linear regression model, making up the matrix $\mathbf{X}$ (the first column is a column of ones). The return on the portfolio consisting of the companies with the smallest size and BM ratios is the dependent variable y. In addition, returns recorded for the months from January 1990 to December 1994 (a total of 60 time periods) are employed to compute the hyperparameters of the informative prior distributions, in the manner explained in the previous section. Our interest centers primarily on the posterior inference for the regression coefficients, β_k, $k = 1, \ldots, 6$—the intercept and the five factor exposures (in the terminology of multifactor models).

Posterior Distributions The prior and posterior parameter values for $\boldsymbol{\beta}$ are given in Exhibit 4.1 Part A of the exhibit presents the results under the diffuse improper prior assumption and Part B under the informative prior assumption. In parentheses are the posterior standard deviations, computed using the expression in (3.26) in Chapter 3. The OLS estimates of the regression coefficients are, of course, given by the posterior means in the diffuse prior scenario. Notice how the posterior mean of $\boldsymbol{\beta}$ under the informative prior is shrunk away from the OLS estimate and toward the prior value, for the chosen value of $\tau = 1$. We could introduce more uncertainty into the prior distribution of $\boldsymbol{\beta}$ (make it less informative) by choosing a smaller value of τ—the posterior mean of $\boldsymbol{\beta}$ would then be closer to the OLS estimate. Conversely, the stronger our prior belief about the mean of $\boldsymbol{\beta}$, the closer the posterior mean would be to the prior mean.

Credible Intervals Since the marginal posterior distribution of β_k, $k = 1, \ldots, 6$, is of known form—Student's t—we can compute analytically the Bayesian confidence intervals for the regression coefficients. We provide several quantiles from the distribution of each β_k. For example, under the diffuse improper prior, the 95% (symmetric) Bayesian interval for β_2 is $(-0.3187, -0.3029)$, while, under the informative prior, the 99% (symmetric) Bayesian interval for β_6 is $(-0.0162, 0.1180)$.[11]

Hypothesis Comparison In the frequentist regression tradition, testing the significance of the regression coefficients is of great interest—the validity of the null hypothesis $\beta_k = 0$ is examined. In the Bayesian setting, we could evaluate and compare the posterior probabilities, $P(\beta_k \rangle 0 \mid y, \mathbf{X})$ and $P(\beta_k < 0 \mid y, \mathbf{X})$ (given in Exhibit 4.1 for each factor exposure). We could safely conclude that the exposures on Factor 1 through Factor 4 are different from zero—the mass of their posterior distributions is concentrated on

[11]Notice that, since the Student's t-distribution is unimodal, these (symmetric) intervals are also the HPD intervals.

		β_1	β_2	β_3	β_4	β_5	β_6
		Intercept	Factor1	Factor 2	Factor 3	Factor 4	Factor 5
A.	**Prior Mean**	–	–	–	–	–	–
	Posterior Mean	0.0048	–0.3108	–0.3997	0.0648	–0.4132	–0.0042
	Posterior Standard Deviation	(0.0011)	(0.0048)	(0.0103)	(0.0202)	(0.0297)	(0.0410)
	$b_{0.01}$	0.0021	–0.3219	–0.4238	0.0174	–0.4826	–0.1000
	$b_{0.05}$	0.0029	–0.3187	–0.4168	0.0312	–0.4624	–0.0721
	$b_{0.25}$	0.0040	–0.314	–0.4067	0.0511	–0.4333	–0.0319
	$b_{0.75}$	0.0055	–0.3075	–0.3928	0.0784	–0.3931	–0.0235
	$b_{0.95}$	0.0067	–0.3029	–0.3827	0.0983	–0.364	0.0636
	$b_{0.99}$	0.0075	–0.2996	–0.3757	0.1121	–0.3438	0.0915
B.	**Prior Mean**	0.0037	–0.2952	–0.4217	0.038	–0.2784	0.1063
	Posterior Mean	0.0042	–0.303	–0.4107	0.0514	–0.3458	0.0510
	Posterior Standard Deviation	(0.0008)	(0.0033)	(0.0072)	(0.0142)	(0.0208)	(0.0287)
	$b_{0.01}$	0.0024	–0.3108	–0.4276	0.0182	–0.3945	–0.0162
	$b_{0.05}$	0.0029	–0.3085	–0.4226	0.0280	–0.3801	0.0038
	$b_{0.25}$	0.0037	–0.3052	–0.4156	0.0418	–0.3598	0.0318
	$b_{0.75}$	0.0048	–0.3007	–0.4059	0.0609	–0.3318	0.0703
	$b_{0.95}$	0.0056	–0.2975	–0.3986	0.0747	–0.3115	0.0983
	$b_{0.99}$	0.0061	–0.2952	–0.3939	0.0844	–0.2972	0.1180

EXHIBIT 4.1 Posterior inference for β
Note: Part A contains posterior results under the diffuse improper prior; Part B contains posterior results under the informative prior.

either positive or negative values. For the exposure on Factor 5, the picture is less than clear-cut. Under the diffuse, improper prior, a bit over 50% of the posterior mass is below zero and the rest—above zero. Therefore, one would perhaps take the pertinence of this factor for explaining the variability of the return on the small-cap/small-BM portfolio with a grain of salt. Notice, however, how the situation changes in the informative-prior case. More than 95% of the posterior mass is above zero. The strong prior beliefs about a positive mean of β_6 lead to the conclusion that the exposure of the portfolio returns to Factor 5 is not zero. Exhibit 4.2 further illustrates these observations.

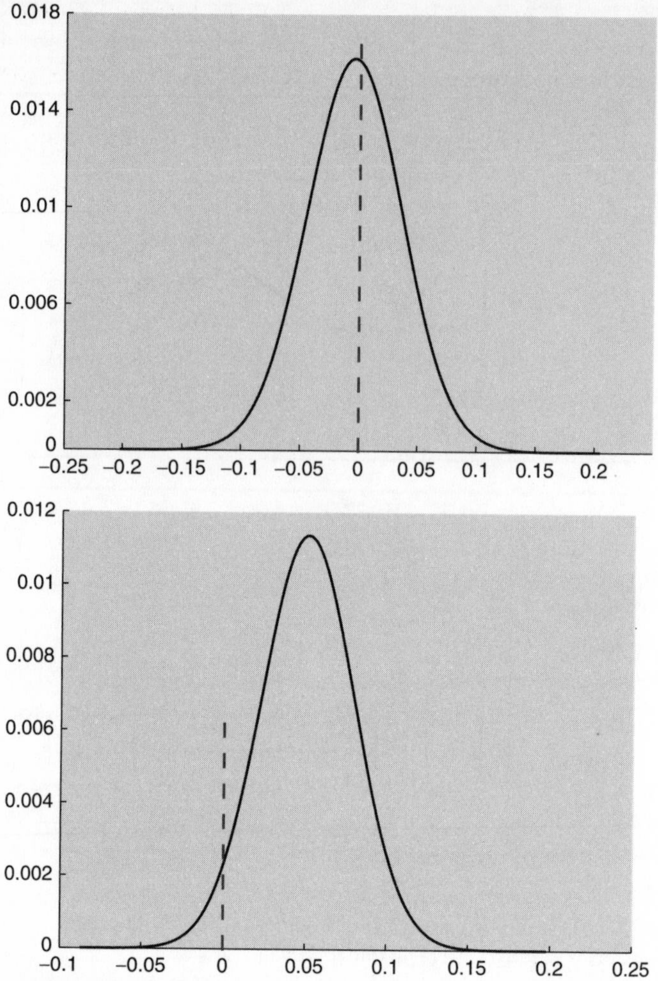

EXHIBIT 4.2 Posterior densities of β_6 under the two prior scenarios

Note: The plot on the top refers to the diffuse improper prior; the plot on the bottom—to the informative prior.

THE MULTIVARIATE LINEAR REGRESSION MODEL

Quite often in finance, and especially in investment management, one is faced with modeling data consisting of many assets whose returns or other attributes are not independent. Casting the problem in a multivariate framework is one way to tackle dependencies between assets.[12] In this section, we outline the basics of multivariate regression estimation within the Bayesian setting. For applications to portfolio construction, see Chapters 6 through 9.

Suppose that T observations are available on N dependent variables. We arrange these in the $T \times N$ matrix, $\boldsymbol{Y}$,

$$\boldsymbol{Y} = \begin{pmatrix} \boldsymbol{y}_1 \\ \vdots \\ \boldsymbol{y}_t \\ \vdots \\ \boldsymbol{y}_T \end{pmatrix} = \begin{pmatrix} y_{1,1} & y_{1,2} & \cdots & y_{1,N} \\ \cdots & \cdots & \cdots & \cdots \\ y_{t,1} & y_{t,2} & \cdots & y_{t,N} \\ \cdots & \cdots & \cdots & \cdots \\ y_{T,1} & y_{T,2} & \cdots & y_{T,N} \end{pmatrix}.$$

The multivariate linear regression is written as

$$\boldsymbol{Y} = \boldsymbol{X}\boldsymbol{B} + \boldsymbol{U}, \tag{4.31}$$

where: $\boldsymbol{X}$ = $T \times K$ matrix of observations of the K independent variables,

$$\boldsymbol{X} = \begin{pmatrix} \boldsymbol{x}_1 \\ \vdots \\ \boldsymbol{x}_t \\ \vdots \\ \boldsymbol{x}_T \end{pmatrix} = \begin{pmatrix} x_{1,1} & x_{1,2} & \cdots & x_{1,K} \\ \cdots & \cdots & \cdots & \cdots \\ x_{t,1} & x_{t,2} & \cdots & x_{t,K} \\ \cdots & \cdots & \cdots & \cdots \\ x_{T,1} & x_{T,2} & \cdots & x_{T,K} \end{pmatrix},$$

$\boldsymbol{B}$ = $K \times N$ matrix of regression coefficients,

$$\boldsymbol{B} = \begin{pmatrix} \boldsymbol{\alpha} \\ \boldsymbol{\beta}_1 \\ \cdots \\ \boldsymbol{\beta}_K \end{pmatrix} = \begin{pmatrix} \alpha_1 & \alpha_2 & \cdots & \alpha_N \\ \beta_{1,1} & \beta_{1,2} & \cdots & \beta_{1,N} \\ \cdots & \cdots & \cdots & \cdots \\ \beta_{K,1} & \beta_{K,2} & \cdots & \beta_{K,N} \end{pmatrix},$$

[12] We note, in passing, that although the multivariate normal distribution is usually assumed because of its analytical tractability, dependencies among asset returns could be somewhat more complex than what the class of elliptical distributions (to which the normal distribution belongs) is able to describe. Alternative distributional assumptions could be made at the expense of analytical convenience and occasional substantial estimation problems (especially, in high-dimensional settings). A more flexible way of dependence modeling is provided through the use of copulas. Unfortunately, copula estimation could also suffer from estimation problems. We briefly discuss copulas in Chapter 13.

$U = T \times N$ matrix of regression disturbances,

$$U = \begin{pmatrix} u_1 \\ \vdots \\ u_t \\ \vdots \\ u_T \end{pmatrix} = \begin{pmatrix} u_{1,1} & u_{1,2} & \dots & u_{1,N} \\ \dots & \dots & \dots & \dots \\ u_{t,1} & u_{t,2} & \dots & u_{t,N} \\ \dots & \dots & \dots & \dots \\ u_{T,1} & u_{T,2} & \dots & u_{T,N} \end{pmatrix}.$$

The first column of $\boldsymbol{X}$ usually consists of ones to reflect the presence of an intercept. In the multivariate setting, the usual linear regression assumption that the disturbances are i.i.d. means that each row of $\boldsymbol{U}$ is an independent realization from the same N-dimensional multivariate distribution. We assume that this distribution is multivariate normal with zero mean and covariance matrix, $\boldsymbol{\Sigma}$,

$$\boldsymbol{u}_t \sim \mathrm{N}(\boldsymbol{0}, \boldsymbol{\Sigma}), \tag{4.32}$$

for $t = 1, \ldots, T$. The off-diagonal elements of $\boldsymbol{\Sigma}$ are nonzero, as we assume the dependent variables are correlated, and the covariance matrix contains N variances and $N(N-1)/2$ distinct covariances.

Using the expression for the density of the multivariate normal distribution in (3.28), we write the likelihood function for the unknown model parameters, $\boldsymbol{B}$ and $\boldsymbol{\Sigma}$, as[13]

$$L(\boldsymbol{B}, \boldsymbol{\Sigma} \mid \boldsymbol{Y}, \boldsymbol{X}) \propto |\boldsymbol{\Sigma}|^{-T/2} \exp\left(-\frac{1}{2}\sum_{t=1}^{T}(\boldsymbol{y}_t - \boldsymbol{x}_t\boldsymbol{B})\Sigma^{-1}(\boldsymbol{y}_t - \boldsymbol{x}_t\boldsymbol{B})'\right), \tag{4.33}$$

where $|\boldsymbol{\Sigma}|$ is the determinant of the covariance matrix. We now turn to specifying the prior distributional assumptions for $\boldsymbol{B}$ and $\boldsymbol{\Sigma}$.

Diffuse Improper Prior

The lack of specific prior knowledge about the elements of $\boldsymbol{B}$ and $\boldsymbol{\Sigma}$ can be reflected by employing the Jeffreys' prior, which in the multivariate setting

---

[13]The expression in the exponent in (4.33) could also be written as

$$-\frac{1}{2}\mathrm{tr}(\boldsymbol{Y} - \boldsymbol{X}\boldsymbol{B})'(\boldsymbol{Y} - \boldsymbol{X}\boldsymbol{B})\boldsymbol{\Sigma}^{-1},$$

where tr denotes the trace operator, which sums the diagonal elements of a square matrix.

takes the form[14]

$$\pi(B, \Sigma) \propto |\Sigma|^{-\frac{N+1}{2}}. \tag{4.34}$$

The posterior distributions parallel those in the univariate case. With the risk of stating the obvious, note that B is a random matrix; therefore, its posterior distribution, conditional on Σ, will be a generalization of the multivariate normal posterior distribution in (4.9). To describe it, we first vectorize (expand column-wise) the matrix of regression coefficients, B, and denote the resulting $KN \times 1$ vector by β,

$$\beta = \text{vec}(B) = \begin{pmatrix} \alpha' \\ \beta_1' \\ \vdots \\ \beta_K' \end{pmatrix},$$

by stacking vertically the columns of B'. It can be shown that β's posterior distribution, conditional on Σ, is a multivariate normal given by

$$p(\beta \mid Y, X, \Sigma) = \text{N}\left(\widehat{\beta}, \Sigma \otimes (X'X)^{-1}\right), \tag{4.35}$$

where $\widehat{\beta} = \text{vec}(\widehat{B}) = \text{vec}\left((X'X)^{-1}(X'Y)\right)$ is the vectorized OLS estimator of B and $\otimes$ denotes the Kronecker product.[15]

The posterior distribution of Σ can be shown to be the inverted Wishart distribution (the multivariate analog of the inverted gamma distribution),[16]

$$p(\Sigma \mid Y, X) = \text{IW}(\nu^*, S), \tag{4.36}$$

---

[14] As in the univariate case, we assume independence between (the elements of) B and Σ.

[15] The Kronecker product is an operator for direct multiplication of matrices (which are not necessarily compatible). For two matrices, A of size $m \times n$ and B of size $p \times q$, the Kronecker product is defined as

$$A \otimes B = \begin{pmatrix} a_{1,1}B & a_{1,2}B & \ldots & a_{1,n}B \\ \ldots & \ldots & \ldots & \ldots \\ a_{m,1}B & a_{m,2}B & \ldots & a_{m,n}B \end{pmatrix},$$

resulting in an $mp \times nq$ block matrix.

[16] See the appendix to Chapter 3 for the definition of the inverted Wishart distribution.

where the degrees of freedom parameter is $\nu^* = T - K + N + 1$ and the scale matrix is $S = (Y - X\widehat{B})'(Y - X\widehat{B})$.

A full Bayesian informative prior approach to estimation of the multivariate linear regression model would require one to specify proper prior distributions for the regression coefficients, $\boldsymbol{\beta}$, and the covariance matrix, $\boldsymbol{\Sigma}$. The conjugate prior scenario is invariably the scenario of choice so as to keep the regression estimation within analytically manageable boundaries. That scenario consists of a multivariate normal prior for $\boldsymbol{\beta}$ and inverted Wishart for $\boldsymbol{\Sigma}$. See Chapters 6 and 7 for further details.

SUMMARY

In this chapter, we discussed Bayesian inference for the univariate and multivariate linear regression models. In a normal setting and under conjugate priors, the posterior and predictive results are standard. Increased flexibility can be achieved by employing alternative distributional assumptions. Model estimation then is aided by numerical computational methods. We cover the most important posterior simulation and approximation methods in the next chapter; many of them we extend in the following chapters.

CHAPTER 5

Bayesian Numerical Computation

The advances in numerical computation methods in the last two decades have been the driving force behind the growing popularity of the Bayesian framework in empirical statistical and financial research. These methods provide a very flexible computational setting for estimating complex models in which the traditional, frequentist framework sometimes requires much more effort and may encounter estimation problems. The goal of the numerical computational framework is to generate samples from the posterior distribution of the parameters as well as the predictive distribution in situations when analytical results are unavailable. Increased model manageability comes at a cost, however. Careful design of the sampling schemes is required to ensure that posterior and predictive inference are reliable.

In this chapter, we lay the foundation for the numerical computation framework. We revisit different aspects of it in the following chapters—in the context of particular financial applications.

MONTE CARLO INTEGRATION

In (natural) conjugate scenarios, such as the ones discussed in Chapters 2 and 3 (normal-inverse gamma and binomial beta), the posterior parameter distributions and the predictive distributions are recognizable as known distributions. If one is, for example, interested in estimating the posterior (predictive) mean, analytical expressions for it are readily available. Equivalently, the integral defining the posterior mean can be computed analytically. Denoting the unknown parameter vector by $\boldsymbol{\theta}$ and the observed data by y, the posterior mean of a function $g(\boldsymbol{\theta})$ is given by

$$\mathrm{E}g(\boldsymbol{\theta}) \mid y) = \int g(\boldsymbol{\theta})\, p(\boldsymbol{\theta} \mid y)\, \mathrm{d}\boldsymbol{\theta}, \tag{5.1}$$

where $p(\boldsymbol{\theta} \mid y)$ is $\boldsymbol{\theta}$'s posterior distribution. In the general case, it might not be possible to evaluate the integral in (5.1) analytically. Then, one can compute an approximation of it which, by a fundamental result in statistics, called the *Law of Large Numbers*, can be made arbitrarily close to the integral above. Suppose we have been able to obtain a sample $\boldsymbol{\theta}^{(1)}, \boldsymbol{\theta}^{(2)}, \ldots, \boldsymbol{\theta}^{(M)}$ from $p(\boldsymbol{\theta} \mid y)$.[1] The quantity

$$\widehat{g_M(\boldsymbol{\theta})} = \frac{1}{M} \sum_{m=1}^{M} g(\boldsymbol{\theta}^{(m)}) \tag{5.2}$$

can be shown to converge to $\mathrm{E}g(\boldsymbol{\theta}) \mid y)$ as M goes to infinity.[2] That is, the larger the sample from θ's posterior distribution, the more accurately we can approximate (estimate) the expected value of $g(\boldsymbol{\theta})$. This approximation procedure lies at the center of *Monte Carlo integration*. The Monte Carlo approximation, $\widehat{g_M(\boldsymbol{\theta})}$, is nothing more than a sample average. Using results from asymptotical statistics, one could evaluate the quality of the approximation (i.e., what the imprecision in estimating $\mathrm{E}g(\boldsymbol{\theta}) \mid y)$ is from using only a finite sample of observations). The asymptotic variance of $\widehat{g_M(\boldsymbol{\theta})}$ is σ^2/M.[3] The variance of $g(\boldsymbol{\theta})$, σ^2, can be estimated with the sample variance,

$$s_M^2 = \sqrt{\frac{1}{M} \sum_{m=1}^{M} \left(g(\boldsymbol{\theta}^{(m)}) - \widehat{g_M(\boldsymbol{\theta})}\right)^2}.$$

The measure of numerical accuracy is then provided by the *Monte Carlo Standard Error* (MCSE),[4]

$$\mathrm{MCSE} = \sqrt{\frac{S_M^2}{M}}. \tag{5.3}$$

[1]The Law of Large Numbers requires that $\boldsymbol{\theta}^{(i)}$ are independent realizations (simulations) from the distribution of θ. Similar results hold, however, for dependent realizations as well, as will be the case with the Markov Chain Monte Carlo simulations that we discuss later in the chapter.

[2]The convergence is in probability, given the sample of realizations $\boldsymbol{y}$ and provided the expectation in (5.1) exists. See any text in basic probability theory such as Feller (2001) and Chung (2000).

[3]The asymptotic distribution of the estimator of $g(\boldsymbol{\theta})$, $\widehat{g_M(\boldsymbol{\theta})}$, is normal, $N(g(\boldsymbol{\theta}), \sigma^2/M)$.

[4]The expression in (5.3) could be used as a practical indication for the number of draws, M, necessary for an adequate approximation to $g(\boldsymbol{\theta})$. For example, M = 10,000 means that the error due to approximation is 1% of the standard deviation of $g(\boldsymbol{\theta})$'s posterior distribution.

The usefulness of Monte Carlo approximation becomes apparent when one considers the fact that probabilities can be expressed as expectations. For example, the probability of some subset A of values of θ is expressed as the expectation

$$P(\boldsymbol{\theta} \text{ is in A}) = \mathrm{E}\left(I_{\{A\}}(\boldsymbol{\theta})\right),$$

where $I_{\{A\}}(\boldsymbol{\theta})$ is an indicator function taking value of 1 if $\boldsymbol{\theta}$ is in A and a value of 0 if $\boldsymbol{\theta}$ is not in A. The Monte Carlo approximation of the expectation above would give

$$P(\boldsymbol{\theta} \text{ is in A}) \approx \frac{1}{M}\sum_{m=1}^{M} I_{\{A\}}(\boldsymbol{\theta}^{(m)}).$$

That is, to approximate the probability, one would simply compute the proportion of times $\boldsymbol{\theta}$ takes a value in A in the simulated sample of size M.

Even though the Monte Carlo approximation might seem like an easy way to deal with complicated situations, it turns out not to be the best approach in practice. First, the estimators produced as a result do not necessarily have the smallest approximation error. Second, while obtaining samples from standard distributions is usually easy, the posterior distributions one comes across in practice are often not of familiar form. Direct simulation from the posterior (as above) is then not possible, and posterior and predictive inferences require the use of simulation algorithms. We discuss posterior simulations next.

ALGORITHMS FOR POSTERIOR SIMULATION

Algorithms for simulation from the posterior distribution can be divided into categories:

- *Independent simulation.* Algorithms that produce an independent and identically distributed (i.i.d.) sample from the posterior.[5]
- *Dependent simulation.* Algorithms whose output (after convergence) is a sample of (nearly) identically distributed (but not independent) draws from the posterior.

[5]Although, formally, the direct posterior simulation is a member of this category, here we only include algorithms targeted at cases when the posterior cannot be sampled directly.

The algorithms from the first category can be seen as precursors to the ones from the second category. Posterior simulation in practice frequently uses a mixture of the algorithms in the two categories, as we see in the chapters ahead.

Representatives of the first category are importance sampling and rejection sampling. In the second category fall all algorithms based on generation (simulation) of a Markov chain—the so-called *Markov Chain Monte Carlo* (MCMC) methods. We discuss both categories next.

Rejection Sampling

Rejection sampling, one of the early algorithms for posterior simulation, rests on a simple idea: find an "envelope" of the posterior density, obtain draws from the envelope, and discard those that do not belong to the posterior distribution. In order to employ the rejection sampling algorithm, the posterior must be known (up to a constant of proportionality), although not recognizable as a standard distribution. Recall that the constant of proportionality is given by the denominator of the ratio in the Bayes' theorem (see Chapter 3).

More formally, suppose that a function $h(\boldsymbol{\theta})$ is available, such that

$$p(\boldsymbol{\theta} \mid y) \leq K h(\boldsymbol{\theta}),$$

where K is a constant greater than 1. Then, $h(\boldsymbol{\theta})$ plays the role of the envelope function. Notice that $h(\boldsymbol{\theta})$ could be a density function itself, but this is not necessary.[6] The role of K is to make sure that the inequality is satisfied for all values of $\boldsymbol{\theta}$.

The rejection sampling algorithm procedure for obtaining one draw from the posterior of $\boldsymbol{\theta}$ consists of the following steps:

1. Draw $\boldsymbol{\theta}$ from $h(\boldsymbol{\theta})$ and denote the draw by $\boldsymbol{\theta}^*$.
2. Compute the ratio

$$a = \frac{p(\boldsymbol{\theta}^* \mid y)}{K h(\boldsymbol{\theta}^*)}. \tag{5.4}$$

3. With probability a, accept the draw $\boldsymbol{\theta}^*$ as a draw from the posterior, $p(\boldsymbol{\theta} \mid y)$. If $\boldsymbol{\theta}^*$ is rejected, go back to step (1). To decide whether to accept

[6] In Chapter 12, for example, in the context of stochastic volatility modeling, we mention the adaptive rejection algorithm of Gilks and Wild (1992) for a univariate posterior, in which $h(\theta)$ is a piecewise linear approximation to the posterior and is not a density.

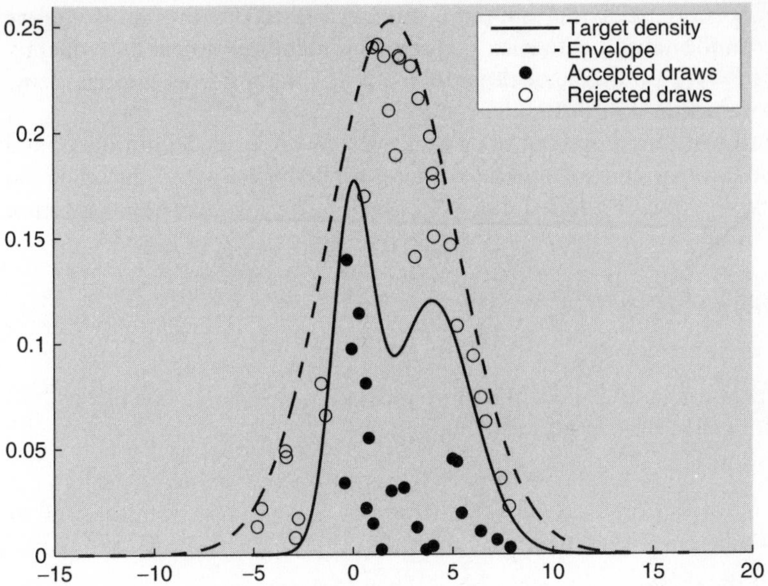

EXHIBIT 5.1 The rejection sampling algorithm

or not, draw one observation, u, from the uniform distribution on (0, 1) $U(0, 1)$ if $u \leq a$, accept $\boldsymbol{\theta}^*$. If $u > a$, reject $\boldsymbol{\theta}^*$.

We can observe that the greater is K, the bigger the "discrepancy" between $p(\boldsymbol{\theta} \mid \boldsymbol{y})$ and the lower the probability of accepting draws from $h(\boldsymbol{\theta})$. Finally, repeating the steps of the rejection sampling algorithm many times produces a sample exactly from the posterior density. This is graphically illustrated in Exhibit 5.1 for the univariate case. Draws of θ, corresponding to points under the posterior density curve (the filled circles on the graph), are accepted, while draws corresponding to points falling in the area outside of the posterior density curve (the empty circles on the graph) are rejected. The acceptance probability, a, represents the ratio of the heights of the posterior density curve and the envelope curve at a particular value of θ.

Importance Sampling

An algorithm, related to rejection sampling, for approximating expectations is the importance sampling algorithm. Its underlying idea is to increase the accuracy (decrease the variance) of an estimator by weighting more the simulations that are more important (likely), hence its name. Unlike the rejection sampling algorithm, importance sampling draws are obtained from a density approximating the posterior density. The posterior density kernel (unnormalized posterior density) is, as before, denoted as $p(\boldsymbol{\theta} \mid \boldsymbol{y})$. Suppose $h(\boldsymbol{\theta})$ is a probability density function, sampling from which is easy. (It may be a function of the data $\boldsymbol{y}$, but we suppress this notationally.) As explained earlier, many quantities of interest (such as probabilities) can be expressed as expectations; therefore, here we simply suppose that the posterior expectation of a function $g(\boldsymbol{\theta})$ needs to be evaluated. The expectation is written as[7]

$$E\big(g(\boldsymbol{\theta}) \mid \boldsymbol{y}\big) = \frac{\int g(\boldsymbol{\theta}) p(\boldsymbol{\theta} \mid \boldsymbol{y})\, d\boldsymbol{\theta}}{\int p(\boldsymbol{\theta} \mid \boldsymbol{y})\, d\boldsymbol{\theta}} = \frac{\int g(\boldsymbol{\theta}) h(\boldsymbol{\theta}) p(\boldsymbol{\theta} \mid \boldsymbol{y}) / h(\boldsymbol{\theta})\, d\boldsymbol{\theta}}{\int p(\boldsymbol{\theta} \mid \boldsymbol{y}) h(\boldsymbol{\theta}) / h(\boldsymbol{\theta})\, d\boldsymbol{\theta}}. \tag{5.5}$$

The expression in (5.5) becomes more palatable when we define the following ratio, called the "importance weight,"

$$\omega(\boldsymbol{\theta}) = \frac{p(\boldsymbol{\theta} \mid \boldsymbol{y})}{h(\boldsymbol{\theta})}, \tag{5.6}$$

which is the same as a in (5.4) above. Then (5.5) becomes

$$E\big(g(\boldsymbol{\theta}) \mid \boldsymbol{y}\big) = \frac{\int g(\boldsymbol{\theta}) h(\boldsymbol{\theta}) \omega(\boldsymbol{\theta})\, d\boldsymbol{\theta}}{\int h(\boldsymbol{\theta}) \omega(\boldsymbol{\theta})\, d\boldsymbol{\theta}} \approx \frac{\frac{1}{M} \sum_{m=1}^{M} g\big(\boldsymbol{\theta}^{(m)}\big) \omega\big(\boldsymbol{\theta}^{(m)}\big)}{\frac{1}{M} \sum_{m=1}^{M} \omega\big(\boldsymbol{\theta}^{(m)}\big)},$$

where $\boldsymbol{\theta}^{(m)}$, $m = 1, \ldots, M$, are (i.i.d.) simulations from $h(\boldsymbol{\theta})$. The estimator above has a smaller approximation variance the less variable the weights, $\omega(\boldsymbol{\theta}^{(m)})$, are. Therefore, the choice of approximating density, $h(\boldsymbol{\theta})$, is essential. In practice, one would select $h(\boldsymbol{\theta})$ so as to match the mode and shape (scale) of the target density. (See the discussion of the Independence-Chain M-H algorithm later in this chapter.)

MCMC Methods

Simulating i.i.d. draws from a complicated posterior density (or from an appropriately chosen approximating density) is not always possible. The posterior simulation algorithms, collectively known as MCMC methods, provide iterative procedures to approximately sample from complicated

[7]Notice that, since $p(\boldsymbol{\theta} \mid \boldsymbol{y})$ is unnormalized, it is not possible to evaluate the expectation unless we know the constant of proportionality—the integral in the denominator of (5.5). We can, however, approximate it together with the numerator, as we see shortly.

posterior densities (including in high-dimensional settings) by avoiding the independence assumption. At each step, the algorithm attempts to find parameter values with higher posterior probability, so that the approximation moves closer to the target (posterior) density. The purpose of applying the algorithms remains the same—to approximate the expectations of functions of interest with their sample averages. The difference is that the simulations of θ, at which the sample averages are computed, are obtained as the realizations of Markov chains.[8] In fact, the Markov chain needs to run for a sufficiently long time in order to ensure that the simulations are indeed draws from θ's posterior distribution.[9] Then, we say that the chain has converged. We discuss some practical rules to determine whether convergence has occurred later in the chapter. We now proceed with a closer look at the two most commonly employed MCMC methods—the Metropolis-Hastings algorithm and the Gibbs sampler.

The Metropolis-Hastings Algorithm The Metropolis-Hastings (M-H) algorithm is related to both rejection sampling and importance sampling discussed earlier.[10] Let $p(\boldsymbol{\theta} \mid \boldsymbol{y})$ again denote the unnormalized posterior density, sampling from which is not possible. Here, we consider the general case in which $\boldsymbol{\theta}$ is a K-dimensional parameter vector, $\boldsymbol{\theta} = (\theta_1, \theta_2, \ldots, \theta_K)$. Denote by $q(\boldsymbol{\theta} \mid \boldsymbol{\theta}^{(t-1)})$ the approximating density, called the "proposal density" or the "candidate-generating density." The purpose of the proposal

[8]A Markov chain is a random process in discrete time (a sequence of random variables) such that any state of the process depends on the previous state only and not on any earlier state. We say that the process possesses the Markov property. Denoting the random process by $\{X_n\}_{n=1}^{\infty}$, the Markov property is expressed as

$$P(X_n = x_n \mid X_{n-1} = x_{n-1}, X_{n-2} = x_{n-2}, \ldots, X_1 = x_1) = P(X_n = x_n \mid X_{n-1} = x_{n-1}).$$

The collection of all possible values of the process is called the *state space*. In the context of posterior simulations, the state space is the parameter space. For more information on Markov Chains, see, for example, Norris (1998).

[9]A Markov chain has to satisfy a number of properties (such as irreducibility and ergodicity) in order to be able to converge to its so-called "stationary distribution" (and for its stationary distribution to exist at all). Generally, these properties mean that the chain can reach any state from any other state in a finite number of steps (including a single step). See any probability text for rigorous definitions of the properties of Markov chains. Usually, the chains arising in MCMC satisfy these prerequisites.

[10]The algorithm was developed by Metropolis, Rosenbluth, Rosenbluth, Teller, and Teller (1953) and extended by Hastings (1970).

density is to randomly generate a realization of $\boldsymbol{\theta}$ given the value at the previous iteration of the algorithm.

The algorithm consists of two basic stages: first, a draw from the proposal density is obtained and second, that draw is either retained or rejected. More precisely, to obtain a sample from the posterior of $\boldsymbol{\theta}$, the M-H algorithm iterates the following sequence of steps 2 through 5:

1. Initiate the algorithm with a value $\boldsymbol{\theta}^{(0)}$ from the parameter space of $\boldsymbol{\theta}$.
2. At iteration t, draw a (multivariate) realization, $\boldsymbol{\theta}^*$, from the proposal density, $q(\boldsymbol{\theta} \mid \boldsymbol{\theta}^{(t-1)})$, where $\boldsymbol{\theta}^{(t-1)}$ is the parameter value at the previous step.
3. Compute the acceptance probability, given by

$$a\left(\boldsymbol{\theta}^*, \boldsymbol{\theta}^{(t-1)}\right) = \min\left\{1, \frac{p(\boldsymbol{\theta}^*) \,/\, q(\boldsymbol{\theta}^* \mid \boldsymbol{\theta}^{(t-1)})}{p\left(\boldsymbol{\theta}^{(t-1)}\right) \,/\, q\left(\boldsymbol{\theta}^{(t-1)} \mid \boldsymbol{\theta}^*\right)}\right\}, \tag{5.7}$$

   where we suppress notationally the dependence on the data, $\boldsymbol{y}$, for simplicity.
4. Draw u from the uniform distribution on (0, 1), $U(0, 1)$. Then,
   - If $u \leq a\left(\boldsymbol{\theta}^{(t)}, \boldsymbol{\theta}^{(t-1)}\right)$, set $\boldsymbol{\theta}^{(t)} = \boldsymbol{\theta}^*$.
   - Otherwise, set $\boldsymbol{\theta}^{(t)} = \boldsymbol{\theta}^{(t-1)}$.
5. Go back to step 2.

The algorithm is iterated (steps 2 through 5 repeated) a large number of times. Only the simulations obtained after the chain converges are regarded as an approximate sample from the posterior distribution and used for posterior inference. (See the discussion on convergence diagnostics later in the chapter for further details.) Notice that knowledge of the constant of proportionality of $\boldsymbol{\theta}$'s posterior density is not necessary; since the constant is present in both the numerator and the denominator in (5.7), it cancels out anyway.

The adequate selection of proposal densities has been the focus of considerable research efforts. We outline two main classes of proposal densities, giving rise to two versions of the M-H algorithm.

Random Walk M-H Algorithm Suppose one does not have in mind a distribution that could be regarded as a good approximation of the posterior density. Then, one would simply want to construct a chain that can explore the parameter space well (visit areas of both high and low posterior probability). The relation between successive states of the chain (realizations of $\boldsymbol{\theta}$) could be described by

$$\boldsymbol{\theta}^{(t+1)} = \boldsymbol{\theta}^{(t)} + \boldsymbol{\epsilon}^{(t+1)}, \tag{5.8}$$

where $\boldsymbol{\epsilon}^{(t+1)}$ is a (K-dimensional) zero-mean random variable distributed with q. The proposed draw of $\boldsymbol{\theta}$ at each iteration of the algorithm is then equal to the current draw plus random noise. The choice of $\boldsymbol{\epsilon}$'s distribution is driven by convenience and most often a multivariate normal distribution. The proposal distribution is then[11]

$$q\left(\boldsymbol{\theta}^{*}|\boldsymbol{\theta}^{(t-1)}\right) = \mathrm{N}\left(\boldsymbol{\theta}^{(t-1)}, \boldsymbol{\Sigma}\right) \tag{5.9}$$

When the proposal distribution, q, is symmetric (which is not required, although usually the case), the acceptance probability in (5.7) is simplified to

$$a\left(\boldsymbol{\theta}^{*}, \boldsymbol{\theta}^{(t-1)}\right) = \min\left\{1, \frac{p(\boldsymbol{\theta}^{*})}{p\left(\boldsymbol{\theta}^{(t-1)}\right)}\right\}. \tag{5.10}$$

The algorithm can now be given an intuitive explanation: When the proposed draw has a higher posterior probability than the current draw, it is always accepted (a is then equal to 1); when the proposed draw has a lower posterior probability than the current draw, it is accepted with probability a.

The simplicity of the random walk M-H algorithm might be deceptive. If the jumps the chain makes are "too" large, chances are that the generated (proposed) draws come from areas of the parameter space that have low posterior probability. Then the acceptance probability would be very low and most proposed draws would be rejected. The chain would "get stuck" at a particular value of $\boldsymbol{\theta}$ and move only rarely. If the jumps the chain makes are too small, then the chain would tend to remain in the same area of the parameter space (of either high or low posterior probability). The acceptance probability would then be very high and most proposed draws would be accepted. Clearly, both scenarios are not desirable since, in order to achieve convergence of the chain, one would have to waste substantial computing time. The quantity that regulates the jump size and requires careful tuning is the covariance matrix, $\boldsymbol{\Sigma}$, of the proposal distribution in (5.9).

The easiest way to select $\boldsymbol{\Sigma}$ is to set it equal to the scaled covariance matrix, S, where S is estimated as the negative inverse Hessian evaluated at the mode (see the discussion of the independence chain M-H algorithm below),

$$\boldsymbol{\Sigma} = cS.$$

The scale constant, c, is the tuning parameter that can be adjusted to yield a reasonable acceptance rate (proportion of accepted draws of $\boldsymbol{\theta}$). It

[11]See the appendix to Chapter 3 for the definition of the multivariate normal distribution.

has been shown that when the proposal distribution is one-dimensional, the optimal acceptance rate is around 0.5, whereas when it is multidimensional, the optimal acceptance rate is around 0.23.[12] We should note that these rates are asymptotic results and might not be achieved if, for instance, the chain has been run for an insufficient amount of time. However, they are useful as guidelines. In practice, one should perform any tuning of the covariance of the proposal distribution (by increasing or decreasing c, so as to match the desired acceptance probability) in a preliminary run of the algorithm; then, using fixed $\boldsymbol{\Sigma} = c\boldsymbol{S}$, run the chain until its convergence. (Otherwise, adjusting c during the algorithm's main run might result in the chain converging to a distribution different from the posterior.)

Independence Chain M-H Algorithm In contrast to the random walk M-H algorithm, where the proposal distribution at each iteration is centered at the most recent draw, the independence chain M-H algorithm, candidate draws are obtained regardless of the chain's current state. Employing this version of the M-H algorithm is appropriate when an adequate approximating density has been determined. The multivariate normal and multivariate Student's t-distributions are the common choices for a proposal density (and they, of course, best approximate unimodal and nearly symmetric posteriors[13]). In fact, when a diffuse prior has been specified for the model parameters, and especially when the data sample is not large, the multivariate Student's t-distribution is preferable to the multivariate normal distribution, as it can better approximate the tails of the posterior distribution.

The next step after selecting the proposal density is to center it and scale it to match the posterior as closely as possible. To do this, one needs to:

1. Find the posterior mode, $\widehat{\boldsymbol{\theta}}$, of the (unnormalized) posterior distribution.[14] Since, most often, the posterior density is complicated, one would have to resort to numerical optimization, which can be performed with most commercial software products.[15]
2. Compute the Hessian, $\boldsymbol{H}$, of the logarithm of the (unnormalized) posterior density, evaluated at $\widehat{\boldsymbol{\theta}}$. The Hessian is simply the matrix of

[12]See Gelman, Roberts, and Gilks (1996) and Roberts, Gelman, and Gilks (1997).
[13]See Geweke (1989) for a discussion of the so-called "split–normal" and "split-Student's t" distributions designed to accommodate skewed posteriors.
[14]The mode is the value of $\boldsymbol{\theta}$ that maximizes the posterior. In practice, it is easier to maximize the logarithm of the posterior distribution.
[15]For instance, MATLAB, S-PLUS or SAS/IML.

second partial derivatives of a function. In this case, $\boldsymbol{H}$ is the matrix of second derivatives of $\log(p(\boldsymbol{\theta} \mid y))$ with respect to the components of $\boldsymbol{\theta}$. The Hessian (evaluated at the mode) is usually provided by commercial software products as a byproduct of the numerical optimization routine for finding the maximum-likelihood estimate, $\widehat{\boldsymbol{\theta}}$.

The multivariate normal proposal density becomes[16]

$$q\left(\boldsymbol{\theta} \mid \boldsymbol{\theta}^{(t-1)}\right) = q\left(\boldsymbol{\theta}\right) = \mathrm{N}\left(\widehat{\boldsymbol{\theta}}, -\boldsymbol{H}^{-1}\right). \tag{5.11}$$

In order to ensure that the proposal density adequately envelops the posterior density, it might be a good idea to scale up (inflate) the normal covariance matrix in (5.11). The scale could be employed, as explained earlier, to adjust the acceptance rate. For example, Geweke (1994) uses a factor of 1.2^2, so that the covariance matrix becomes $-1.2^2\,\boldsymbol{H}^{-1}$.

The multivariate Student's t proposal density is written as[17]

$$q\left(\boldsymbol{\theta} \mid \boldsymbol{\theta}^{(t-1)}\right) = q\left(\boldsymbol{\theta}\right) = t\left(\nu, \widehat{\boldsymbol{\theta}}, -(\boldsymbol{H})^{-1}(\nu - 2)/\nu\right), \tag{5.12}$$

where the degrees-of-freedom parameter, ν, is usually set at a low value such as $\nu = 5$ (thus producing a heavy-tailed proposal density).[18] To sample from the proposal distribution in (5.12), draw $\widetilde{\boldsymbol{\theta}}$ from the (standardized) multivariate Student's t with ν degrees of freedom, centered around 0 and with scale equal to the identity matrix, $t\left(\nu, 0, \boldsymbol{I}_K\right)$. Then, transform $\widetilde{\boldsymbol{\theta}}$ by scaling and centering to obtain the draw of $\boldsymbol{\theta}$,

$$\boldsymbol{\theta} = \widehat{\boldsymbol{\theta}} + \widetilde{\boldsymbol{\theta}}\left[-(\boldsymbol{H})^{-1}(\nu - 2)/\nu\right].$$

---

[16]This result comes from maximum likelihood theory. The multivariate normal distribution in (5.11) is the asymptotic distribution of the maximum-likelihood estimator, $\widehat{\boldsymbol{\theta}}$.

[17]In Chapter 3, we adopted the notation $t(\nu, \boldsymbol{\mu}, \boldsymbol{S})$ for the multivariate Student's t-distribution, where $\boldsymbol{S}$ is the distribution's scale matrix and ν is the degrees-of-freedom parameter. The quantity $-\boldsymbol{H}^{-1}$ is the estimator of the (asymptotic) covariance matrix of the maximum-likelihood estimator, $\widehat{\boldsymbol{\theta}}$, while the covariance matrix of the multivariate Student's t-distribution is given by $\boldsymbol{\Sigma} = \boldsymbol{S}\nu/(\nu - 2)$. Whence, the form of the scale matrix in (5.12).

[18]Recall that when ν is equal to 2 or less, the Student's t-distribution is so heavy-tailed that its covariance does not exist. As ν increases, the tails become thinner and for values of ν exceeding 30, the univariate Student's t-distribution behaves approximately like a normal distribution. (In general, for a given dimension of the random variable, the higher ν is, the closer the Student's t is to the normal distribution.)

We can observe that, in the case of the independence chain M-H algorithm, the acceptance probability, $a(\boldsymbol{\theta}^*, \boldsymbol{\theta}^{(t-1)})$, becomes

$$a(\boldsymbol{\theta}^*, \boldsymbol{\theta}^{(t-1)}) = \min\left\{1, \frac{\omega(\boldsymbol{\theta}^*)}{\omega(\boldsymbol{\theta}^{(t-1)})}\right\}, \tag{5.13}$$

where $\omega(\boldsymbol{\theta}) = p(\boldsymbol{\theta})/q(\boldsymbol{\theta})$ is the importance weight in (5.6).

Block Structure M-H Algorithm Finally, as a transition to our discussion of an important special case of the M-H algorithm, the Gibbs sampler, we consider one M-H algorithm's implementation issue. Most often than not, it is not possible to identify an adequate proposal (approximating) density, $q(\boldsymbol{\theta})$, for the posterior distribution of the whole parameter vector, $\boldsymbol{\theta}$. Instead, one can easily specify proposals for blocks of the parameter vector. Suppose, for example, that $\boldsymbol{\theta}$ is partitioned as

$$\boldsymbol{\theta} = (\boldsymbol{\theta}_1, \boldsymbol{\theta}_2),$$

where the blocks, $\boldsymbol{\theta}_i$, $i = 1, 2$, could be vectors themselves or scalars.

Further, suppose that one determines two suitable proposals for the conditional posterior densities $p_1(\boldsymbol{\theta}_1 \mid \boldsymbol{\theta}_2, y)$ and $p_2(\boldsymbol{\theta}_2 \mid \boldsymbol{\theta}_1, y)$. Denote the respective proposal densities by

$$q_1(\boldsymbol{\theta}_1 \mid \boldsymbol{\theta}_1^{(t-1)}, \boldsymbol{\theta}_2)$$

and

$$q_2(\boldsymbol{\theta}_2 \mid \boldsymbol{\theta}_2^{(t-1)}, \boldsymbol{\theta}_1).$$

Certainly, q_1 and q_2 could be independent of $\boldsymbol{\theta}_1^{(t-1)}$ and $\boldsymbol{\theta}_2^{(t-1)}$, respectively, as is the case in the independent chain M-H algorithm. It can be shown that successive sampling from these two proposal densities produces an approximate sample from the joint posterior density, $p(\boldsymbol{\theta} \mid y)$. Steps 2 through 4 at iteration t of the M-H algorithm outlined earlier are modified as follows to accommodate this successive sampling. At iteration t,

1. Draw a realization $\boldsymbol{\theta}_1^*$ from the conditional proposal density, $q_1(\boldsymbol{\theta}_1 \mid \boldsymbol{\theta}_1^{(t-1)}, \boldsymbol{\theta}_2^{(t-1)})$, where $\boldsymbol{\theta}_i^{(t-1)}$, $i = 1, 2$, are the values of the two blocks at the previous iteration of the algorithm.
2. Compute the acceptance probability in (5.7) modified in the obvious way.
3. Accept or reject $\boldsymbol{\theta}_1^*$ as explained earlier.

4. Draw a realization $\boldsymbol{\theta}_2^*$ from the conditional proposal density, $q_2(\boldsymbol{\theta}_2 \mid \boldsymbol{\theta}_1^{(t)}, \boldsymbol{\theta}_2^{(t-1)})$, where $\boldsymbol{\theta}_1^{(t)}$ is the value of $\boldsymbol{\theta}_1$ obtained in step (4.1) and $\boldsymbol{\theta}_2^{(t-1)}$ is the value of $\boldsymbol{\theta}_2$ at the previous iteration of the algorithm.
5. Compute the acceptance probability in (5.7) modified in the obvious way.
6. Accept or reject $\boldsymbol{\theta}_2^*$ as explained earlier.

Often, the estimated model itself suggests the block structure of the parameter vector, $\boldsymbol{\theta}$. Functional characteristics of the parameters could be one structure criterion. In a linear regression model, for example, the regression parameter vector, $\boldsymbol{\beta}$, could constitute one block and the disturbance variance, σ^2 another.[19]

The Gibbs Sampler The Gibbs sampler could be seen as a special version of the M-H algorithm and, more specifically, an extension to the block structure M-H algorithm discussed earlier. It requires that one be able to sample directly from the (full) conditional posterior distributions of the (blocks of) components of $\boldsymbol{\theta}$. Let the K-dimensional parameter vector be partitioned into q components as $\boldsymbol{\theta} = (\boldsymbol{\theta}_1, \boldsymbol{\theta}_2, \ldots, \boldsymbol{\theta}_q)$. Then, the full conditional posterior distribution of $\boldsymbol{\theta}_i$, $i = 1, \ldots, q$, is given by

$$p(\boldsymbol{\theta}_i \mid \boldsymbol{\theta}_1, \ldots, \boldsymbol{\theta}_{i-1}, \boldsymbol{\theta}_{i+1}, \ldots, \boldsymbol{\theta}_q, y) \equiv p(\boldsymbol{\theta}_i \mid \boldsymbol{\theta}_{-i}, y). \tag{5.14}$$

Assuming these are all standard distributions, the Gibbs sampler algorithm is given by the following steps:

1. Initialize the chain by selecting the starting values for all components, $\boldsymbol{\theta}_i^{(0)}$, $i = 1, \ldots, q$.
2. At iteration t, obtain the draw of $\boldsymbol{\theta} = (\boldsymbol{\theta}_1, \boldsymbol{\theta}_2, \ldots, \boldsymbol{\theta}_q)$ by drawing and updating successively its components, as follows:
   - Draw an observation, $\boldsymbol{\theta}_1^{(t)}$ from $p(\boldsymbol{\theta}_1 \mid \boldsymbol{\theta}_2^{(t-1)}, \boldsymbol{\theta}_3^{(t-1)}, \ldots, \boldsymbol{\theta}_q^{(t-1)}, y)$.
   - Draw an observation, $\boldsymbol{\theta}_2^{(t)}$ from $p(\boldsymbol{\theta}_2 \mid \boldsymbol{\theta}_1^{(t)}, \boldsymbol{\theta}_3^{(t-1)}, \ldots, \boldsymbol{\theta}_q^{(t-1)}, y)$.
   - Cycle through the rest of the components, $\boldsymbol{\theta}_3, \ldots, \boldsymbol{\theta}_q$, in a similar way.
3. Repeat step (2) until convergence is achieved.

Knowledge of the full conditional posterior distributions amounts to using an acceptance probability equal to one in the M-H algorithm, and there is no need for a rejection step.

---

[19]See further the discussion of volatility models estimation in Chapters 11 and 12.

In many situations, the full conditional posterior distribution of at least one component would not be recognizable as a standard distribution. Then a proposal density for that conditional posterior distribution needs to be identified and the algorithm above modified by including a rejection step in the manner discussed earlier in the chapter. We thus obtain a hybrid M-H algorithm.

Predictive Inference When one's objective is to carry the model analysis further than posterior inference and perform predictions for future periods, simulation of the predictive distribution turns out to be straightforward, given a posterior sample already obtained. Recall the definition of predictive density from Chapter 3,

$$f(x_{+1} \mid \boldsymbol{x}) = \int f(x_{+1} \mid \boldsymbol{\theta}) \pi(\boldsymbol{\theta} \mid \boldsymbol{x})\, d\boldsymbol{\theta},$$

where x_{+1} denotes the one-step-ahead realization of the random variable of interest, $f(x_{+1} \mid \boldsymbol{\theta})$ is the density of the data distribution, and $\pi(\boldsymbol{\theta} \mid \boldsymbol{x})$ is the posterior density of $\boldsymbol{\theta}$. It can be shown that a draw from $f(x_{+1} \mid \boldsymbol{x})$ can be obtained as follows:

1. Draw from the posterior, $\pi(\boldsymbol{\theta} \mid \boldsymbol{x})$, and denote the draw by $\boldsymbol{\theta}^*$.
2. Draw from the data density, $f(x_{+1} \mid \boldsymbol{\theta}^*)$.

The first step is already accomplished in the posterior inference stage. Simulating a sample from the predictive distribution, as well as performing numerical analysis, such as predictive interval construction and hypothesis comparison, then require minimal additional effort.

Convergence Diagnostics Reliability of posterior inference based on a simulation algorithm depends mostly on whether the Markov chain has reached convergence, so that the simulated sample is indeed a sample from the desired posterior distribution.[20] In posterior simulation, our goal is to construct a Markov chain which explores the parameter space well, that is, a chain that "mixes" well. Situations in which the simulations get trapped in a certain part of the parameter space for long periods of time are undesirable and can occur when the autocorrelations between successive parameter draws are high and decay slowly (simple autocorrelation plots would reveal if that is the case). High autocorrelations would not prevent convergence. However,

[20]See Cowles and Carlin (1996) for a comparative review of various MCMC convergence diagnostics.

convergence might take longer to reach. Therefore, some adjustment of the sampling scheme (for instance, a different partitioning of the parameter vector and/or selection of different proposal distributions) is usually in order. (See, for example, the discussion on stochastic volatility estimation in Chapter 12.)

Because of the nature of the Markov chain (its Markov property in particular), the influence of its starting point diminishes with an increasing number of iterations and eventually vanishes. In order to minimize the effect of the chain's initial state, a fraction of the chain's simulations, referred to as *burn-in fraction*, is discarded and only the subsequent draws are employed in posterior inference. There is no hard-and-fast rule to determine the size of the burn-in fraction, which clearly depends on the chain's mixing speed. Fast-mixing chains might "forget their origin" after only several iterations, while chains displaying high serial correlation of the draws might need up to half of the iterations discarded (although that would demonstrate quite a cautious approach). Convergence monitoring discussed below assumes that the burn-in fraction of simulations has already been discarded.

Methods for assessing convergence rely on examining the stability (through iterations) of the behavior of various quantities characterizing the posterior distribution. Intuitively, if these quantities take very divergent values at different points of the simulation sequence, then the chain has not reached its stationary distribution yet.

Cumsum Convergence Monitoring A simple monitoring tool is to visually inspect the plot of the standardized posterior means as functions of the number of iterations—a stable dynamics indicates convergence.[21] The statistic is given by

$$CS_{i,m} = \frac{1}{m}\frac{\sum_{j=1}^{m}\left(\theta_i^{(j)} - \widehat{\theta}_i\right)}{\widehat{\sigma}_i}, \tag{5.15}$$

for $m = 1, \ldots, M$, where M is the after-burn-in number of simulations and $\widehat{\theta}_i$ and $\widehat{\sigma}_i$ are, respectively, the posterior mean and standard deviation of θ_i. The statistic $CS_{i,m}$ is expressed in terms of a parameter, θ_i; one could, of course, monitor convergence for the simulations of any function of θ_i in the same way. Convergence of the Markov chain is indicated by the statistic settling to values close to zero.

Parallel Chains Convergence Monitoring In less complicated models, when simulations are not very computationally intensive, a widely recommended approach is the one of Gelman and Rubin (1992). It is based on running

[21] See Yu and Mykland (1994) and Bauwens and Lubrano (1998).

in parallel several independent chains, with pronouncedly different starting values. Convergence is present when outputs from the chains are similar enough. The degree of similarity is measured by how close the average variance of the (after-burn-in) simulations for a particular chain is to the variance of the posterior means across chains. To simplify notation, suppose we are only interested in inference for one parameter, denoted by θ (this could be a function of θ as well). Suppose that R parallel chains are run. The ith ($i = 1, \ldots, M$) simulation of θ from the rth ($r = 1, \ldots, R$) chain is denoted by $\theta^{(i,r)}$. The average within-sequence variation is estimated by

$$W = \frac{1}{R}\sum_{r=1}^{R}\widehat{\sigma_r^2}, \tag{5.16}$$

where

$$\widehat{\sigma_r^2} = \frac{\sum_{i=1}^{M}(\theta^{(i,r)} - \widehat{\theta^{(r)}})^2}{M-1}$$

and

$$\widehat{\theta^{(r)}} = \frac{\sum_{i=1}^{M}\theta^{(i,r)}}{M}. \tag{5.17}$$

The between-sequence variation is estimated by

$$B = \frac{M}{R-1}\sum_{r=1}^{R}(\widehat{\theta^{(r)}} - \widehat{\theta})^2, \tag{5.18}$$

where

$$\widehat{\theta} = \frac{1}{R}\sum_{r=1}^{R}\widehat{\theta^{(r)}}. \tag{5.19}$$

The posterior variance of θ can be estimated in two ways. On the one hand, one estimate is simply the within-sequence variation estimate, W. On the other hand, the variance of θ can be estimated as a weighted average of W and B,

$$\widehat{\text{var}(\theta)} = \frac{M-1}{M}W + \frac{1}{M}B, \tag{5.20}$$

where we suppress notationally the conditioning on the data, y. Since the chains are started from very far-apart initial parameter values, the between-sequence variation will be larger than the within-sequence variation before convergence. When convergence is present, one would expect that $\widehat{\text{var}}(\theta)$ is very close to W. Then one can compute the statistic,

$$Q = \frac{\widehat{\text{var}}(\theta)}{W}, \tag{5.21}$$

whose value nears 1 at convergence. If the value of Q is much higher than 1, the chain run must be continued until convergence.

Linear Regression with Semiconjugate Prior

We now revisit the univariate regression model from Chapter 4 and illustrate some of the posterior simulation techniques discussed above. We refer the reader to Chapter 4 for the relevant notation.

In the previous chapter, in order to obtain analytically convenient results, we considered the natural conjugate prior case for the parameters of the normal regression model. In that scenario, the prior distribution of $\boldsymbol{\beta}$ is conditional on the variance, σ^2, while its covariance matrix is often made proportional to the matrix $\mathbf{X}'\mathbf{X}$ (see Chapter 3)—assumptions that might be considered unnecessarily restrictive.

Here, the prior variance of $\boldsymbol{\beta}$ is asserted independently of σ^2 and $\mathbf{X}$, while we still assume normal prior for $\boldsymbol{\beta}$ and inverted χ^2 prior for σ^2. These assumptions give rise to the so-called "semiconjugate" prior scenario,

$$\pi(\boldsymbol{\beta}) = \mathrm{N}\big(\boldsymbol{\beta}_0, \boldsymbol{\Sigma}_\beta\big)$$

and

$$\pi(\sigma^2) = \text{Inv-}\chi^2(\nu_0, c_0^2), \tag{5.22}$$

where $\boldsymbol{\beta}_0$, $\boldsymbol{\Sigma}_\beta$, ν_0, and c_0^2 are the hyperparameters determined in advance (for example, estimated from running the model on a prior sample of data or reflecting the researcher's prior knowledge and intuition). Combining (5.22) with the normal likelihood (see Chapter 3) gives the unnormalized joint posterior of the model parameters,

$$\begin{aligned} p(\boldsymbol{\beta}, \sigma^2) \propto\ & (\sigma^2)^{-\left(\frac{n+\nu_0}{2}+1\right)} \\ & \times \exp\left[-\frac{1}{2\sigma^2}(\mathbf{y} - \mathbf{X}\boldsymbol{\beta})'(\mathbf{y} - \mathbf{X}\boldsymbol{\beta}) \right. \\ & \left. - \frac{1}{2}(\boldsymbol{\beta} - \boldsymbol{\beta}_0)'\boldsymbol{\Sigma}_\beta^{-1}(\boldsymbol{\beta} - \boldsymbol{\beta}_0) - \frac{\nu_0 c_0^2}{\sigma^2}\right], \end{aligned} \tag{5.23}$$

where n is the number of data records. The joint posterior density does not assume a convenient analytical form as in the natural conjugate case. However, if we consider it as a function of $\boldsymbol{\beta}$ (for a fixed σ^2) and as a function of σ^2 (for a fixed $\boldsymbol{\beta}$), we can obtain the full conditional posterior distributions of $\boldsymbol{\beta}$ and σ^2 which do have standard distributional forms. The conditional posterior of $\boldsymbol{\beta}$ can be shown to be multivariate normal,

$$p(\boldsymbol{\beta} \mid \sigma^2, y, X) = \mathrm{N}(\boldsymbol{\beta}^*, V_\beta), \tag{5.24}$$

where

$$V_\beta = \left(\frac{1}{\sigma^2} X'X + \boldsymbol{\Sigma}_\beta^{-1}\right)^{-1} \tag{5.25}$$

and

$$\boldsymbol{\beta}^* = V_\beta \left(\frac{1}{\sigma^2} X'X\widehat{\boldsymbol{\beta}} + \boldsymbol{\Sigma}_\beta^{-1}\boldsymbol{\beta}_0\right). \tag{5.26}$$

The conditional posterior of σ^2 is an inverted χ^2 distribution,

$$p(\sigma^2 \mid \boldsymbol{\beta}, y, X) = \text{Inv-}\chi^2(\nu^*, c^{2*}), \tag{5.27}$$

where

$$\nu^* = n + \nu_0 \tag{5.28}$$

and

$$c^{2*} = \frac{\nu_0 c_0^2 + (y - X\boldsymbol{\beta})'(y - X\boldsymbol{\beta})}{\nu^*}. \tag{5.29}$$

The availability of the parameters' full conditionals means that we can now employ the Gibbs sampler to generate a sample from the joint posterior distribution of $\boldsymbol{\beta}$ and σ^2 in (5.23).

Illustration To illustrate the posterior simulation, we use the same set of data as in the regression illustration in Chapter 4 and regress the returns on the small-cap/small-BM portfolio on the returns on the five factors with greatest explanatory power, obtained with principal components analysis. The sample consists of 132 observations for each variable. In addition, we use data recorded in an earlier period to compute the values of the hyperparameters. We run the Gibbs sampler for 10,000 iterations, discard the first 1,000 (the burn-in iterations), and use the rest to compute the posterior means and numerical standard errors. Part A of Exhibit 5.2 presents these, as well as the 5th and 95th numerical percentiles. To visualize the posterior distributions better, we can plot the histogram of

		β_1	β_2	β_3	β_4	β_5	β_6	σ^2
		Intercept	Factor 1	Factor 2	Factor 3	Factor 4	Factor 5	
A.	**Prior Mean**	0.0037	−0.2952	−0.4217	0.038	−0.2784	0.1063	1.67e-04
	Posterior Mean	0.0044	−0.3051	−0.4084	0.0696	−0.3709	0.0424	1.54e-04
	Posterior Standard Deviation	(0.0008)	(0.0038)	(0.009)	(0.0157)	(0.023)	(0.0337)	(1.67e-05)
	$b_{0.05}$	0.003	−0.3112	−0.4232	0.0438	−0.4081	−0.0139	1.29e-04
	$b_{0.95}$	0.0057	−0.2988	−0.3937	0.0956	−0.3326	0.0979	1.83e-04
B.	**Prior Mean**	0.0037	−0.2952	−0.4217	0.038	−0.2784	0.1063	1.67e-04
	Posterior Mean	0.0043	−0.3047	−0.4093	0.0687	−0.3687	0.0446	1.47e-4
	Posterior Standard Deviation	(0.0009)	(0.0036)	(0.0084)	(0.0153)	(0.0232)	(0.0332)	1.53e-05
	$b_{0.05}$	0.003	−0.311	−0.4218	0.0448	−0.4062	−0.0097	1.24e-04
	$b_{0.95}$	0.0058	−0.2993	−0.3943	0.0949	−0.3339	0.0994	1.78e-04

EXHIBIT 5.2 Posterior summaries: Gibbs sampler and M-H algorithm

the simulated observations; the histogram of the posterior draws of σ^2, for instance, together with the "raw" simulations, can be seen in Exhibit 5.3.

Although superfluous for our analysis, for the sake of illustration, we consider a M-H sampling scheme as well, in particular, a random walk M-H algorithm. We use a multivariate normal jumping distribution for the regression coefficients, $\boldsymbol{\beta}$, and a univariate normal jumping kernel for σ^2. To account for the positivity restriction of σ^2, any negative draws are simply discarded.[22] Notice that the posterior means and numerical errors in Part B of Exhibit 5.2 are very close to those resulting from the Gibbs sampler (and provide an indication that both chains have converged; see below as well). The acceptance proportion for this M-H sampling scheme turns out to be just above 0.18.

As a visual check of whether the chains (in the Gibbs sampler case and the M-H algorithm case) have reached convergence, we examine the plots of the parameters' standardized ergodic averages (computed using the post-burn-in simulations) against the number of iterations. For example, Exhibit 5.4 provides this plot (from the Gibbs output) for β_4 on the bottom. Based on it, convergence has been achieved. The second graph in Exhibit 5.4

[22]This is, in general, an easy way to deal with parameter restrictions. No equivalent approach exists in the classical, frequentist setting. However, if a large number of the draws for a given parameter violate the parameter restriction and need to be discarded, this might be a signal that the model is misspecified.

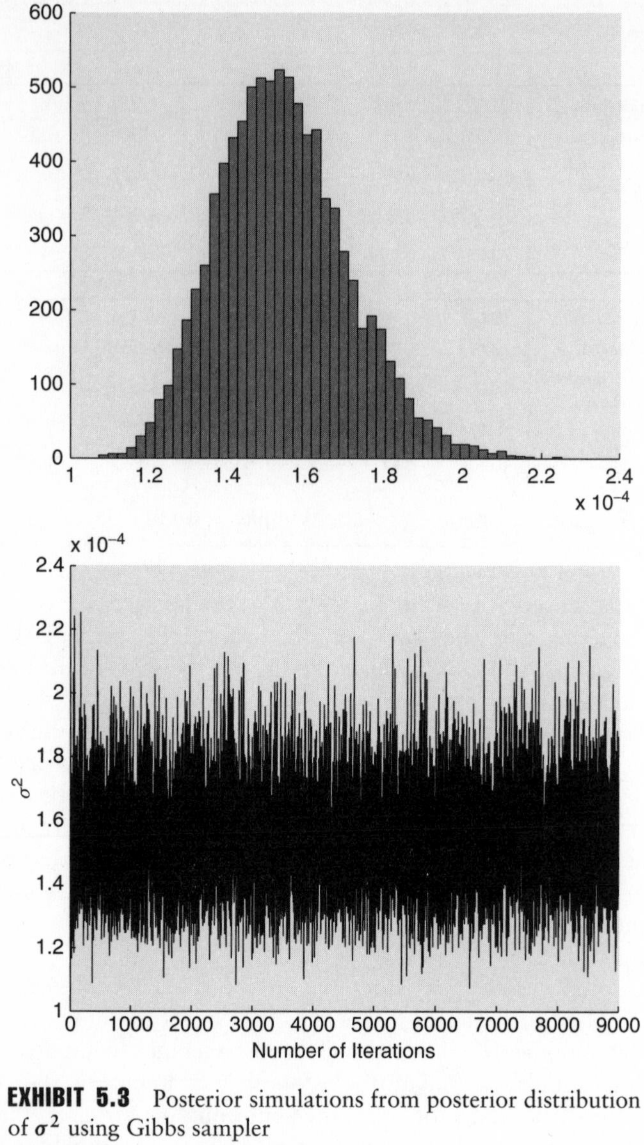

EXHIBIT 5.3 Posterior simulations from posterior distribution of σ^2 using Gibbs sampler

is the plot of the sample autocorrelation of the simulated sequence from the distribution of β_4. Since the autocorrelations decay very fast, we conclude that the chain in this simple model mixes very well. The plots for the remaining parameters are very similar.

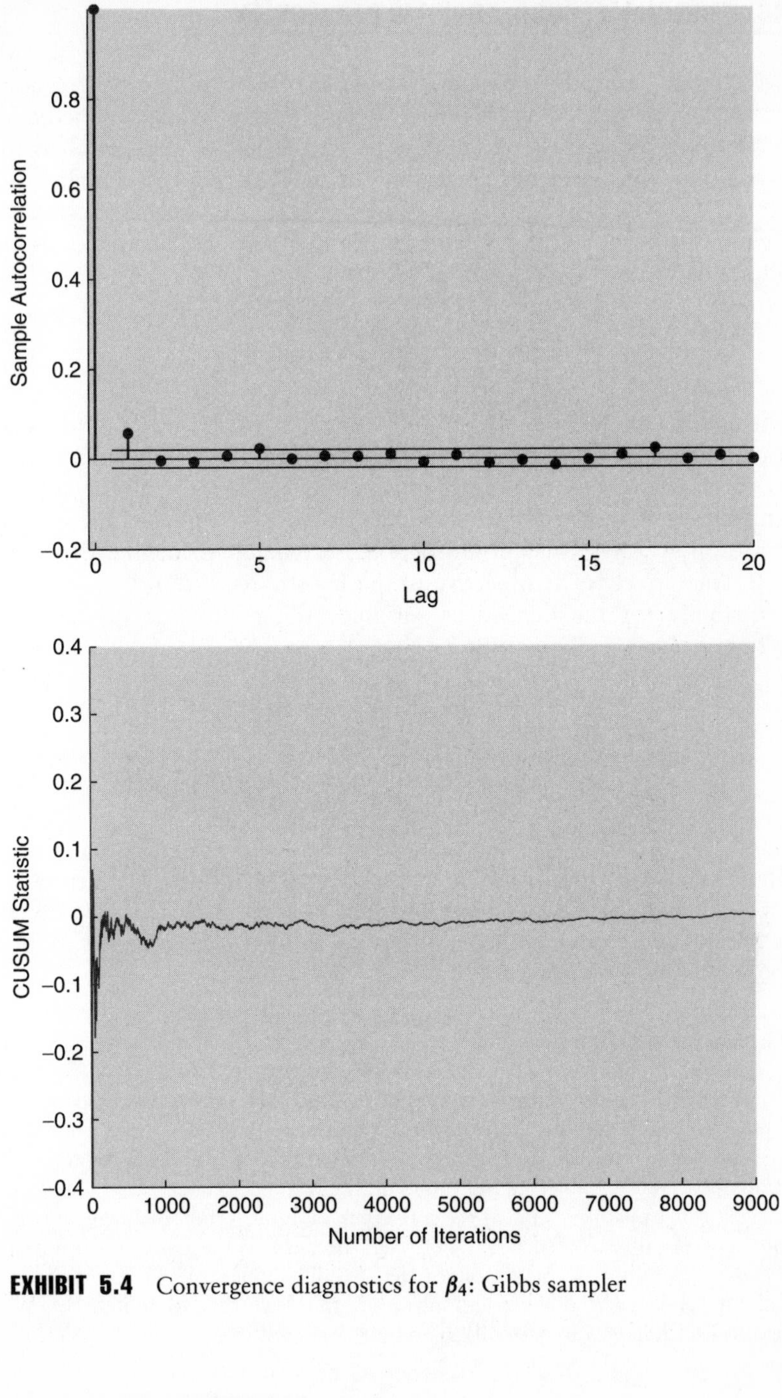

EXHIBIT 5.4 Convergence diagnostics for β_4: Gibbs sampler

APPROXIMATION METHODS: LOGISTIC REGRESSION

In this section, we consider the estimation of one type of nonlinear regression model, the logistic regression, to illustrate the way approximation methods work. The logistic regression's most important financial application is in credit-risk modeling and, in particular, in modeling the probability of default.

Denote the probability of default of a company by θ. Then the odds of default are defined as

$$\frac{\theta}{1-\theta}.$$

The logistic regression models the logarithm of the odds ratio as a linear combination of a number of explanatory variables.[23] The underlying dependent variable, Y, in the regression is a binary (categorical) variable.[24] It manifests itself in two states—default or no default—and these two states are observable. For convenience, it is common to denote them by 1 and 0, respectively. The objective of the logistic regression is to predict the probability for the dependent variable falling into one of the two categories,

$$P(Y=1)=\theta$$

and

$$P(Y=0)=1-\theta. \tag{5.30}$$

The explanatory variables (which presumably influence the probability of default) could be company-specific characteristics or macroeconomic variables. Suppose we have observations of the dependent variable

---

[23]In the logistic regression, the probability of default is estimated indirectly, through the log-odds ratio. The reason for that transformation is to remove the boundedness of the support of θ (defined on the interval $[0, 1]$). The odds transformation converts $[0, 1]$ into $[0, \infty)$, while the log transformation converts $[0, \infty)$ into $(-\infty, \infty)$. It is then possible to model the logarithm of the odds as a linear combination of empirically observed variables taking values on the whole real line.

[24]The logistic regression is one of several types of models for analyzing binary data but it is usually favored by practitioners because of the ease of parameter interpretation. Another is the probit model. Models applicable to situations in which the dependent variable can fall into more than two categories (*polytomous data*) exist. See Chapter 5 in McCullagh and Nelder (1999).

and the $p-1$ explanatory variables for n companies, $y_1, y_2, \ldots, y_n$ and $x_1, x_2, \ldots, x_{p-1}$, respectively. Then, the logistic regression is represented by

$$\alpha_i \equiv \log\left(\frac{\theta_i}{1-\theta_i}\right) = \beta_0 + \beta_1 x_{i,1} + \ldots + \beta_{p-1} x_{i,p-1} = \boldsymbol{x}_i'\boldsymbol{\beta}, \tag{5.31}$$

for $i = 1, \ldots, n$, where $\boldsymbol{x}_i = (1, \ x_{i,1}, \ x_{i,2}, \ldots, x_{i,p-1})'$ and $\boldsymbol{\beta} = (\beta_0, \beta_1, \beta_2, \ldots, \beta_{p-1})'$.[25] The probability of default is then given by

$$\theta_i = \frac{\exp(\boldsymbol{x}_i'\boldsymbol{\beta})}{1+\exp(\boldsymbol{x}_i'\boldsymbol{\beta})}. \tag{5.32}$$

The coefficients of the logistic regression, β_j, $j = 1, \ldots, p-1$, take on the interpretation of the amount of change in the log-odds ratio for a unit increase in x_j.[26]

The binary dependent variable, Y, has the Bernoulli distribution. Therefore, the likelihood function for the vector of regression coefficients, $\boldsymbol{\beta}$, is

$$\begin{aligned} L(\boldsymbol{\beta} \mid \boldsymbol{y}) &\propto \prod_{i=1}^{n} \theta_i^{y_i}(1-\theta_i)^{1-y_i} \\ &= \prod_{i=1}^{n}\left[\frac{\exp(\boldsymbol{x}_i'\boldsymbol{\beta})}{1+\exp(\boldsymbol{x}_i'\boldsymbol{\beta})}\right]^{y_i}\left[\frac{1}{1+\exp(\boldsymbol{x}_i'\boldsymbol{\beta})}\right]^{1-y_i} \\ &= \frac{\exp(\boldsymbol{t}'\boldsymbol{\beta})}{\prod_{i=1}^{n}[1+\exp(\boldsymbol{x}_i'\boldsymbol{\beta})]}, \end{aligned} \tag{5.33}$$

where $\boldsymbol{t} = \sum_{i=1}^{n} \boldsymbol{x}_i y_i$.

Let $\pi(\boldsymbol{\beta})$ be the prior density of $\boldsymbol{\beta}$. The (unnormalized) posterior distribution of $\boldsymbol{\beta}$ is then given by

$$\begin{aligned} p(\boldsymbol{\beta} \mid \boldsymbol{y}) &\propto L(\boldsymbol{\beta} \mid \boldsymbol{y})\pi(\boldsymbol{\beta}) \\ &= \frac{\exp(\boldsymbol{t}'\beta)}{\prod_{i=1}^{n}[1+\exp(\boldsymbol{x}_i'\boldsymbol{\beta})]}\pi(\boldsymbol{\beta}). \end{aligned} \tag{5.34}$$

Suppose we are interested in performing posterior inference with respect to (functions of) the regression coefficients, β_i, or the unknown probabilities,

[25]The log-odds ratio, $\log(\theta_i/(1-\theta_i))$, can also be written as $\text{logit}(\theta_i)$.

[26]Sometimes, the effect of a change in x_j is termed "multiplicative" since the unit increase in x_j translates into multiplying the odds ratio, $\theta/(1-\theta)$, by $\exp(\beta_j)$.

θ_i. Denote such a function by the generic $g(\boldsymbol{\beta})$. The posterior mean of $g(\boldsymbol{\beta})$ is given by

$$\begin{aligned} \mathrm{E}g(\boldsymbol{\beta}) \mid y) &= \int g(\boldsymbol{\beta}) p(\boldsymbol{\beta} \mid y)\, d\boldsymbol{\beta} \\ &= c^{-1} \int g(\boldsymbol{\beta}) \frac{\exp(\boldsymbol{t}'\beta)}{\prod_{i=1}^{n}[1+\exp(\boldsymbol{x}_i'\boldsymbol{\beta})]} \pi(\boldsymbol{\beta}) d\boldsymbol{\beta}, \end{aligned} \tag{5.35}$$

where c is the constant of proportionality omitted in (5.34). That constant needs to be known in order to compute the expectation above and can be found by the p-dimensional integration,[27]

$$c = \int \frac{\exp(\boldsymbol{t}'\beta)}{\prod_{i=1}^{n}[1+\exp(\boldsymbol{x}_i'\boldsymbol{\beta})]} \pi(\boldsymbol{\beta}) d\boldsymbol{\beta}. \tag{5.36}$$

The p-dimensional integrals in (5.35) and (5.36) are in general not straightforward to compute, and even more so for dimensions greater than 4 ($p > 4$).

In what follows, we discuss how to use the approximations to the posterior density to compute the posterior moments of (functions of) the parameters, as well as the parameter's marginal posterior densities.

The Normal Approximation

The normal approximation to the posterior density relies on a Taylor expansion of the logarithm of the posterior density around the posterior mode.[28] The posterior mode of complicated posterior densities is usually found numerically, using a computer software package. Consider a generic

[27] Recall, from Chapter 3, that this is the denominator in the Bayes formula.

[28] In mathematics, the Taylor series of a function is an infinite sum of the derivatives of the function, evaluated at a single point. Denote the function by $f(x)$ and take a point a. Then, under some conditions about $f(x)$, the Taylor series of $f(x)$ is given by

$$\begin{aligned} T(x,a,n) &= f(a) + \left.\frac{df(x)}{dx}\right|_{x=a}(x-a) + \frac{1}{2}\left.\frac{d^2 f(x)}{dx^2}\right|_{x=a}(x-a)^2 \\ &+ \frac{1}{3!}\left.\frac{d^3 f(x)}{dx^3}\right|_{x=a}(x-a)^3 + \ldots + \frac{1}{3!}\,\frac{1}{n!}\left.\frac{d^n f(x)}{dx^n}\right|_{x=a}(x-a)^n, \end{aligned}$$

where ! denotes factorial and $\left.\frac{df(x)}{dx}\right|_{x=a}$ is a notation for the first derivative of $f(x)$ with respect to x, evaluated at a (it could be written alternatively as $f'(a)$). The posterior density function of a parameter vector, η, denoted by $p(\eta \mid y)$. Denote the posterior mode by $\widehat{\eta}$. Then, under certain regularity conditions, the logarithm of the posterior density can be approximated by its second-order Taylor expansion around $\widehat{\eta}$ as follows,

$$\log(p(\eta \mid y)) \approx \log(p(\widehat{\eta} \mid y)) + \left.\frac{d \log(p(\eta \mid y))}{d\eta}\right|_{\eta=\widehat{\eta}} (\eta - \widehat{\eta}) + \frac{1}{2}(\eta - \widehat{\eta})' \left.\frac{d^2 \log(p(\eta \mid y))}{d\eta\eta'}\right|_{\eta=\widehat{\eta}} (\eta - \widehat{\eta}). \quad (5.37)$$

The second term on the right-hand side above is zero, since it represents the first derivative of a function evaluated at the function's maximum, while the first term on the right-hand side is a constant with respect to η. Therefore, the log-posterior is approximated as

$$\log(p(\eta \mid y)) = \text{const} + \frac{1}{2}(\eta - \widehat{\eta})' \left.\frac{d^2 \log(p(\eta \mid y))}{d\eta\eta'}\right|_{\eta=\widehat{\eta}} (\eta - \widehat{\eta}).$$

The second derivative of the log-posterior with respect to the components of η, evaluated at the posterior mode, is the Hessian matrix, $\boldsymbol{H}$. Taking the exponential on both sides above, we obtain

$$p(\eta \mid y) \propto \exp\left(-\frac{1}{2}(\eta - \widehat{\eta})'(-\boldsymbol{H})(\eta - \widehat{\eta})\right), \quad (5.38)$$

which we can recognize as the kernel of a multivariate normal distribution with mean the posterior mode, $\widehat{\eta}$, and covariance matrix—the negative of

---

notation of the remaining terms in the infinite sum has an analogous meaning. With a few exceptions for $f(x)$, we can write that

$$f(x) = T(x, a, n) + R_n,$$

where R_n is a remainder term which approaches zero as n becomes infinitely large. The Taylor expansion above can be used to provide an approximation to $f(x)$. In practice, a second-order Taylor series approximation usually provides results with sufficient accuracy,

$$f(x) \approx T(x, a, 2) = f(a) + \left.\frac{df(x)}{dx}\right|_{x=a} + \frac{1}{2} \left.\frac{d^2 f(x)}{dx^2}\right|_{x=a} (x - a)^2.$$

the inverse Hessian matrix, $-H^{-1}$. Notice that this normal approximation is the same as the normal proposal density used in the independence chain M-H algorithm. Provided that the sample size is large enough, the approximation turns out to be very accurate.

The posterior moments of any function, $g(\eta)$, of the parameter vector can now be computed easily. First, simulate η from the normal distribution in (5.38) above, then compute the values of $g(\eta)$ at those simulations, and, finally, use Monte Carlo integration discussed earlier in the chapter.

Illustration The normal approximation discussed above can be used to approximate the posterior distribution of $\boldsymbol{\beta}$ with density given in (5.34) in the logistic regression case. As an illustration, we consider the dataset of Johnson and Wichern (2002) for 46 companies recorded in a particular year—two years prior to the default of 21 of them. The four variables used as predictors for the probability of default are the following financial ratios: cash flow/total debt, net income/total assets, current assets/current liabilities, and current assets/net sales. Their values are observed for each of the 46 companies in the sample. We consider the logistic regression model in (5.31). The two categories of the binary dependent variable, Y, are coded as "$1 =$ *default*" and "$0 =$ *no default*." The vectors of explanatory variables, $\mathbf{x}_i$, $i = 1, \ldots, 46$, have 1 as their first component and the four financial ratios as the remaining four components. The dataset is given in Exhibit 5.5.

We employ the logistic regression to investigate the relationship between the explanatory variables and the probability of default, and to predict the probability, θ, that a company k with a given set of financial ratios, $x_{k,1}$, $x_{k,2}$, $x_{k,3}$, $x_{k,4}$, will default in two-years time.

Suppose that the prior for the regression coefficients, $\boldsymbol{\beta}$, is an uninformative, improper prior,

$$\pi(\boldsymbol{\beta}) \propto 1. \tag{5.39}$$

The posterior mode found by numerical maximization of the posterior of $\boldsymbol{\beta}$ in (5.34) is

$$\hat{\boldsymbol{\beta}} = (5.31, -7.06, 3.50, -3.41, 2.98)',$$

while the negative inverse Hessian matrix evaluated at the posterior mode is

$$\begin{pmatrix} 5.60 & -7.70 & 15.86 & -2.24 & -2.04 \\ -7.70 & 35.73 & -70.60 & 2.89 & 1.87 \\ 15.86 & -70.60 & 185.18 & -7.05 & -0.68 \\ -2.24 & 2.89 & -7.05 & 1.45 & -1.22 \\ -2.04 & 1.87 & -0.68 & -1.22 & 9.41 \end{pmatrix}.$$

Companies in Future Default					Companies in No Future Default				
y_i	$x_{i,1}$	$x_{i,2}$	$x_{i,3}$	$x_{i,4}$	y_i	$x_{i,1}$	$x_{i,2}$	$x_{i,3}$	$x_{i,4}$
1	–0.45	–0.41	1.09	0.45	0	0.51	0.10	2.49	0.54
1	–0.56	–0.31	1.51	0.16	0	0.08	0.02	2.01	0.53
1	0.06	0.02	1.01	0.40	0	0.38	0.11	3.27	0.35
1	–0.07	–0.09	1.45	0.26	0	0.19	0.05	2.25	0.33
1	–0.10	–0.09	1.56	0.67	0	0.32	0.07	4.24	0.63
1	–0.14	–0.07	0.71	0.28	0	0.31	0.05	4.45	0.69
1	0.04	0.01	1.50	0.71	0	0.12	0.05	2.52	0.69
1	–0.06	–0.06	1.37	0.40	0	–0.02	0.02	2.05	0.35
1	0.07	–0.01	1.37	0.34	0	0.22	0.08	2.35	0.40
1	–0.13	–0.14	1.42	0.44	0	0.17	0.07	1.80	0.52
1	–0.22	–0.30	0.33	0.18	0	0.15	0.05	2.17	0.55
1	0.07	0.02	1.31	0.25	0	–0.10	–0.01	2.50	0.58
1	0.01	0.00	2.15	0.70	0	0.14	–0.03	0.46	0.26
1	–0.28	–0.23	1.19	0.66	0	0.14	0.07	2.61	0.52
1	0.15	0.05	1.88	0.27	0	0.15	0.06	2.23	0.56
1	0.37	0.11	1.99	0.38	0	0.16	0.05	2.31	0.20
1	–0.08	–0.08	1.51	0.42	0	0.29	0.06	1.84	0.38
1	0.05	0.03	1.68	0.95	0	0.54	0.11	2.33	0.48
1	0.01	–0.00	1.26	0.60	0	–0.33	–0.09	3.01	0.47
1	0.12	0.11	1.14	0.17	0	0.48	0.09	1.24	0.18
1	–0.28	–0.27	1.27	0.51	0	0.56	0.11	4.29	0.45
					0	0.20	0.08	1.99	0.30
					0	0.47	0.14	2.92	0.45
					0	0.17	0.04	2.45	0.14
					0	0.58	0.04	5.06	0.13

EXHIBIT 5.5 Logistic regression illustration: data

Then, using (5.38), these two quantities are, respectively, the mean and the covariance matrix of the normal approximation to $\boldsymbol{\beta}$'s posterior. The marginal posterior distributions of each of the regression coefficients, β_j, $j = 0, \ldots, 4$, are straightforward to obtain. For example, the posterior density of β_0 is approximately normal with mean $\hat{\beta}_0 = 5.31$ and variance $\sigma_0^{2*} = 5.60$, while that of β_2 has a mean $\hat{\beta}_2 = 3.50$ and variance $\sigma_2^{2*} = 185.18$.

Using Exhibit 5.6, one can evaluate visually the quality of the normal approximation for β_0 and β_2. The histograms are constructed using draws obtained with the importance sampling algorithm. Because of the nature of the importance sampling algorithm, they practically represent histograms of draws from the exact distributions of β_0 and β_2. One can observe that the normal approximations to the posteriors of the two regression coefficients are not very good, possibly due to the small sample size in this illustration.

Suppose now that we would like to compute the posterior mean of the probability of default of company k. Let the four financial ratios considered

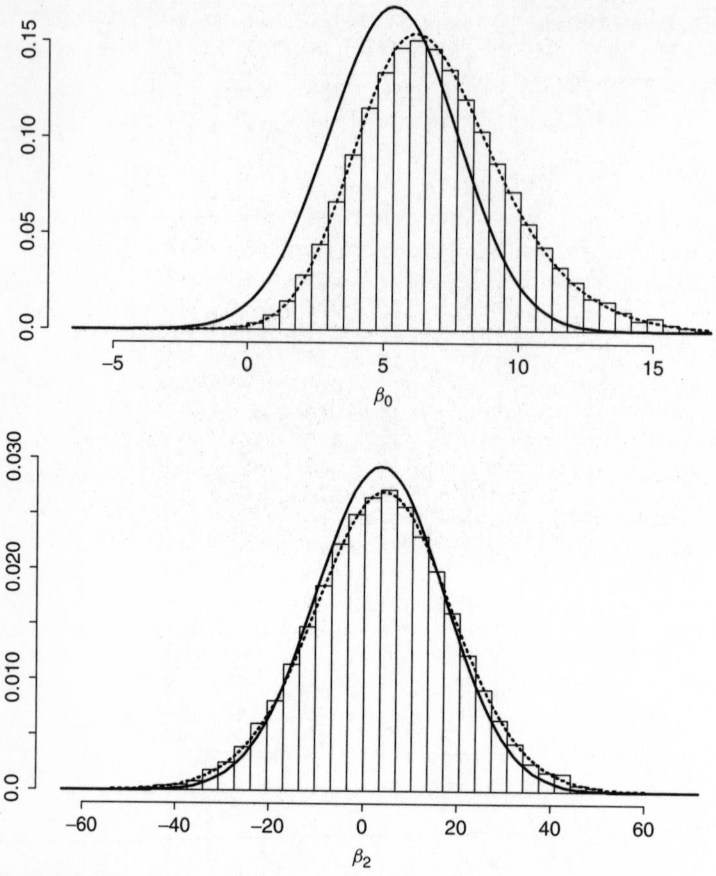

EXHIBIT 5.6 Approximations to the posterior densities of $\boldsymbol{\beta}_0$ and $\boldsymbol{\beta}_2$
Note: The solid curves represent density curves of the normal approximations to the posteriors of β_0 and β_2. The dotted curves represent the Laplace approximations to the posteriors. The histograms are constructed from draws obtained with the importance sampling algorithm.

above have the following values for company k: $x_{k,1} = 0.05$, $x_{k,2} = 0.05$, $x_{k,3} = 1.80$, and $x_{k,4} = 0.50$. The probability of default, θ_k, is then (by (5.32))

$$\theta_k = \frac{\exp(\beta_0 + 0.05\beta_1 + 0.05\beta_2 + 1.8\beta_3 + 0.5\beta_4)}{1 + \exp(\beta_0 + 0.05\beta_1 + 0.05\beta_2 + 1.8\beta_3 + 0.5\beta_4)}. \tag{5.40}$$

One could compute the posterior distribution of θ_k by substituting the draws of $\boldsymbol{\beta}$ from the normal approximation into the expression above. The posterior mean of θ_k is thus found to be 0.42.

Generally, when only a small data sample is available, a more adequate approximation to the posterior distribution is provided by the Laplace approximation, which we discuss next.

The Laplace Approximation

Consider again the generic parameter vector $\boldsymbol{\eta}$ with a posterior distribution $p(\boldsymbol{\eta} \mid y)$. Suppose that one would like to approximate directly the marginal posterior density of a component of $\boldsymbol{\eta}$, η_1, where the parameter vector is partitioned as $\boldsymbol{\eta} = (\eta_1, \boldsymbol{\eta}_2)$ and $\boldsymbol{\eta}_2 = (\eta_2, \cdots, \eta_p)$. The posterior density of $\boldsymbol{\eta}$ is then written as

$$p(\boldsymbol{\eta} \mid y) = p(\eta_1, \boldsymbol{\eta}_2 \mid y)$$

and we can apply a second-order Taylor expansion of the log-posterior around the conditional posterior mode of $\boldsymbol{\eta}_2$, that is, the value $\widehat{\boldsymbol{\eta}}$ that maximizes $p(\eta_1, \boldsymbol{\eta}_2 \mid y)$ for a fixed η_1. Based on the Taylor expansion, we can write

$$\begin{aligned}\log(p(\eta_1, \boldsymbol{\eta}_2 \mid y)) \approx {} & \log(p(\eta_1, \widehat{\boldsymbol{\eta}_2} \mid y)) \\ & + \left. \frac{d \log(p(\eta_1, \boldsymbol{\eta}_2 \mid y))}{d\, \boldsymbol{\eta}_2} \right|_{\boldsymbol{\eta}_2 = \widehat{\boldsymbol{\eta}_2}} (\boldsymbol{\eta}_2 - \widehat{\boldsymbol{\eta}_2}) \\ & + \frac{1}{2}(\boldsymbol{\eta}_2 - \widehat{\boldsymbol{\eta}_2})' \boldsymbol{H} (\boldsymbol{\eta}_2 - \widehat{\boldsymbol{\eta}_2}),\end{aligned}$$

where, for a fixed η_1, the second term on the right-hand side is zero and $\boldsymbol{H}$ is the Hessian matrix. Then the marginal posterior density of η_1 is obtained by computing the following integral:

$$\begin{aligned} p(\eta_1 \mid y) &= \int p(\eta_1, \boldsymbol{\eta}_2 \mid y)\, d\boldsymbol{\eta}_2 \\ &= \int \exp\left(\log(p(\eta_1, \boldsymbol{\eta}_2 \mid y))\right) d\boldsymbol{\eta}_2 \\ &\approx \int \exp\left(\log(p(\eta_1, \widehat{\boldsymbol{\eta}_2} \mid y)) - \frac{1}{2}(\boldsymbol{\eta}_2 - \widehat{\boldsymbol{\eta}_2})'(-\boldsymbol{H})(\boldsymbol{\eta}_2 - \widehat{\boldsymbol{\eta}_2})\right) d\boldsymbol{\eta}_2 \\ &= p(\eta_1, \widehat{\boldsymbol{\eta}_2} \mid y) \int \exp\left(-\frac{1}{2}(\boldsymbol{\eta}_2 - \widehat{\boldsymbol{\eta}_2})'(-\boldsymbol{H})(\boldsymbol{\eta}_2 - \widehat{\boldsymbol{\eta}_2})\right) d\boldsymbol{\eta}_2 \qquad (5.41) \\ &\propto p(\eta_1, \widehat{\boldsymbol{\eta}_2} \mid y) \left|-\boldsymbol{H}^{-1}\right|^{-1/2}, \qquad (5.42)\end{aligned}$$

where the last line follows from recognizing the integrand in (5.41) as the kernel of a multivariate normal distribution. The method for computing the integral above is known as the *Laplace method*.[29]

The dotted curves in Exhibit 5.6 represent the density curves of the approximated marginal posterior distributions of β_0 and β_2 in the logistic regression illustration. We can observe that even for the small sample size, the approximations are very accurate.

In conclusion, we briefly describe how Tierney and Kadane (1986) use the Laplace method to compute the approximate posterior expectation of a function $g(\eta)$,

$$
\begin{aligned}
\mathrm{E}\left(g(\eta)\,|\,y\right) &= \int g(\eta)p(\eta\,|\,y)\,\mathrm{d}\eta \\
&= \frac{\int \exp\left[\log(g(\eta)) + \log(L(\eta\,|\,y)) + \log(\pi(\eta))\right]\,\mathrm{d}\eta}{\int \exp\left[\log(L(\eta\,|\,y)) + \log(\pi(\eta))\right]\,\mathrm{d}\eta} \\
&\equiv \frac{\int \exp\left[h(\eta)^*\right]\,\mathrm{d}\eta}{\int \exp\left[h(\eta)\right]\,\mathrm{d}\eta},
\end{aligned}
\tag{5.43}
$$

where $L(\eta\,|\,y)$ and $\pi(\eta)$ are, respectively, the likelihood function and the prior distribution of η. The numerator and the denominator in (5.43) can both be approximated using the Laplace method, as in (5.41) to obtain

$$
\mathrm{E}\left(g(\eta)\,|\,y\right) \approx \frac{|\boldsymbol{R}^*|^{1/2}\exp\left(h(\widehat{\eta}^*)\right)}{|\boldsymbol{R}|^{1/2}\exp\left(h(\widehat{\eta})\right)},
\tag{5.44}
$$

where $\boldsymbol{R}^*$ and $\boldsymbol{R}$ are the negative inverse Hessian matrices of $h(\eta)^*$ and $h(\eta)$, respectively, and $\widehat{\eta}^*$ and $\widehat{\eta}$ are the maximal values of $h(\eta)^*$ and $h(\eta)$, respectively.[30]

SUMMARY

The recent surge in popularity of the Bayesian framework among practitioners is undoubtedly due to the large strides made in developing computational

[29]See also Leonard (1982) for a derivation of the approximation to the marginal posterior distribution of η_1 in a related way.

[30]Leonard, Hsu, and Tsui (1989) and Kass, Tierney, and Kadane (1989) show how to approximate the marginal posterior density of $g(\eta)$. See also Hsu (1995) and Leonard and Hsu (1999).

algorithms and in the advancement of computing power. In this chapter, we discussed the main methods for posterior simulation, along with those for approximation.[31] In the chapters that follow, we provide additional details in the context of specific financial applications. We hope that we conveyed the idea that even though the computational algorithms (especially the MCMC methods) greatly facilitate estimation of complicated models, they are not black-box solutions—thoughtful algorithm design, as well as convergence monitoring, are necessary on part of the researcher.

[31] See Gilks, Richardson, and Spiegelhalter (1996) for more details on the application of MCMC methods.

CHAPTER 6

Bayesian Framework for Portfolio Allocation

The Mean-Variance Setting

Markowitz's 1952 paper set the foundations for what is now popularly referred to as "modern portfolio theory" and had a profound impact on the financial industry. Individual security selection lay at the heart of the standard investment practice until then. Afterward, the focus shifted toward diversification and assessment of the contribution of individual securities to the risk-return profile of a portfolio. Mean-variance analysis rests on the assumption that rational investors select among risky assets on the basis of expected portfolio return and risk (as measured by the portfolio variance).

However, the reputation of this classical framework among practitioners has suffered due to numerous implementation difficulties. Portfolio weights derived from it are notoriously sensitive to the inputs,[1] especially expected returns, and often represent unintuitive or extreme allocations exposing an investor to unintended risks.[2] These inputs (expected returns, variances, and covariances) are all subject to estimation errors that an optimizer picks up and then leverages. Chopra and Ziemba,[3] for example, examine the relative impact of errors in the three groups of parameter inputs on optimal weights and find that errors in the means can be up to 10 or 11 times more important than errors in variances.[4]

---

[1] Best and Grauer (1991).
[2] Black and Litterman (1992).
[3] Chopra and Ziemba (1993).
[4] Merton (1980) points out that variances and covariances of return are more stable over time than expected returns, and, therefore, estimation errors in them affect portfolio choice less seriously than estimation errors in the means.

Estimation risk must be, then, a component of any comprehensive approach to the investment management process. The focus is on making the portfolio selection problem more robust. Several extensions to the classical mean-variance framework dealing with this issue have been developed. Among them are extensions targeting estimation of the input parameters, factor models, robust optimization techniques, and portfolio resampling. All of them help address the errors intrinsic in parameter estimation.

Factor models describe the behavior of asset returns by means of a small number (relative to the number of assets in a typical portfolio) of factors (sources of risk). They are especially useful in the estimation of the asset covariance matrix by reducing dramatically the dimension of the estimation problem, introducing structure into the covariance estimator, and improving it compared to the historical covariance estimator.

The robust approach to portfolio selection introduces the estimation error directly into the optimization process. Robust optimization focuses most often on estimation errors in the means than in the covariance matrix (likely due to the greater relative importance of the errors in the means). In its simplest form, the idea is to consider portfolio optimization as a two-stage problem. In the first stage, expected utility is minimized with respect to expected return (reflecting the "worst" estimate case that could be realized). In the second stage, the minimum expected utility is maximized with respect to the portfolio weights, for a given risk-aversion parameter.

Extensions of the robust framework to modeling of the estimation error in other parameter inputs beyond expected returns and to accounting for model risk exist.[5]

Portfolio resampling has emerged as a heuristic approach to partially capture estimation error.[6] It relies on a Monte Carlo simulation to obtain a large number of samples from the distribution of historical returns, treating the sample parameters as the true parameters. An efficient frontier is computed for each of the samples and the average (resampled) frontier is obtained. The portfolios on the resampled frontier are more diversified than the portfolios on the traditional mean-variance frontier, thus addressing a major weakness of mean-variance analysis. However, the estimation error in the parameter estimates (of the mean and covariance, if normality is assumed) is carried on to the resampled frontier.

The Bayesian approach addresses estimation risk from a conceptually different perspective. Instead of treating the unknown true parameters as fixed, it considers them random. The investor's belief (prior knowledge)

---

[5]See Ben-Tal and Nemirovksi (1998, 1999), El Ghaoui and Lebret (1997), and Goldfarb and Iyengar (2003), among others.
[6]See Jorion (1992), Michaud (1998), and Scherer (2002).

about the parameter inputs, combined with the observed data, yield an entire distribution of predicted returns which explicitly takes into account the estimation and predictive uncertainty.

In this chapter, we begin with an overview of the classical portfolio selection problem. Then, we examine the Bayesian approach to dealing with estimation risk in portfolio optimization, briefly discussing shrinkage estimators. Finally, we turn out attention to the case when assets with return histories of unequal length compose the investment universe.

The next chapter focuses on a further refinement of the Bayesian asset allocation approach, namely incorporating asset pricing models into the investment decision-making framework, while Chapter 8 presents a well-known example—the Black-Litterman model.

Chapter 13 extends the mean-variance optimization framework and discusses asset allocation assuming nonnormality of returns—higher moments, as well as expected tail loss optimization, are considered.

CLASSICAL PORTFOLIO SELECTION

Mean-variance analysis presumes that return and risk (as measured by the portfolio variance) are all investors consider when making portfolio-selection decisions. Therefore, a rational investor would prefer a portfolio with a higher expected return for a given level of risk. An equivalent way to express the mean-variance principle is: a preferred portfolio is one that minimizes risk for a given expected return level. The portfolios that are optimal in these two equivalent senses make up the *efficient frontier*. No rational investor would invest in a portfolio lying below the efficient frontier since that would mean accepting a lower return for the same amount of risk as an efficient portfolio (equivalently, undertaking greater risk for the same expected return). How do we obtain the efficient frontier? It has been shown that three formulations of the investor's mean-variance problem provide the same optimal portfolio solution, under some conditions generally satisfied in practice.[7]

More formally, it is usually accepted that mean-variance analysis is grounded in either of two conditions: asset returns have a multivariate normal distribution or investor preferences are described by quadratic utilities.[8] (We discussed the multivariate normal distribution in Chapter 3.)

---

[7]See Rockafellar and Uryasev (2002) for the proof of equivalence of the three portfolio problem formulations.

[8]In fact, Markowitz and Usmen (1996) point out that neither of the two conditions is indispensable. Almost optimal asset allocations can be obtained using a variety

We start with some portfolio selection preliminaries. Suppose that there are N assets in which an investor may invest. Denote by $\boldsymbol{R}_t$ the excess returns on the N assets at time t,

$$\boldsymbol{R}_t = (R_{1,t}, \ldots, R_{N,t})',$$

and assume that they have a multivariate normal distribution,

$$p(\boldsymbol{R}_t \mid \boldsymbol{\mu}, \boldsymbol{\Sigma}) = N(\boldsymbol{\mu}, \boldsymbol{\Sigma}),$$

with mean and covariance matrix given by the $N \times 1$ vector $\boldsymbol{\mu}$ and the $N \times N$ matrix $\boldsymbol{\Sigma}$, respectively. The portfolio weights are the proportions of wealth invested in each of the N assets and are given by the $N \times 1$ vector $\boldsymbol{\omega} = (\omega_1, \ldots, \omega_N)'$. A portfolio's return at time t is then given by

$$R_p = \sum_{i=1}^{N} \omega_i R_{i,t} = \boldsymbol{\omega}' \boldsymbol{R}_t.$$

Its expected return and variance are defined, respectively, as

$$\mu_p = \sum_{i=1}^{N} \omega_i \mu_i = \boldsymbol{\omega}' \boldsymbol{\mu},$$

where μ_i is the expected return on asset i and

$$\sigma_p^2 = \sum_{i=1}^{N} \sum_{j=1}^{N} \omega_i \omega_j \mathrm{cov}(\boldsymbol{R}_i, \boldsymbol{R}_j) = \boldsymbol{\omega}' \boldsymbol{\Sigma} \boldsymbol{\omega}.$$

where $\mathrm{cov}(\boldsymbol{R}_i, \boldsymbol{R}_j)$ is the covariance between the returns on assets i and j.

Portfolio Selection Problem Formulations

Suppose that the investor has a portfolio holding period of length τ. We assume that the investor's objective is to maximize his wealth at the end of his investment horizon, $T + \tau$, where T is the time of portfolio composition (equivalently, the last period for which return data are available).

---

of utility functions. The quadratic utility function approximates well several more general utility functions, as explained in Chapter 2 in Fabozzi, Focardi, and Kolm (2006). The multivariate normal distribution assumption can also be relaxed. Rachev, Ortobelli, and Schwartz (2004) show that the so-called location-scale family of distributions results in optimal solutions as well.

The mean-variance principle can be expressed through the following dual portfolio problems:

$$\begin{aligned} \min_{\omega} \sigma_p^2 &= \min_{\omega} \boldsymbol{\omega}' \boldsymbol{\Sigma}_{T+\tau} \boldsymbol{\omega} \\ \text{subject to} \quad & \boldsymbol{\omega}' \boldsymbol{\mu}_{T+\tau} \geq \mu^* \\ & \boldsymbol{\omega}' \mathbf{1} = 1, \end{aligned} \tag{6.1}$$

where $\mathbf{1}$ is a vector of ones compatible with $\boldsymbol{\omega}$, that is, of dimension $N \times 1$, and μ^* is the portfolio's minimum acceptable return, and

$$\begin{aligned} \max_{\omega} \mu_p &= \max_{\omega} \boldsymbol{\omega}' \boldsymbol{\mu}_{T+\tau} \\ \text{subject to} \quad & \boldsymbol{\omega}' \boldsymbol{\Sigma}_{T+\tau} \boldsymbol{\omega} \leq \sigma^{2*} \\ & \boldsymbol{\omega}' \mathbf{1} = 1, \end{aligned} \tag{6.2}$$

where σ^* is the portfolio's maximum acceptable risk. We have added the subscripts $T + \tau$ in the notation for the expected returns and covariance to stress that these refer to attributes of yet unobserved asset returns. For an investor who pursues an indexing strategy (i.e., a strategy to replicate or track the performance of a designated benchmark), μ^* in (6.1) is the benchmark's return.

In its third formulation, the portfolio optimization problem is expressed as the maximization of the investor's expected utility of end-period portfolio value,

$$\begin{aligned} \max_{\omega} \mathrm{E}\left[U\left(\omega' \boldsymbol{R}_{T+\tau}\right)\right] &= \max_{\omega} \int U\left(\omega' \boldsymbol{R}_{T+\tau}\right) p_{T+\tau}\left(\boldsymbol{R}_{T+\tau} \mid \boldsymbol{\mu}, \boldsymbol{\Sigma}\right) \mathrm{d}\boldsymbol{R}_{T+\tau} \\ \text{subject to} \quad & \boldsymbol{\omega}' \mathbf{1} = 1. \end{aligned} \tag{6.3}$$

Notice that the expected utility is expressed with respect to the distribution of future returns, $p_{T+\tau}$. We can think of this as computing the weighted sum of the utilities of portfolio returns, with the probabilities of future asset returns serving as weights.

It can be shown that the expected quadratic utility function of investor's wealth at time $T + \tau$ has the form

$$\mathrm{E}\left[U\left(\omega' \boldsymbol{R}_{T+\tau}\right)\right] = \mu_p - \frac{A}{2}\sigma_p^2, \tag{6.4}$$

where A is the relative risk aversion parameter, a measure for the rate at which the investor is willing to accept additional risk for a one unit increase in expected return.

The composition of the investor's optimal portfolio (vector of optimal weights) is given by

$$\boldsymbol{\omega}^* = \frac{\boldsymbol{\Sigma}_{T+\tau}^{-1}\,\boldsymbol{\mu}_{T+\tau}}{\mathbf{1}'\,\boldsymbol{\Sigma}_{T+\tau}^{-1}\,\boldsymbol{\mu}_{T+\tau}}. \tag{6.5}$$

More constraints are usually added to the three optimization problems just given. For example, many institutional investors are not permitted to take short positions. In such cases, the portfolio weights are constrained to be positive, $\omega_i > 0$, $i = 1, \ldots, N$.[9]

Mean-Variance Efficient Frontier

By varying the values of A in (6.4), μ^* in (6.1) or σ^{2*} in (6.2), we obtain a sequence of optimal portfolios. Their corresponding risk-return combinations, (σ_p^2, μ_p), are represented geometrically by the *mean-variance frontier*. The upward-sloping portion of it is called the *efficient frontier*—the geometric locus of the *efficient portfolios*, providing the highest return for a given level of risk (lowest risk for a given level of return).

How do the portfolios on the efficient frontier compare with each other and which one is the investor's optimal portfolio? A measure of portfolio performance, called the *Sharpe ratio*, can be used to help answer these questions. The Sharpe ratio of a portfolio is its expected return per unit of standard deviation (risk),[10]

$$SR_P = \frac{\mu_p}{\sigma_p} = \frac{\boldsymbol{\omega}'\boldsymbol{\mu}}{\sqrt{\boldsymbol{\omega}'\boldsymbol{\Sigma}\boldsymbol{\omega}}}. \tag{6.6}$$

It can be shown that the portfolio with the highest Sharpe ratio (among the efficient portfolios) and, therefore, the most desirable to an investor, is the portfolio corresponding to the risk-return combination such that the efficient frontier and a line passing through the origin are tangent to each other.[11] Thus we can see that the selection of the optimal portfolios can be viewed as a two-step process: first the efficient frontier is constructed and then the optimal portfolio located. See Exhibit 6.1.

We emphasized earlier that, since we assume the investor's objective is maximization of the terminal portfolio value, the parameter inputs of the portfolio problem pertain to the period of the investment horizon.

---

[9] See Chapter 4 in Fabozzi, Focardi, and Kolm (2006) for the portfolio constraints commonly used in practice.
[10] See Sharpe (1994).
[11] The portfolio problem is sometimes also expressed as maximization of the Sharpe ratio in (6.6).

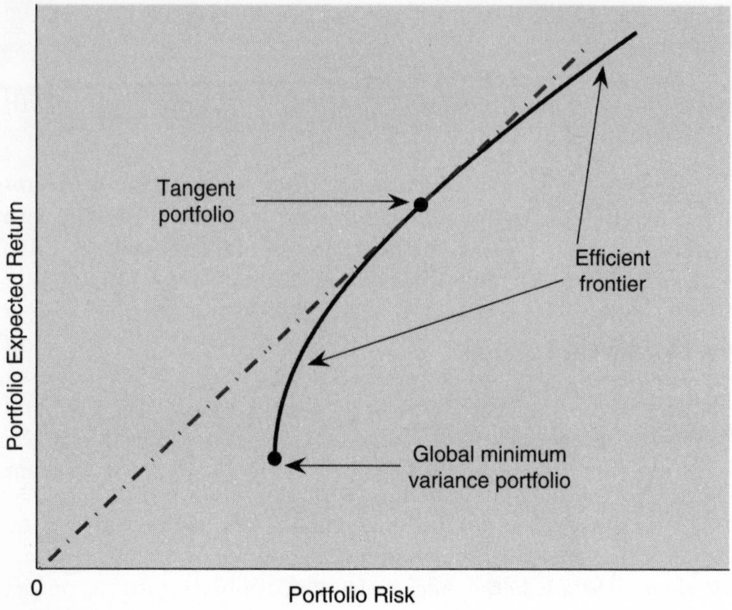

EXHIBIT 6.1 The efficient frontier

The classical mean-variance approach relies on the following two points. First, the unknown parameters are estimated from the sample of available data and the sample estimates are then treated as the true parameters. Second, it is implicitly assumed that the distribution of returns at the time of portfolio construction remains unchanged until the end of the portfolio holding period. Usually, the sample estimates of $\boldsymbol{\mu}$ and $\boldsymbol{\Sigma}$ are computed as

$$\widehat{\boldsymbol{\mu}} = \frac{1}{T}\sum_{t=1}^{T} \boldsymbol{R}_t, \tag{6.7}$$

and

$$\widehat{\boldsymbol{\Sigma}} = \frac{1}{T-1}\sum_{t=1}^{T} (\boldsymbol{R}_t - \widehat{\boldsymbol{\mu}})(\widehat{\boldsymbol{R}}_t - \widehat{\boldsymbol{\mu}})'. \tag{6.8}$$

These two estimates are unbiased. From statistical theory we know that the maximum likelihood estimate of the mean coincides with $\widehat{\boldsymbol{\mu}}$, while the maximum likelihood of the covariance is not unbiased,

$$\boldsymbol{\Sigma}_{mle} = \frac{1}{T}\sum_{t=1}^{T} (\boldsymbol{R}_t - \widehat{\boldsymbol{\mu}})(\widehat{\boldsymbol{R}}_t - \widehat{\boldsymbol{\mu}})' = \frac{T-1}{T}\widehat{\boldsymbol{\Sigma}}. \tag{6.9}$$

We reexpress the vector of optimal portfolio positions in (6.5) as

$$\omega_{ce}^{*} = \frac{\widehat{\Sigma}^{-1}\widehat{\mu}}{1'\widehat{\Sigma}^{-1}\widehat{\mu}}. \tag{6.10}$$

The optimal solution, ω_{ce}^{*}, is known as the *certainty-equivalence solution* since it treats the estimated parameters as if they were the true ones. Such an approach fails to recognize the fact that $\widehat{\mu}$ and $\widehat{\Sigma}$ may contain nonnegligible amounts of estimation error. The resulting portfolio is quite often badly behaved, leveraging on assets with high estimated mean returns and low estimated risks, which are the ones most likely to contain high estimation errors. To deal with this, practitioners usually impose tight constraints on asset positions. However, this could lead to an optimal portfolio determined by the constraints instead of the optimization procedure. Moreover, the assumption that the return distribution remains the same till the investment horizon, $T+\tau$, can only be justified if the holding period, τ, is very short.

Illustration: Mean-Variance Optimal Portfolio with Portfolio Constraints

As an illustration, we consider the daily excess returns on ten MSCI European country indexes—Denmark, Germany, Italy, the United Kingdom, Portugal, the Netherlands, France, Sweden, Norway, and Ireland—for the period January 2, 1998, through May 5, 2004, a total 1,671 observations per country index. Their summary statistics (mean returns, standard deviations, and correlations) are presented in Exhibit 6.2. In Exhibit 6.3, we give the weights of the efficient portfolios in the cases when short sales are allowed and when short sales are restricted. Notice the large long and short positions when no short sales are allowed—some of these tilts do not seem to bear direct correspondence to the returns summary statistics. When we restrict short sales, we obtain a significant number of zero weights. For the sole purpose of this illustration, we also provide optimal portfolio weights when long and short positions are restricted to be no larger than 30%. It is, of course, not a realistic restriction in practice. As in the case when no short sales are allowed, the constraint results in a number of corner positions.

Explicit consideration of estimation risk is provided within the Bayesian approach to portfolio selection, which uses the predictive distribution of returns as an input to the portfolio problem. Furthermore, as we will see in the next two chapters, combining information about the model parameters from different sources helps to alleviate the problems with the classical portfolio selection illustrated above. We turn next to discussing the foundations of Bayesian portfolio selection.

	Mean Return	St. Dev.	Correlations									
Denmark	2.3	20.7	1	0.51	0.51	0.47	0.48	0.54	0.55	0.51	0.51	0.46
Germany	−0.6	27.2		1	0.74	0.69	0.52	0.77	0.81	0.65	0.48	0.45
Italy	2.4	23.0			1	0.68	0.57	0.76	0.81	0.62	0.50	0.47
UK	−2.3	19.6				1	0.45	0.77	0.77	0.61	0.48	0.50
Portugal	−3.1	20.0					1	0.51	0.56	0.48	0.43	0.43
Netherlands	−3.3	24.3						1	0.85	0.65	0.55	0.50
France	4.0	23.6							1	0.71	0.53	0.49
Sweden	5.2	31.2								1	0.51	0.43
Norway	−0.1	22.6									1	0.46
Ireland	−1.7	21.2										1

EXHIBIT 6.2 Summary statistics of the monthly returns on the 10 MSCI country indexes
Note: The summary statistics of the 10 MSCI country indexes are computed using daily returns in excess of one-month LIBOR. The mean returns and standard deviations are annualized percentages.

Target Return	1.08%	1.59%	1.08%	3.16%	3.05%	3.16%	5.24%	5.24%	5.24%
	Short Sales Allowed	No Short Sales	Each Weight Within ± 30%	Short Sales Allowed	No Short Sales	Each Weight Within ± 30%	Short Sales Allowed	No Short Sales	Each Weight Within ± 30%
Denmark	30.2	39.8	30	35.0	47.9	30	39.8	0	30
Germany	−14.7	0	−15.2	−18.8	0	−24.3	−23.0	0	−24.2
Italy	15.5	12.5	15.7	20.8	7.9	30	26.0	0	30
UK	37.0	0	30	31.0	0	17.5	25.0	0	−0.1
Portugal	19.3	4.1	19.7	12.1	0	6.4	5.0	0	−8.5
Netherlands	−35.1	0	−30	−50.5	0	−30	−65.9	0	−30
France	22.8	18.7	23.2	42.5	36.9	30	62.2	0	30
Sweden	−7.1	0	−6.8	−4.2	5.5	6.4	−1.3	100	30
Norway	15.6	11.2	15.8	16.2	1.8	17.6	16.8	0	24.7
Ireland	16.6	13.8	17.6	16.0	0	16.5	15.4	0	18.0

EXHIBIT 6.3 Optimal portfolio weights under three different constraints
Note: Portfolio weights are in percentages. Weights might not sum up to 1 due to rounding errors.

BAYESIAN PORTFOLIO SELECTION

The effect of parameter uncertainty on optimal portfolio choice is naturally accounted for by expressing the investor's problem in terms of the predictive distribution of the future excess returns. Recall, from the discussion in Chapter 3, that the predictive distribution essentially weighs the distribution of returns with the joint posterior density of the parameters.

Denoting the (yet unobserved) next-period excess return data by $\boldsymbol{R}_{T+1}$, we write the predictive return density as

$$p(\boldsymbol{R}_{T+1} \,|\, \boldsymbol{R}) \propto \int p(\boldsymbol{R}_{T+1} \,|\, \boldsymbol{\mu}, \boldsymbol{\Sigma})\, p(\boldsymbol{\mu}, \boldsymbol{\Sigma} \,|\, \boldsymbol{R}) \mathrm{d}\boldsymbol{\mu}\, \mathrm{d}\boldsymbol{\Sigma}, \tag{6.11}$$

where: $\boldsymbol{R}$ = return data available up to period T—a $T \times N$ matrix.
$p\,(\boldsymbol{\mu},\ \boldsymbol{\Sigma}\ |\ \boldsymbol{R})$ = joint posterior density of the two parameters of the multivariate normal distribution.
$p\,(\boldsymbol{R}_{T+1}\ |\ \boldsymbol{\mu},\ \boldsymbol{\Sigma})$ = multivariate normal density.
$\propto$ = proportional to.

Notice that we account for estimation risk by averaging over the posterior distribution of the parameters. Therefore, the distribution of $\boldsymbol{R}_{T+1}$ does not depend on the parameters, but only on the past return data, $\boldsymbol{R}$. When returns are assumed to have a multivariate normal distribution, as in this chapter, the predictive density can be shown to be a known distribution (given that standard prior distributional assumptions are made as discussed further below). Once we depart from the normality assumption the predictive density may not have a closed form. In both cases, however, it is possible to evaluate the integral on the right-hand side of (6.11) as explained in Chapter 4. Applications in which no analytical expressions exist for the likelihood and some of the prior distributions are discussed in Chapters 13 and 14.

Substituting in the predictive density of excess returns, the portfolio problem in (6.3) becomes

$$\max_{\omega} \mathrm{E}\left[U(\omega'\boldsymbol{R}_{T+1})\right] = \max_{\omega} \int U(\omega'\boldsymbol{R}_{T+1})\, p(\boldsymbol{R}_{T+1}|\boldsymbol{R})\, \mathrm{d}\boldsymbol{R}_{T+1}$$

$$\text{subject to} \quad \boldsymbol{\omega}'\mathbf{1} = 1. \tag{6.12}$$

Let us denote the mean and covariance of next-period returns, R_{T+1}, by $\widetilde{\mu}$ and $\widetilde{\Sigma}$, respectively. Then the problem in (6.1) is expressed as[12]

$$\min_{\omega} \sigma_p^2 = \min_{\omega} \omega' \widetilde{\Sigma}\, \omega$$
$$\text{subject to} \quad \omega' \widetilde{\mu} \geq \mu^*$$
$$\omega' 1 = 1, \tag{6.13}$$

and the one in (6.2) is rewritten analogously. The expression for the optimal portfolio weights in (6.5) becomes then

$$\omega^* = \frac{\widetilde{\Sigma}^{-1}\, \widetilde{\mu}}{1'\, \widetilde{\Sigma}^{-1}\, \widetilde{\mu}}. \tag{6.14}$$

In what follows, we outline two basic portfolio selection scenarios depending on the amount of prior information the investor is assumed to have about the parameters of the return distribution and we examine their effects on optimal portfolio choice. We extend the prior distribution framework in the next two chapters by including asset pricing models in it.

The likelihood function for the mean vector, $\boldsymbol{\mu}$, and covariance matrix, $\boldsymbol{\Sigma}$, of a multivariate normal distribution, as shown in Chapter 3, is given by

$$L(\boldsymbol{\mu}, \boldsymbol{\Sigma} \mid R) \propto |\boldsymbol{\Sigma}|^{-T/2} \exp\left(-\frac{1}{2} \sum_{t=1}^{T} (R_t - \boldsymbol{\mu})' \boldsymbol{\Sigma}^{-1} (R_t - \boldsymbol{\mu}) \right), \tag{6.15}$$

where $|\boldsymbol{\Sigma}|$ is the determinant of the covariance matrix.

Prior Scenario 1: Mean and Covariance with Diffuse (Improper) Priors

We consider the case when the investor is uncertain about the distribution of both parameters, $\boldsymbol{\mu}$ and $\boldsymbol{\Sigma}$, and has no particular prior knowledge of them. This uncertainty can be represented by a flat (diffuse) prior, which is

[12] Notice a key difference between the Bayesian approach to portfolio selection and the resampled frontier approach of Michaud (1998). In the Bayesian setting, uncertainty is taken into account before solving the investor's optimization problem in (6.13)—$\widetilde{\mu}$ and $\widetilde{\Sigma}$ already reflect the estimation error. In contrast, Michaud's approach involves solving a number of optimization problems, based on sample estimates, and then, by averaging out the optimal allocations, incorporating parameter uncertainty.

typically taken to be the Jeffreys' prior, discussed in Chapter 3,

$$p(\boldsymbol{\mu}, \boldsymbol{\Sigma}) \propto |\boldsymbol{\Sigma}|^{-(N+1)/2}. \tag{6.16}$$

Note that $\boldsymbol{\mu}$ and $\boldsymbol{\Sigma}$ are independent in the prior, and $\boldsymbol{\mu}$ is not restricted as to the values it can take. The prior is uninformative in the sense that small changes in the data exert a large influence on the posterior distribution of the parameters.

It can be shown that the predictive distribution of the excess returns is a multivariate Student's t-distribution with $T - N$ degrees of freedom.[13] The predictive mean and covariance matrix of returns are, respectively,[14]

$$\widetilde{\boldsymbol{\mu}} = \widehat{\boldsymbol{\mu}}$$

and

$$\widetilde{\boldsymbol{\Sigma}} = \frac{(1 + \frac{1}{T})(T - 1)}{T - N - 2}\widehat{\boldsymbol{\Sigma}},$$

where $\widehat{\boldsymbol{\Sigma}}$ is given in (6.8). The predictive covariance here represents the sample covariance scaled up by a factor, reflecting estimation risk. For a given number of assets N, parameter uncertainty decreases as more return data become available (T grows). When a fixed number of historical observations are considered (T is fixed), increasing the number of assets leads to higher uncertainty and estimation risk, since the relative amount of available data declines. (Statisticians would say that there are less degrees of freedom to estimate the unknown parameters.

Prior Scenario 2: Mean and Covariance with Proper Priors

Suppose now that the investor has informative beliefs about the mean vector and the covariance matrix of excess returns. We consider the case of conjugate priors.

---

[13]We assume that $T - N \geq 2$ to ensure that the predictive distribution of returns has a finite variance.

[14]Since the predictive distribution in scenario 1 is not normal, the assumption of a concave utility function is needed for mean-variance optimization. In general, the predictive distribution is normal when the covariance is assumed known and the mean has a conjugate (normal) prior. When neither the mean nor the variance are known and either a diffuse prior is assumed, as in scenario 1, or conjugate priors for both are assumed, as in scenario 2 below, the predictive density is Student's t.

The conjugate prior for the unknown covariance matrix of the normal distribution is the inverted Wishart distribution (see (3.66)), while the conjugate prior for the mean vector of the normal distribution (conditional on $\boldsymbol{\Sigma}$) is multivariate normal:

$$\begin{aligned} \boldsymbol{\mu} \mid \boldsymbol{\Sigma} &\sim \mathrm{N}\left(\boldsymbol{\eta}, \frac{1}{\tau}\boldsymbol{\Sigma}\right) \\ \boldsymbol{\Sigma} &\sim \mathrm{IW}(\boldsymbol{\Omega}, \nu), \end{aligned} \tag{6.17}$$

The prior parameter τ determines the strength of the confidence the investor places on the value of $\boldsymbol{\eta}$, while ν reflects the confidence about $\boldsymbol{\Omega}$. The lower τ and ν are, the higher the uncertainty about those values. When $\tau = 0$, the variance of $\boldsymbol{\mu}$ is infinite and its prior distribution becomes completely flat—the investor has no knowledge or intuition about the mean and lets it vary uniformly from $-\infty$ to $+\infty$. (This is another way to inject "uninformativeness" in the prior distribution—just make the prior covariance (determinant) very large.)

It is important to notice that $\boldsymbol{\mu}$ and $\boldsymbol{\Sigma}$ are no longer independent in the conjugate prior in (6.17), unlike scenario 1. This prior dependence might not be unreasonable if the investor believes that higher risk could entail greater expected returns.

The predictive distribution of next-period's excess returns can be shown to be multivariate Student's t. The mean of the predicted excess returns and their covariance matrix can be shown to be, respectively,

$$\widetilde{\boldsymbol{\mu}} = \frac{\tau}{T+\tau}\boldsymbol{\eta} + \frac{T}{T+\tau}\widehat{\boldsymbol{\mu}} \tag{6.18}$$

and

$$\widetilde{\boldsymbol{\Sigma}} = \frac{T+1}{T(\nu+N-1)}\left(\boldsymbol{\Omega} + (T-1)\widehat{\boldsymbol{\Sigma}} + \frac{T\tau}{T+\tau}(\boldsymbol{\eta}-\widehat{\boldsymbol{\mu}})(\boldsymbol{\eta}-\widehat{\boldsymbol{\mu}})'\right). \tag{6.19}$$

In contrast with scenario 1, the predictive mean and predictive covariance matrix are not proportional to the sample estimates $\widehat{\boldsymbol{\mu}}$ and $\widehat{\boldsymbol{\Sigma}}$. This is characteristic of the impact "informativeness" of the prior distributions has on Bayesian inference. We will see below how this difference from scenario 1 is reflected in the efficient frontier and the optimal portfolio choice. First, let us briefly examine more closely the expressions in (6.18) and (6.19).

The predictive mean in (6.18) is a weighted average of the prior mean, $\boldsymbol{\eta}$, and the sample mean, $\widehat{\boldsymbol{\mu}}$—the sample mean is shrunk toward the prior mean. The stronger the investor's belief in the prior mean is (the higher $\tau/(T+\tau)$ is), the larger the degree to which the prior mean influences the predictive mean (the degree of shrinkage). In the extreme case, when the investor has 100% confidence in the prior mean, the predictive mean is equal to the prior mean, $\widetilde{\mu} = \eta$, and the observed data in fact become irrelevant to the determination of the predictive mean. Conversely, when an investor is completely sceptical about the prior, only the data determine the predictive mean and $\widetilde{\mu} = \widehat{\mu}$—there is no correction for estimation risk in the mean estimate in this case, as we are back to the certainty-equivalence scenario of the classical mean-variance approach.

Notice that in scenario 1 the predictive expected return is not shrunk towards the prior mean. Therefore, the full amount of any sampling error in the sample mean is transferred to the predictive mean (the same is true for the posterior mean). This scenario is, thus, appropriate to employ when we do not suspect that the sample mean contains (substantial) estimation errors. Otherwise, the informative proper prior of scenario 2 might be the better prior alternative.

We learn more about the interplay between the strength of prior beliefs and Bayesian inference in the next two chapters, where asset pricing models enter into the picture to make the analysis more refined.

Next, we discuss how the efficient frontier and the optimal portfolio choice change under the certainty-equivalence scenario and the two prior scenarios outlined above.

The Efficient Frontier and the Optimal Portfolio

The vector of optimal portfolio positions, ω^*, is a function of the predictive mean, $\widetilde{\mu}$, and the predictive covariance, $\widetilde{\Sigma}$, of future returns and is given by (6.14). The efficient frontier is traced out by the optimal pairs $\left(\mu_p^*, \sigma_p^{2\,*}\right)$, where

$$\mu_p^* = \omega^{*\prime}\,\widetilde{\mu}$$

and

$$\sigma_p^{2\,*} = \omega^{*\prime}\,\widetilde{\Sigma}\,\omega^*,$$

for varying values of the risk-aversion parameter, A, in (6.4), the required portfolio return, μ^*, in (6.1) or the minimum portfolio variance, σ^{2*}, in (6.2).

First, consider the certainty-equivalence scenario together with scenario 1. In the classical mean-variance setting, the sample estimates, $\widehat{\mu}$ and $\widehat{\Sigma}$, are treated as the true values of the unknown mean and covariance. In scenario 1, the moments of the predictive distributions are proportional to the sample estimates (equivalently, the maximum-likelihood estimates); the portfolio mean μ_p is unchanged, while the portfolio variance σ_p^2 is just scaled up with a constant. Consequently, the efficient frontier in scenario 1 is shifted to the right compared with the certainty-equivalence case.

Incorporating parameter uncertainty into the investor problem leads to a different perception of the risk and the risk-return trade-off. For each level of expected portfolio return, the risk of holding the efficient portfolio is higher than when parameter uncertainty is ignored. The investor faces not only the risk originating from return variability but also the risk intrinsic in the estimation process.

When informative prior beliefs are introduced into the portfolio problem, such as in scenario 2, no clear comparison can be made between the composition of the efficient portfolios in the Bayesian setting and in the classical (certainty-equivalence) setting—the predictive mean and variance in (6.18) and (6.19), respectively, are no longer proportionate to the sample moments. See the illustration that follows.

Illustration: Bayesian Portfolio Selection

We continue with our illustration based on the daily excess returns of the ten MSCI country indexes. To elicit the hyperparameters in the Bayesian scenario with proper priors, we obtain a presample of daily excess returns, nonoverlapping with the data we use for portfolio optimization. The presample data consist of 520 observations. Denote these data by $\boldsymbol{R}_{-S}$, where S is the length of the presample period. We choose the hyperparameters in (6.17) as follows:

- η is equal to the a vector of zeros. The reason for not specifying η as the sample mean of $\boldsymbol{R}_{-S}$ instead is that we are sceptical that the mean level of returns from the economic-upturn period of the mid-1990s is representative of the mean-return level in our sample.
- τ is equal to 200. τ often takes on the interpretation of the size of a hypothetical sample drawn from the prior distribution: the larger the sample size, the greater our confidence in the prior parameter, η. We have around 6.5 years of (calibration) data available. A τ of 200 could be interpreted as weighting the prior on the mean of returns with about one eighth of the weight of the sample data.
- $\boldsymbol{\Omega}$ is equal to $\widehat{\boldsymbol{\Sigma}}_{-S}(\nu - N - 1)$, where the subscript of $\widehat{\boldsymbol{\Sigma}}$ refers to its being estimated from the presample data, $\boldsymbol{R}_{-S}$.[15]
- ν is equal to 12. We choose a low value for the degrees of freedom to make the prior for $\boldsymbol{\Sigma}$ uninformative and reflect our uncertainty about $\boldsymbol{\Omega}$.[16]

[15] $\boldsymbol{\Sigma}$ is distributed as $IW(\boldsymbol{\Omega}, \nu)$. The prior mean of $\boldsymbol{\Sigma}$ is $E(\boldsymbol{\Sigma}) = \boldsymbol{\Omega}/(\nu - N - 1)$. We estimate $E(\boldsymbol{\Sigma})$ with its sample counterpart, $\widehat{\boldsymbol{\Sigma}}$, given in (6.8).

[16] The mean of the inverse Wishart random variable exists if $\nu > N + 1$.

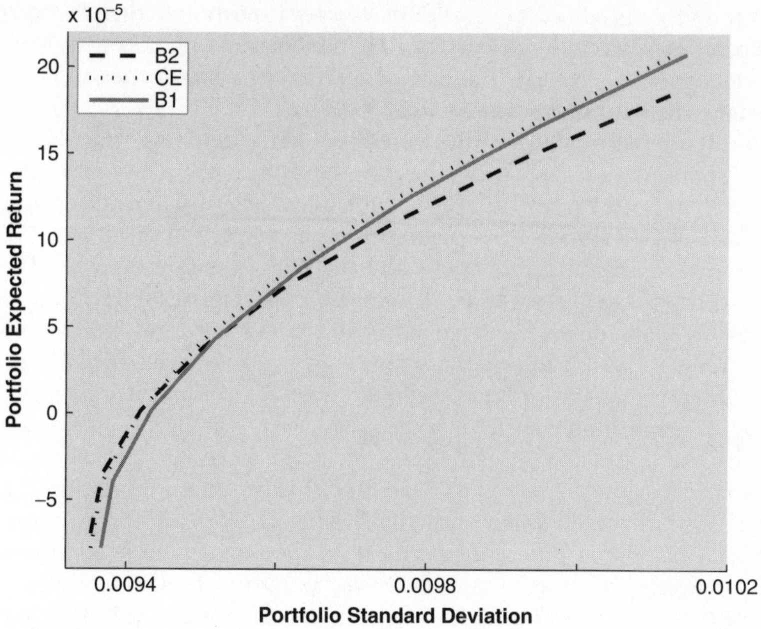

EXHIBIT 6.4 Comparison of the efficient frontiers in the certainty-equivalence setting and the two Bayesian scenarios

Note: CE = certainty-equivalence setting; B1 = Bayesian scenario with diffuse (improper) priors; and B2 = Bayesian scenario with proper priors. The portfolio expected returns and standard deviations are on a daily basis.

In Exhibit 6.4, we present plots of the efficient frontiers in the certainty-equivalence scenario and the two Bayesian scenarios. Given our earlier discussion, the plots appear as expected: The greater risk perceived by the investor in the Bayesian setting is reflected by a shift of the frontier to the right in the two Bayesian scenarios compared to the certainty-equivalence case. The frontier in the Bayesian scenario 1 is very close to the one in the certainty-equivalence setting because of the large number of data points (1,671) available for portfolio optimization. Increasing the amount of sample information even more will eventually make the two frontiers coincide. The rate at which the frontier of scenario 2 moves closer to the certainty-equivalence frontier depends on the strength of the prior beliefs—the values of τ and ν. The degrees-of-freedom parameter, ν, does not affect the risk-return trade-off, since only the predictive covariance depends on it. Changes in it, however, will shift the efficient frontier in a parallel fashion, as uncertainty about the covariance matrix changes.

The parameter τ does affect the relationship between the predictive mean and the predictive covariance matrix in a nonlinear way, as can be seen from the expressions in (6.18) and (6.19), with the consequence that the effect on the efficient frontier is not clear a priori.

More illuminating about the difference between the classical and Bayesian approaches is an illustration on the sensitivity of optimal allocations to changes in the portfolio problem inputs. Suppose that the sample mean of MSCI Germany is 10% higher than the value in Exhibit 6.1. We perform portfolio optimization with all remaining inputs as before. The efficient frontier is constructed from the expected return-standard deviation pairs corresponding to eight portfolios, for varying rates of required portfolio return. Exhibit 6.5 presents the result from our sensitivity check. We can observe that the optimal weights under the certainty-equivalence scenario are much more sensitive to the change in a single component of $\widehat{\mu}$ than are the optimal weights derived under the Bayesian scenario—22 of the certainty-equivalence optimal weights changed by more than 30%, compared to 0 of the Bayesian optimal weights. The reason for the divergent sensitivities is the different treatment of the sample estimates in the certainty-equivalence setting and in the Bayesian setting. In the former case, the sample estimates are considered to be the true parameter values; in the latter case, the sample estimates are considered for what they are—sample estimates—and the uncertainty about the true parameter values is embodied in the portfolio problem. The predictive mean, $\widetilde{\mu}$, and covariance, $\widetilde{\Sigma}$, reflect the uncertainty and this serves as a cushion to soften the impact of the change in the sample mean of MSCI Germany's daily returns.

SHRINKAGE ESTIMATORS

A *shrinkage estimator* is a weighted average of the sample estimator and another estimator. Stein (1956) showed that shrinkage estimators for the mean, although not unbiased, possess more desirable qualities than the sample mean. The so-called *James-Stein estimator* of the mean has the general form:

$$\mu_{JS} = (1-\kappa)\,\widehat{\mu} + \kappa \mathbf{1}'\mu_0, \tag{6.20}$$

where the weight κ, called the *shrinkage intensity*, is given by

$$\kappa = \min\left\{1, \frac{N-2}{T\,(\widehat{\mu} - \mathbf{1}'\mu_0)'\,\mathbf{\Sigma}\,(\widehat{\mu} - \mathbf{1}'\mu_0)}\right\},$$

and $\mathbf{1}$ is a $N \times 1$ vector of ones. It is interesting to notice that any point μ_0 can serve as the shrinkage target. The resulting shrinkage estimator is still

Bayesian Scenario 2

Target Return	−1.8%	−0.9%	0.04%	1.0%	1.9%	2.8%	3.8%	4.7%
Denmark	0.00	−0.01	−0.03	−0.05	−0.07	−0.08	−0.10	−0.11
Germany	0.00	0.43	0.73	0.94	1.10	1.22	1.32	1.40
Italy	−0.00	0.04	0.04	0.04	0.04	0.04	0.04	0.04
UK	0.00	0.02	0.05	0.09	0.13	0.18	0.25	0.33
Portugal	0.00	0.03	0.09	0.17	0.29	0.48	0.83	1.68
Netherlands	−0.00	−0.12	−0.22	−0.28	−0.31	−0.34	−0.35	−0.37
France	0.00	0.18	−0.01	−0.04	−0.05	−0.06	−0.06	−0.06
Sweden	−0.00	−0.02	−0.02	−0.02	−0.02	−0.02	−0.02	−0.03
Norway	0.00	−0.01	−0.02	−0.03	−0.04	−0.05	−0.06	−0.07
Ireland	−0.00	−0.00	−0.01	−0.01	−0.01	−0.01	−0.02	−0.02

Certainty-Equivalence Scenario

Target Return	−2.0%	−1.0%	0.04%	1.1%	2.1%	3.2%	4.2%	5.2%
Denmark	−4.18	0.22	0.13	0.51	7.90	14.27	19.82	24.69
Germany	7.48	11.54	7.86	−2.84	−26.72	−27.47	−16.70	−2.19
Italy	−19.14	−3.11	−1.88	−1.48	−22.34	−44.56	−28.30	−15.33
UK	34.64	30.36	25.09	18.96	24.63	44.33	68.62	102.16
Portugal	−0.99	−7.44	−6.54	−1.94	17.39	48.57	107.47	272.63
Netherlands	34.26	31.64	17.29	14.50	29.90	40.59	48.46	54.48
France	64.79	−10.06	−1.88	−1.96	8.04	29.36	42.66	51.74
Sweden	3.14	−1.47	−1.32	4.01	65.72	254.3	786.81	2480.0
Norway	−6.89	−4.79	−3.61	−1.20	−0.95	−8.62	−24.15	−46.73
Ireland	−16.61	−14.68	−11.47	−5.93	−0.60	−3.32	−9.31	−16.84

EXHIBIT 6.5 Optimal weights sensitivity to changes in the sample means
Note: The table entries are the percentage changes in the optimal portfolio weights resulting from a 10% increase in the sample mean of the daily MSCI Germany return.

better than the sample mean. However, the closer μ_0 is to the true mean μ, the greater the gains are from using $\boldsymbol{\mu}_{JS}$ in place of $\widehat{\boldsymbol{\mu}}$. Therefore, μ_0 is often chosen to be the prediction of a model for the unknown parameter μ—we say, in this case, that μ_0 has structure.

For example, in the context of portfolio selection, Jorion (1986) proposed as a shrinkage target the return on the global-minimum-variance portfolio—the efficient portfolio with smallest risk (see Exhibit 6.1)—given by[17]

$$\mu_0 = \frac{\mathbf{1}'\boldsymbol{\Sigma}^{-1}}{\mathbf{1}'\boldsymbol{\Sigma}^{-1}\mathbf{1}}\widehat{\boldsymbol{\mu}}. \tag{6.21}$$

The optimal portfolio is then shrunk toward this minimum-variance portfolio. Jorion showed that the shrinkage estimator he proposed could also be derived within a Bayesian setting. Several studies document that employing a shrinkage estimator in mean-variance portfolio selection leads to increased stability of optimal portfolio weights across time periods and, possibly, improved portfolio performance.[18]

Recall that in scenario 2, the predictive mean of returns is in fact a shrinkage estimator. The shrinkage target there was the prior mean η, which, in the general case, does not need to have a particular structure. In the two chapters that follow, we will see how to introduce structure into the prior distribution.

Shrinkage estimators for the covariance matrix have also been developed. For example, Ledoit and Wolf (2003) propose that the covariance matrix from the single-factor model of Sharpe (1963) (where the single factor is the market) be used as a shrinkage target:

$$\widehat{\boldsymbol{\Sigma}}_{LW} = (1-\kappa)S + \kappa\boldsymbol{\Psi}, \tag{6.22}$$

where S is the sample covariance matrix and $\boldsymbol{\Psi}$ is the covariance matrix estimated from the single-factor model. The shrinkage intensity κ can be shown to be inversely proportional to number of return observations. The constant of proportionality is dependent on the correlation between the estimation error in S and the misspecification error in $\boldsymbol{\Psi}$.

UNEQUAL HISTORIES OF RETURNS

Consider the tasks of constructing a portfolio of emerging market equities, a portfolio of non-U.S. bonds, or a portfolio of hedge funds. Although of completely different nature, these three endeavors have one common aspect: All are likely to run into the problem of dealing with return series of different lengths. An easy fix is to base one's analysis only on the overlapping parts of the series and to discard portions of the longer series. However, unless a

[17] Shrinkage estimators were introduced to the portfolio selection by Jobson, Korkie, and Ratti (1979). See also Jobson and Korkie (1980) and Frost and Savarino (1986), among others.
[18] See, for example, Jorion (1991), and Larsen and Resnick (2001).

researcher is concerned that the return-generating process (or the distribution of returns) has changed during the longer sample period, this truncation procedure is not desirable since the longer series may carry information useful for estimation. It could be expected that using all of the available data will help reduce uncertainty about the true parameters (which exists by default in dealing with finite samples) and improve estimation results. Stambaugh's framework (Stambaugh (1997)) offers a way to do this.[19]

Suppose that there are a total of N assets available for investment:

1. For N_1 of them, the return history spans T periods (from period 1 to period T). Denote the return data by $\boldsymbol{R}^1$ (a $N_1 \times T$ matrix).
2. The remaining N_2 assets have returns recorded for S periods (from period s to period T). Denote the return data by $\boldsymbol{R}^2$ (a $N_2 \times S$ matrix).
3. Denote by $\boldsymbol{R}^S$ the $N_1 + N_2 \times S$ matrix of overlapping data. That is,

$$\boldsymbol{R}^S = \begin{pmatrix} \boldsymbol{R}^{1,S} \\ \boldsymbol{R}^2 \end{pmatrix},$$

   where $\boldsymbol{R}^{1,S}$ is the matrix of returns of the N_1 assets from the most recent S periods.

Although, for simplicity, we discuss the case of only two starting dates, it is possible to consider multiple starting dates as well, and even to model the starting date as a random variable (see Stambaugh (1997) for these extensions). In this section, our goal is to find out how the long return series (or more precisely, the first $T - S$ observations of them) can contribute in obtaining more precise estimates for the mean and covariance of the short series. Our starting point is to evaluate to what extent the short series and the overlapping part of the long series covary (that is, how much of the information content of the short series is explained by the long series). We can expect that they are not independent if there are common factors that influence them.

Before plunging into the details of the calculations, we outline the basic steps of the approach:

Step 1: Analyze the dependence of the short series on the long series by running ordinary least squares (OLS) regressions.

Step 2: Compute the maximum likelihood estimates (MLEs) of the expected return and covariance of the short and long series. The MLEs of the long series are computed in the usual way. The MLEs

[19] Stambaugh (1997) proposes both a frequentist and a Bayesian approach to combining series of different lengths. Here, we only discuss the latter.

of the short series have additional terms reflecting their dependence on the long series.

Step 3: Compute the predictive mean and covariance of next-period returns.

Step 4: Proceed to portfolio optimization as discussed earlier in the chapter.

We discuss next each of the first three steps in detail.

Dependence of the Short Series on the Long Series

We regress, using OLS, each of the N_2 short series in $\boldsymbol{R}^2$ on the truncated long series in $\boldsymbol{R}^{1,S}$. The regressions have the general form

$$\boldsymbol{R}_j^2 = \alpha_j + \beta_{j1}\boldsymbol{R}_1^{1,S} + \ldots + \beta_{jN_1}\boldsymbol{R}_{N_1}^{1,S} + \epsilon_j, \tag{6.23}$$

where $\boldsymbol{R}_j^2$ denotes the S returns on asset j (the jth row of $\boldsymbol{R}^2$, $j = 1, \ldots, N_2$), $\boldsymbol{R}_i^{1,S}$ denotes the truncated long return history of asset i, $i = 1, \ldots, N_1$, and β_{ji} denotes the "exposure" of the short series of asset j to the overlapping portion of the long series of asset i.

Denote the matrix of estimated slope coefficients by $\boldsymbol{B}$:

$$\widehat{\boldsymbol{B}} = \begin{pmatrix} \beta_{1,1} & \ldots & \beta_{1,N_1} \\ \vdots & \ddots & \vdots \\ \beta_{N_2,1} & \ldots & \beta_{N_2,N_1} \end{pmatrix}. \tag{6.24}$$

The rows of the $N_2 \times N_1$ matrix $\boldsymbol{B}$ will serve as weights on the information from the long series that feeds through to the moment estimates of the short series. Before we proceed to show this, we briefly outline the Bayesian setup.

Bayesian Setup

Assume that $\boldsymbol{R}^S$ has a multivariate normal distribution, independent across periods, with mean vector

$$\boldsymbol{E} = \begin{pmatrix} \boldsymbol{E}_1 \\ \boldsymbol{E}_2 \end{pmatrix},$$

where $\boldsymbol{E}_1$ and $\boldsymbol{E}_2$ are the mean vectors of $\boldsymbol{R}^{1,S}$ and $\boldsymbol{R}^2$, respectively, and covariance matrix

$$\boldsymbol{V} = \begin{pmatrix} \boldsymbol{V}_{11} & \boldsymbol{V}_{12} \\ \boldsymbol{V}_{21} & \boldsymbol{V}_{22} \end{pmatrix},$$

where V_{11} and V_{22} are the covariance matrices of $R^{1,S}$ and R^2, respectively, and $V_{12} = V_{21}$—the matrices of covariances of $R^{1,S}$ and R^2. Consider an uninformative Bayesian setup, such that, the joint prior density is as in (6.16),

$$p(E, V) \propto |V|^{-(N+1)/2}.$$

Recall, from the discussion in scenario 1 above, that (in the equal-history case) the mean and covariance of the predictive density of next-period's returns (given by the $N \times 1$ vector R_{T+1}) are, respectively,

$$\widetilde{E} = \widehat{E} = E^{mle} \tag{6.25}$$

and

$$\widetilde{V} = \frac{(1 + 1/T)(T - 1)}{T - N - 2}\widehat{V} = \frac{T + 1}{T - N - 2}V^{mle}, \tag{6.26}$$

where $\widehat{E}$ and $\widehat{V}$ are the sample moments defined in (6.7) and (6.8), while V^{mle} is given by (6.9).

The general form of the predictive moments in the *un*equal-history setting is the same as in the two expressions above. However, the *maximum-likelihood estimators* (MLEs) now reflect the "feed-through" effect the long series have on the short series. Next, we analyze this effect.

Predictive Moments

Before proceeding to explain the predictive moments of next-period's excess returns, we review the MLEs of the mean and the covariance of returns.

Considering only the overlapping portions of the return series, we can compute the so-called "truncated" MLEs (as we would do if we wanted an easy but suboptimal fix to the problem of unequal histories). The truncated MLE of the joint mean vector E is the usual sample mean of the truncated return data R^S, given by the $N_1 + N_2 \times 1$ vector

$$E_S^{mle} = \begin{pmatrix} E_{1,S}^{mle} \\ E_{2,S}^{mle} \end{pmatrix} = \frac{1}{S} R^S \mathbf{1}_S,$$

where $\mathbf{1}_S$ is a $S \times 1$ vector of ones.

The truncated MLE of the covariance matrix of excess returns is given by

$$V_S^{mle} = \begin{pmatrix} V_{11,S}^{mle} & V_{12,S}^{mle} \\ V_{21,S}^{mle} & V_{22,S}^{mle} \end{pmatrix},$$

where the $V_{11,S}^{mle}$ and $V_{22,S}^{mle}$ are the estimators of the covariance matrices of the truncated long and short series, respectively, and $V_{12,S}^{mle} = V_{21,S}^{mle\,\prime}$ is the estimator of the covariance between the long and short series.

Most notable here is the use of a familiar result from the analysis of multifactor models (see Chapter 14) to write the following decomposition of the truncated covariance estimator of the short series of returns:

$$V_{22,S}^{mle} = \widehat{B}' V_{11,S}^{mle} \widehat{B} + \Sigma, \tag{6.27}$$

which follows from the regression in (6.23). The first term in (6.27) is the portion of the covariance of the short-series explained by the long series. The second term is the unexplained, residual portion of the covariance of the short series.

Combined-Sample MLE of the Mean It can be demonstrated that, when one takes the unequal histories into account and allows for dependencies of the short series on the long series, the *combined-sample* MLE of the mean of the short series is

$$E_2^{mle} = E_{2,S}^{mle} - \widehat{B}\left(E_{1,S}^{mle} - E_1^{mle}\right), \tag{6.28}$$

where

$$E_1^{mle} = \frac{1}{T} R^1 \mathbf{1}_T \tag{6.29}$$

is the combined-sample MLE of the mean of the long series and $\mathbf{1}_T$ is a $T \times 1$ vector of ones.

Let us take a closer look at the expression in (6.28). The first term is the truncated MLE of the short series. The second term is an adjustment factor reflecting the additional information that the long series carries. Since E_1^{mle} is estimated using a larger number of returns, it is a more precise estimate of (is closer to) the true mean of returns than $E_{1,S}^{mle}$. Therefore, the difference $\left(E_{1,S}^{mle} - E_1^{mle}\right)$ represents the error in estimating the true mean by using $E_{1,S}^{mle}$ instead of E_1^{mle}.

What portion of this error is fed through to the truncated MLE, E_2^{mle}? The exposure of the short series to the long series is given by the matrix of regression slopes $\widehat{B}$ in (6.24). Therefore, the portion of estimation error in the long series reflected in the estimator of the short series is $\widehat{B}\left(E_{1,S}^{mle} - E_1^{mle}\right)$.

Notice that the adjustment factor in (6.28) is subtracted from $E_{2,S}^{mle}$, not added. When E_1^{mle} exceeds $E_{1,S}^{mle}$ and the long and short series are positively correlated, $E_{2,S}^{mle}$ is adjusted upward since the information coming from the long series is that the truncated estimator underestimates the true mean, compared to the full estimator. Conversely, when E_1^{mle} is lower than $E_{1,S}^{mle}$ and the series are positively correlated, $E_{2,S}^{mle}$ is adjusted downward.

Combined-Sample MLE of the Covariance Matrix The combined-sample MLE of the covariance matrix of excess returns is given by

$$V^{mle} = \begin{pmatrix} V_{11}^{mle} & V_{1,2}^{mle} \\ V_{2,1}^{mle} & V_{2,2}^{mle} \end{pmatrix}.$$

We now consider each of its components separately;

- V_{11}^{mle} is the usual MLE of the covariance of the long series:

$$V_{11}^{mle} = \frac{1}{T}\sum_{t=1}^{T}\left(R_t^1 - E_1^{mle}\right)'\left(R_t^1 - E_1^{mle}\right), \tag{6.30}$$

  where R_t^1 is the $N_1 \times 1$ vector of returns at time t, t, $t = 1, \ldots, T$.
- V_{12}^{mle} is given by

$$V_{12}^{mle} = V_{12,S}^{mle} - \widehat{B}\left(V_{11,S}^{mle} - V_{11}^{mle}\right); \tag{6.31}$$

- V_{22}^{mle} can be shown to be

$$V_{22}^{mle} = V_{22,S}^{mle} - \widehat{B}\left(V_{11,S}^{mle} - V_{11}^{mle}\right)\widehat{B}' = \widehat{B}V_{11}^{mle}\widehat{B}' + \Sigma. \tag{6.32}$$

Suppose that we only have two assets: Asset 1 with a long return history and asset 2 with a short return history. Then V_{11}^{mle} is the MLE of the variance of asset 1, $V_{12,S}^{mle}$ is the truncated estimator of the covariance between the two assets, and $V_{22,S}^{mle}$ is the truncated estimator of the variance of asset 2.

The adjustment factors in (6.31) and (6.32) rest on a similar intuition to that of the mean estimator in (6.28). When the variance of asset 1 in the most recent S periods is higher (lower) than the variance over the entire sample, $V_{12,S}^{mle}$ and $V_{22,S}^{mle}$ are corrected for this over-underestimation error. The amount of the correction depends on the exposure asset 2 has to asset 1, as in (6.28).

Predictive Moments of Future Excess Returns Finally, we are ready to put all elements together to obtain the moments of the predictive distribution of next-period's returns.

From (6.25), the predictive mean coincides with the MLE. The predictive covariance matrix can be written as

$$\widetilde{V} = \begin{pmatrix} \widetilde{V}_{11} & \widetilde{V}_{12} \\ \widetilde{V}_{21} & \widetilde{V}_{22} \end{pmatrix}. \tag{6.33}$$

Each of the components of $\widetilde{V}$ are given below:

$$\widetilde{V}_{11} = \left(\frac{T+1}{T-N-2}\right) V_{11}^{mle}, \tag{6.34}$$

$$\widetilde{V}_{12} = \left(\frac{T+1}{T-N-2}\right) V_{12}^{mle}, \tag{6.35}$$

and

$$\widetilde{V}_{22} = \left(c\boldsymbol{\Sigma} + \left(\frac{T+1}{T-N-2}\right) \widehat{\boldsymbol{B}} V_{11}^{mle} \widehat{\boldsymbol{B}}'\right), \tag{6.36}$$

where

$$c = \left(\tfrac{S}{S-N_2-2}\right)\left(1 + \tfrac{1}{S}\left[1 + \tfrac{T+1}{T-N-2} tr\left({V_{11,S}^{mle}}^{-1} V_{11}^{mle}\right)\right.\right.$$
$$\left.\left. + \left(E_1^{mle} - E_{1,S}^{mle}\right)' {V_{11,S}^{mle}}^{-1} \left(E_1^{mle} - E_{1,S}^{mle}\right)\right]\right). \tag{6.37}$$

The components of the covariance matrix estimator in (6.34) (6.35), and (6.36) are all, not surprisingly, scaled-up versions of the respective MLEs (recall that we assumed diffuse priors). In the same way as in the equal-histories setting, the difference between the predictive covariance and the sample covariance (that is, the estimation error) decreases as more data become available (T increases).

The combined-sample predictive moments of returns can now be substituted in (6.14) to compute the optimal portfolio positions in the $N_1 + N_2$ assets.

SUMMARY

In this chapter, we presented an overview of the mean-variance portfolio selection and got acquainted with the basic framework of the Bayesian portfolio selection. The classical framework uses the sample estimates of the mean and the covariance of returns as if they were the true parameters. This failure to account for parameter uncertainty leads to optimal portfolio weights that are too sensitive to small changes in the inputs of the portfolio optimization problem. Casting the problem in a Bayesian framework helps deal with this sensitivity. The advantages of applying Bayesian methods to portfolio selection go beyond accounting for uncertainty, as we will see in the chapters ahead—they provide a sound theoretical platform for combining information coming from different sources, while their computational toolbox allows for great modeling flexibility.

CHAPTER 7

Prior Beliefs and Asset Pricing Models

Students of financial theory and practice can be overwhelmed by the multitude of financial models describing the behavior of asset returns. Do they use a general equilibrium asset pricing model such as the *capital asset pricing model* (CAPM), an econometric model such as the Fama and French's (FF) *three-factor model* (Fama and French, 1992), or an arbitrage pricing model such as *arbitrage pricing theory* (APT)?

Being a theoretical abstraction, no single model provide's a completely accurate and infallible description of financial phenomena. Should decision making then discard all models as worthless? In this chapter, we demonstrate how the Bayesian framework conveniently allows an investor to incorporate an asset pricing model into the analysis and combine it with prior beliefs. In doing this, an investor is able to express varying degrees of confidence in the validity of the model—from complete belief to complete skepticism.

Moreover, decision making need not be constrained to utilizing a single asset pricing model. Suppose that an investor entertains the CAPM and the FF models as possible alternatives to model the returns on a portfolio of risky assets. The Bayesian framework provides an elegant tool to account for the uncertainty about which model is true and to produce a return forecast which averages out the forecasts of the individual models.

In this and the next chapters, we expand the simple Bayesian applications to portfolio selection discussed in Chapter 6. This chapter provides a description of how to enrich prior beliefs with the implications of an asset pricing model. We also explain model uncertainty. In the following chapter, we present a prominent example which incorporates an equilibrium model into portfolio selection, the Black-Litterman model.

PRIOR BELIEFS AND ASSET PRICING MODELS

More than three decades ago, Treynor and Black[1] demonstrated the integration of security analysis with Markowitz's approach to portfolio selection. An investor's special insights about individual securities can be combined with CAPM's implication that a rational (market-neutral) investor holds the market portfolio. Although Treynor and Black's analysis did not involve Bayesian estimation, it is clear that the problem they posed is a perfect candidate for it. The "special insights" about securities could be based on a bottom-up valuation analysis, an asset pricing model or simply intuition. In all cases, this "extra market" information is easily combined with the available data within a Bayesian framework. A prominent example of this is the model developed by the Quantitative Resources Group at Goldman Sachs Asset Management, which originated with the work of Black and Litterman (1991). We examine it in the next chapter. Here we offer a treatment of a more general methodology of combining prior beliefs and asset pricing models. Our exposition is based on the frameworks by Pástor (2000) and Pástor and Stambaugh (1999), with some modifications.

Preliminaries

Suppose that the CAPM is the true model of asset returns. Since it is an equilibrium model and all market participants are assumed to possess identical information, each investor optimally holds a combination of the market portfolio and the risk-free asset. The allocation to the risk-free asset in the optimal portfolio depends on the degree of risk aversion (more generally, on the investment objectives).

An econometric model describes prices or returns as functions of exogenous variables, called *factors* or *factor portfolios*, which are often measures of risk. If a given econometric model is believed to be valid, the investor's optimal portfolio consists of a combination of the factor portfolios exposing the investor only to known sources of risk priced by the model.

When a decision maker is completely skeptical with regards to an asset pricing model and only wishes to account for the error intrinsic in parameter estimation, he could accomplish a "no-frill" portfolio selection in the manner described in Chapter 6. It is more likely, however, that although aware of the deficiencies of pricing models, he is not prepared to discard them altogether. Before we describe how to express in a quantitative way the uncertainty about model validity, we briefly review both the CAPM and a general factor model.

[1]Treynor and Black (1973).

The CAPM is based on two categories of assumptions: (1) the way investors make decisions and (2) the characteristics of the capital market. Investors are assumed to be risk-averse and to make one-period investment decisions based on the expected return and the variance of returns. Capital markets are assumed to be perfectly competitive; it is assumed that a risk-free asset exists at which investors can lend and borrow. Based on these assumptions, the CAPM is written as

$$E(R_i) - R_f = \beta_i(E(R_M) - R_f), \tag{7.1}$$

where: $E(R_i)$ = expected return of the risky asset i.
R_f = risk-free rate (assumed constant).
$E(R_M)$ = expected return on the market portfolio.
β_i = measure of systematic risk of asset i (referred to as *beta*).

The CAPM states that, given the assumptions, the expected return of an asset is a linear function of its measure of systematic risk (beta). No other factors, apart from the market, should systematically affect the expected asset return. Risk coming from all other sources can be diversified away.

The empirical analogue of the CAPM is written in the form of a linear regression:

$$R_{i,t} - R_f = \alpha + \beta\left(R_{M,t} - R_f\right) + \epsilon_{i,t}, \tag{7.2}$$

for $i = 1, \ldots, K$, where: $R_{i,t}$ = asset i's return at time t
$R_{M,t}$ = market portfolio's return at time t
$\epsilon_{i,t}$ = asset i's specific return at time t

A factor-based model states that the expected return of an asset is proportional to a linear combination of premia on risk factors:

$$E(R_i) - R_f = \beta_{i,1}\left(E\left(f_1\right) - R_f\right) + \cdots + \beta_{i,k}\left(E\left(f_k\right) - R_f\right), \tag{7.3}$$

where: $E\left(f_j\right)$ = expected return on factor j.
$\beta_{i,j}$ = sensitivity of the expected return of asset i to factor j.

To estimate the factor sensitivities, we write (7.3) in its empirical form as

$$R_{i,t} - R_f = \alpha + \beta_{i,1}\left(f_{1,t} - R_f\right) + \cdots + \beta_{i,K}\left(f_{K,t} - R_f\right) + \epsilon_{i,t}. \tag{7.4}$$

The coefficient α in (7.2) and (7.4) are often referred to as *alpha* and in the context of realized performance sometimes interpreted as an ex post measure of skill of an active portfolio manager.[2] In the context of security selection, a positive (negative) ex post α is a signal that an asset is underpriced (overpriced). The investor would gain from a long position in an asset with positive alpha and a short position in an asset with a negative alpha.[3] Ex ante, α is the forecast of the active stock (portfolio) return.

Quantifying the Belief about Pricing Model Validity

A correct asset pricing model prices the stock/portfolio of stocks exactly. Therefore, if the model is valid, it is the case that the *true (population)* α is zero. Equivalently, to use a tautology, we say that a correct model implies *no mispricing*. Consider an investor who is skeptical about the pricing implications in (7.1) and (7.3). This skepticism is reflected in a belief that the pricing relationship is in fact "off" by some amount λ:

$$E(R_i) - R_f = \lambda + \beta_i\big(E(R_M) - R_f\big)$$

or

$$E(R_i) - R_f = \lambda + \beta_1\big(E(f_1) - R_f\big) + \cdots + \beta_k\big(E(f_k) - R_f\big).$$

That is, the investor's subjective belief is expressed as a perturbation of the "ideal" model.

Perturbed Model

Our goal is to estimate the *perturbed model* in a Bayesian setting so as to be able to reflect the investor's uncertainty about the pricing power of a model. Certainly, the observed data also provide (objective) validation of the pricing model. The resulting predictive distribution of returns not only reflects parameter estimation risk but also the investor's prior uncertainty updated with the data.

We are interested in modeling the excess return on a risky asset (an individual stock or a portfolio of stocks). Throughout the rest of the chapter,

---

[2]In asset pricing, *ex ante* refers to expected or predicted quantities, and *ex post*—to realized (observed) or estimated quantities. In Chapter 9, we come across the important distinction between the two once again in the context of market efficiency testing.

[3]The reason is that adding (shorting) an asset with a positive (negative) alpha to the holding of the market portfolio increases (decreases) the resulting active portfolio's Sharpe ratio. (See equation (6.6) in Chapter 6.)

we write "return" instead of "excess return" for simplicity—and denote the asset's return by R_t. In addition, we observe the returns on K benchmark (factor) portfolios, $f_{1,t}$, $f_{2,t}$, $\ldots$, $f_{K,t}$. In the case of the CAPM, $K = 1$ since there is a single benchmark portfolio—the market portfolio. Data are available for T periods, $t = 1, \ldots, T$. The investor allocates funds between the risky asset and the K benchmark portfolios. The model we estimate is then given by

$$R_t = \alpha + \beta_1 f_{t,1} + \cdots + \beta_K f_{t,K} + \epsilon_t. \tag{7.5}$$

To write (7.5) compactly in matrix notation, denote by $\boldsymbol{R}$ the $T \times 1$ vector of excess returns on the risky asset. The $T \times K$ matrix of benchmark excess returns is denoted by $\boldsymbol{F}$. Then, we write

$$\boldsymbol{R} = \boldsymbol{X}\boldsymbol{b} + \boldsymbol{\epsilon}. \tag{7.6}$$

where $\boldsymbol{X}$ is defined as $(\boldsymbol{1}\,\boldsymbol{F})$, $\boldsymbol{1}$ is a $T \times 1$ vector of ones, and $\boldsymbol{\epsilon}$ is the $T \times 1$ vector of asset-specific returns (regression disturbances). The $(K+\ 1) \times 1$ vector of regression coefficients $\boldsymbol{b}$ is expressed as

$$\boldsymbol{b} = \begin{pmatrix} \alpha \\ \boldsymbol{\beta} \end{pmatrix},$$

where $\boldsymbol{\beta}$ is the $K \times 1$ vector of exposures of the risky asset to the K risk sources, that is, the factor loadings.

As discussed in Chapter 3, estimation of (7.6) involves the following steps: specification of the likelihood for the model parameters, expressing subjective beliefs in the form of prior distributions, and deriving (computing) the posterior distributions. We describe each of these steps in the next sections.

Likelihood Function

We adopt standard assumptions for the regression parameters in (7.6). Disturbances are assumed uncorrelated with the regressors (the benchmark return series) and independently and identically distributed (i.i.d.) with a normal distribution, centered at zero and variance σ^2. Therefore, asset returns are distributed normally with mean $\boldsymbol{X}\boldsymbol{b}$ and variance σ^2:

$$\boldsymbol{R} \sim \mathrm{N}(\boldsymbol{X}\boldsymbol{b}, \sigma^2 \boldsymbol{I}_T),$$

where $\boldsymbol{I}_T$ is a $T \times T$ identity matrix. The likelihood function of the model parameters, $\boldsymbol{b}$ and σ^2, is given (as in Chapter 3) by

$$L\left(\boldsymbol{b}, \sigma \,|\boldsymbol{R}, \boldsymbol{X}\right) \propto (\sigma^2)^{-T/2} \exp\left(-\frac{1}{2\sigma^2}(\boldsymbol{R} - \boldsymbol{X}\boldsymbol{b})'(\boldsymbol{R} - \boldsymbol{X}\boldsymbol{b})\right). \tag{7.7}$$

Now, the question of whether to treat the K benchmark returns (premia) in $\boldsymbol{F}$ as nonstochastic (constants) or stochastic (random variables) arises. The importance of this distinction is highlighted by some empirical evidence, suggesting that estimation errors in the risk premia have a stronger impact on the (im)precision in estimating the expected asset returns than estimation errors in β_k, $k = 1, \ldots, K$.[4] Therefore, in order to take the uncertainty about the components of $\boldsymbol{F}$ into account, we make the assumption that benchmark returns are stochastic and follow a multivariate normal distribution:

$$\boldsymbol{F}_t \sim \mathrm{N}(\boldsymbol{E}, \boldsymbol{V}),$$

where: $\boldsymbol{F}_t = 1 \times K$ vector of benchmark returns at time t (the tth row of $\boldsymbol{F}$).
$\boldsymbol{E} = 1 \times K$ vector of expected benchmark returns.
$\boldsymbol{V} = K \times K$ covariance matrix of the benchmark returns.

The likelihood function for $\boldsymbol{E}$ and $\boldsymbol{V}$ is written as

$$L(\boldsymbol{E}, \boldsymbol{V} \mid \boldsymbol{F}) \propto |\boldsymbol{V}|^{-K/2} \exp\left(-\frac{1}{2}\sum_{t=1}^{T}(\boldsymbol{F}_t - \boldsymbol{E})'\boldsymbol{V}^{-1}(\boldsymbol{F}_t - \boldsymbol{E})\right). \tag{7.8}$$

Prior Distributions

The perturbation of the ideal model discussed earlier is easily expressed as a prior probability distribution on α. The mean of α is set equal to zero to reflect the default scenario of no mispricing. The standard deviation of α, σ_α, is a parameter whose value is chosen by the investor to reflect the degree of his confidence in the asset pricing model. Suppose, on the other hand, that, instead of an asset pricing model, the investor would like to incorporate the predictions of a stock analyst in his decision-making process. Then, α's prior distribution will be centered on those predictions, and σ_α will represent the confidence in them. The lower σ_α is, the stronger the belief in the model's implications. At one extreme is $\sigma_\alpha = 0$—the prior distribution of α degenerates to a single point, its mean of zero—the investor is certain that (7.1) ((7.3)) holds exactly. At the other extreme, $\sigma_\alpha = \infty$, that is, the prior distribution of α is completely flat (diffuse) and the investor rejects the model as worthless.

We assume that the model parameters (the regression coefficients and the disturbance variance) have a natural conjugate prior distributions,

$$\boldsymbol{b} \mid \sigma^2 \sim \mathrm{N}(\boldsymbol{b}_0, \sigma^2 \boldsymbol{\Omega}_0) \tag{7.9}$$

$$\sigma^2 \sim \text{Inv-}\chi^2(\nu_0, c_0^2), \tag{7.10}$$

[4]For example, see Pástor and Stambaugh (1999) and the references therein.

where $\mathbf{\Omega}_0$ is a positive definite matrix and Inv-$\chi^2(\nu_0, c_0^2)$ denotes the scaled inverted χ^2 distribution with degrees of freedom ν_0 and scale parameter c_0^2 given in (3.62).

The prior mean of the vector of regression coefficients is

$$\boldsymbol{b}_0 = \begin{pmatrix} \alpha_0 \\ \boldsymbol{\beta}_0 \end{pmatrix}, \tag{7.11}$$

with $\alpha_0 = 0$, as explained above, while $\mathbf{\Omega}_0$ can be expressed as

$$\mathbf{\Omega}_0 = \begin{pmatrix} \sigma_\alpha^2 \frac{1}{\sigma^2} & 0 \\ 0 & \mathbf{\Sigma}_\beta \end{pmatrix}. \tag{7.12}$$

We set the off-diagonal elements in (7.12) equal to zero since we do not have a priori reasons to believe that the intercepts are correlated with the regression slopes—that is, that the mispricing is correlated with the factor loadings. Since we are not interested in inference about the factor loadings, $\boldsymbol{\beta}$, we impose a weak prior on them by specifying $\mathbf{\Sigma}_\beta$ as a diagonal matrix with large diagonal elements. Notice our choice for the first diagonal element of $\mathbf{\Omega}_0$—the aim of this formulation is to make the variance of α equal to the investor-specified σ_α^2, which reflects the skepticism about the pricing model's implications. We soon investigate the influence different choices of σ_α^2 have on the optimal portfolio composition.

The prior for the mean vector, $\boldsymbol{E}$, and the covariance matrix, $\boldsymbol{V}$, of the benchmark returns is assumed to be Jeffreys' prior (see Chapter 3),

$$\boldsymbol{E}, \boldsymbol{V} \propto |\boldsymbol{V}|^{-(T+1)/2}. \tag{7.13}$$

Posterior Distributions

Posterior Distribution of $\boldsymbol{b}$, conditional on σ^2 Since we made natural conjugate prior assumptions about the parameters of the normal model, we obtain posterior distributions of the same form as the prior distributions.

The posterior distribution of $\boldsymbol{b}$, conditional on σ^2, is multivariate normal with mean $\boldsymbol{b}^*$ and covariance matrix $\sigma^2\mathbf{\Omega}^*$,

$$\boldsymbol{b} \mid \sigma^2, \boldsymbol{R}, \boldsymbol{X} \propto \mathrm{N}\left(\boldsymbol{b}^*, \sigma^2\mathbf{\Omega}^*\right), \tag{7.14}$$

where (from (3.39) and (3.40))

$$\mathbf{\Omega}^* = \left(\mathbf{\Omega}_0^{-1} + \boldsymbol{X}'\boldsymbol{X}\right)^{-1} \tag{7.15}$$

and

$$b^* \equiv \begin{pmatrix} \alpha^* \\ \beta^* \end{pmatrix} = \boldsymbol{\Omega}^* \left(\boldsymbol{\Omega}_0^{-1} b_0 + X'X\widehat{b} \right). \qquad (7.16)$$

In (7.16), $\widehat{b}$ denotes the least-squares estimate of b, which is also its *maximum-likelihood estimate* (MLE). The posterior mean, b^*, is, as expected, a shrinkage estimator of b—a weighted average of its prior mean, b_0, and its MLE, $\widehat{b}$. The weights are functions of the sample precision $(\sigma^2(X'X)^{-1})^{-1}$ and the prior precision $(\sigma^2\boldsymbol{\Omega}_0)^{-1}$, and reflect the shrinkage of the sample estimate of b toward the prior mean.[5]

Posterior Distribution of σ^2 The posterior distribution of σ^2 is an inverted χ^2 distribution,

$$\sigma^2 \sim \text{Inv-}\chi^2(\nu^*, c^{2*}), \qquad (7.17)$$

with the posterior parameters ν^* and c^{2*} given by (as in (3.42) and (3.43))

$$\nu^* = T + \nu_0 \qquad (7.18)$$

and

$$c^{2*} = \frac{1}{\nu^*}\left(\nu_0 c_0^2 + (R - X\widehat{b})'(R - X\widehat{b}) + (b_0 - \widehat{b})'K(b_0 - \widehat{b}) \right). \qquad (7.19)$$

where $K = \left(\boldsymbol{\Omega}_0 + (X'X)^{-1}\right)^{-1}$.

Posterior Distributions of the Benchmark Parameters The posterior distributions of the moments of the benchmark returns are normal and inverted Wishart,

$$E \,|\, V, F \sim \mathrm{N}\left(\widehat{E}, \frac{V}{T}\right) \qquad (7.20)$$

$$V \,|\, F \sim \mathrm{IW}\left(\boldsymbol{\Psi}, T - 1\right), \qquad (7.21)$$

---

[5]To see that, rewrite the expression for b^* in (7.16) as

$$b^* = \sigma^2 \boldsymbol{\Omega}^* \left((\sigma^2 \boldsymbol{\Omega})^{-1} b_0 + (\sigma^2 (X'X)^{-1})^{-1} \widehat{b} \right).$$

From standard results of multivariate regression analysis, we can recognize $\sigma^2(X'X)^{-1}$ as the covariance matrix of $\widehat{b}$.

where

$$\widehat{E} = \frac{1}{T}\sum_{t=1}^{T} F_t$$

and

$$\Psi = \sum_{t=1}^{T}(F_t - \widehat{E})'(F_t - \widehat{E}).$$

Predictive Distributions and Portfolio Selection

In Chapter 6, we provided the foundations of Bayesian portfolio selection and we explained that the key input for the portfolio problem is the predictive distribution of next-period returns. The optimal portfolio weights are as given in (6.14) in Chapter 6.

Denote by F_{T+1} the $1 \times K$ vector of next-period's benchmark returns. Let R_{T+1} denote next-period excess return on the risky asset. Since the investor allocates funds among the risky asset and the K benchmark portfolios, the predictive moments, $\widetilde{\mu}$ and $\widetilde{\Sigma}$, are in fact the joint predictive mean and covariance of (R_{T+1}, F_{T+1}).

Since we assume that benchmark returns are random variables themselves, we first need to predict F_{T+1} before we are able to predict R_{T+1}. As in Chapter 6, the predictive distribution of F_{T+1} is multivariate Student's t-distribution with $T-K$ degrees of freedom. The predictive mean and covariance of F_{T+1} are, respectively

$$\widetilde{E}_F = \widehat{E} \quad \text{and} \quad \widetilde{V}_F = \frac{T+1}{T(T-K-2)}\Psi. \tag{7.22}$$

The predictive distribution of next-period's returns is Student's t with $T + \nu_0$ degrees of freedom, with predictive mean given by

$$\widetilde{E}_R = \widetilde{E}_X b^* \tag{7.23}$$

and variance

$$\widetilde{V}_R = \frac{T+\nu_0}{T+\nu_0-2}\, c^{2*}\left(1 - \widetilde{E}_X \Omega^* \widetilde{E}_X\right), \tag{7.24}$$

where $\widetilde{E}_X$ is $\left(1\, \widetilde{E}_F\right)$. Finally, the predictive covariance between next-period's risky asset's return, R_{T+1}, and next-period's return on benchmark j, $F_{j,T+1}$, is obtained from[6]

$$\widetilde{V}_{R,F} = \boldsymbol{\beta}_j^* \widetilde{V}_{F,jj}, \tag{7.25}$$

where $\boldsymbol{\beta}_j^*$ is the posterior mean of the jth factor loading and $\widetilde{V}_{F,jj}$ is the jth diagonal component of $\widetilde{V}_F$.

Now, combining the results in (7.22), (7.23), (7.24) and (7.25), we obtain the joint predictive mean and covariance used for portfolio optimization,

$$\widetilde{\boldsymbol{\mu}} = \begin{pmatrix} \widetilde{E}_R \\ \widetilde{E}_F \end{pmatrix}$$

and

$$\widetilde{\boldsymbol{\Sigma}} = \begin{pmatrix} \widetilde{V}_R & \widetilde{V}_{R,F} \\ \widetilde{V}_{R,F} & \widetilde{V}_F \end{pmatrix}.$$

Applying (6.14), we compute the optimal portfolio weights. We stress that we do not need to have analytical expressions for the posteriors nor the predictive densities. As long as we are able to simulate from them, we can compute the optimal portfolio weights. Appendix A of this chapter outlines the step-by-step procedure to do so.

Prior Parameter Elicitation

The hyperparameters whose values we need to specify for the calculations in the previous section are the vector of prior means, $\boldsymbol{b}_0$, and the prior covariance matrix, $\boldsymbol{\Omega}_0$, from the prior distribution of $\boldsymbol{b}$, as well as the degrees of freedom ν_0 and the scale parameter c_0^2 from the prior distribution of σ^2.

- The first element of $\boldsymbol{b}_0$, α_0, is set equal to 0 to reflect the "default" case of no mispricing in the asset pricing model.
- The prior means of the benchmark loadings, $\boldsymbol{\beta}_0$, could be specified to be zero as well, in case no other prior intuition exists about their values. Presample estimates of the loadings could be employed as well.

---

[6] Recall that an asset's beta with respect to a risk factor is defined as the covariance of the asset's return with the factor's return divided by the variance of the factor's return.

- Since inference about σ^2 is not of particular interest to us in this chapter, we could make its prior relatively uninformative (flat) by specifying a small value (greater than 4) for the prior degrees of freedom parameter ν_0.[7] Thus, we let the data dominate in determining the posterior distribution of σ^2. The scale parameter c_0^2 is determined indirectly from the expression for the expectation of an inverse χ^2 random variable, $E(\sigma^2) = \nu_0 c_0^2/(\nu_0 - 2)$. The expectation, $E(\sigma^2)$, is estimated from the presample data as the residual variance.
- Specifying the elements of the prior covariance matrix, σ_α^2 and $\boldsymbol{\Sigma}_\beta$, in (7.12) requires only a small additional effort. As mentioned earlier, we make the prior on the factor loadings uninformative by letting their covariance, $\boldsymbol{\Sigma}_\beta$, equal to a diagonal matrix with very large diagonal elements, for example,

$$\boldsymbol{\Sigma}_\beta = 100\boldsymbol{I}_K, \tag{7.26}$$

where $\boldsymbol{I}_K$ is a $K \times K$ identity matrix. The value of σ_α^2 depends on the investor's confidence in the validity of the asset pricing model. It ranges from zero (full confidence) to infinity (complete skepticism).

Illustration: Incorporating Confidence about the Validity of an Asset Pricing Model

In this section, we present an illustration of the previous discussion.[8] We consider an investor entertaining the CAPM as an asset-pricing model option (corresponding to $K = 1$ in (7.6)). Our goal is to examine the asset allocation decision for varying degrees of confidence in the pricing model. The investor allocates his funds between the risky asset and the market portfolio. The risky asset is represented by the monthly return on IBM stock. The data on the stock and portfolios cover the period January 1996 to December 2005. Exhibit 7.1 presents the posterior means of the intercept and the loading on the market, as well as the optimal allocations for five different values of σ_α^2, representing five levels of scepticism about the model's pricing power.

We can observe that as uncertainty about the pricing model increases, the allocation to the risky asset increases—strong belief in the validity of the pricing model implies that the stock is priced correctly and, therefore, the investor optimally invests his whole wealth in the market portfolio; conversely, as σ_α^2 increases, the investor gives more credence to the positive posterior alpha of IBM and reallocates funds to the IBM stock accordingly.

[7] An inverse χ_ν^2 random variable has a finite variance if its degrees of freedom parameter, ν, is greater than 4.
[8] The illustration is based on an application in Pástor (2000).

	IBM Stock					Market
Skepticism (σ_α)	None $\sigma_\alpha 0 = 0\%$	Small $\sigma_\alpha = 1\%$	Medium $\sigma_\alpha = 5\%$	Big $\sigma_\alpha = 15\%$	Complete $\sigma_\alpha = \infty$	
Sample Means	$\hat{\alpha} = 0.068 \quad \hat{\beta} = 1.307$					$\tilde{E} = 0.067$
Prior Means	$\alpha_0 = 0 \quad \beta_0 = 0.617$					-
Posterior Means	$\tilde{\alpha} = 0.0$ $\tilde{\beta} = 1.296$	$\tilde{\alpha} = 0.001$ $\tilde{\beta} = 1.296$	$\tilde{\alpha} = 0.017$ $\tilde{\beta} = 1.293$	$\tilde{\alpha} = 0.052$ $\tilde{\beta} = 1.286$	$\tilde{\alpha} = 0.068$ $\tilde{\beta} = 1.292$	$\tilde{E} = 0.067$
Optimal Allocation	0%	1.29%	26 .6%	86.5%	101%	

EXHIBIT 7.1 Optimal allocation of the IBM stock given varying degrees of uncertainty in the validity of the CAPM
Note: The standard deviations, values for alpha, as well as expected market returns are annualized.

Next, we explicitly account for the uncertainty about which model is the correct one and discuss portfolio choice based on the combined posterior inference.

MODEL UNCERTAINTY

In the previous section, we considered separately two out of a number of possible asset pricing models. Typically, data analysis is initiated by selecting a single "best" model, which is then treated as the true one and used for inferences and predictions. Sound familiar? This practice mirrors on a magnified level the one of treating the sample estimate of a parameter as the true parameter in inferences and predictions. No matter which model we select to assist us in the decision-making process, we could never be certain it is correctly specified to describe the true data-generating process. Since all models employed in finance are inevitably only approximations, accounting for *model risk* (i.e., the ambiguity associated with model selection) is an important element of the inference process.[9]

[9]Treatment of model risk has not yet become the norm in the empirical finance literature. Cremers (2002) and Avramov (2002) discuss it in the context of predictability; and Pástor and Stambaugh (1999) provide a brief overview in the context of asset pricing models.

Two principal sources of model risk in empirical finance are:

- Suppose a researcher analyzes a set of data and detects the presence of a certain structure in it. It is possible that the data are in fact nearly random and the apparent structure is due simply to a spurious relationship.
- A common simplification is to specify a static model for the data, when in fact they have been generated by a process with a time-varying structure; if a dynamic model is assumed, there is a risk of misspecifying the dynamic structure.

The first source of risk is due to the large degree of noise present in financial data. The model could leverage this noise, interpreting it as a regularity of the data. Consider, for example, the extensive debate in the empirical finance literature about whether stock returns are predictable. The critics of predictability have argued that the predictive relationships found between stock returns and certain fundamental or macroeconomic variables are spurious or the result of data mining.[10] Even supporters of predictability have not been able to achieve consensus—neither about the identity of the predictive variables, nor about the combination of them that would best describe the behavior of stock returns. No doubt both camps would agree that model risk plays a major role in their analyses. (We examine predictability in Chapter 9.)

The second source of error is often the more serious one. Consider estimation of a financial model with quarterly data. Then, in order to collect a large enough data sample, one has to consider a sufficiently long period of financial data history. However, it is possible that the economic paradigm has undergone changes during that period. A static model could be a misspecification for the underlying time-varying, data-generating process, thus producing large forecasting errors. One way of dealing with time-variation is by means of regime-switching models. We discuss these models in Chapter 11.

In general, model risk is a factor that dilutes our inferences. We can think of specifying a single model as giving up a part of our degrees of freedom—there is less information left available to estimate the model parameters. As a result, we end up with noisier parameter estimates and predictions.

In the illustration in the previous section, we selected a model (the CAPM) and discussed how to account for the uncertainty about its pricing ability, that is, for the *within-model* uncertainty. In doing so, we implicitly conditioned our analysis on the single model. The *Bayesian model*

---

[10]See, for example, Lo and MacKinlay (1990).

averaging (BMA) methodology allows one to explicitly incorporate model uncertainty by conditioning on all models from the universe of models considered. Each model is assigned a posterior probability, which serves as a weight in the "mega" composite model. Thus we are able to evaluate the *between-model* uncertainty and, more importantly, draw inferences based on the composite model.

In the next section, we describe the systematic framework of BMA.[11]

Bayesian Model Averaging

It is helpful to think of the BMA setting as a hierarchical parameter setting. We start at the highest level of the hierarchy with a true, unknown model. We regard each of the candidate models as a perturbation of the true model. Assuming we entertain N models as plausible, denote model j by M_j, $j = 1, \ldots, N$. M_j is a parameter associated with the particular model that governs its "credibility share" of the true model. We assert a prior distribution on M_j, based on our belief about how credible a candidate the model is, we update the prior with the information contained in the data sample and arrive at a posterior distribution reflecting the model's updated credibility. At the lower hierarchical level, we find the parameter vectors $\boldsymbol{\theta}_j$ of each model j. The updating procedure of their distributions is essentially the one discussed earlier in the chapter.

Prior Distributions The choice of prior model distributions is naturally based on the existence of a particular intuition about the relative plausibility of the models in consideration. For example, there is now little disagreement among academics and practitioners that more than one pervasive factor influence the comovement of stock returns. Therefore, a single-factor model might get less of a prior weight than a multifactor model.

As in the previous section, let's consider only two models—the CAPM and the FF three-factor model—as potential candidates for the true asset pricing model. Denote the prior probability of model j by $p_j \equiv p\ (M_j)$, where $j = 1$ refers to the CAPM and $j = 2$ corresponds to the FF model. It is not unusual, in the absence of specific intuition about model plausibility, to assume that the models are equally likely. Then, each of them will be assigned a prior model probability $p_j = 1/2$.[12]

---

[11]See Hoeting et al. (1999) for an introduction to BMA.

[12]In the context of predictability, Cremers (2002) suggests the following intuitive approach to asserting a model prior. Suppose there are K variables which, one believes, are potential predictors for the excess stock returns. The number of possible

The prior distributions of the parameters under model j are conditional on the model. Denote the prior by $p(\boldsymbol{\theta}_j \mid M_j) = p(\boldsymbol{b} \mid \sigma^2)p(\sigma^2)$, where $\boldsymbol{\theta}_j$ is the vector of parameters of model j, $\boldsymbol{\theta}_j = (\boldsymbol{b}_j, \sigma^2)$. The vector $\boldsymbol{b}_1$ is a 2×1 vector, consisting of the intercept, α_1 and β_1, the sensitivity of the risky asset to market risk (the CAPM setting). The vector $\boldsymbol{b}_2$ is a 4×1 vector consisting of the intercept α_2 and the vector of exposures to the three factor risks, $\boldsymbol{\beta}_2$ (the FF three-factor setting). Assume that the priors of the model parameters (the elements of $\boldsymbol{\theta}$) are as given in (7.9) and (7.10). For simplicity, we consider the factor returns nonstochastic in the current discussion.

Posterior Model Probabilities and Posterior Parameter Distributions The posterior model probabilities play a key role in deriving the posterior parameter distributions. The posterior probability of model j is computed using Bayes' formula from Chapter 2:

$$p(M_j \mid \boldsymbol{R}) = \frac{p(\boldsymbol{R} \mid M_j)\, p(M_j)}{\sum_{k=1}^{2} p(\boldsymbol{R} \mid M_k)\, p(M_k)}. \tag{7.27}$$

In the following discussion, we suppress the dependence on $\boldsymbol{X}$ for notational simplicity. The term $p(\boldsymbol{R} \mid M_j)$ in (7.27) is the marginal likelihood of model j and is computed by integrating model j's parameters from their likelihood:

$$p(\boldsymbol{R} \mid M_j) = \int L(\boldsymbol{b}, \sigma^2 \mid \boldsymbol{R}, M_j)\, p\,(\boldsymbol{b}, \sigma^2 \mid M_j)\, \mathrm{d}\boldsymbol{b}\, \mathrm{d}\sigma^2, \tag{7.28}$$

where $L(\boldsymbol{b}, \sigma^2 | \boldsymbol{R}, M_j)$ is the likelihood for the parameters of model j (given in (7.7)) and $p(\boldsymbol{b}, \sigma^2 | M_j)$ is the joint prior distribution for model j's parameters (which factors into the densities given in (7.9) and (7.10)). See Appendix B of this chapter for the computation of the likelihood of model j in the setting of this chapter.

---

distinct combinations of these variables is 2^K and there are as many (linear) models that could describe the return-generating process. Let each variable's inclusion in a model is equally likely and independent, with probability ρ. Denote by 1 the event that variable j is included in model i, and by 0 the event that it is not. This describes a Bernoulli trial. The prior probability of model i can then be viewed as the joint probability of the particular combination of variables or the Bernoulli likelihood function (see Chapter 4). It is given by $p\,(M_i) = \rho^{\kappa}(1-\rho)^{K-\kappa}$, where κ is the number of variables included in the ith model. Note that when $\rho = 1/2$, all models are equally likely. It is easy to generalize this prior model probability and assign different probabilities, ρ, to different (groups of) variables.

Given a particular model, M_j, the posterior distribution of the parameter vector is $p(\boldsymbol{\theta}_j \mid \boldsymbol{R}, M_j)$ and can be factored into

$$p\,(\boldsymbol{\theta}_j \mid \boldsymbol{R}, M_j) = p(\boldsymbol{b} \mid \sigma^2, \boldsymbol{R}, M_j)\, p(\sigma^2 \mid \boldsymbol{R}, M_j). \tag{7.29}$$

The marginal posterior distributions $p\,(\boldsymbol{b} \mid \sigma^2, \boldsymbol{R}, M_j)$ and $p\,(\sigma \mid \boldsymbol{R}, M_j)$ are the same as in (9.21) and (7.17), respectively.

To remove the conditioning on model j, and to obtain the overall posterior distribution of θ, we average the posterior parameter distributions across all models:

$$p\,(\boldsymbol{b} \mid \sigma^2, \boldsymbol{R}) = \sum_{j=1}^{2} p\,(\boldsymbol{b} \mid \sigma^2, \boldsymbol{R}, M_j)\, p\,(M_j \mid \boldsymbol{R}) \tag{7.30}$$

and

$$p\,(\sigma^2 \mid \boldsymbol{R}) = \sum_{j=1}^{2} p\,(\sigma^2 \mid \boldsymbol{R}, M_j)\, p\,(M_j \mid \boldsymbol{R}). \tag{7.31}$$

The posterior distribution under each model is weighted by the posterior probability of the respective model. That represents one of the most attractive features of BMA—the posterior mean and variance of the model parameters $\boldsymbol{b}$ and σ^2 are computed as averages over the posterior moments from all models. The predictive ability is thus improved in comparison with using a single model.[13] Denote by $\boldsymbol{b}_j^*$ and σ_j^{2*} the posterior means of $\boldsymbol{b}$ and σ^2 under model j. The (unconditional) posterior means across all models are, respectively,

$$\boldsymbol{b}^* = \sum_{j=1}^{2} \boldsymbol{b}_j^*\, p\,(M_j \mid \boldsymbol{R}), \tag{7.32}$$

and

$$\sigma^{2*} = \sum_{j=1}^{2} \sigma_j^{2*}\, p\,(M_j \mid \boldsymbol{R}). \tag{7.33}$$

Predictive Distribution and Portfolio Selection The overall predictive distribution of excess returns next period is a weighted average of the predictive distributions of returns across the individual models:

$$p\,(R_{T+1} \mid \boldsymbol{R}) = \sum_{j=1}^{2} p\,(M_j \mid \boldsymbol{R})\, p\,(R_{T+1} \mid \boldsymbol{R}, M_j). \tag{7.34}$$

---

[13]See Madigan and Raftery (1994).

Sampling from the overall predictive distribution is accomplished by sampling from the predictive distribution under each model and then computing the weighted average of the draws across models. The predictive mean and variance are obtained as weighted averages as well (in the same way as the posterior parameter moments were obtained earlier).

Illustration: Combining Inference from the CAPM and the Fama and French Three-Factor Model

Here, we provide an example of computing posterior model probabilities for two models—the CAPM and the Fama and French (FF) three-factor model, using again IBM stock as the risky asset. Fama and French (1992) assert that, in addition to the market, there are two more risk factors—value and size—that drive stock returns and should, therefore, be priced by the model. It has been empirically observed that small-capitalization stocks and stocks with high book-to-market value outperform large-capitalization stocks and stocks with low book-to-market value, respectively. To capture these size and value premiums, the two risk factors are represented by zero-investment (factor) portfolios. The size-factor portfolio consists of a long position in small-capitalization stocks and a short position of equal size in large-capitalization stocks. The value-factor portfolio is constructed by going long in high book-to-market value stocks and going short in low book-to-market value stocks. These factor portfolios have been called, respectively, *small minus big* (SMB) and *high minus low* (HML). (For more details on multifactor models, see Chapter 14.) Given the prior and data assumptions made earlier in the chapter, we calculate the posterior model probabilities; 98.9% for the CAPM and 1.11% for the FF model.

Simulating from the predictive distribution of IBM returns is accomplished using (7.34) and the simulation procedure in Appendix A, as follows. First, select the CAPM with probability 98.9% and the FF model with probability 1.11%. To do this, draw an observation, U, from uniform [0,1] distribution. If $U \leq 0.989$, select the CAPM; if $U \leq 0.11$, select the FF model. Second, conditional on the selected model, draw from the posteriors of $\boldsymbol{b}$ and σ^2. Third, draw R_{T+1} from its normal distribution.

We simulate a sample of 30,000 observations of R_{T+1} and obtain an (annualized) predictive mean for the returns on IBM equal to 8.52%. These are simulations from the composite model, thus accounting for model risk. In a model with more than one risky asset, we could produce simulations from the composite model in the way just described and then use these to determine the optimal portfolio composition.

SUMMARY

Combining prior beliefs with asset pricing models introduces structure and economic justification into Bayesian portfolio selection. We continue along these lines in the following two chapters. In Chapter 8, we review the Black-Litterman model, while in Chapter 9 we explore market efficiency and predictability.

Whenever possible, model uncertainty should be incorporated into the decision-making process in order to reflect the risk investors face, in addition to parameter uncertainty.

APPENDIX A: NUMERICAL SIMULATION OF THE PREDICTIVE DISTRIBUTION

In this appendix, we outline the steps for simulating from the predictive distributions of next-period's risky asset's return, R_{T+1} and next-period's benchmark returns, $\boldsymbol{F}_{T+1}$, as well as for computing their predictive moments.

We write the predictive distribution of R_{T+1} as

$$p\left(R_{T+1} \mid \boldsymbol{R}\right) = \int p\left(R_{T+1} \mid \boldsymbol{b}, \sigma^2, \boldsymbol{X}_{T+1}, \boldsymbol{R}\right) \times p\left(\boldsymbol{b}, \sigma^2 \mid \boldsymbol{R}, \boldsymbol{X}\right) p\left(\boldsymbol{F}_{T+1} \mid \boldsymbol{F}\right) \mathrm{d}\boldsymbol{F}_{T+1}\, \mathrm{d}\boldsymbol{b}\, \mathrm{d}\sigma^2, \quad (7.35)$$

where $\boldsymbol{X}_{T+1}$ is $(\mathbf{1}\, \boldsymbol{F}_{T+1})$, while $\boldsymbol{R}$ and $\boldsymbol{F}$ denote, respectively, the returns on the risky asset and the benchmarks available up to time T. Since $\boldsymbol{F}_{T+1}$ is random, it needs to be integrated out, together with the parameters, to compute the predictive density. Thus, not only the parameter uncertainty about $\boldsymbol{b}$ and σ^2 is accounted for but the uncertainty about $\boldsymbol{F}_{T+1}$ as well. All densities on the right-hand side in (7.35) are known densities:

- $p\left(R_{T+1} \mid \boldsymbol{b}, \sigma, \boldsymbol{X}_{T+1}, \boldsymbol{R}\right)$ is a normal density with mean zero and variance σ^2. To see that, consider (7.6) and roll it forward one period.
- $p\left(\boldsymbol{b}, \sigma^2 \mid \boldsymbol{R}, \boldsymbol{X}\right)$ factors into $p\left(\boldsymbol{b} \mid \sigma^2, \boldsymbol{R}, \boldsymbol{X}\right) p\left(\sigma^2 \mid \boldsymbol{R}, \boldsymbol{X}\right)$, which are the posterior densities in (9.21) and (7.17).
- $p\left(\boldsymbol{F}_{T+1} \mid \boldsymbol{F}\right)$ is the multivariate Student's t predictive distribution of $\boldsymbol{F}_{T+1}$ with parameters given in (7.22).

The predictive distribution of F_{T+1} is written in a similar way as

$$p\left(F_{T+1}\,|\,F\right) = \int p\left(F_{T+1}\,|\,F, E, V\right) \times p\left(E\,|\,V, F\right) p\left(V\,|\,F\right) \mathrm{d}E\, \mathrm{d}V. \tag{7.36}$$

The distributions on the right-hand side are known as well; $p\left(F_{T+1}\,|\,F, E, V\right)$ is a multivariate normal with mean E and covariance V, $p\left(E\,|\,V, F\right)$ and $p\left(V\,|\,F\right)$ are the posteriors given in (7.20) and (7.21), respectively.

Sampling from the Predictive Distribution

We turn now to sampling (simulation) from the joint predictive distribution of $\left(R_{T+1}, F_{T+1}\right)$. We focus on the joint predictive distribution since the joint mean and the joint covariance of $\left(R_{T+1}, F_{T+1}\right)$ are required to solve the portfolio optimization problem, as explained in the chapter. A draw from the joint predictive distribution is obtained using the following sequence of steps:

1. Draw a $K \times 1$ vector F_{T+1} from the predictive distribution $p\left(F_{T+1}\,|\,F\right)$:
   a. Draw V from its inverse Wishart posterior density in (7.21).
   b. Conditional on the draw of V, draw E from its normal posterior density in (7.21).
   c. Conditional on the draws of V and E, draw F_{T+1} from the multivariate normal distribution $\mathrm{N}(E, V)$.
2. Draw R_{T+1} from its predictive distribution:
   a. Draw σ^2 from its inverse χ^2 posterior density in (7.17).[14]
   b. Conditional on the draw of σ^2, draw b from its normal posterior density in (9.21).
   c. Conditional on the draws of F_{T+1}, b, and σ^2, draw R_{T+1} from the normal distribution $\mathrm{N}(X_{T+1}b, \sigma^2)$.

Repeating the procedure a large number of times and collecting the pairs $\left(R_{T+1}, F_{T+1}\right)$, we obtain a sample from the joint predictive distribution of next-period's excess returns, R_{T+1}, and next-period's returns on the K benchmark portfolios, F_{T+1}. We now explain how to compute the joint predictive mean and covariance.

[14]To obtain a draw of σ^2 from its inverse $\chi^2(\nu^*, c^{2*})$ distribution, we draw τ from χ^2_ν and set σ^2 equal to $\nu^* c^{2*}/\tau$. Notice also that drawing from χ^2_ν is equivalent to drawing from $\Gamma(\nu/2, 1/2)$.

Suppose we have obtained M draws from the joint predictive distribution. Denote by SM the $M \times (K+1)$ matrix of simulated draws. The mth row of SM is given by

$$SM^m = \left(R^m_{T+1}, F^{m\,\prime}_{T+1}\right),$$

where R^m_{T+1} and F^m_{T+1} are the mth draws from their respective (marginal) predictive distributions.

Joint Predictive Mean The $(K+1) \times 1$ joint predictive mean vector, $\widetilde{\mu}$, is computed by taking the average along the columns of the matrix SM:

$$\widetilde{\mu} = \left(\frac{1}{M}\sum_{m=1}^{M} R^m_{T+1}, \frac{1}{M}\sum_{m=1}^{M} F^{m\,\prime}_{T+1}\right). \tag{7.37}$$

Joint Predictive Covariance Let's recall two expressions for the variance and covariance of random variables, which can be found in any intermediate statistics textbook. The variance of a random variable Y is given by

$$\text{var}(Y) = \text{E}(Y^2) - \text{E}(Y)^2, \tag{7.38}$$

where E denotes the expectation. The covariance between two random variables Y and Z is

$$\text{cov}(Y, Z) = \text{E}(YZ) - \text{E}(Y)\text{E}(Z). \tag{7.39}$$

The $(K+1) \times (K+1)$ joint predictive covariance matrix, $\widetilde{\Sigma}$, of $\left(R_{T+1}, F_{T+1}\right)$ can be written as follows:

$$\widetilde{\Sigma} = \begin{pmatrix} \widetilde{\Sigma}_{1,1} & \widetilde{\Sigma}_{1,2} & \ldots & \widetilde{\Sigma}_{1,K+1} \\ \vdots & \vdots & \ddots & \vdots \\ \widetilde{\Sigma}_{K+1,1} & \widetilde{\Sigma}_{K+1,2} & \ldots & \widetilde{\Sigma}_{K+1,K+1} \end{pmatrix}.$$

Let's see how each of the elements of $\widetilde{\Sigma}$ is computed:

- $\widetilde{\Sigma}_{1,1}$ denotes the predictive variance of R_{T+1}. We use (7.38) to compute $\widetilde{\Sigma}_{1,1}$, but we replace the expectations with sample means:

$$\widetilde{\Sigma}_{1,1} = \frac{1}{M}\sum_{m=1}^{M}\left(R^m_{T+1}\right)^2 - \left(\frac{1}{M}\sum_{m=1}^{M} R^m_{T+1}\right)^2, \tag{7.40}$$

- $\widetilde{\Sigma}_{j,j}, j = 2, \ldots, K+1$, denotes the predictive variance of the jth benchmark's returns. For $j = 2, \ldots, K+1$, we compute each $\widetilde{\Sigma}_{j,j}$ as in (7.40), substituting $F_{T+1}^{m,j-1}$ for R_{T+1}^{m},
- $\widetilde{\Sigma}_{1,j}, j = 2, \ldots, K+1$, denotes the predictive covariance between the returns on the risky asset and the returns on the $(j-1)$st benchmark. We use (7.39) to obtain

$$\widetilde{\Sigma}_{1,j} = \frac{1}{M}\sum_{m=1}^{M} R_{T+1}^{m} F_{T+1}^{m,j-1} - \left(\frac{1}{M}\sum_{m=1}^{M} R_{T+1}^{m}\right)\left(\frac{1}{M}\sum_{m=1}^{M} F_{T+1}^{m,j}\right), \tag{7.41}$$

where $F_{T+1}^{m,j}$, denotes the mth draw of the predictive return on the $(j-1)$st benchmark.
- $\widetilde{\Sigma}_{i,j}, i \neq j, i, j > 1$ denotes the predictive covariance between the returns on the ith and jth benchmarks. Each of them is computed as in (7.41), substituting $F_{T+1}^{m,i-1}$ for R_{T+1}^{m}.

The computations above are applications of Monte Carlo integration (see Chapter 5). Having obtained $\widetilde{\mu}$ and $\widetilde{\Sigma}$, it is just a matter of straightforward algebra to arrive at the optimal portfolio weights in (6.14).

APPENDIX B: LIKELIHOOD FUNCTION OF A CANDIDATE MODEL

Here, we derive the likelihood of model j in (7.28). Let's substitute the likelihood for the parameters, $\boldsymbol{b}$ and σ^2, given in (7.7), and their full priors into (7.28). We obtain

$$\begin{aligned} p\left(M_j \mid \boldsymbol{R}, \boldsymbol{X}\right) = & \int \left(\sigma^2\right)^{-T/2} \exp\left[-\frac{1}{2\sigma^2}\left(\boldsymbol{R} - \boldsymbol{X}\boldsymbol{b}\right)'\left(\boldsymbol{R} - \boldsymbol{X}\boldsymbol{b}\right)\right] \\ & \times \left(\sigma^2\right)^{-1/2}|\boldsymbol{\Omega}|^{-1/2} \exp\left[-\frac{1}{2\sigma^2}\left(\boldsymbol{b} - \boldsymbol{b}_0\right)'\boldsymbol{\Omega}^{-1}\left(\boldsymbol{b} - \boldsymbol{b}_0\right)\right] \\ & \times \frac{\left(\frac{\nu_0}{2}\right)^{\nu_0/2}}{\Gamma\left(\frac{\nu_0}{2}\right)} c_0^{\nu}\left(\sigma^2\right)^{-\left(\frac{\nu_0}{2}+1\right)} \exp\left[-\frac{\nu_0 c_0^2}{2\sigma^2}\right] \mathrm{d}\boldsymbol{b}\, \mathrm{d}\sigma^2. \end{aligned} \tag{7.42}$$

Notice that our objective is to compute a probability, not the kernel of a density. Therefore, we do not discard the constants with respect to $\boldsymbol{b}$ and σ^2 as we would do when deriving posterior or predictive distributions.

Rearranging, we obtain

$$p\left(M_j \mid \mathbf{R}, \mathbf{X}\right) = \int (\sigma^2)^{-\left(\frac{\nu_0+T+1}{2}+1\right)} Q \times \exp\left[-\frac{1}{2\sigma^2}\left(S + (b-\widehat{b})'\mathbf{X}'\mathbf{X}(b-\widehat{b})\right)\right] \times \exp\left[-\frac{1}{2\sigma^2}\left((b-b_0)'\mathbf{\Omega}^{-1}(b-b_0) + \nu_0 c_0^2\right)\right] \mathrm{d}b\, \mathrm{d}\sigma^2, \tag{7.43}$$

where we denote by Q the expression

$$|\mathbf{\Omega}|^{-1/2} \frac{\left(\frac{\nu_0}{2}\right)^{\nu_0/2}}{\Gamma\left(\frac{\nu_0}{2}\right)} c_0^{\nu},$$

by $\widehat{\boldsymbol{b}}$ the least-squares estimate of $\boldsymbol{b}$, we use the following result from linear regression algebra:

$$(\mathbf{R} - \mathbf{X}b)'(\mathbf{R} - \mathbf{X}b) = (\mathbf{R} - \mathbf{X}\widehat{b})'(\mathbf{R} - \mathbf{X}\widehat{b}) + (b-\widehat{b})'\mathbf{X}'\mathbf{X}(b-\widehat{b}),$$

and we denote $S = \left(\mathbf{R} - \mathbf{X}\widehat{b}\right)'\left(\mathbf{R} - \mathbf{X}\widehat{b}\right)$.

Next, we combine the two quadratic forms in (7.43), involving $\boldsymbol{b}$ to get

$$(b-b^*)'(\mathbf{\Omega}^{-1} + \mathbf{X}'\mathbf{X})(b-b^*) + (\widehat{b}-b_0)'(\mathbf{\Omega} + (\mathbf{X}'\mathbf{X})^{-1})^{-1}(\widehat{b}-b_0) \tag{7.44}$$

where $b^* = (\mathbf{\Omega}^{-1} + \mathbf{X}'\mathbf{X})^{-1}(\mathbf{\Omega}^{-1}b_0 + (\mathbf{X}'\mathbf{X})^{-1}\widehat{b})$.

It is easy now to recognize the kernel of a normal density with mean $\boldsymbol{b}^*$ and covariance $\sigma^2 M^{-1}$, where $M = \left(\mathbf{\Omega}^{-1} + (\mathbf{X}'\mathbf{X})\right)$. The density integrates to 1 and we are left with

$$p\left(M_j \mid \mathbf{R}, \mathbf{X}\right) = Q|M|^{1/2} \int (\sigma^2)^{-\left(\frac{\nu+T}{2}+1\right)} \times \exp\left[-\frac{1}{\sigma^2}(\mathbf{R} - \mathbf{X}\widehat{b})'(\mathbf{R} - \mathbf{X}\widehat{b})\right] \times \exp\left[-\frac{1}{\sigma^2}(\widehat{b}-b_0)'(\mathbf{\Omega} + (\mathbf{X}'\mathbf{X})^{-1})^{-1}(\widehat{b}-b_0) + \nu_0 c_0^2\right] \mathrm{d}\sigma^2. \tag{7.45}$$

Recognizing the kernel of an inverse χ^2 distribution above, we finally obtain the posterior probability of model j:

$$p\left(M_j \mid \mathbf{R}, \mathbf{X}\right) = \frac{\left(\frac{\nu_0}{2}\right)^{\nu_0/2} \Gamma\left(\frac{\nu_0+T}{2}\right)}{\Gamma\frac{\nu_0}{2}\left(\frac{\nu_0+T}{2}\right)^{(\nu_0+T)/2}} c_0^{\nu_0} |M|^{1/2} |\boldsymbol{\Omega}|^{-1/2}$$
$$\times \Big[\left(\mathbf{R} - \mathbf{X}\widehat{\boldsymbol{b}}\right)'\left(\mathbf{R} - \mathbf{X}\widehat{\boldsymbol{b}}\right) + \left(\widehat{\boldsymbol{b}} - \boldsymbol{b}_0\right)'\left(\boldsymbol{\Omega} + \left(\mathbf{X}'\mathbf{X}\right)^{-1}\right)^{-1}\left(\widehat{\boldsymbol{b}} - \boldsymbol{b}_0\right)$$
$$+ \nu_0 c_0^2\Big]^{-(\nu+T)/2}. \tag{7.46}$$

CHAPTER 8

The Black-Litterman Portfolio Selection Framework

In the early 1990s, the Quantitative Resources Group at Goldman Sachs proposed a model for portfolio selection (Black and Litterman, 1991, 1992). This model, popularly known as the *Black-Litterman* (BL) *model*, has become the single most prominent application of the Bayesian methodology to portfolio selection. Its appeal to practitioners because:

- *Portfolio managers specify views on the expected returns on as many or as few assets as they desire.* Classical mean-variance optimization requires that estimates for the means and (co)variances of all assets in the investment universe be provided. Given the number of securities available for investment, this task is impractical—portfolio managers typically have knowledge and expertise to provide reliable forecasts of the returns of only a few assets. This is arguably one of the major reasons why portfolio managers opt out of mean-variance optimization in favor of heuristic (nonquantitative) allocation schemes. The BL model provides an easy to employ mechanism for incorporating the views of qualitative asset managers into the mean-variance problem.
- *Corner allocations in which only a few assets are assigned nonzero weights are avoided.* As explained in Chapter 6, traditional mean-variance optimization is haunted by the problem of unrealistic asset weights. The sample means and (co)variances are often plugged in as inputs into the mean-variance optimizer, which overweights securities with large expected returns and low standard deviations and underweights those with low expected returns and high standard deviations. Therefore, large estimation errors in the inputs are automatically propagated through to portfolio allocations. The Bayesian approach to portfolio selection, and in particular the BL model, takes into account the uncertainty in estimation.

- *If no views are expressed on given securities' expected returns, these are centered on the equilibrium expected returns.* Bayesian methodology is commonly criticized for the "arbitrariness" involved in the prior parameters choice. The BL framework helps fend off this criticism by using an asset pricing model as a reference point. The CAPM provides the "center of gravity" for expected returns.

In Chapter 7, we discussed a related framework that incorporated various degrees of confidence in the validity of an asset pricing model into the investor's prior beliefs. The BL model goes a step further and offers the investor the opportunity to specify beliefs (views) exogenous to the asset pricing model. At its core lies the recognition that an investor, who is market-neutral with respect to all securities in his (or her) investment universe, will make the rational choice of holding the market portfolio. Only when he is more bullish or bearish than the market with respect to a given security and/or he believes some relative mispricing exists in the market, will his portfolio holdings differ from the market holdings.

Our first task in this chapter is a step-by-step description of the BL methodology. Then we show how trading strategies could be integrated into BL framework and how to translate the BL framework to an active return-active risk setting. Finally, since the covariance matrix of asset returns is an important input into the BL model, we briefly review Goldman Sachs' approach to its estimation. In Chapter 13, we discuss two extensions of the BL model that represent mechanisms for introducing distributional assumptions other than normality into the portfolio allocation framework, namely Meucci (2006) and Giacometti, Bertocchi, Rachev, and Fabozzi (2007).

PRELIMINARIES

We now lay the groundwork for the discussion of the BL model and explain its core inputs.

Equilibrium Returns

One of the basic assumptions of the BL model is that unless an investor has specific views on securities, the securities' expected returns are consistent with market equilibrium returns. Therefore, an investor with no particular views holds the market portfolio.

The expected equilibrium risk premiums, serving the role of the neutral views, may be interpreted in either of two equivalent ways—as the expected risk premiums produced by an equilibrium asset pricing model, such as the *capital asset pricing model* (CAPM), or as the carrier of the prevailing information on the capital markets (which are assumed to be in equilibrium). The equivalence derives from the fact that, in equilibrium, all investors hold the market portfolio combined with cash (or leverage). Let's look at these two interpretations within the context of the CAPM.

Suppose the asset universe (the market portfolio) consists of N assets. Denote by $\mathbf{\Pi}$ the $N \times 1$ vector of equilibrium risk premiums:

$$\mathbf{\Pi} = \boldsymbol{R} - R_f \mathbf{1},$$

where $\boldsymbol{R}$ is the $N \times 1$ vector of asset returns, $\mathbf{1}$ is an $N \times 1$ vector of ones, and R_f is the risk-free rate.

Denote by $\boldsymbol{\omega}_{\text{eq}}$ the market-capitalization weights of the market portfolio. Assuming the CAPM holds, $\mathbf{\Pi}$ is given by[1]

$$\mathbf{\Pi} = \boldsymbol{\beta}\left(R_M - R_f\right), \tag{8.1}$$

where:

$R_M - R_f$ is the market risk premium.

$\beta = \text{cov}(\boldsymbol{R}, \boldsymbol{R}'\boldsymbol{\omega}_{\text{eq}})/\sigma_M^2$ is the $N \times 1$ vector of asset betas, where $\boldsymbol{R}'\boldsymbol{\omega}_{\text{eq}}$ is the market return.

$\boldsymbol{R}$ is the $N \times 1$ vector of asset returns.

$\boldsymbol{\omega}_{\text{eq}}$ is the $N \times 1$ vector of market capitalization weights.

σ_M^2 is the variance of the market return, i.e., $\sigma_M^2 = \boldsymbol{\omega}_{\text{eq}}'\mathbf{\Sigma}\boldsymbol{\omega}_{\text{eq}}$, where $\mathbf{\Sigma}$ is the asset return covariance matrix.[2]

Denote by δ the expression $\left(R_M - R_f\right)/\sigma_M^2$. The vector of equilibrium risk premiums, $\mathbf{\Pi}$, can then be written as

$$\mathbf{\Pi} = \delta\mathbf{\Sigma}\boldsymbol{\omega}_{\text{eq}}. \tag{8.2}$$

We could rearrange (8.2) to obtain the expression

$$\boldsymbol{\omega}_{\text{eq}} = \frac{1}{\delta}\mathbf{\Sigma}^{-1}\mathbf{\Pi}. \tag{8.3}$$

This is in fact the vector of market capitalization positions (unnormalized weights) and δ takes on the interpretation of the risk-aversion

[1] See Satchell and Scowcroft (2000) for this derivation.

[2] The covariance matrix, $\mathbf{\Sigma}$, is estimated outside of the BL model. We discuss its estimation later in the chapter.

parameter, A, from Chapter 6. The expression for market capitalization weights given in (6.5) in Chapter 6 is obtained by dividing the right-hand side of (8.3) by the sum of the portfolio positions (δ will cancel out in that case).

The equivalent approach to the derivation of the equilibrium risk premiums relies on the assumption that capital markets are in equilibrium and clear. Solving the unconstrained portfolio problem from Chapter 6, $\mathbf{\Pi}$ can be obtained (backed out) from (6.5) in that chapter, where the optimal weights are regarded as the market capitalization weights, $\boldsymbol{\omega}_{eq}$.

Investor Views

Investors' views are expressed as deviations from the equilibrium returns, $\mathbf{\Pi}$. Suppose the investment universe consists of four assets, A, B, C, and D. An *absolute view* could be formulated as "next-period's expected returns of assets A and B are 7.4% and 5.5%." A *relative view* is expressed as "C will outperform A, B, and D by 2% next period." It is easy to see why relative views are likely to be the predominant type, especially among qualitatively oriented portfolio managers. Many portfolio strategies produce relative rankings of securities (securities are expected to underperform/outperform other securities) rather than absolute expected returns.

Views are expressed by means of the returns on portfolios composed of the securities involved in the respective views. For example, the absolute views above correspond to two *view portfolios*, one long in asset A and the another long in asset B. Relative views are usually expressed by means of zero-investment view portfolios, which are long in the security expected to outperform and short in the security expected to underperform.

Distributional Assumptions

In the following presentation, we outline the BL model's original distributional assumptions. We assume that asset returns, $\boldsymbol{R}$, follow a multivariate normal distribution with mean vector $\boldsymbol{\mu}$ and covariance matrix $\mathbf{\Sigma}$.

Market Information Although we expect the market to be on average in equilibrium, at any given point in time this equilibrium could be perturbed by shocks; for example, shocks related to the arrival of information relevant for the pricing of securities. Therefore, we write

$$\boldsymbol{\mu} = \mathbf{\Pi} + \boldsymbol{\epsilon},$$

where the $N \times 1$ vector $\boldsymbol{\epsilon}$ embodies the perturbations to the equilibrium and is assumed to have a multivariate normal distribution, so that the prior distribution on $\boldsymbol{\mu}$ is given by

$$\boldsymbol{\mu} \sim \mathrm{N}(\boldsymbol{\Pi}, \tau\boldsymbol{\Sigma}). \tag{8.4}$$

The prior covariance matrix of the mean is simply the scaled covariance matrix of the sampling distribution. We can interpret the scale parameter, τ, as reflecting the investor's uncertainty that the CAPM holds. Alternatively, τ represents the uncertainty in the accuracy with which $\boldsymbol{\Pi}$ is estimated. A small value of τ corresponds to a high confidence in the equilibrium return estimates.[3]

Subjective Views Suppose that an investor expresses K views and denote the $K \times N$ matrix of view portfolios by $\boldsymbol{P}$. Each row of $\boldsymbol{P}$ represents a view portfolio, where an element of $\boldsymbol{P}$ is nonzero if the respective asset is involved in the view and zero otherwise. Based on our earlier discussion, when a relative view is expressed, the elements of a row sum up to zero; when an absolute view is expressed, the corresponding row consists of a 1 in the place of asset C and zeros everywhere else—the sum of its elements is 1. Suppose that the investment universe consists of four assets, A, B, C, and D, and consider the two absolute and one relative views above. The matrix $\boldsymbol{P}$ becomes then the 3×4 matrix

$$\begin{pmatrix} 1 & 0 & 0 & 0 \\ 0 & 1 & 0 & 0 \\ -1/3 & -1/3 & 1 & -1/3 \end{pmatrix},$$

where equal weighting is used to form the third view portfolio (market-capitalization weighting scheme can also be employed). The $K \times 1$ vector of expected returns on the view portfolios is then given by $\boldsymbol{P\mu}$. Assuming it is normally distributed, we obtain the distributional assumption regarding the investor's subjective views:

$$\boldsymbol{P\mu} \sim \mathrm{N}(\boldsymbol{Q}, \boldsymbol{\Omega}). \tag{8.5}$$

[3]In Chapter 7, uncertainty about the validity of an asset pricing relationship was represented with the help of a prior distribution on the intercept α in $\boldsymbol{R}_i = \alpha + \beta \boldsymbol{R}_M + \epsilon_i$, centered around zero ($\boldsymbol{R}_i$ and $\boldsymbol{R}_M$ are excess returns). The prior relation in (8.4) is an equivalent way to express the same source of uncertainty. To see this, rewrite (8.4) as $\boldsymbol{\mu} - \boldsymbol{\Pi} \sim \mathrm{N}(0, \tau\boldsymbol{\Sigma})$ and recognize that $\boldsymbol{\mu} - \boldsymbol{\Pi}$ is the expected superior return (mispricing), α.

The vector Q contains the investor's views on the securities' expected returns. Continuing with our example,

$$Q = \begin{pmatrix} 7.4 \\ 5.5 \\ 2 \end{pmatrix}.$$

The degree of confidence an investor has in his views is reflected in the diagonal elements, ω_{kk}, $k = 1, \ldots, K$, of the $K \times K$ prior covariance matrix $\boldsymbol{\Omega}$. Its off-diagonal elements are usually set equal to zero, since views are assumed to be uncorrelated. The value of ω_{kk} is inversely proportional to the strength of the investor's confidence in the kth view.

COMBINING MARKET EQUILIBRIUM AND INVESTOR VIEWS

Bayes' theorem (see Chapter 2) is applied to combine the two sources of information represented by the "objective information" embodied in (8.4) and the subjective information in (8.5).

The posterior distribution of expected returns, $\boldsymbol{\mu}$, is normal with mean and covariance given, respectively, by

$$\begin{aligned} \boldsymbol{M} &= \left((\tau\boldsymbol{\Sigma})^{-1} + \boldsymbol{P}'\boldsymbol{\Omega}^{-1}\boldsymbol{P}\right)^{-1}\left((\tau\boldsymbol{\Sigma})^{-1}\boldsymbol{\Pi} + \boldsymbol{P}'\boldsymbol{\Omega}^{-1}\boldsymbol{Q}\right) \\ &= \left((\tau\boldsymbol{\Sigma})^{-1} + \boldsymbol{P}'\boldsymbol{\Omega}^{-1}\boldsymbol{P}\right)^{-1}\left((\tau\boldsymbol{\Sigma})^{-1}\boldsymbol{\Pi} + \boldsymbol{P}'\boldsymbol{\Omega}^{-1}\boldsymbol{P}\hat{\mu}\right), \end{aligned} \tag{8.6}$$

where $\hat{\mu}$ is the estimate of expected returns implied by the views, $\hat{\mu} = (\boldsymbol{P}'\boldsymbol{P})^{-1}\boldsymbol{P}'\boldsymbol{Q}$, and

$$\boldsymbol{V} = \left((\tau\boldsymbol{\Sigma})^{-1} + \boldsymbol{P}'\boldsymbol{\Omega}^{-1}\boldsymbol{P}\right)^{-1}. \tag{8.7}$$

When no views are expressed ($\boldsymbol{P}$ is a matrix consisting of zeros only), the posterior estimate of the expected return becomes $\boldsymbol{M} = \boldsymbol{\Pi}$; when the views uncertainty (i.e., ω_{kk}, $k = 1, \ldots, K$) is very large, $\boldsymbol{M}$ is dominated by $\boldsymbol{\Pi}$ (and in the limit is equal to it). In those cases, a rational investor ends up holding the market portfolio and the riskless asset. The efficient frontier representing the investor's risk-return trade-off, given his risk preferences, will simply be the Markowitz efficient frontier resulting from classical mean-variance optimization.

Observe that the posterior mean in (8.6) is the usual shrinkage estimator. The lower investor's confidence in his views, the closer expected returns are to the ones implied by market equilibrium; conversely, the higher confidence in subjective views causes expected returns to tilt away from equilibrium expected returns.

The posterior covariance matrix in (8.7) is an expression involving the prior precisions (inverse covariance matrices) of the expected returns implied by market equilibrium and the expected returns implied by the views (similar to the expression for the posterior covariance in (4.17) in Chapter 4).

THE CHOICE OF τ AND ω

The choices of τ and ω_{ii} are the major roadblocks in practical applications of the BL model—no guideline exists for the selection of their values. Since uncertainty about the expected returns is less than the variability of returns themselves, τ is usually set to a value less than 1. Black and Litterman (1992) advocate a value close to 0, while Satchell and Scowcroft (2000) choose $\tau = 1$. Suppose that we take sequentially larger and larger samples of data. We would expect that the larger the dataset, the less influential the impact of the perturbations, $\boldsymbol{\epsilon}$, is and the more accurate our estimate of $\boldsymbol{\Pi}$ becomes—the value of τ decreases. Therefore, we could interpret τ as the remaining uncertainty in the estimate of $\boldsymbol{\Pi}$, given a sample of length T, and set $\tau = 1/T$. For example, a sample of length 10 years would correspond to $\tau = 1/10$.

To minimize the subjectivity in τ's choice, a different approach would be to calibrate τ from historical return data. Consider the distributional assumption in (8.4). Simple statistical arguments show that the distribution of the vector $\boldsymbol{\mu} - \boldsymbol{\Pi}$ is

$$\boldsymbol{\mu} - \boldsymbol{\Pi} \sim \mathrm{N}(0, \tau\boldsymbol{\Sigma}), \tag{8.8}$$

where $\boldsymbol{\Sigma}$ is the covariance matrix of returns computed separately. To obtain τ, we estimate the covariance matrix, V, of $\boldsymbol{\mu} - \boldsymbol{\Pi}$ using observed return data and solve the equation[4]

$$||\boldsymbol{V}|| = \tau\, ||\boldsymbol{\Sigma}||. \tag{8.9}$$

[4]The norm of a $p \times q$ matrix, A, denoted by $||A||$ is a number associated with $\boldsymbol{A}$. Different kinds of matrix norms exist. The simplest one is the so-called *Euclidean norm*, also known as *Frobenius norm* and is simply given by the square root of the sum of squared elements of A,

$$||A|| = \sqrt{a_{11}^2 + a_{12}^2 + \cdots + a_{pq}^2}.$$

The matrix V is the covariance matrix of $(R_s - \Pi_s)$, where:

R_s = $1 \times N$ vector of observed returns on N stocks at time s.
Π_s = $1 \times N$ vector of equilibrium returns on the N stocks at time s, computed (using (8.2)) over a moving window of certain length; for example, the length could be 250 days (equivalent to one year), if daily data are employed.

The diagonal elements of Ω, ω_{ii}, could also be computed through a calibration (backtesting) procedure, which we explain later in the chapter. Another possible approach is to make a statistical assumption about the distribution of a view. For example, suppose that the portfolio manager expresses the view that stock A will outperform stock B by 6% and, in addition, he can evaluate his confidence that his projection will fall between 5% and 7% at 95%. If we assume that the view is normally distributed and we treat the interval [5%, 7%] as a confidence interval with a confidence level of 95%, we could use elementary statistical arguments to derive the implied standard deviation of 0.5%. Therefore, we could set $\omega_{ii} = (0.5\%)^2 = 0.25\%$. This is, in fact, a customary approach to eliciting the parameters of the prior distributions, as we discussed in Chapter 3.

THE OPTIMAL PORTFOLIO ALLOCATION

As discussed in Chapter 6, solving the investor's mean-variance optimization problem requires knowledge of the mean and covariance of the predictive distribution of (future) excess returns. It can be shown that the mean of the predictive returns distribution is the same as the posterior mean of expected returns, while the covariance of the predictive distribution includes a term reflecting the estimation error. The predictive mean and covariance are, respectively,

$$\widetilde{\mu} = M \qquad \text{and} \qquad \widetilde{\Sigma} = \Sigma + V. \tag{8.10}$$

The solution to the unconstrained investor's portfolio problem is then given by the vector of optimal portfolio positions,

$$\omega^* = \frac{1}{A}\widetilde{\Sigma}^{-1}\widetilde{\mu}. \tag{8.11}$$

As shown by He and Litterman (1999), (8.11) can be decomposed into

$$\omega^* = \frac{1}{1+\tau}\left(\omega_{\text{eq}} + P'\Lambda\right). \tag{8.12}$$

where $\omega_{eq} = 1/A\Sigma^{-1}\Pi$ are the market capitalization (equilibrium) positions (see (8.3)). The elements of the $K \times 1$ vector Λ represent the weights assigned to each of the view portfolios.[5]

What the representation in (8.12) tells us is that the investor's optimal portfolio can essentially be viewed as a combination of two portfolios—the market portfolio and a weighted sum of the view portfolios. In the absence of particular views on assets' expected returns, the investor optimally holds a fraction of the market portfolio $(\omega_{eq}/(1+\tau))$. The size of this fraction is inversely proportional to the degree of investor's skepticism about the estimates of equilibrium returns (alternatively, about the CAPM).

Illustration: Black-Litterman Optimal Allocation

Next we illustrate the mechanism through which views affect the optimal portfolio. Our data sample consists of daily returns and market capitalizations on the eight constituents of the MSCI World Index with the largest market capitalization (as of the beginning of the sample period): United Kingdom (UK), United States (US), Japan (JP), France (FR), Germany (DE), Canada (CA), Switzerland (CH), and Australia (AU). The data span the period from 1/2/1990 through 12/31/2003. Part A of Exhibit 8.1 contains the sample covariance matrix of the eight return series, while the equilibrium implied expected returns for the eight country indices, as well as their equilibrium-implied (market-capitalization) weights, are in Part B.

Purely as an illustration, we formulate two views:

- CH will outperform US by 5%.
- JP will return 10% on an annual basis.

The first view is a relative one, while the second view is an absolute one. Thus, the view matrix, P, and the subjective expected returns vector, Q, take the form,

$$P = \begin{pmatrix} 0 & -1 & 0 & 0 & 0 & 0 & 1 & 0 \\ 0 & 0 & 1 & 0 & 0 & 0 & 0 & 0 \end{pmatrix} \quad \text{and} \quad Q = \begin{pmatrix} 0.05 \\ 0.1 \end{pmatrix},$$

[5]The elements of Λ are given by

$$\Lambda = \frac{1}{A}\tau\Omega^{-1}Q - S^{-1}P\frac{\Sigma}{1+\tau}\omega_{eq} - S^{-1}\frac{1}{A}P\frac{\Sigma}{1+\tau}P'\tau\Omega^{-1}Q, \tag{8.13}$$

where $S = \Omega/\tau + P\Sigma/(1+\tau)P'$.

		UK	US	JP	FR	DE	CA	CH	AU
A	UK	0.0246	0.0081	0.0054	0.0204	0.0196	0.0085	0.0161	0.0055
	US		0.0228	0.0019	0.0102	0.0121	0.0141	0.0072	0.0017
	JP			0.0332	0.0064	0.0070	0.0034	0.0060	0.0079
	FR				0.0350	0.0284	0.0110	0.0212	0.0060
	DE					0.0438	0.0125	0.0234	0.0075
	CA						0.0234	0.0075	0.0049
	CH							0.0276	0.0052
	AU								0.0246
B	Π	0.0179	0.0188	0.0409	0.0214	0.0238	0.0160	0.0174	0.0122
	ω_{eq}	0.09	0.34	0.43	0.03	0.04	0.03	0.02	0.02

EXHIBIT 8.1 MSCI sample and equilibrium-implied information
Note: The covariance and expected return entries are expressed on an annual basis. Part A contains the covariance matrix of MSCI excess returns. Part B contains the equilibrium-implied expected returns and market-capitalization weights.

where we use equal weighting of the relative view portfolio. Notice that the view on JP implies a doubling of its equilibrium-implied expected return (of 4.9% annually). The equilibrium expected returns imply that US outperforms CH by 0.14% annually, in contrast to the relative view. In our computations, we use a coefficient of risk aversion, A, equal to 2.5 and a scale parameter, τ, equal to 0.5. The matrix $\mathbf{\Omega}$ reflecting the view uncertainty is as follows,

$$\mathbf{\Omega} = \begin{pmatrix} \omega_{11} & 0 \\ 0 & \omega_{22} \end{pmatrix},$$

where $\omega_{11}^H = 0.0001$ or $\omega_{11}^L = 0.04$ and $\omega_{22} = 0.0004$.

The subscripts H and L above refer to the high-confidence and low-confidence cases with respect to the relative view that we consider. The values of ω_{11}, ω_{22}^H, and ω_{22}^L are determined using the confidence-interval argument outlined in our earlier discussion on the choice of τ and $\mathbf{\Omega}$. When we consider the absolute and relative views separately, $\boldsymbol{P}$, $\boldsymbol{Q}$, and $\mathbf{\Omega}$ are transformed accordingly.

In Exhibit 8.2 we can observe that since returns are correlated, views expressed on only several assets would imply changes in the expected returns on all assets. The mechanism for this propagation of views is

	UK	US	JP	FR	DE	CA	CH	AU
Absolute View Only	0.0271	0.022	0.0986	0.0324	0.0358	0.0216	0.0278	0.0256
Relative View Only, High Confidence	0.0291	−0.0026	0.0492	0.0368	0.0397	0.0068	0.0458	0.0174
Relative View Only, Low Confidence	0.0206	0.0136	0.0429	0.0251	0.0277	0.0137	0.0243	0.0135
Both Views	0.0292	0.0175	0.0987	0.0353	0.0388	0.0196	0.0334	0.0263

EXHIBIT 8.2 Views-implied expected returns
Note: The expected return entries are expressed on an annual basis.

the $N \times K$ matrix $\boldsymbol{P}'\boldsymbol{\Omega}^{-1}$, which "maps" the K views onto the N securities through the term $\boldsymbol{P}'\boldsymbol{\Omega}^{-1}\boldsymbol{Q}$. Through this mapping, errors in the investor's forecasts of expected returns are spread out over all securities, thus mitigating estimation error and preventing corner solutions (which could be the case if only the expected returns on some securities are adjusted).

Consider the optimal portfolio when only the absolute view on JP is expressed. The outcome is illustrated in the left-hand side of Exhibit 8.3. As expected, the portfolio loads on JP (relative to the market capitalization weights). Since JP is positively correlated with the rest of the country indices, their weights decrease proportionately to their market capitalizations. Notice the adjustment in the whole expected returns vector—the expected returns on all assets increased, since they are all positively correlated with JP.

We now compare the effect of the high-confidence and low-confidence relative view on CH and US. See Exhibit 8.4. The optimal portfolio weight of CH increases at the expense of the weight of US. The impact of the high-confidence view is dramatic, while the low-confidence view has a more moderate effect. In both cases, only the weights of the indexes involved in the relative view change; the remaining weights are preserved at the equilibrium values. All components of the vectors of expected returns in the high-confidence and low-confidence cases are adjusted, as explained above.

Finally, the right-hand side of Exhibit 8.3 depicts the case when both views are incorporated into the optimal portfolio construction (low

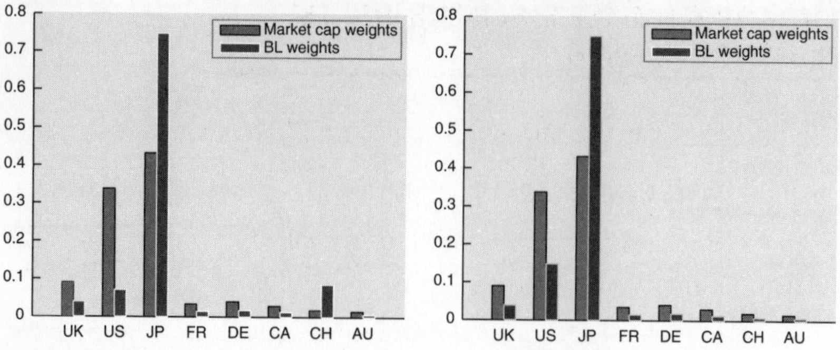

EXHIBIT 8.3 Optimal portfolio weights: absolute view and both views together
Note: The plot on the left-hand side corresponds to the absolute view, while the plot on the right-hand side reflects the joint impact on both the absolute and the relative view.

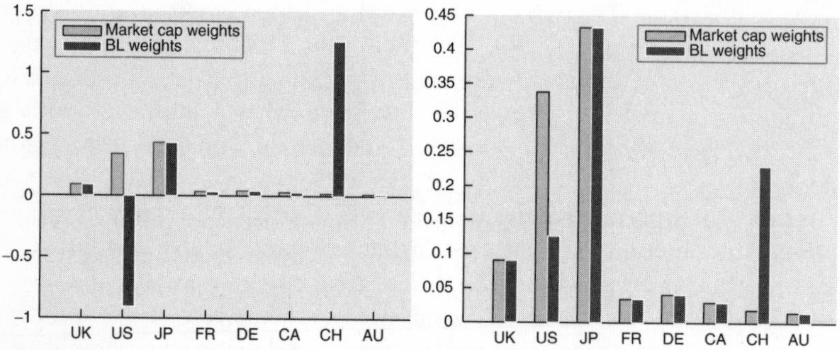

EXHIBIT 8.4 Optimal portfolio weights: relative view
Note: The plot on the left-hand side corresponds to the high-confidence view, while the plot on the right-hand side—to the low-confidence view.

confidence is assigned to the relative view). We can clearly see that the resulting optimal portfolio is a combination of the effects we observed in the individual cases above. Notice that since we only incorporate two simple views and all country indices are positively correlated, the allocations reflecting both views are still very intuitive. This will likely not be the case in more complicated situations; however, one can still be certain that the investor's views are accurately reflected in the optimal portfolio weights.

INCORPORATING TRADING STRATEGIES INTO THE BLACK-LITTERMAN MODEL

Trading strategies can be introduced into the BL framework. The sole requirement for that is to be able to identify the components of the strategy with the respective inputs of the BL model. Of course, the trading strategy is simply a way to formulate the views of the portfolio manager. Let us consider the momentum strategy example of Fabozzi, Focardi, and Kolm (2006).

Momentum is the tendency of securities or equity indexes to preserve their good (poor) performance for a certain period in the future.[6] Empirical findings show that stocks that outperformed (underperformed) the market in the past 6 to 12 months continue to do so in the next 3 to 12 months. A cross-sectional momentum strategy would consist in ranking the securities according to their past performance; then, a *long-short portfolio* is formed by purchasing the "winners" and selling the "losers." The expected view return, Q, is then a scalar, equal to the expected return on the long-short portfolio. The variance of the view could be determined through a backtesting procedure, which we explain in the following paragraphs.

Fabozzi, Focardi, and Kolm (2006) use daily returns of the country indexes making up the MSCI World Index over a period of 24 years (1980 to 2004). The momentum (long-short) portfolio is constructed at a particular point in time, t (hence a "cross-sectional" strategy) and held for one month. Winners and losers are determined on the basis of their performance over the past nine months—the quantity used to rank them is their normalized nine-month return (lagged by one day):

$$z_{t,\,i} = \frac{\boldsymbol{P}_{t-1,\,i} - \boldsymbol{P}_{t-1-189,\,i}}{\boldsymbol{P}_{t-1-189,\,i}\sigma_i}, \tag{8.14}$$

where:

$\boldsymbol{P}_{t-1,\,i}$ = price of country index i at time $t - 1$.
$\boldsymbol{P}_{t-1-189,\,i}$ = price of country index i nine months (approximately, 189 days) before $t - 1$.
σ_i = volatility of country index i.

[6]The momentum phenomenon was first described by Jegadeesh and Titman (1993). See also Rouwenhorst (1998).

The top half and the bottom half of the country indexes are then assigned weights, respectively, of

$$w_i = \frac{1}{\sigma_i \kappa} \quad \text{and} \quad w_i = -\frac{1}{\sigma_i \kappa}. \tag{8.15}$$

That is, the view matrix, $\boldsymbol{P}$, consists of a single row with elements one of the two quantities above. Weights are dependent on a country indexes' volatilities in order to avoid corner solutions. The parameter κ is a constant whose role is to constrain the annual portfolio volatility to a certain level (20% in the application of Fabozzi, Focardi, and Kolm).

The confidence in the view represented by the cross-sectional momentum strategy could be determined through backtesting in the following way. For each period t:

1. Construct the momentum portfolio using (8.14).
2. Hold the portfolio for one month and observe its return, $R_{M,t}$, over the holding period.
3. For the same holding period, observe the realized return, $R_{A,\,t}$, on the portfolio of the actual winners and losers.
4. Compute the "residual" return, $E_t = R_{M,t} - R_{A,t}$.
5. Move the performance-evaluation period one month forward and repeat the steps above.

Then, calculate the variance of the series of residuals, E_t, and set

$$\omega_{ii} = \text{var}(E_t).$$

Fabozzi, Focardi, and Kolm compute the covariance matrix of returns, $\boldsymbol{\Sigma}$, as the daily-returns, geometrically weighted covariance matrix. (See the discussion later in the chapter on exponential (geometric)-weighting schemes.)

Finally, the predictive mean and covariance of returns are computed using (13.27) and the optimal portfolio constructed. Fabozzi, Focardi, and Kolm use a scale parameter τ equal to 0.1. Exhibits 8.5 and 8.6 present, respectively, the realized returns and volatilities of the optimized momentum strategy and the MSCI World Index.

ACTIVE PORTFOLIO MANAGEMENT AND THE BLACK-LITTERMAN MODEL

A fund manager generates return by undertaking two types of risk—market risk and active risk. The market exposure comes as a result of the strategic

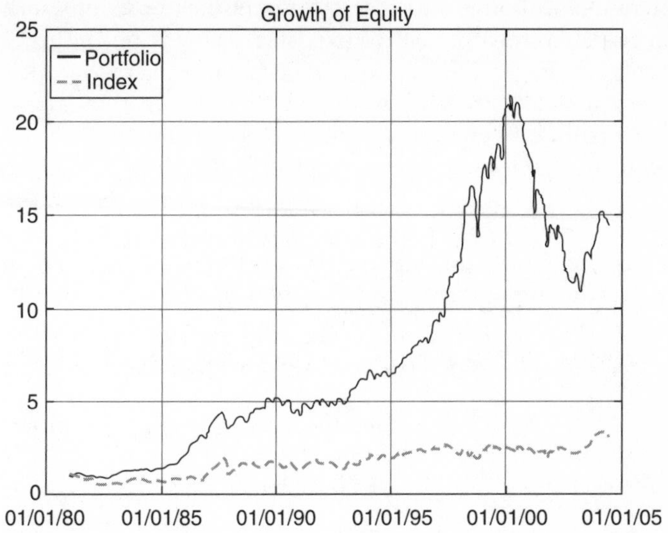

EXHIBIT 8.5 Realized returns on the optimized momentum strategy and the MSCI world index

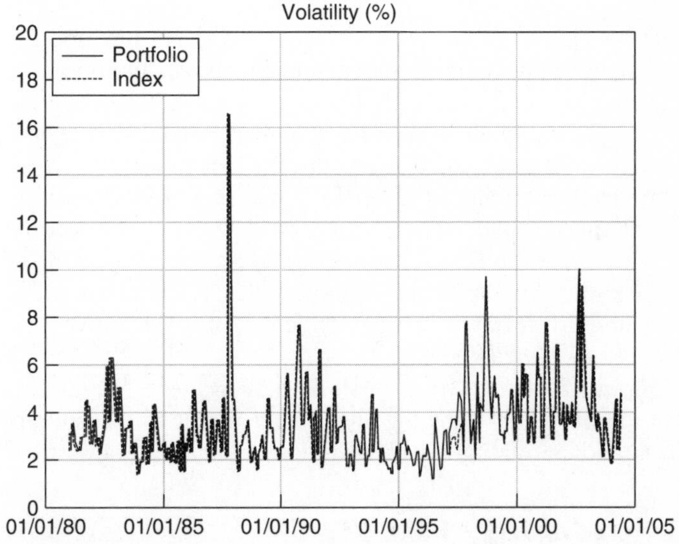

EXHIBIT 8.6 Realized volatilities on the optimized momentum strategy and the MSCI world index

allocation decision—how the funds available for investment are allocated among the major asset classes. The active exposure depends on the risks taken by a portfolio manager relative to the benchmark against which performance is measured. There are two main reasons why an active strategy might be capable of generating abnormal returns relative to the benchmark: benchmark inefficiency and investment constraints. The more inefficient a benchmark is and the less investment constraints there are, the greater the opportunity for a skilled manager to achieve active returns.[7]

Active return is the return on a particular portfolio strategy minus the return on the benchmark. Active return has two sources—one due to benchmark exposure (and originating from market movements) and another due to stock picking (the "residual return"). The decomposition is given by,[8]

$$\boldsymbol{R}_{P,A} = \boldsymbol{R}_{P,R} + \beta_{P,A}\boldsymbol{R}_{B}, \tag{8.16}$$

where:

$\boldsymbol{R}_{P,\,A}$ = active return of portfolio P.
$\boldsymbol{R}_{P,\,R}$ = residual return on portfolio P.
$\beta_{P,A}$ = active beta.
$\boldsymbol{R}_{B}$ = benchmark return.

Adjusting the benchmark exposure (the active beta) on a period-by-period basis is what typically constitutes benchmark timing ("loading" on the benchmark in market upturns and "unloading" in market downturns). Institutional investors usually do not engage in benchmark timing and maintain an active beta of close to 1.0 relative to the benchmark. Then, all active return comes from the skill of the portfolio manager at stock-picking and coincides with the residual return; that is, the optimal portfolio is market-neutral. We assume this is the case below and use "active return" to refer to both active and residual return. The expected active return is called *alpha*, while the standard deviation of the active return is the active risk, commonly referred to as *tracking error*.

In this section, our focus is active portfolio management. We discuss a modification of the BL model allowing an active manager to incorporate his (or her) views (either qualitative or quantitative) into the allocation process.

---

[7]See Winkelmann (2004).

[8]See, for example, Grinold and Kahn (1999). The decomposition of active return into its two components is obtained by regressing it against the return on the benchmark.

Views on Alpha and the Black-Litterman Model

The setup for the BL model modified for the active-returns case essentially mirrors the setup for the "total-return" BL model discussed earlier. We adopt the same distributional assumption for active returns as for total returns earlier in the chapter,

$$\boldsymbol{R}_A \sim \mathrm{N}(\boldsymbol{\alpha}, \boldsymbol{\Sigma}_A).$$

The source of neutral, equilibrium information is represented by a normal distribution on alpha centered around zero. That is, the residual return on the benchmark is not systematically different from zero unless the benchmark is inefficient (see Chapter 9 for more details on market efficiency),

$$\boldsymbol{\alpha} \sim \mathrm{N}(0, \tau \boldsymbol{\Sigma}_A), \tag{8.17}$$

where $\boldsymbol{\Sigma}_A$ is the covariance matrix of active returns, and the scaling factor τ could be interpreted as the confidence in the benchmark's efficiency. The active manager expresses views on the assets' alphas if he believes he could outperform the benchmark. These views are described in distributional terms by

$$\boldsymbol{P}\boldsymbol{\alpha} \sim \mathrm{N}(\boldsymbol{Q}, \boldsymbol{\Omega}), \tag{8.18}$$

where $\boldsymbol{P}$, $\boldsymbol{Q}$, and $\boldsymbol{\Omega}$ take on the same interpretations as described previously.

When a manager is able to specify a level of confidence in his views, the values of the diagonal elements of $\boldsymbol{\Omega}$, ω_{ii}, can be computed as explained earlier in the chapter. Herold (2003) suggests that fundamental managers, who do not have quantitative insight (but rather simply express a bullish/bearish view on an asset or a group of assets), set ω_{ii} equal to the respective diagonal element of the matrix $\boldsymbol{P}\boldsymbol{\Sigma}_A\boldsymbol{P}'$.[9] Since views can be represented by view portfolios, the diagonal elements of $\boldsymbol{P}\boldsymbol{\Sigma}_A\boldsymbol{P}'$ are, in fact, the tracking errors of these view portfolios.

The posterior moments of $\boldsymbol{\alpha}$'s distribution, as well as the predictive moments of the distribution of next-period's active returns, are as given in (8.6), (8.7), and (13.27) (with the obvious change in notation). The unconstrained portfolio selection problem is expressed in terms of the portfolio's predictive alpha and tracking error,

$$\max_{\omega_A} \left(\boldsymbol{\omega}_A' \widetilde{\boldsymbol{\alpha}} - \frac{A}{2} \boldsymbol{\omega}_A' \widetilde{\boldsymbol{\Sigma}}_A \boldsymbol{\omega}_A \right), \tag{8.19}$$

[9] The approach by He and Litterman (1999) is similar. They choose to calibrate the ratio ω_{ii}/τ by setting it equal to $\boldsymbol{p}_i \boldsymbol{\Sigma} \boldsymbol{p}_i'$, where $\boldsymbol{p}_i$ is the ith row of the $\boldsymbol{P}$ matrix.

where A is the risk-aversion coefficient, $\boldsymbol{\omega}_A$ is the vector of active portfolio weights, and $\widetilde{\boldsymbol{\alpha}}$ and $\widetilde{\boldsymbol{\Sigma}}_A$ are, respectively, the predictive mean and covariance of the active returns. Active managers are usually constrained as to the maximum tracking error they can assume. Then, the active portfolio selection problem can be represented as a maximization of $\boldsymbol{\omega}_A'\widetilde{\boldsymbol{\alpha}}$, subject to the tracking error constraint as explained in Chapter 6.

Translating a Qualitative View into a Forecast for Alpha

To translate a qualitative view into a forecast value for alpha, a portfolio manager could employ two fundamental concepts from the field of active asset management—the information ratio and the information coefficient.[10]

The *information ratio* (IR) is a measure of the investment value of active strategies, representing the amount of active return per unit of active risk. The IR of a portfolio p is defined as

$$IR_p = \frac{\alpha_p}{\psi_p}, \tag{8.20}$$

where $\alpha_p = \boldsymbol{\omega}_A'\boldsymbol{\alpha}\boldsymbol{\omega}_A$ is the portfolio's alpha and $\psi_p = \boldsymbol{\omega}_A'\boldsymbol{\Sigma}_A\boldsymbol{\omega}_A'$ is the portfolio's active risk. The IR is, then, a natural tool to employ in the selection of portfolio managers. The *information coefficient* (IC) is defined as the correlation between the forecast and the realized active return, and is considered an indicator of the portfolio manager's skill.

Grinold (1989) and Grinold and Kahn (1999) show that the information ratio and the information coefficient are related through the following (approximate) relationship:

$$IR \approx IC \times \sqrt{BR}, \tag{8.21}$$

where BR (breadth) is the number of independent, active bets made by the portfolio manager in a period. We assume that IC is the same for all forecasts. Since each view portfolio represents one active bet, $BR = 1$ and $IR = IC$ in our discussion. We obtain the forecast value of $\boldsymbol{\alpha}$, in fact, the mean vector, $\boldsymbol{Q}$, as

$$\boldsymbol{\alpha} = IC \times \boldsymbol{\psi}, \tag{8.22}$$

where $\boldsymbol{\psi} = \text{diag}(\boldsymbol{\Omega}) = \text{diag}(\boldsymbol{P\Sigma P}')$ is the vector of tracking errors of the view portfolios. A higher degree of uncertainty in the expressed views logically corresponds to a lower value of the information coefficient, IC; therefore,

[10]See also Grinold and Kahn (1999).

IC could be manually adjusted to reflect uncertainty (as in Herold (2003)), although, certainly, this procedure would lack mathematical rigor.

COVARIANCE MATRIX ESTIMATION

Variance (covariance matrix) is the input traditionally used as a measure of risk in portfolio optimization, and financial practice in general. As expected returns, the covariance matrix needs to be estimated from historical data. It has been argued (Best and Grauer, 1991, 1992) that estimation errors in expected returns affect mean-variance optimization to a much larger degree than errors in the covariance matrix, while errors in variances are about twice as important as errors in covariances. Nevertheless, the search for a better estimate of the covariance matrix goes on. In this section, we discuss some covariance matrix estimation techniques. (See also our brief discussion in Chapter 6 on the shrinkage estimator of the covariance matrix.)

The simplest approach to estimation of the covariance matrix of excess returns, $\mathbf{\Sigma}$, relies on computing the sample estimates of variances and covariances at time T, given, respectively, by

$$\widehat{var^T}(r_{it}) \equiv \sigma_{ii}^T = \frac{\sum_{t=0}^{T} r_{it}^2}{t-1} \tag{8.23}$$

and

$$\widehat{cov^T}\left(r_{it}, r_{jt}\right) \equiv \sigma_{ij}^T = \frac{\sum_{t=0}^{T} r_{it} r_{jt}}{t-1}, \tag{8.24}$$

where r_{it} is the return on asset i at time t. We assume that the mean of each return series is subtracted from the returns, so that they have a mean of zero.

The major shortcoming of the estimators above is that they assign equal weights to all return observations in the sample. This precludes the possibility to account for the fact that variances and covariances might have changed over time and data from the distant past might be less relevant than more recent data.[11]

One way to take into account time variation is to compute variances (covariances) as weighted sums of squared returns (products of returns). The

[11]There is an extensive literature documenting the time variability of volatilities and correlations. See our discussions in Chapters 10, 11, and 12.

expressions for the weighted estimators of the variances and covariances of returns are, respectively,

$$\widehat{var^T}(r_i) \equiv \sigma_{ii}^T = \frac{\sum_{t=1}^T w_t r_{i,t}^2}{\sum_{t=1}^T w_t} \tag{8.25}$$

and

$$\widehat{cov^T}(r_i, r_j) \equiv \sigma_{ij}^T = \frac{\sum_{t=1}^T w_t r_{it} r_{jt}}{\sum_{t=1}^T w_t}. \tag{8.26}$$

Notice that when weights are equal, (8.23) and (8.24) are the same as (8.25) and (8.26). Generally, the weights reflect the length of return history to which an investor attaches relatively greater importance. For example, when daily data are used in estimating the covariance matrix, it is not uncommon to weigh more heavily data that pertain to the most recent month than data from, say, one year ago. That is, a weighting scheme with *decaying* (declining with time) weights is employed. A term often used in this context is *half-life*. A half-life of k periods means that an observation from k periods ago receives half of the weight of an observation in the current period. Alternatively, we talk of *decay rate*, defined as $d \equiv 1 - w_{t-1}/w_t$. The decay rate d and the half-life k are related by

$$d^k = 0.5.$$

For example, the decay rate such that data three months (36 business days, if daily data is used) ago is given twice as little weight as current data is approximately 0.98. That is, an observation at day $t - 1$ receives 98% of the weight of the following observation (at day t) for all t.[12]

Various refinements of volatility estimation have been developed and applied in empirical work. We discuss *generalized autoregressive heteroskedasticity* (GARCH) and stochastic volatility models in chapters 10, 11, and 12. Factor models of returns are widely used to both provide economic intuition about common forces driving expected returns, and to

[12] It is clear from (8.25) and (8.26) that the decay rate plays a key part in the estimation of the return variances and covariances. Therefore, it is necessary to select a decay rate that is "best" or optimal in some sense. From a statistical viewpoint, the optimal rate could be the one that maximizes the likelihood function of returns.

reduce the dimension of the problem of covariance matrix estimation.[13] (See Chapter 14 for more details on Bayesian factor model estimation.)

In recent years, a tremendous push has been made for employing measures of risk other than variance, as well as higher moments, in portfolio risk modeling. See Chapter 13 for a brief outline of these alternative risk measures, as well as a discussion of some of advanced portfolio techniques.

SUMMARY

The Black-Litterman model allows for a smooth and elegant integration of investors' views about the expected returns of assets into the portfolio optimization process. The basic idea of the model is that an asset's expected return should be consistent with market equilibrium unless an investor holds views on it. Therefore, the asset allocations induced from the views represent tilts away from the neutral, equilibrium-implied, market-capitalization weights. In the absence of views, the optimal portfolio is the market portfolio.

We consider two extensions to the Black-Litterman model. The first extension incorporates a momentum strategy; the second extension reflects views on the expected active returns (alphas).

[13]Given N assets, the covariance matrix of returns contains $N(N+1)/2$ distinct elements that need to be estimated. A factor model reduces the number of unknown elements to $K(K+1)/2+N$, where K is the number of factors in the model. The first term gives the factor covariance matrix and the second one, the vector of specific variances. In practical applications, K is a much smaller number than N.

CHAPTER 9

Market Efficiency and Return Predictability

Market efficiency is one of the paradigms of modern finance that has created the most vibrant debate and prolific literature since Fama (1970) coined the *Efficient Market Hypothesis* (EMH). Without doubt, an engaging and controversial aspect of the debate is the presence of predictable components in asset returns (or lack thereof). The most intuitive implication of return predictability for asset allocation decisions is the ability to "time" the market—buy assets when the market is up and sell assets when it is down. The presence of return predictability also affects the way return variance scales with the investment horizon. Suppose that returns are negatively serially correlated—that is, a high return today is followed by a low return tomorrow. We say that the daily return exhibits *mean-reversion*. The variance of long-horizon returns is then smaller than the daily variance multiplied by the horizon. A buy-and-hold investor would find a long-term investment more attractive than a short-term one. The opposite is true when returns are positively serially correlated (high return today is followed by a high return tomorrow). In general, whether an investor decides to pursue a passive or an active strategy within a certain asset class depends on his belief that the market for this asset class is efficient. In an efficient market, strategies designed to outperform a broad-based market index cannot achieve consistently superior returns, after adjusting for risk and transaction costs.

According to the EMH, the market is efficient if asset prices reflect all available information at all times.[1] This requirement is cast in terms

[1]Fama(1991) points out a more realistic version of this strong condition. In determining the amount of information that prices reflect, one takes into account the trade-off between the costs of acquiring the information and the profits that could be made from acting on it.

of expected asset returns—random variables which adjust in response to changes in the available information. Fama (1970) classified the efficiency of a market into three forms, depending on the scope of information reflected in prices: weak form, semistrong form, and strong form. *Weak efficiency* means that past prices and trading information are incorporated into asset prices and current price changes cannot be predicted from past changes. The *semistrong efficiency* requires that prices reflect all publicly available information. Finally, a market is *strong efficient* if prices reflect all information, whether or not it is publicly available.

Tests of weak-form efficiency have the most controversial implications. While early tests (up to the early 1980s) considered only the forecast power of past returns, more recent studies focus on the predictive ability of variables such as dividend yield (D/P), book value to market value ratio (B/M), earnings-to-price ratio (E/P) or interest rates. Since predictability of returns implies that the expected asset returns vary through time, these tests are time-series tests. It is clear that expected returns play a very important role in reaching conclusions about the presence and amount of predictability. Expected returns are the "normal" returns against which abnormal performance is gauged. Therefore, since expected return is the return predicted from a pricing model, each test of market efficiency is in fact a joint test of efficiency and the assumed pricing model. If we find that returns are predictable, is this evidence against efficiency or evidence against the validity of the pricing model? This so-called "joint hypothesis problem" makes it impossible to unequivocally prove or disprove the EMH. The cross-sectional tests of predictability are tests on the validity of asset-pricing models, such as the *capital asset pricing model* (CAPM) and the *arbitrage pricing theory* (APT).

Some commonly found results are that past returns might help explain as much as 40% of the variability of long-horizon (2- to 10-year) stock returns. Predictive variables such as D/P and E/P also have long-horizon predictive power, explaining around 25% of the variability of two- to five-year returns. The overall evidence is that, after a shock, stock returns tend to return slowly to their preshock levels, so that they exhibit mean-reversion.[2]

Both the time-series and the cross-sectional predictability tests are performed with the help of regression analysis. For example, in time-series tests, individual asset returns or portfolio returns are regressed on past returns or on predictor variables to find out what their predictable component is. Tests on pricing models typically employ a *two-pass regression*, which we briefly review in this chapter.

---

[2]See Fama (1991) for a review of the literature on efficiency testing and predictability, in the frequentist setting.

Suppose that, based on regression evidence, a quantitative portfolio manager designs a strategy that "beats" the market, with projected return, after transaction costs, is 1.5%. Given that the regression coefficients are estimated with error, how much confidence should the manager place on the projection?

In this chapter, we offer the Bayesian perspective on testing for market efficiency. We start with a brief discussion of a "classical" test of the CAPM, and then move on to Bayesian tests of asset pricing models. Finally, we discuss return predictability in the presence of uncertainty.

TESTS OF MEAN-VARIANCE EFFICIENCY

In Chapter 7, we saw that the empirical analogues of the CAPM and the APT are given, respectively, by

$$R_i = \alpha + \beta_M R_M + \epsilon_i \tag{9.1}$$

and

$$R_i = \alpha + \beta_1 f_1 + \cdots + \beta_K f_K + \epsilon_i \tag{9.2}$$

for $i = 1, \ldots, N$, where:
- R_i = $T \times 1$ vector of excess returns on asset i.
- R_M = $T \times 1$ vector of excess returns on the market portfolio.
- f_j = $T \times 1$ vector of excess returns on risk factor j.
- β_M = sensitivity of asset i's return to the market risk factor.
- β_j = sensitivity of asset i's return to the jth risk factor.
- ϵ_i = $T \times 1$ vector of specific returns on asset i.
- α = intercept.

For the CAPM and the APT to hold, the intercept, α, in (9.1) and (9.2) must be zero.

The classical tests of the CAPM and the APT are typically based on a two-stage procedure. Here we will consider the tests of the CAPM. Tests of the APT have a similar methodology. In the first stage, an estimate of the sensitivity (beta) to the market risk factor is obtained for each asset. For example, Fama and MacBeth (1973) propose that the stock beta be estimated using a time-series regression of asset returns on the market portfolio. The beta represents the market risk of an asset (equivalently, the contribution of an asset to the risk of the market portfolio). Since the CAPM implies that the asset's expected return is linear in beta, in the second stage, a cross-sectional regression is run to find out if the betas explain the variability in expected returns across assets, at a given point in time:[3]

$$\boldsymbol{R}_t = b_0 + b_1\boldsymbol{\beta} + \boldsymbol{\epsilon}_t, \tag{9.3}$$

where: $\boldsymbol{R}_t = N \times 1$ vector of excess asset returns at time t.
$\boldsymbol{\beta} = N \times 1$ vector of asset betas.
$\boldsymbol{\epsilon}_t = N \times 1$ vector of asset specific returns at time t.
b_0, b_1 = parameters to be estimated.

The main implications of the CAPM that we can test are:

- The intercept, b_0, in the cross-sectional regression is zero.
- The regression coefficient, b_1, is equal to the market risk premium (market excess return), $\boldsymbol{R}_M$.

A likelihood-ratio test is usually employed to test the first implication and the hypothesis that $b_0 = 0$ is most often rejected.

However, inference using classical hypothesis tests suffers from the so-called "errors-in-variables" problem: The estimated rather than the true values of the regression coefficients are used in the tests, potentially leading to wrong inferences (conclusions). Moreover, the interpretation of the p-value from a hypothesis test is somewhat counterintuitive. The p-value certainly does not give the probability that $b_0 = 0$, which is the information one would really want to have. The Bayesian methodology deals with the problem of uncertainty in the estimates of the regression parameters, and allows one to compute the posterior probability of the hypothesis that $b_0 = 0$.

Throughout our discussion of the CAPM tests, we refer often to the "market" or the "market portfolio." A broad-based index, such as the S&PII500 or the NYSE Composite Index, represents the market portfolio in most of the empirical tests of the CAPM. The market portfolio in reality is much broader in scope and includes global equity, as well as global bonds and currencies. The benchmark portfolio used for testing the CAPM is, thus, only an imperfect proxy for the unobservable market portfolio, and objections can be raised about the validity of CAPM tests. This was one

[3]See Chapter 14 for a discussion of the fundamental multifactor model estimation, which makes use of the Fama-MacBeth regressions.

of the points of the famous CAPM critique by Roll (1977): If the market portfolio is misspecified, the validity of the CAPM will be rejected; if the market portfolio is correctly specified but the CAPM is wrong, its validity will be rejected again. Therefore, is the CAPM testable at all?

It is easy to show that, since the CAPM is an equilibrium pricing model, its pricing relationship,

$$E(\boldsymbol{R}_i) = \beta_i E(\boldsymbol{R}_M),$$

in fact says that "the market portfolio is mean-variance efficient"; that is, the market portfolio minimizes risk for a given level of expected return. Therefore, an alternative way to test the implication of the CAPM is to test whether the portfolio chosen to represent the market portfolio (i.e., the proxy for the market portfolio) is ex ante efficient.[4]

In addition to dealing with parameter uncertainty, the Bayesian methodology offers another advantage. Suppose we are not interested in the rather restrictive conclusion of a classical hypothesis test (reject or fail to reject the hypothesis of mean-variance efficiency). Instead, we would prefer to explore the degree of market inefficiency and its economic significance. (We will see a way to do this within a Bayesian framework in this chapter.)

We could divide into two categories the Bayesian empirical tests of mean-variance efficiency. The first category focuses on the intercepts in (9.1). Since the hypothesis of efficiency of the market portfolio is analogous to the hypothesis that there is zero mispricing in the model, we are in fact interested in testing the same restriction, whose impact on portfolio selection we explored in Chapter 7. These tests rely on the computation of a posterior odds ratio to test the null hypothesis of mean-variance efficiency.[5] We briefly discussed the posterior odds ratio approach to hypothesis testing in Chapter 3. Tests in the second category are based on the computation of the posterior distributions of measures of portfolio inefficiency. We discuss these next.[6]

---

[4]*Ex ante efficiency* refers to mean-variance efficiency based on expected returns and covariances. Contrast this with *ex post efficiency*, which is based on realized (observed) returns. Since the CAPM is an equilibrium model of returns, we focus on the ex ante efficiency of the market portfolio in testing it. An ex ante inefficient benchmark portfolio shows a potential for an active portfolio manager to achieve superior returns. Ex post, we are able to assess the contribution of a manager's active strategy to his performance. See, for example, Baks, Metrick, and Wachter (2001) and Busse and Irvine (2006).

[5]See Harvey and Zhou (1990).

[6]Our discussion is based on Kandel, McCulloch, and Stambaugh (1987) and Wang (1998).

INEFFICIENCY MEASURES IN TESTING THE CAPM

Construction of the inefficiency measure for a certain benchmark portfolio involves a comparison of that portfolio with a portfolio lying on the efficient frontier (see Chapter 6). Implicit in building the efficient frontier is the choice of risky assets. Different sets of risky assets give rise to different efficient frontiers. Therefore, a robust test would require that the set of assets used to construct the efficient frontier be widely diversified.

Suppose we are interested in testing the efficiency of portfolio p. Denote the $N \times 1$ vector of risky asset excess returns at time t by $\boldsymbol{R}_t = (R_{1,t}, \ldots, R_{N,t})$. Portfolio p is one of the N risky assets. It is common to select portfolios to represent the N risky assets for the purpose of diversification mentioned already. Consider, for example, the *size effect*—an "anomaly" of asset return behavior which was historically uncovered in tests of the CAPM: Firm size (market capitalization) helps to explain variations in average stock returns beyond market betas—small stocks have higher average returns than large stocks. Then firm size provides a criterion for sorting stocks into portfolios. Another sorting criterion is the ratio of firms' book value to market value.[7] Our goal is to construct the efficient frontier based on the N assets and then use one of the efficient portfolios to calculate the measure of inefficiency for portfolio p.

Let's first look at the case of no investment (holding) restrictions. Denote by x the efficient portfolio with the same variance as p, $\sigma_p^2 = \sigma_x^2$. Then, $\mu_p < \mu_x$, if p is inefficient; and $\mu_p = \mu_x$, if p is efficient. The difference between the expected returns of p and x can be interpreted as the expected loss from holding the inefficient portfolio, p, instead of the efficient portfolio, x, with the same risk as p. An intuitive measure of the inefficiency of p is then[8]

$$\Delta = \mu_x - \mu_p. \tag{9.4}$$

Better still, we could examine the difference between the risk-adjusted returns:

$$\Delta^R = \frac{\mu_x}{\sigma_x} - \frac{\mu_p}{\sigma_p}, \tag{9.5}$$

[7]See, for example, Fama and French (1992).

[8]There are other inefficiency measures, treated in the Bayesian literature, with roots in the classical (frequentist) analysis. For example, one measure is based on the maximum correlation ρ between p and an efficient portfolio with the same expected return. If p is efficient, the maximum correlation, ρ, is one. Otherwise, $\rho < 1$. The loss due to inefficiency of p is measured in terms of the ratio of standard deviations of the two portfolios with equal means. See Kandel, McCulloch, and Stambaugh (1987) and Harvey and Zhou (1990).

where x is the portfolio with the best risk-return trade-off—the portfolio with the maximal Sharpe ratio (see our discussion in Chapter 6). Portfolio p is efficient if and only if $\Delta = 0$ or $\Delta^R = 0$. Therefore, the goal is to compute and examine the posterior distribution of Δ (Δ^R). Geometrically, Δ measures the vertical distance between p and the efficient frontier. Since x is an efficient portfolio, Δ cannot be smaller than zero, while Δ^R is in practice always positive. We would be skeptical about the efficiency of p if, after computing Δ's (Δ^R's) distribution, we find that the greater part of its mass is located far above zero.

Next, we turn to a discussion of the distributional assumptions and the posterior distributions.

Distributional Assumptions and Posterior Distributions

Let us assume that the $N \times 1$ vector of returns, $\boldsymbol{R}_t$, $t = 1, \ldots, T$, has a multivariate normal distribution, independent across t, with mean $\boldsymbol{\mu}$ and covariance matrix $\boldsymbol{\Sigma}$. Assume that the parameters of the normal distribution follow a diffuse prior (Jeffreys') distribution (see Chapter 3),

$$\boldsymbol{\mu}, \boldsymbol{\Sigma} \sim |\boldsymbol{\Sigma}|^{-(N+1)/2}. \tag{9.6}$$

The posterior distributions of $\boldsymbol{\mu}$ and $\boldsymbol{\Sigma}$ are given, respectively, by

$$\boldsymbol{\Sigma} \mid \boldsymbol{R} \sim \text{IW}(\boldsymbol{\Psi}, T-1) \tag{9.7}$$

and

$$\boldsymbol{\mu} \mid \boldsymbol{\Sigma}, \boldsymbol{R} \sim \text{N}\left(\widehat{\boldsymbol{\mu}}, \frac{1}{T}\boldsymbol{\Sigma}\right), \tag{9.8}$$

where $\boldsymbol{R}$ is the $T \times N$ matrix of asset return data, the $N \times 1$ vector $\widehat{\boldsymbol{\mu}}$ denotes the sample mean of returns and $\boldsymbol{\Psi}$ is a $N \times N$ matrix defined as[9]

$$\boldsymbol{\Psi} = \sum_{t=1}^{T} (\boldsymbol{R}_t - \widehat{\boldsymbol{\mu}})'(\boldsymbol{R}_t - \widehat{\boldsymbol{\mu}}).$$

The inefficiency measure, Δ, is a nonlinear function of $\boldsymbol{\mu}$ and $\boldsymbol{\Sigma}$. To see this, consider the steps we need to compute it. First, using the techniques from Chapter 6, we construct the efficient frontier. Second, we identify the efficient portfolio, x, with the same risk as p. Finally, we compute the difference between μ_x and μ_p. Therefore, no analytical expression of the

[9]See Chapter 4, as well as our discussion in Chapter 7.

posterior density, $p(\Delta \mid \boldsymbol{\mu}, \boldsymbol{\Sigma}, \boldsymbol{R})$, of Δ is available. However, as discussed in Chapter 5, we can simulate Δ's (exact) posterior distribution by repeating a large number of times the following algorithm:

1. Draw $\boldsymbol{\Sigma}$ from its posterior inverse Wishart distribution in (9.7).
2. Given the draw of $\boldsymbol{\Sigma}$, draw $\boldsymbol{\mu}$ from its posterior normal distribution in (9.8).
3. For each pair $(\boldsymbol{\mu}, \boldsymbol{\Sigma})$, go through the three steps outlined in the previous paragraph, and compute the corresponding value of Δ (Δ^R).

We now show how to incorporate investment constraints into the analysis. The efficient frontier is, naturally, affected by constraints. Sharpe (1991) shows that the market portfolio might be inefficient when short-sale constraints are imposed. For example, restrictions on short sales reduce the possibility to mitigate return variability and to manage risk efficiently. Typically, a mutual fund's manager would achieve a given expected return at the expense of greater risk than a hedge fund's manager. The average loss from investing in an inefficient portfolio is then greater for an investor under short-sale constraints.

Efficiency under Investment Constraints

The inefficiency measure, Δ (Δ^R), is easily adapted to account for investment constraints. Wang (1998) proposes to modify it, in the case of short-sale restrictions, as

$$\tilde{\Delta} = \max_{x_i} \left\{ \mu_x - \mu_p \mid x_i \geq 0, \quad i = 1, \ldots, = N \right\}, \tag{9.9}$$

where x_i, $i = 1, \ldots, N$ denotes asset i's weight in portfolio x.

Consider a different constraint, one that applies to all margin accounts at brokerage houses. The Federal Reserve Board's Regulation T sets a 50% margin requirement—a customer may borrow 50% of the cost of a new asset position. We can incorporate a constraint reflecting a 50% margin modifying (9.9) with $x_i \geq -0.5$, $i = 1, \ldots, i = N$.

As shown earlier, efficiency of the benchmark portfolio, p, is equivalent to $\tilde{\Delta} = 0$. To compute the posterior distribution of $\tilde{\Delta}$ under the investment constraints, we follow the exact same steps as for the posterior distribution of Δ with one difference: The efficient frontier is constructed subject to the investment constraints that we would like to reflect. (We perform the constrained optimization in (9.9) for each pair $(\boldsymbol{\mu}, \boldsymbol{\Sigma})$).

Now, we illustrate the computation of the posterior distribution of Δ^R and analyze the implications for the efficiency of the market portfolio.

Illustration: The Inefficiency Measure, Δ^R

The sample in this illustration[10] consists of the monthly returns on 26 portfolios. The first 25 of them are the Fama-French portfolios. Stocks in them are ranked in five brackets according to size (as measured by market capitalization). Within each size bracket, stocks are ordered in five categories, according their book-to-market ratio. Thus 25 portfolios are constructed. The 26th portfolio is the value-weighted NYSE-AMEX stock portfolio, whose efficiency we are interested in—portfolio p from the previous section. The return on the one-month T-Bill is used as the risk-free rate. The sample period starts in January 1995 and ends in December 2005. The histograms in Exhibit 9.1 are based on 1,000 draws from the distribution of Δ^R computed as explained earlier, for the cases of no investment constraints and of short-sale constraints. The values of Δ^R are annualized, therefore, we can think of the histograms as representing the annual loss (in terms of risk-adjusted return) from holding the NYSE-AMEX

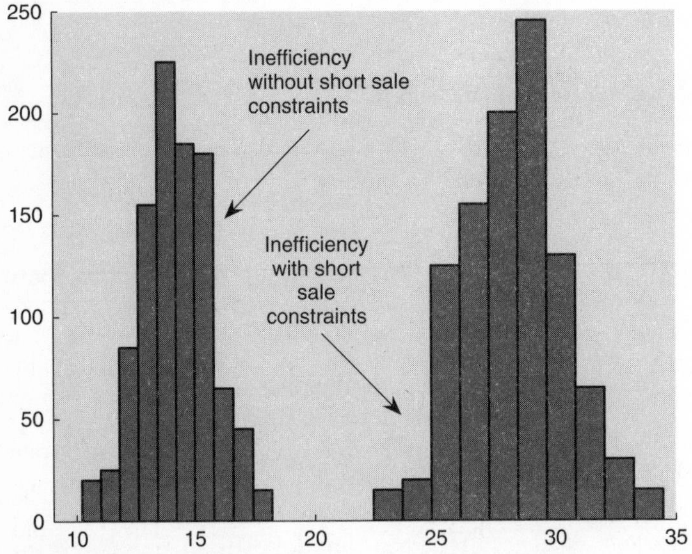

EXHIBIT 9.1 Distribution of the inefficiency measure, Δ^R
Note: The histograms are based on 1,000 draws from the distribution of Δ^R. The values of Δ^R are annualized.

[10]The illustration is based on the illustrations in Kandel, McCulloch, and Stambaugh (1987) and Wang (1998).

portfolio, instead of the efficient portfolio. As expected, the loss under short-sale constraints is greater than under no investment constraints.

TESTING THE APT

In the previous section, we discussed how to assess the efficiency of a portfolio in terms of an inefficiency measure, Δ^R. We could also examine the economic implications of the divergence between a (possibly) inefficient portfolio p and an efficient portfolio x in terms of utility losses, thus answering the question: How much does an investor value the validity of an asset pricing model? One possible way to answer this question is to compare the expected utilities of the investor's optimal portfolio choice under the scenarios of efficiency and inefficiency. Here we examine this approach in the context of testing the APT.[11]

Rewriting the empirical form of the APT in (9.2) in vector form, we obtain:

$$R = \boldsymbol{\alpha} + F\boldsymbol{\beta}' + \boldsymbol{\epsilon}, \tag{9.10}$$

where: $\boldsymbol{R} = T \times N$ matrix of excess return data.
$F = T \times K$ matrix of excess factor returns (factor premiums).
$\boldsymbol{\beta} = N \times K$ matrix of factor sensitivities.
$\boldsymbol{\alpha} = N \times 1$ vector of intercepts.
$\boldsymbol{\epsilon} = T \times N$ matrix of stock-specific returns series.

See Chapter 14 for more details on multifactor models, in particular, the types of factor models and their estimation.

A close parallel has been shown to exist between the mean-variance efficiency concept in the context of the CAPM and the APT. Testing the pricing implication of the APT (the linear restriction that $\boldsymbol{\alpha} = 0$) is equivalent to testing for mean-variance efficiency of the portfolio composed of the K factor portfolios in (9.2).

We denote the case when mean-variance efficiency holds ($\boldsymbol{\alpha} = 0$) as the "restricted case" and the case when mean-variance efficiency does not hold ($\boldsymbol{\alpha} \neq 0$) as the "unrestricted case." The metric to assess the economic significance of $\boldsymbol{\alpha}$'s distance from 0 is provided by the difference in the maximum expected utilities (of portfolio return) under the restricted case and the unrestricted case. Since different returns are generally associated with different

[11]Our discussion is based on McCulloch and Rossi (1990).

risk levels, utilities cannot be compared directly. Instead, utilities need to be computed using a uniform measurement unit called *the certainty-equivalent return*. Suppose the annual expected return of asset A is 7% with volatility (standard deviation of the return) of 13%. The *certainty-equivalent rate of return* is the risk-free rate of return (the "certain" return), R_{ce}, which provides the same utility as the return from holding asset A,

$$U(R_{ce}, 0\%) = U(7\%, 13\%),$$

where the volatility of the risk-free return is 0%, and U denotes a generic utility function of two variables (expected return and volatility). Comparison between the certainty equivalent levels in the restricted and unrestricted cases is equivalent to the comparison between the utility levels corresponding to these two cases.

Distributional Assumptions, Posterior and Predictive Distributions

In Chapter 6, we reviewed the Bayesian approach to portfolio selection. We apply it again here as an intermediate step in computing the certainty-equivalent returns under the hypotheses of efficiency and inefficiency. We proceed as follows. First, we find the optimal portfolio under each hypothesis; second, we compute the expected utility of next-period's return on the optimal portfolio; third, we compute and compare the certainty-equivalent returns. We start with deriving the predictive distribution of next-period's returns.

Suppose that the disturbances $\boldsymbol{\epsilon}$ in (9.10) have a multivariate normal distribution with covariance matrix $\boldsymbol{\Sigma}$. Denote by $\boldsymbol{E}$ and $\boldsymbol{E}_0$, respectively, the mean vector of excess returns, $\boldsymbol{R}$, in the unrestricted and the restricted cases. They are given, respectively, by

$$\boldsymbol{E} = \boldsymbol{\alpha} + \widehat{\boldsymbol{\mu}}_F \boldsymbol{\beta}'$$

and

$$\boldsymbol{E}_0 = \widehat{\boldsymbol{\mu}}_F \boldsymbol{\beta}',$$

where $\widehat{\boldsymbol{\mu}}_F$ is the sample mean vector of the time-series of factor returns. The covariance return matrix is the same in the restricted and unrestricted cases:[12]

$$\boldsymbol{V} = \boldsymbol{\beta}\,\widehat{\boldsymbol{\Omega}}_F\,\boldsymbol{\beta}' + \boldsymbol{\Sigma},$$

[12]See Chapter 14.

where $\widehat{\mathbf{\Omega}}_F$ is the sample covariance matrix of factor returns. As in Chapter 7, the moments of the factor returns, $\boldsymbol{\mu}_F$ and $\mathbf{\Omega}_F$, could be treated as random variables, and prior distributions asserted on them in order to reflect the estimation error contained in them. For the sake of simplicity, here we assume that $\widehat{\boldsymbol{\mu}}_F$ and $\widehat{\mathbf{\Omega}}_F$ are the true moments.

Consider a diffuse prior for the regression parameters, $\boldsymbol{\alpha}$, $\boldsymbol{\beta}$, and $\mathbf{\Sigma}$, as in (9.6), where the mean parameter is $\boldsymbol{E}$ in the restricted case and $\boldsymbol{E}_0$ in the unrestricted case. Then, the posterior densities of $\boldsymbol{\beta}$ and $\mathbf{\Sigma}$ (in the restricted case) or $(\boldsymbol{\alpha}, \boldsymbol{\beta})$ and $\mathbf{\Sigma}$ (in the unrestricted case) are multivariate normal and inverted Wishart (as in (9.7) and (9.8), where $\widehat{\boldsymbol{\mu}}$ is $\widehat{\boldsymbol{\alpha}} + \boldsymbol{F}\widehat{\boldsymbol{\beta}}'$ in the unrestricted case, $\boldsymbol{F}\widehat{\boldsymbol{\beta}}'$ in the restricted case, and "hats" denote least-squares estimates).

In Chapter 6, we discussed that the predictive distribution of excess returns is needed to solve the Bayesian portfolio selection problem. Next period's excess returns, $\boldsymbol{R}_{T+1}$, have a multivariate Student t, with $T-K-N$ degrees of freedom in the unrestricted case and $T-K-N+1$ degrees of freedom in the restricted case (we have one less parameters to estimate, hence one more degree of freedom).[13] Denote next period's observation of factor returns by $\boldsymbol{F}_{T+1}$ (a $1\times K$ vector). The predictive mean and covariance of future excess returns in the unrestricted case are given, respectively, by

$$\widetilde{E} = \widehat{\boldsymbol{\alpha}} + \boldsymbol{F}_{T+1}\widehat{\boldsymbol{\beta}}' \tag{9.11}$$

and

$$\widetilde{V} = \frac{1}{\nu - 2} S \left(1 - \boldsymbol{F}_{T+1}(\boldsymbol{F}'\boldsymbol{F} + \boldsymbol{F}_{T+1}'\boldsymbol{F}_{T+1})^{-1}\boldsymbol{F}_{T+1}'\right)^{-1}, \tag{9.12}$$

where ν is the degrees-of-freedom parameter equal to $T-K-N$ or $T-K-N+1$, as explained above, and

$$S = (\boldsymbol{R} - \widehat{\boldsymbol{\alpha}} + \boldsymbol{F}\widehat{\boldsymbol{\beta}}')' (\boldsymbol{R} - \widehat{\boldsymbol{\alpha}} + \boldsymbol{F}\widehat{\boldsymbol{\beta}}'). \tag{9.13}$$

The predictive mean and covariance under the restricted case, $\widetilde{E}_0$ and $\widetilde{V}_0$, are obtained by substituting $\widehat{\boldsymbol{\alpha}} = 0$ in (9.11) and (9.13).

Certainty Equivalent Returns

McCulloch and Rossi (1990) use a negative exponential utility function to describe investors' preferences, given by

$$U(W) = -\exp(-AW), \tag{9.14}$$

[13] See Chapter 3 for the definition of the multivariate Student's t-distribution.

where A is the coefficient of risk aversion. The end-of-period wealth, W, is defined as $(1 + R_f + R_p)W_0$, where R_f is the risk-free rate, R_p is the excess portfolio return (different in the restricted and the unrestricted cases), and W_0 is the initial amount of invested funds. The expected utility can be shown to be

$$\mathrm{E}\left(U(W)\right) = -\exp\left\{-AW_0(1 + R_f + \mu) + A^2 W_0^2 \frac{\sigma^2}{2}\right\}, \tag{9.15}$$

with μ and σ^2 denoting the mean and variance of portfolio return, R_p. Using the methodology of Chapter 6, we obtain the efficient frontiers in the unrestricted and the restricted case.

Denote by $\boldsymbol{\omega}^*$ and $\boldsymbol{\omega}_0^*$ the vectors of optimal portfolio weights in the unrestricted and restricted case, respectively. Then, the expected returns and risks of the optimal portfolio could be computed under the hypothesis of efficiency (restricted case)—μ_0^* and $\sigma_0^{2^*}$—and the hypothesis of inefficiency (unrestricted case)—μ^* and σ^{2^*}. To assess the degree of inefficiency, we compute the difference in certainty equivalent returns under the two hypotheses,

$$R_{ce}(\boldsymbol{\alpha}, \boldsymbol{\beta}, \boldsymbol{\Sigma}) - R_{ce}(0, \boldsymbol{\beta}, \boldsymbol{\Sigma}). \tag{9.16}$$

McCulloch and Rossi (1990) construct 10 size-based portfolios, whose weekly returns for the period January 1967 through December 1987 constitute the $T \times N$ matrix R. They use principal components analysis to extract the factors driving returns[14] and examine the evidence for mean-variance efficiency in one-, three-, and five-factor models. For an initial wealth, W, and a degree of risk aversion equal to $15/W$, McCulloch and Rossi find a 1% annual difference in certainty equivalence for all three-factor models. A lower degree of risk aversion ($2/W$) leads to an increase in the difference in certainty equivalents to around 8% annually for the three models. This increase is a reflection of the fact that a lower risk aversion leads to greater riskiness of the optimal portfolio. McCulloch and Rossi observe that the five-factor model does not imply a larger degree of efficiency than the one-factor model.

If a certain degree of inefficiency is observed in the market, can it be exploited to obtain higher returns? In the next section, we explore stock return predictability in the Bayesian setting.

[14]The principal components analysis procedure is briefly described in Chapter 14.

RETURN PREDICTABILITY

Suppose an empirical investigation has shown that there exists a predictable component in the returns of a market index. How would this affect the investor's optimal portfolio selection? What impact does return predictability have on the ability to obtain estimates closer to the true values of the unknown parameters as we acquire more information with time? In this section, we discuss the asset allocation problem of a buy-and-hold investor (i.e., an investor who constructs a portfolio at the beginning of a period and does not rebalance untill the end of his investment horizon) in the context of predictability.

The regression employed by most of the predictability studies has the following form:

$$R_t = \alpha + \beta x_{t-1} + \epsilon_t, \tag{9.17}$$

where: R_t = stock's excess return at time t.
x_{t-1} = value of a predictive variable at time $t-1$ (lagged predictor value).
ϵ_t = regression's disturbance.

The predictive variable (predictor) is either the lagged stock return or variable(s) related to asset prices. For example, the dividend yield (the ratio of the dividend at time t and the stock price at time t), the book-to-market ratio (the ratio between the book value per share at time t and the stock price at time t), and the term premium (the difference in returns on long-term and short-term Treasury debt obligations) have been found to have predictive power, at least in in-sample investigations.

It is also assumed that the predictive variable is stochastic and follows an autoregressive process of order 1 (AR(1)):

$$x_t = \theta + \gamma x_{t-1} + u_t. \tag{9.18}$$

Suppose that the predictor in (9.17) is the dividend yield (D/P). Let us review a few stylized facts about the relationship between stock returns and predictors (dividend yield, in particular), which will help us gain intuition about the results discussed later in this section.

- *The contemporaneous stock return, R_t is positively related to last period's dividend yield, D/P_{t-1}, that is, $\beta > 0$ in* (9.17).
- *A positive shock to D/P_t leads to a lower contemporaneous return, R_t.* Suppose the simple one-period stock-price valuation model is correct;

that is, the stock price today is equal to the expected discounted cash flows next period. The discount rate is equal to the internal rate of return; that is, the expected stock return. The increase in D/P_t pushes up the expected return at time $t+1$, $E[R_{t+1}]$ (since $\beta > 0$). The future cash flow is thus discounted at a higher rate, which impacts negatively today's price and leads to a decrease in the contemporaneous return, R_t.

- *The disturbance, ϵ_t, in* (9.17) *is negatively correlated with D/P_t and u_t.* The disturbance, ϵ_t, and D/P_t, are correlated because they are both impacted by shocks to the stock price. Consider a positive shock to the stock price at time t. The stock return at time t, R_t, will go up, while the dividend yield at time t, D/P_t, will go down. Since the shock is by default unexpected, it had not been incorporated into the expected return, $E[R_t]$, and the entire increase in R_t will be reflected in the disturbance, ϵ_t. Therefore, ϵ_t and D/P_t are negatively correlated. Consider (9.18): a decrease in D/P_t impacts negatively the disturbance u_t. This implies a negative correlation between the disturbances in (9.17) and (9.18).

Two competing hypotheses aim to explain predictability; one is in line with efficiency, the other one is in contradiction to it. The first one contends that predictability arises as a result of the discount effect explained before. The second one claims that predictability is the result of irrational bubbles in stock prices: low D/P_t signals that the price is irrationally high and will move (in a predictable way) toward its fundamental value. In the rest of this chapter, we are only concerned with the effects of predictability on portfolio choice and we leave the discussion of its causes to researchers of financial theory.

Let us assume the simplest case in which the excess returns on one risky asset—a widely diversified portfolio such as the value-weighted NYSE index—are examined for predictability. A single predictor variable, D/P, is assumed. Then, (9.17) and (9.18) describe the relationship between R_t (the asset return) and x_t (D/P), as well as the evolution of D/P through time. The framework combining the two equations is called *vector autoregressive* (VAR) and explicitly models the dependence of ϵ_t and D/P_{t-1}. In vector notation, we write the model as

$$Y = WB + E, \tag{9.19}$$

or, equivalently,

$$\begin{pmatrix} R_1 & x_1 \\ R_2 & x_2 \\ \vdots & \vdots \\ R_T & x_T \end{pmatrix} = \begin{pmatrix} 1 & x_0 \\ 1 & x_1 \\ \vdots & \vdots \\ 1 & x_{T-1} \end{pmatrix} \begin{pmatrix} \boldsymbol{\alpha}' \\ \boldsymbol{\beta}' \end{pmatrix} + \begin{pmatrix} \epsilon_1 & u_1 \\ \epsilon_2 & u_2 \\ \vdots & \vdots \\ \epsilon_T & u_T \end{pmatrix},$$

where $\boldsymbol{\alpha} = (\alpha\ \theta)'$, and $\boldsymbol{\beta} = (\beta\ \gamma)'$ and the tth row of $\boldsymbol{Y}$ is given by $\boldsymbol{Y}_t' = (R_t, x_t)$.

Assume that the disturbances, ϵ_t and u_t, are jointly normally distributed with zero mean vector and covariance matrix, $\boldsymbol{\Sigma}$:

$$\boldsymbol{\Sigma} = \begin{pmatrix} \sigma_\epsilon^2 & \sigma_{\epsilon u} \\ \sigma_{\epsilon u} & \sigma_u^2 \end{pmatrix}, \tag{9.20}$$

where, as explained above, $\sigma_{\epsilon u} < 0$.

We explore predictability in terms of its effect on the asset selection. As in the previous section, we solve the Bayesian portfolio problem. However, instead of the one-period portfolio allocation, we are now interested in multiperiod allocations and the interplay between predictability and the investment horizon. In this discussion, we follow Barberis (2000).

Posterior and Predictive Inference

We consider the portfolio allocation problem for a buy-and-hold investor who constructs his portfolio at time T and does not rebalance until the end of his investment horizon at time $T + \widehat{T}$ (hence, a static allocation problem). The investor has return and D/P data available for T periods.

Let us derive the predictive distribution of excess returns $\widehat{T}$ periods ahead, assuming diffuse prior information for the parameters of the multivariate regression in (9.19),

$$\boldsymbol{B}, \boldsymbol{\Sigma} \propto |\boldsymbol{\Sigma}|^{-(N+1)/2},$$

where $N = 2$. The posterior distributions of $\boldsymbol{B}$ and $\boldsymbol{\Sigma}$ are normal and inverse Wishart, respectively:

$$\text{vec}(\boldsymbol{B}) \mid \boldsymbol{\Sigma} \sim \text{N}\left(\text{vec}(\widehat{\boldsymbol{B}}),\ \boldsymbol{\Sigma} \otimes \left(\boldsymbol{W}'\boldsymbol{W}\right)^{-1}\right) \tag{9.21}$$

$$\boldsymbol{\Sigma} \sim \text{IW}(\boldsymbol{\Psi}, T-1), \tag{9.22}$$

where:[15] $\widehat{\boldsymbol{B}} = (\boldsymbol{W}'\boldsymbol{W})^{-1}(\boldsymbol{W}'\boldsymbol{Y}) =$ least-squares estimate of $\boldsymbol{B}$.
$\boldsymbol{\Psi} = (\boldsymbol{Y} - \boldsymbol{W}\widehat{\boldsymbol{B}})'(\boldsymbol{Y} - \boldsymbol{W}\widehat{\boldsymbol{B}})$

In (9.21), "vec" is an operator which stacks the columns of a matrix into a column vector, so that vec($\boldsymbol{B}$) is a 4×1 vector and $\otimes$ is the notation for the Kronecker product.[16]

[15] See the appendix to this chapter for more details on the notation.

[16] The Kronecker product between two matrices, $\boldsymbol{A}$ and $\boldsymbol{B}$, of any dimension, is

$$\boldsymbol{A} \otimes \boldsymbol{B} = \begin{pmatrix} a_{11}\boldsymbol{B} & a_{12}\boldsymbol{B} & \cdots & a_{1K}\boldsymbol{B} \\ a_{21}\boldsymbol{B} & a_{22}\boldsymbol{B} & \cdots & a_{2K}\boldsymbol{B} \\ \cdots & & & \\ a_{L1}\boldsymbol{B} & a_{L2}\boldsymbol{B} & \cdots & a_{LK}\boldsymbol{B} \end{pmatrix}.$$

In previous chapters, our goal has been to find the distribution for the $N \times 1$ vector of next-period excess returns (at time $T+1$). Here, we generalize this result to the predictive distribution of the $N \times 1$ vector of excess returns at time $T+\widehat{T}$. It is important to realize that, in the static, multiperiod prediction case, we are interested in predicting the *cumulative* excess return at the end of the investment period. The cumulative excess return is the quantity that a rational buy-and-hold investor would aim to maximize. We take the cumulative excess return, $R_{T,\widehat{T}}$, to be simply the sum of the single-period excess returns:

$$R_{T,\widehat{T}} = R_T + R_{T+1} + \cdots + R_{T+\widehat{T}}.$$

Therefore, we need to derive the predictive distribution of cumulative excess returns at time $T+\widehat{T}$. Moreover, since the VAR framework links the dynamics of the excess returns and the predictive variable, we predict the future *D*/*P* along with future excess returns.

The predictive distribution for $\boldsymbol{Y}_{T,\widehat{T}}$ is given by (see (3.19) in Chapter 3)

$$p\left(\boldsymbol{Y}_{T,\widehat{T}} \mid Y\right) = \int p\left(\boldsymbol{Y}_{T,\widehat{T}} \mid \boldsymbol{B}, \boldsymbol{\Sigma}, Y\right) p\left(\boldsymbol{B}, \boldsymbol{\Sigma} \mid Y\right) \mathrm{d}\boldsymbol{B}\,\mathrm{d}\boldsymbol{\Sigma}, \tag{9.23}$$

where we implicitly assume that the distribution (and distributional parameters) of Y remains unchanged throughout the $\widehat{T}$ periods ahead. In the following chapters on volatility models, including regime-switching models, the assumption of stationarity of the returns distribution is relaxed.

We know that, for $\widehat{T} = 1$, the distribution of $\boldsymbol{Y}_{T+1}$ is normal. For an arbitrary value of $\widehat{T}$, we still have a normal density, since we can simply roll forward (9.19) an arbitrary number of times. Denote the normal distribution of $\boldsymbol{Y}_{T+1}$ by $\mathrm{N}\left(\boldsymbol{\mu}_{T+1}, \boldsymbol{\Sigma}_{T+1}\right)$, the normal distribution of $\boldsymbol{Y}_{T+2}$ by $\mathrm{N}\left(\boldsymbol{\mu}_{T+2}, \boldsymbol{\Sigma}_{T+2}\right)$, and so on. Then, using the properties of the normal distribution, we obtain that $\boldsymbol{Y}_{T,\widehat{T}} = \boldsymbol{Y}_{T+1} + \cdots + \boldsymbol{Y}_{T,\widehat{T}}$ is normally distributed:

$$p\left(\boldsymbol{Y}_{T,\widehat{T}} \mid \boldsymbol{B}, \boldsymbol{\Sigma}, Y\right) = \mathrm{N}\left(\boldsymbol{\mu}_{T+1} + \ldots + \boldsymbol{\mu}_{T+\widehat{T}},\ \boldsymbol{\Sigma}_{T+1} + \ldots + \boldsymbol{\Sigma}_{T+\widehat{T}}\right).$$

To find the means and covariances of each $\boldsymbol{Y}_{T+t}$, $t = 1, \ldots, \widehat{T}$, above, we use the fact that (9.17) and (9.18) establish a recursive relationship between returns and *D*/*P*. To see this, rewrite (9.19) in the following way. At time $T+1$,

$$\boldsymbol{Y}_{T+1} = \boldsymbol{\alpha} + \boldsymbol{\beta}_0 \boldsymbol{Y}_T + \boldsymbol{e}_{T+1}, \tag{9.24}$$

Note that computing the Kronecker product does not require compatibility of the matrix dimensions. The appendix to this chapter explains why the Kronecker product appears in (9.21).

where

$$\boldsymbol{\beta}_0 = \begin{pmatrix} 0 & \beta \\ 0 & \gamma \end{pmatrix},$$

$$\boldsymbol{e}_{T+1} = \begin{pmatrix} \epsilon_{T+1} \\ u_{T+1} \end{pmatrix}.$$

It is easy to verify that (9.24) is equivalent to (9.19). Iterating forward one-period at a time and at each step t substituting the expression for $\boldsymbol{Y}_{t-1}$, we obtain

$$\boldsymbol{Y}_{T+2} = \{\boldsymbol{\alpha} + \boldsymbol{\beta}_0\boldsymbol{\alpha} + \boldsymbol{\beta}_0^2\boldsymbol{Y}_T\} + \{\boldsymbol{\beta}_0\boldsymbol{e}_{T+1} + \boldsymbol{e}_{T+2}\}$$

$$\boldsymbol{Y}_{T+3} = \{\boldsymbol{\alpha} + \boldsymbol{\beta}_0\boldsymbol{\alpha} + \boldsymbol{\beta}_0^2\boldsymbol{\alpha} + \boldsymbol{\beta}_0^3\boldsymbol{Y}_T\} + \{\boldsymbol{\beta}_0^2\boldsymbol{e}_{T+1} + \boldsymbol{\beta}_0\boldsymbol{e}_{T+2} + \boldsymbol{e}_{T+3}\}$$

$$\dots$$

$$\boldsymbol{Y}_{T+\widehat{T}} = \{\boldsymbol{\alpha} + \boldsymbol{\beta}_0\boldsymbol{\alpha} + \ldots + \boldsymbol{\beta}_0^{\widehat{T}-1}\boldsymbol{\alpha} + \boldsymbol{\beta}_0^{\widehat{T}}\boldsymbol{Y}_T\} + \boldsymbol{\beta}_0^{\widehat{T}-1}\{\boldsymbol{e}_{T+1} + \cdots + \boldsymbol{e}_{T+\widehat{T}}\},$$

where $\boldsymbol{\beta}_0^t$ denotes the tth power of the matrix $\boldsymbol{\beta}_0$. The first (bracketed) term in each right-hand-side expression is the mean of the corresponding normal distribution of $\boldsymbol{Y}_{T+t}$, $t = 1, \ldots, \widehat{T}$. The second term is used to derive the covariance in the following way:

$$\begin{aligned}
\text{cov}(\boldsymbol{Y}_{T+2}) &= \boldsymbol{\beta}_0\boldsymbol{\Sigma}\,\boldsymbol{\beta}_0' + \boldsymbol{\Sigma} \\
&= (I + \boldsymbol{\beta}_0)\boldsymbol{\Sigma}(I + \boldsymbol{\beta}_0)', \\
\text{cov}(\boldsymbol{Y}_{T+3}) &= \boldsymbol{\beta}_0^2\,\boldsymbol{\Sigma}\,\boldsymbol{\beta}_0^{2'} + \boldsymbol{\beta}_0\,\boldsymbol{\Sigma}\,\boldsymbol{\beta}_0' + \boldsymbol{\Sigma} \\
&= (I + \boldsymbol{\beta}_0 + \boldsymbol{\beta}_0^2)\,\boldsymbol{\Sigma}\,(I + \boldsymbol{\beta}_0 + \boldsymbol{\beta}_0^2)'.
\end{aligned}$$

and so on, where we use the fact that $\boldsymbol{e}_{T+t}$ has covariance matrix $\boldsymbol{\Sigma}$ for each $t = 1, \ldots, \widehat{T}$.

Finally, we can write out the parameters of the normal distribution of $\boldsymbol{Y}_{T,\widehat{T}}$, $p\,(\boldsymbol{Y}_{T,\widehat{T}}\,|\,\boldsymbol{B}, \boldsymbol{\Sigma}, Y)$, conditional on $\boldsymbol{\alpha}$, $\boldsymbol{\beta}$, and $\boldsymbol{\Sigma}$. The mean is

$$\begin{aligned}
\boldsymbol{\mu}_{T,\widehat{T}} &= \widehat{T}\boldsymbol{\alpha} \\
&+\left((\widehat{T} - 1)\boldsymbol{\beta}_0 + (\widehat{T} - 2)\boldsymbol{\beta}_0^2 + \cdots + \boldsymbol{\beta}_0^{\widehat{T}-1}\right)\boldsymbol{\alpha} \\
&+(\boldsymbol{\beta}_0 + \boldsymbol{\beta}_0^2 + \cdots + \boldsymbol{\beta}_0^{\widehat{T}})\boldsymbol{Y}_T,
\end{aligned} \tag{9.25}$$

and the covariance is

$$\begin{aligned}
\boldsymbol{V}_{T,\widehat{T}} &= \boldsymbol{\Sigma} \\
&+(I + \boldsymbol{\beta}_0)\boldsymbol{\Sigma}(I + \boldsymbol{\beta}_0)' \\
&+(I + \boldsymbol{\beta}_0 + \boldsymbol{\beta}_0^2)\boldsymbol{\Sigma}(I + \boldsymbol{\beta}_0 + \boldsymbol{\beta}_0^2)'
\end{aligned} \tag{9.26}$$

$$+\ldots$$
$$+(I+\boldsymbol{\beta}_0+\boldsymbol{\beta}_0^2+\ldots+\boldsymbol{\beta}_0^{\widehat{T}-1})\boldsymbol{\Sigma}(I+\boldsymbol{\beta}_0+\boldsymbol{\beta}_0^2+\ldots+\boldsymbol{\beta}_0^{\widehat{T}-1})'.$$

To sample from the predictive distribution of $\boldsymbol{Y}_{T,\widehat{T}}$ in (9.23), we employ the following sampling scheme:

- Draw $\boldsymbol{\Sigma}$ from its inverted Wishart posterior distribution in (9.22).
- Given the draw of $\boldsymbol{\Sigma}$, draw $\boldsymbol{B}$ from its normal posterior distribution in (9.21).
- Given the draws of $\boldsymbol{\Sigma}$ and $\boldsymbol{B}$, compute $\boldsymbol{\mu}_{T,\widehat{T}}$ and $\boldsymbol{V}_{T,\widehat{T}}$ and sample from a normal distribution with those parameters to obtain a draw from the predictive distribution of $\boldsymbol{Y}_{T,\widehat{T}} = \left(R_{T,\widehat{T}}, x_{T,\widehat{T}}\right)$.

We perform these steps a large number of times to obtain the simulated predictive distribution of the cumulative excess return at the end of the investment horizon, $T+\widehat{T}$. Now we are ready to compute the optimal portfolio allocation by maximizing the investor's expected utility over the predictive density of cumulative excess return. We do that numerically.

Solving the Portfolio Selection Problem

In Chapters 6 and 7, we assumed that the investor had a quadratic utility, and computed the optimal portfolio weights using (6.14) in Chapter 6. Earlier in this chapter, we used the negative exponential utility function. Here, we consider a power utility, given by[17]

$$U\left(W_{T+\widehat{T}}\right) = \frac{W_{T+\widehat{T}}^{1-A}}{1-A}, \tag{9.27}$$

where A is the risk-aversion parameter and $W_{T+\widehat{T}}$ is the end-of-horizon (terminal) wealth. Assuming continuously compounded returns, the terminal wealth is written as

$$W_{T+\widehat{T}} = W_T\left\{\omega\exp\left(\widehat{T}R_f + R_{T,\widehat{T}}\right) + (1-\omega)\exp\left(\widehat{T}R_f\right)\right\},$$

[17] Power utility is also known as *iso-elastic utility*. It is often taken to be the neutral (benchmark) utility function in investigations of investor preferences because of its distinctive property of *constant* relative *risk aversion* (CRRA). Intuitively, CRRA means that the investor's preferences for risk do not change with his wealth level nor with the time horizon—the same proportion of wealth is invested in risky assets. In contrast, the negative exponential function we employed in the previous section exhibits constant *absolute* risk aversion, which means that the investor becomes more risk averse as his wealth increases—he invests the same absolute amount in risky assets at any wealth level.

where: W_T = wealth at the time of portfolio construction.
R_f = continuously compounded, risk-free rate.
ω = fraction of the portfolio invested in the risky asset.

Without loss of generality, we could take W_T=1. Notice that we add the cumulative risk-free return, $\widehat{T}R_f$, in the terminal wealth equation since $R_{T,\widehat{T}}$ is the cumulative excess return.

Taking the expectation of (9.27) with respect to the predictive distribution of $R_{T,\widehat{T}}$, we obtain

$$\mathrm{E}\left(U\left(W_{T+\widehat{T}}\right)\right) = \int U\left(W_{T+\widehat{T}}\right) p\left(Y_{T,\widehat{T}} \mid \boldsymbol{B}, \boldsymbol{\Sigma}\right) \mathrm{d}R_{T,\widehat{T}}. \tag{9.28}$$

Since no analytical expression is available for the expectation in (9.28), we compute the integral numerically (approximate it with a sum) averaging the utility over the draws of $R_{T,\widehat{T}}$. For a total number of M draws, that sum is expressed as

$$\mathrm{E}\left(U\left(W_{T+\widehat{T}}\right)\right) = \frac{1}{M}\sum_{m=1}^{M} \frac{\left\{\omega \exp\left(\widehat{T}R_f + R^m_{T,\widehat{T}}\right) + (1-\omega)\exp\left(\widehat{T}R_f\right)\right\}^{1-A}}{1-A}, \tag{9.29}$$

where the superscript of $R_{T,\widehat{T}}$ denotes the mth draw from the predictive distribution.

Assuming no short selling and no buying on margin, portfolio weights, ω, can take values between 0 and 0.99.[18] We maximize (9.29) with a constrained optimizer (available in most commercial software packages) or with the following numerical procedure. We evaluate the right-hand side in (9.29) over a grid of values of ω and identify the optimal allocation as the value of ω that produces the greatest value of the expected utility, $\mathrm{E}\left(U\left(W_{T+\widehat{T}}\right)\right)$. For example, the expected utility could be evaluated on the grid [0, 0.01, 0.02, ... ,0.97, 0.98, 0.99].

In order to explore the implication of predictability on optimal allocations at different horizons, the numerical optimization above is performed for different values of $\widehat{T}$.

[18] The upper bound of the weights range is restricted to 0.99 instead of 1 since, when $\omega = 1$, expected utility is equal to $-\infty$. The unboundedness of the utility function from below is a result of the heavy-tailedness of the predictive distribution (the unconditional predictive distribution of $R_{T+\widehat{T}}$ is a multivariate Student's t-distribution). See Barberis (2000) and Kandel and Stambaugh (1996).

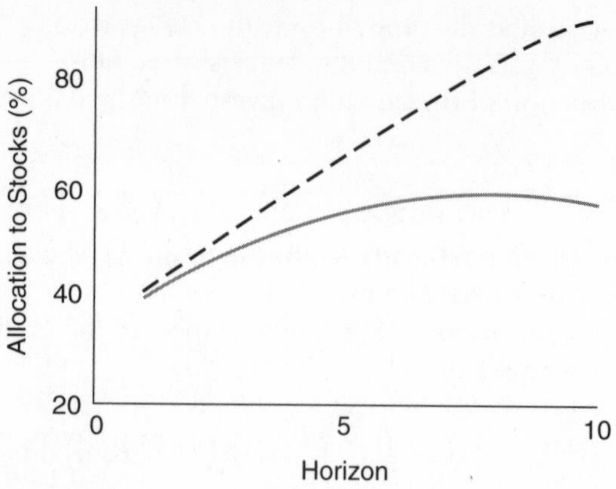

EXHIBIT 9.2 Optimal stock allocation when returns are predictable
Source: Adapted from Figure 2 in Barberis (2000).

ILLUSTRATION: PREDICTABILITY AND THE INVESTMENT HORIZON

Exhibit 9.2 presents the optimal allocation, ω, plotted against the investment horizon from the investigation of Barberis (2000). He uses monthly data on the NYSE stock index and its dividend yield over the period June 1952 through December 1995. The value of the risk aversion parameter, A, used to solve for the optimal portfolio is 10. The lines in the exhibit correspond to two scenarios—predictability with uncertainty taken into account (the solid line) and predictability with no uncertainty taken into account (the dashed line). The former scenario is the one discussed earlier in the chapter. The latter scenario treats the mean and covariance of returns as given; these parameters are fixed at their posterior mean values and for each length of the investment horizon, $\widehat{T}$, the distribution of cumulative returns, $R_{T,\widehat{T}}$, is simulated by drawing a sample from $\mathrm{N}(\widehat{T}\widehat{\mu}, \widehat{T}\widehat{\Sigma})$, where the "hats" on μ and Σ denote posterior moments.

In the absence of uncertainty about the mean and covariance of returns, predictability causes an increasing-with-horizon allocation to the NYSE index—investment in stocks becomes more attractive with time. In contrast, when uncertainty in the parameters is included in the analysis, the effect of predictability is not strong enough to induce ever-increasing allocation to stocks. As time passes, uncertainty begins to dominate and stock allocation declines.

SUMMARY

In this chapter, we consider two of the most debated topics in empirical finance—market efficiency and return predictability. We discuss how to cast both into the Bayesian framework. Accounting for estimation risk has tangible implications for a buy-and-hold investor—at short investment horizons, the effect of predictability dominates the effect of estimation uncertainty; at longer horizons, however, uncertainty "wins over," implying declining portfolio allocations to stocks.

APPENDIX: VECTOR AUTOREGRESSIVE SETUP

The VAR model considered in the chapter is given by

$$Y = WB + E, \tag{9.30}$$

equivalent to

$$\begin{pmatrix} R_1 & x_1 \\ R_2 & x_2 \\ \cdots & \cdots \\ R_T & x_T \end{pmatrix} = \begin{pmatrix} 1 & x_0 \\ 1 & x_1 \\ \cdots & \cdots \\ 1 & x_{T-1} \end{pmatrix} \begin{pmatrix} \alpha & \theta \\ \beta & \gamma \end{pmatrix} + \begin{pmatrix} \epsilon_1 & u_1 \\ \epsilon_2 & u_2 \\ \cdots & \cdots \\ \epsilon_T & u_T. \end{pmatrix} \tag{9.31}$$

In the chapter we assumed that each row of $\boldsymbol{E}$ is normally distributed with zero mean and covariance matrix $\boldsymbol{\Sigma}$. For the purposes of distributional analysis, it is often helpful to vectorize the matrices in (9.31) and represent it as

$$y = Zb + e, \tag{9.32}$$

where:
$$\begin{aligned} \boldsymbol{y} &= \mathrm{vec}(\boldsymbol{Y}) \\ \boldsymbol{Z} &= \boldsymbol{I}_2 \otimes \boldsymbol{W} \\ \boldsymbol{b} &= \mathrm{vec}(\boldsymbol{B}) \\ \boldsymbol{e} &= \mathrm{vec}(\boldsymbol{E}) \end{aligned}$$

The vec operator serves to stack the columns of a matrix into a column vector, while $\otimes$ is the Kronecker product. The expression in (9.32) is equivalent to

$$\begin{pmatrix} R_1 \\ R_2 \\ \vdots \\ R_T \\ x_1 \\ x_2 \\ \vdots \\ x_T \end{pmatrix} = \begin{pmatrix} 1 & x_0 & 0 & 0 \\ 1 & x_1 & 0 & 0 \\ \cdots & \cdots & \cdots & \cdots \\ 1 & x_{T-1} & 0 & 0 \\ 0 & 0 & 1 & x_0 \\ 0 & 0 & 1 & x_1 \\ \cdots & \cdots & \cdots & \cdots \\ 0 & 0 & 1 & x_{T-1} \end{pmatrix} \begin{pmatrix} \alpha \\ \beta \\ \theta \\ \gamma \end{pmatrix} + \begin{pmatrix} \epsilon_1 \\ \epsilon 2 \\ \vdots \\ \epsilon_T \\ u_1 \\ u_2 \\ \vdots \\ u_T \end{pmatrix}. \tag{9.33}$$

The covariance matrix of e is now written as

$$\text{cov}(\boldsymbol{e}) = \boldsymbol{\Sigma} \otimes \boldsymbol{I}_T, \tag{9.34}$$

where $\boldsymbol{I}_T$ is an identity matrix of dimension $T \times T$. The expression in (9.34) can be expanded as

$$\text{cov}(\boldsymbol{e}) = \begin{pmatrix} \sigma_\epsilon^2 & 0 & \cdots & 0 & \sigma_{\epsilon u} & 0 & \cdots & 0 \\ 0 & \sigma_\epsilon^2 & \cdots & 0 & 0 & \sigma_{\epsilon u} & \cdots & 0 \\ \cdots & \cdots & \cdots & \cdots & \cdots & \cdots & \cdots & \cdots \\ 0 & 0 & \cdots & \sigma_\epsilon^2 & 0 & 0 & \cdots & \sigma_{\epsilon u} \\ & & & & & & & \\ \sigma_{\epsilon u} & 0 & \cdots & 0 & \sigma_u^2 & 0 & \cdots & 0 \\ 0 & \sigma_{\epsilon u} & \cdots & 0 & 0 & \sigma_u^2 & \cdots & 0 \\ \cdots & \cdots & \cdots & \cdots & \cdots & \cdots & \cdots & \cdots \\ 0 & 0 & \cdots & \sigma_{\epsilon u} & 0 & 0 & \cdots & \sigma_u^2 \end{pmatrix}. \tag{9.35}$$

CHAPTER 10

Volatility Models

An Overview

Volatility describes the variability of a financial time series, that is, the magnitude and speed of the time series' fluctuations. In some sense, it most clearly conveys the uncertainty in which financial decision making is accomplished. Volatility is often expressed as the standard deviation of asset returns and, more generally, when returns are assumed to be nonnormal, as the scale of the return distribution.[1]

In financial modeling, volatility is a forward-looking concept. It is the variance of the yet unrealized asset return conditional on all relevant, available information. Denote by $\Im_{t-1}$ the set of information available up to time $t - 1$. This information set includes, for example, past asset returns and information about past trading volume. The volatility at time t is given by

$$\sigma^2_{t|t-1} = \mathrm{var}\left(r_t|\Im_{t-1}\right) = \mathrm{E}\left(\left(r_t - \mu_{t|t-1}\right)^2 \mid \Im_{t-1}\right),$$

where r_t and $\mu_{t|t-1}$ are the asset's return and conditional expected return at time t, respectively

As the previous equation suggests, the volatility of returns is not constant through time. In such cases, we say that returns are *heteroskedastic*. An important phenomenon, called *volatility clustering*, is characteristic of the dynamics of asset returns. Mandelbrot (1963) was one of the first to note that "large changes [in asset prices] tend to be followed by large changes—of either sign—and small changes tend to be followed by small changes." In other words, volatility clustering describes the tendency of asset returns to alternate between periods of high volatility and low volatility. The periods

[1]Measures of risk other than the standard deviation are increasingly popular among both finance practitioners and academics. We discuss some of them in Chapter 13.

of high volatility see large magnitudes of asset returns (both positive and negative), while in periods of low volatility the market is "calm" and returns do not fluctuate much. Clearly, this stylized fact about financial time series contradicts the efficient market hypothesis, which we discussed in Chapter 9. In an efficient market, investors would react immediately to the arrival of new information so that its effect is quickly dissipated; changes in asset returns are independent through time.

Two other empirically observed features of returns are that returns exhibit skewness and heavier tails (higher kurtosis) than suggested by the normal distribution and that volatility displays an asymmetric behavior to positive and negative return shocks—it tends to be higher when the market falls than when it rises. Volatility models attempt to explain these stylized facts about asset returns.

Since the volatility (and the expected return) today depends on the volatility (and the expected return) yesterday, it is clear that today's asset return is not independent from yesterday's asset return. Therefore, we can write an expression describing the evolution of returns through time—the *stochastic process*—incorporating the time-varying conditional volatility. In general, although asset returns can be thought of as evolving in a continuous fashion, the return-generating process is often modeled in the discrete time domain.

We can represent the one-period, discretely sampled (e.g., daily) return, r_t, as the sum of a conditional expected return, $\mu_{t|t-1}$, and an innovation (a random component), u_t, with zero mean and nonzero conditional variance, $\sigma^2_{t|t-1}$:

$$r_t = \mu_{t|t-1} + u_t. \tag{10.1}$$

A further decomposition gives

$$r_t = \mu_{t|t-1} + \sigma_{t|t-1}\epsilon_t, \tag{10.2}$$

where $\sigma_{t|t-1}$ is positive. The term ϵ_t is the building block of all time-series models. It denotes a *white noise process*—a sequence of independent and identically distributed (i.i.d.) random variables with zero mean and variance equal to one.

The expression in (10.2) is the underlying basis common to the two major groups of volatility models—the *autoregressive conditionally heteroskedastic* (ARCH) *-type models* and the *stochastic volatility* (SV) *models.* The conceptual difference between the two lies in the degree of determinacy of σ_t at time $t-1$. In the simplest ARCH-type model, volatility is described by a deterministic function of past squared returns; volatility at time t can be uniquely determined at time $t-1$. In an SV model, the conditional volatility is subject to random shocks; the unpredictable component makes it *latent* and unobservable. The distinction can be further visualized by considering the set of available information. The former setting assumes that, when estimating σ_t, all relevant information, embodied in $\Im_{t-1}$, is available and observable at time $t-1$. In contrast, in the latter setting, only a part of $\Im_{t-1}$ is directly observable; the "true" volatility thus becomes unobservable or latent.[2]

In this chapter, we provide an overview of ARCH-type and SV models. We discuss their Bayesian estimation in the next two chapters. In Chapter 14, we put volatility estimation into perspective and integrate it into the multifactor-model framework, thus presenting its main applications to risk management and to portfolio selection.

GARCH MODELS OF VOLATILITY

The analytical tractability of the GARCH-type models has made them the predominant choice in volatility modeling. Furthermore, the various extensions to the original ARCH model of Engle (1982) and the GARCH model of Bollerslev (1986) provide a large degree of flexibility in capturing empirically observed features of returns.

The volatility updating expression is given by

$$\sigma^2_{t|t-1} = \omega + \alpha u^2_{t-1} + \beta\sigma^2_{t-1|t-2}, \tag{10.3}$$

where u_t is a residual defined as $u_t = r_t - \mu_{t|t-1} = \sigma_{t|t-1}\epsilon_t$. The parameters of the GARCH(1,1) process are restricted to be nonnegative, $\omega > 0$, $\alpha \geq 0$, and $\beta \geq 0$, in order to ensure that $\sigma^2_{t|t-1}$ is positive for all values of the white noise process, ϵ_t. Notice how the information available at time $t-1$ impacts the conditional variance at time t, $\sigma^2_{t|t-1}$. The new information at time $t-1$ is embodied in the ARCH term, the squared residual, u^2_{t-1}. The carrier of the old information at time $t-1$ is the GARCH term, $\sigma^2_{t-1|t-2}$.

Rewriting (10.3) as

$$\sigma^2_{t|t-1} = (1-\alpha-\beta)\frac{\omega}{1-\alpha-\beta} + \alpha u^2_{t-1} + \beta\sigma^2_{t-1|t-2}, \tag{10.4}$$

one can see that the GARCH(1,1) model specifies the conditional variance of returns as a weighted average of three components:

- The long-run (unconditional) variance, $\omega/(1-\alpha-\beta)$.
- Last period's predicted variance, $\sigma^2_{t-1|t-2}$.
- The new information at time $t-1$, u^2_{t-1}.

[2] See Andersen, Bollerslev, Christoffersen, and Diebold (2005) for this interpretation.

The specification of $\sigma^2_{t|t-1}$ in (10.3), as a function of the lagged squared innovations, u^2_{t-1}, only corresponds to Engle's (1982) original ARCH(1) model.

The expression in (10.3) can be easily extended by including additional lagged squared innovations and lagged conditional variances to arrive at higher-order GARCH(p,q) models. It has been found, however, that the GARCH(1,1) specification generally describes return volatility sufficiently well.

Certainly, the model in (10.3) is incomplete unless we specify a distributional assumption for the asset return at time t. Since we are modeling temporally dependent asset returns, our focus naturally lies on the *conditional* return distribution. The original treatments of the GARCH(1,1) model by Bollerslev (1986) and Taylor (1986) assumed that returns are conditionally normally distributed:

$$r_t \mid \Im_{t-1} \sim \mathrm{N}\left(\mu_{t|t-1}, \sigma^2_{t|t-1}\right). \tag{10.5}$$

Before we discuss the properties of the GARCH model and different distributional assumptions, let us review how the GARCH(1,1) model defined by (10.2), (10.3), and (10.5) explains some of the known stylized facts about asset returns.

Stylized Facts about Returns

Volatility Clustering It is possible, by recursive substitution, to express (10.3) only in terms of the lagged squared residuals, $u^2_{t-1}, u^2_{t-2}, \ldots$:[3]

$$\begin{aligned}\sigma^2_{t|t-1} &= \frac{\omega}{1-\beta} + \alpha u^2_{t-1} + \alpha\beta u^2_{t-2} + \alpha\beta^2 u^2_{t-3} + \ldots \\ &= \frac{\omega}{1-\beta} + \alpha \sum_{j=1}^{\infty} \beta^{j-1} u^2_{t-j}.\end{aligned}$$

It is easy to see, then, that recent large fluctuations of asset returns around their conditional means, that is, recent, large squared residuals, u^2_{t-j}, imply a high value for the conditional variance, $\sigma^2_{t|t-1}$, in period t, since $\alpha \geq 0$ and $\beta \geq 0$. The result is a cluster of high volatility. Conversely, if the recent history of returns is one of small fluctuations around the conditional mean, $\sigma^2_{t|t-1}$ is expected to be small, and a cluster of low volatility occurs.

Nonnormality of Asset Returns GARCH models can partially explain the empirically observed heavy tails and high-peakedness of asset returns, even

[3]Technically, we obtain an ARCH model with an infinite number of lags, ARCH(∞).

with the assumption that returns are conditionally normally distributed. Consider the expression in (10.2). The unconditional (marginal) distribution of r_t can be represented as a combination of normal distributions; a different normal distribution corresponds to the different realizations of $\sigma^2_{t|t-1}$ that could occur. We say that r_t is distributed as a mixture of normals. The tails of the mixture are heavier and the peakedness—higher than these of a normal distribution.

The GARCH effects, however, are insufficient to account fully for the nonnormality of returns. Alternative distributional assumptions could thus be adopted.

Asymmetric Volatility The "plain vanilla" GARCH(1,1) model above does not capture the volatility asymmetry observed in practice. Notice that both positive return shocks (when the return is above its conditional expectation and $u_{t-1} > 0$) and negative return shocks (when the return is below its conditional expectation and $u_{t-1} < 0$) have an identical (symmetric) impact on the conditional variance, $\sigma^2_{t|t-1}$, since the residual, u_{t-1}, in (10.3) appears in a squared form.[4] Many extensions accounting for the asymmetric effect exist in the volatility literature. One of them, for example, is the model of Glosten, Jagannathan, and Runkle (1993) in which the conditional variance reacts in a different way to positive and negative shocks,

$$\sigma^2_{t|t-1} = \omega + \alpha u^2_{t-1} + \gamma u^2_{t-1} I_{(u_{t-1}<0)} + \beta \sigma^2_{t-1|t-2},$$

where $I_{(u_{t-1}<0)}$ is an indicator taking a value of 1 if $u_{t-1} < 0$ and 0 if $u_{t-1} \geq 0$. Another one is Nelson (1991)'s popular exponential GARCH (EGARCH) model.[5]

Modeling the Conditional Mean

The mean of returns in (10.2) is often assumed to be a constant when the goal is modeling the return's conditional variance. However, there is no reason why it cannot be specified conditionally as well. For example, a specification that has been found to describe the behavior of returns

[4]Black (1976) put forward the so-called leverage effect as a possible explanation of the asymmetric response of volatility to stock price movements. Everything else held constant, declining stock prices lead to decreased market capitalizations and higher leverage (debt/equity) ratios. This, in turn, implies a higher perceived risk of the respective stocks and greater volatility. It has been found, however, that the leverage effect is insufficient to explain the extent of asymmetries in the market.

[5]See Fornari and Mele (1996) for a comparison of several of the more popular asymmetric volatility models.

well is the ARMA(1,1)–GARCH(1,1) process, in which an autoregressive moving average (ARMA) model of returns is combined with the GARCH specification:[6]

$$r_t = \eta_0 + \eta_1 r_{t-1} + \eta_2 u_{t-1} + \sigma_{t|t-1}\epsilon_t \tag{10.6}$$
$$\sigma^2_{t|t-1} = \omega + \alpha u^2_{t-1} + \beta\sigma^2_{t-1|t-2}.$$

The autoregressive parameter, η_1, takes values between -1 and 1 and measures the impact of the last-period return observation, while the moving average parameter, η_2, represents the influence of last period's return shock. The parameters of the ARMA (1,1) process are estimated together with the GARCH(1,1) parameters.

A different conditional mean specification is provided by the *ARCH-in-mean model*, relating the expected asset return to the asset risk, represented by the conditional standard deviation of returns:[7]

$$\mu_{t|t-1} = \lambda_0 + \lambda_1 \sigma_{t|t-1}. \tag{10.7}$$

The parameter λ_1 can be interpreted as the compensation investors require (in the form of higher expected return) for an increase in the risk of the asset, that is, as the price of risk. The parameter λ_0 could also be given an economic interpretation—as the risk-free rate of return (the required compensation for holding an asset with no risk ($\sigma_{t|t-1} = 0$)).

Although providing increased flexibility, modeling the conditional mean of returns in an ARCH-type model context is not critical. Nelson and Foster (1994) show that the measurement error due to a misspecification in the conditional mean could be trivial in comparison to the measurement error induced by failure to capture nonnormality of the conditional return distribution or the effects of asymmetry in the volatility.

Properties and Estimation of the GARCH(1,1) Process

We review three of the most important properties of the GARCH(1,1) process.

1. The most important property of the GARCH(1,1) process defined in the previous section is *stationarity* (more specifically, covariance (or weak) stationarity). Stationarity of a stochastic process requires that the process has finite moments (means, variances, and covariances) that do not change with time. The covariance between any two components

[6] See Rachev, Stoyanov, Biglova, and Fabozzi (2004).
[7] See Engle, Lilien, and Robins (1987).

of the process, r_{t-h} and r_t, depends only on the distance between them, h. An obvious implication of this requirement is that, if non-stationarity is suspect, we cannot assume that the same distribution governs the return process throughout the time period under consideration.[8] Regime-switching models are an extension that deals with nonstationarity, and we discuss them in the next chapter.

In the setting of normality, the GARCH(1,1) process is stationary if the sum of its coefficients, $\alpha + \beta$, is less than 1. The sum, $\alpha + \beta$, is known as the *GARCH process persistence parameter* since it determines the speed of the mean-reversion of volatility (another empirically observed feature) to its long-term average. A higher value for $\alpha + \beta$ implies that the effect of the shocks to volatility, u_t^2, dies out slowly. In many financial applications, the persistence parameter is close to 1.

When a Student's t-distribution (with ν degrees of freedom) is assumed for returns, the relevant (covariance) stationarity inequality is given by

$$\alpha \frac{\nu}{\nu - 2} + \beta < 1. \tag{10.8}$$

2. The long-run (unconditional) variance of return is given by

$$\sigma^2 = \frac{\omega}{1 - \alpha - \beta}, \tag{10.9}$$

for $0 \leq \alpha + \beta < 1$. The term $1 - \alpha - \beta$ is the weight given to the long-run variance component of the conditional variance $\sigma_{t|t-1}$ (see (10.4)).

3. The autocorrelation of returns is zero, since the autocovariance is

$$\operatorname{cov}(r_{t-h}, r_t) = 0.$$

The autocorrelation of the squared residuals,

$$\operatorname{corr}(u_{t-h}^2, u_t^2) = (\alpha + \beta)^h \frac{\alpha(1 - \alpha\beta - \beta^2)}{(\alpha + \beta)(1 - 2\alpha\beta - \beta^2)},$$

is positive but declines as the distance, h, between the time periods increases.

---

[8] Strictly speaking, covariance stationarity guarantees that the distribution remains unchanged throughout the time period only in the case of normal distribution (since the normal distribution is completely determined by its first two moments). In all other cases, a stronger condition, called *strict stationarity* is needed.

The parameters of the GARCH model are estimated in the classical framework with the help of maximum likelihood methods. Denote the parameter vector of the GARCH process by $\boldsymbol{\theta} = (\omega, \alpha, \beta)$ and the information set at the start of the process by $\Im_0$. The asset return, r_t, depends on $\sigma^2_{t|t-1}$ and, through it, on the volatilities in each of the preceding time periods (due to the presence of the GARCH component in (10.3)). The unconditional density function of r_t is not available in analytical form, since it is a mixture of densities depending on the dynamics of $\sigma^2_{t|t-1}$. Therefore, the likelihood function for $\boldsymbol{\theta}$ is written in terms of the conditional densities of r_t for each t, $t = 1, 2, \ldots, T$.

Given $\Im_0$, the likelihood function $L(\boldsymbol{\theta} \mid r_1, r_2, \ldots, r_T, \Im_0)$ can be represented as the product of conditional densities:[9]

$$L(\boldsymbol{\theta} \mid \boldsymbol{r}, \Im_0) = f(r_1 \mid \boldsymbol{\theta}, \Im_0) f(r_2 \mid \boldsymbol{\theta}, \Im_1) \ldots f(r_T \mid \boldsymbol{\theta}, \Im_{T-1}), \tag{10.10}$$

where $\boldsymbol{r} = (r_1, r_2, \ldots, r_T)$. Using the distributional assumption in (10.5), the log-likelihood function becomes

$$\begin{aligned} \log L(\boldsymbol{\theta} \mid \boldsymbol{r}, \Im_0) &= \sum_{t=1}^{T} \log f(r_t \mid \boldsymbol{\theta}, \Im_{t-1}) \qquad (10.11) \\ &= \text{const} - \frac{1}{2}\left(\sum_{t=1}^{T} \log(\sigma^2_{t|t-1}) + \sum_{t=1}^{T} \frac{(r_t - \mu_{t|t-1})^2}{\sigma^2_{t|t-1}} \right), \end{aligned}$$

where $\sigma^2_{t|t-1}$ is a function of the parameter vector, $\boldsymbol{\theta}$ (according to (10.3)). Since the likelihood function is nonlinear in the parameters, maximization with respect to $\boldsymbol{\theta}$ is accomplished using numerical optimization techniques. It is necessary to specify starting values for the conditional variance and the squared residuals. Assuming that the GARCH model is stationary, these starting values are often taken to be the sample estimates from an earlier (presample) period.

In (10.11) above, we used the default assumption for the return distribution. Quite frequently, however, this assumption is contradicted empirically. Even though, as discussed earlier, the specification of the GARCH model (with the assumption of normality) itself implies an unconditional distribution (a mixture of normals[10]) with tails heavier than these of the normal distribution, it turns out that we might need different

[9]To see that, notice that when $\Im_t$ is defined as an information set consisting of lagged asset returns, $\Im_1 = \Im_0 \bigcup r_1$, $\Im_2 = \Im_1 \bigcup r_2$, etc.

[10]For more details on mixtures of normals, see Chapter 13.

assumptions for the conditional returns distribution, $f(r_t \mid \boldsymbol{\theta}, \Im_{t-1})$. If the conditional distribution of the innovations of the true data-generating process is as given in (10.5), then the empirical distribution of the standardized filtered (fitted) residuals,

$$\widehat{\epsilon_{t|t-1}} = \frac{r_t - \mu_{t|t-1}}{\sqrt{\widehat{\sigma^2_{t|t-1}}}},$$

should be approximately standard normal. (The term $\widehat{\sigma^2_{t|t-1}}$ in the expression above denotes the estimated conditional variance (computed at the maximum-likelihood estimate of $\boldsymbol{\theta}$).) Instead, when modeling weekly, daily or higher-frequency financial data, the residuals' empirical distribution is found to deviate from normality and exhibit heavy tails and skewness. Alternative assumptions for the conditional distribution have been proposed to adequately model the return process, among them the (a)symmetric Student's t-distribution, the *generalized error distribution* (GED), the stable Pareto distribution, and discrete mixtures of normal distributions. (See Chapter 13 for their definitions.)

Rachev, Stoyanov, Biglova, and Fabozzi (2004) compare the normality and the stable Paretian assumptions when estimating an ARMA(1,1)–GARCH(1,1) model for 382 stocks from the S&P 500 index. They examine the distribution of the standardized filtered residuals and find that normality is rejected at the 99% confidence level for over 80% of the stocks, while the stable assumption is rejected for only 6% of the stocks. Mittnik and Paolella (2000) show an almost uniform improvement in the estimation of an AR(1)–GARCH(1,1) model when using the Student's t-distribution instead of a normal distribution, in a study of seven East Asian currency returns. They also advocate a more general parametrization of the Student's t-distribution, which allows for asymmetries in the returns process.[11]

In the presence of nonnormality, a modification of the parametrization of the volatility equation in (10.3) has been found to provide a better fit than (10.3). Instead of an exponent of two, an exponent of one is used in (10.3),[12]

$$\sigma_{t|t-1} = \omega + \alpha|u_{t-1}| + \beta\sigma_{t|t-1}.$$

[11]For a comprehensive survey of the distributional assumptions for GARCH processes, see Palm (1996).

[12]See Nelson and Foster (1994) and Mittnik and Paolella (2000).

STOCHASTIC VOLATILITY MODELS

Stochastic volatility (SV) models assert that volatility evolves according to a stochastic process. As mentioned earlier, the main difference between ARCH-type models and SV models is that in the latter volatility at time t is a latent, unobservable variable, only partially determined by the information up to time t, contained in $\Im_{t-1}$. The motivation for this concept comes from research linking asset prices to information arrivals, for example macroeconomic and earnings releases, trading volume, and number of trades.[13] Some of these arrivals are unpredictable and give rise to shocks in the volatility dynamics.

Stochastic volatility is also directly linked to the "instantaneous volatility" concept from the area of continuous-time asset pricing. SV models are discrete-time approximations of the continuous-time processes used in finance theory.[14]

In empirical work, the SV models are usually formulated in discrete time. In line with this tradition, we now turn to a description of the discrete-time SV model of Taylor (1982, 1986).

Similar to (10.2), the asset return (in excess of its mean which we assume constant for simplicity) is decomposed as

$$r_t - \mu = \sigma_t \epsilon_t. \tag{10.12}$$

Notice that we do not write $\sigma_{t|t-1}$ here, since volatility is not fully determined given $r_1, r_2, \ldots, r_{t-1}$. We assume that the random variables, ϵ_t, are white noise (i.i.d. with zero mean and unit variance).

Taylor (1986) specifies the logarithm of volatility as an autoregressive process of order 1 (AR(1) process):

$$\log(\sigma_t^2) = \rho_0 + \rho_1 \log(\sigma_{t-1}^2) + \eta_t, \tag{10.13}$$

where ρ_1 is a parameter controlling the persistence of volatility (how slowly its autocorrelations decay); and $-1 < \rho_1 < 1$. It plays the role of the sum

[13]See Clark (1973) and Tauchen and Pitts (1983). This is related to the idea of subordinated stochastic processes. One can consider two different time scales—the physical, calendar time and the *intrinsic* time—of the price dynamics. The intrinsic time is best thought of as the cumulative trading volume up to a point on the calendar-time scale. The asset price process is then "directed" by the process governing the trading volume (or, more generally, the information flow). For a detailed discussion of subordination, see Rachev and Mittnik (2000).

[14]See, for example, Hull and White (1987). They replace the assumption of constant volatility in the Black-Scholes option-pricing formula with a stochastic process for the (instantaneous) volatility.

$\alpha + \beta$ in the context of GARCH models with normal distributional assumption. The innovations, η_t, are the source of the volatility's unpredictability and are assumed to be normally distributed with zero mean and variance τ^2. The disturbances ϵ_t and η_t may or may not be independent for all t, $t = 1, \ldots, T$.

Substituting (10.13) into (10.12), we can see that the dynamics of the asset return is now governed by two sources of variability—ϵ_t and η_t—while only data on a single asset return are available. The unobservable parameters are as many as the sample size, which, we see next, complicates model estimation substantially.

Stylized Facts about Returns

SV models explain the same stylized facts about asset returns as GARCH models. Let us review how:

- *Volatility clustering.* The empirical estimates of ρ_1 are generally close to 1. Thus, a high value for the log-volatility at time $t - 1$ implies a high value in the following period as well, leading to a cluster of high volatility.
- *Nonnormality of returns.* The mixture-of-distributions argument put forward in the GARCH case to partially explain the heavy tails (high kurtosis) of asset returns is valid here as well. Asset return, r_t, is distributed as a mixture with mixing parameter τ^2 (the variance of η_t). The mixture exhibits heavier tails compared to the normal distribution.
- *Asymmetric volatility.* The basic SV model, assuming independence of ϵ_t and η_t for all t, does not allow volatility to react in an asymmetric fashion to return shocks. One way to reflect the empirically observed asymmetry is to permit negative correlation between the innovation processes: $\text{corr}(\epsilon_t, \eta_t) < 0$.

Estimation of the Simple SV Model

The estimation of the parameter vector, $\boldsymbol{\theta} = (\rho_0,\ \rho_1,\ \tau^2)$, of the simple SV model is much less straightforward than estimation of the corresponding parameter vector of the simple GARCH(1,1) model.[15] The likelihood function for $\boldsymbol{\theta}$ can be written as the product of conditional densities. The complicating difference relative to the GARCH case is that the unobserved

[15] We assume that the mean of returns, μ, is estimated outside of the model.

volatility needs to be integrated out, giving rise to an analytically intractable expression. We write the likelihood function as

$$L(\boldsymbol{\theta} \mid r_1, r_2, \ldots, r_T) = \int f(r_1, \ldots, r_T \mid \sigma_1, \ldots, \sigma_T, \boldsymbol{\theta}) f(\sigma_1^2, \ldots, \sigma_T^2 \mid \boldsymbol{\theta})\, d\sigma_1^2 \ldots d\sigma_T^2$$

$$= \int \prod_{t=1}^{T} f(r_t \mid \sigma_t^2, \boldsymbol{\theta}, \boldsymbol{r}_{t-1}) f(\sigma_t^2 \mid \boldsymbol{\theta}, \boldsymbol{\sigma}_{-t}^2)\, d\sigma_1^2 \ldots d\sigma_T^2, \quad (10.14)$$

where $\boldsymbol{r}_{t-1} = (r_1, \ \ldots, \ r_{t-1})$ and $\boldsymbol{\sigma}_{-t}^2 = (\sigma_1^2, \ldots, \sigma_{t-1}^2, \sigma_{t+1}^2, \ldots, \sigma_T^2)$. The volatility density is denoted by $f(\sigma_t^2 \mid \boldsymbol{\theta}, \boldsymbol{\sigma}_{t-1}^2)$. The T-dimensional integral in the equation can only be evaluated with the help of numerical methods.

Shephard (2005) and Ghysels, Harvey, and Renault (1996) offer surveys of SV models and estimation techniques. Among those estimation techniques are various *methods of moments* (MM)[16] and *quasi-maximum likelihood* (QML).[17] MM and QML parameter estimates are generally known to be inefficient, thus implying increased parameter uncertainty and less reliable volatility forecasts.

Simulation-based methods are thought to be the most promising path for estimation of the parameter vector $\boldsymbol{\theta}$ because of both the accuracy of the estimators and the flexibility in dealing with complicated models. We briefly review now one such method, the *Efficient Method of Moments* of Gallant and Tauchen (1996) and explain the Bayesian approach later in Chapter 12.

Efficient Method of Moments Consider the return-generating process in (10.12). As discussed, the likelihood function for the parameter vector, $\boldsymbol{\theta}$, (the vector of *structural parameters*, in the terminology of financial econometrics) is not available in analytical form. Suppose that there is a (competing) model of returns whose parameters are easy to estimate. Denote its parameter vector by $\boldsymbol{\zeta}$. The idea of the *Efficient Method of Moments* (EMM)[18] is to use that model, called the *auxiliary model*, as a "special purpose vehicle" in estimating $\boldsymbol{\theta}$. Since our purpose is to model

[16]See Taylor (1986) and Andersen (1994), among others

[17]See Harvey, Ruiz, and Shephard (1994) for an application to multivariate SV model estimation.

[18]We emphasize the practical aspect of EMM estimation here. For its methodological aspects and the statistical properties of the EMM estimators, see Gallant and Tauchen (1996). For an application of EMM to SV models, see Chernov, Ghysels, Gallant, and Tauchen (2003), among others.

volatility, the natural choice of an auxiliary model is a GARCH model. Then $\boldsymbol{\zeta} = (\omega, \alpha, \beta)$ using the notation established earlier in the chapter. Denote by:

$g(r_t \mid \sigma_t, \boldsymbol{\zeta})$ = conditional density of the asset return under the GARCH (auxiliary) model.
$f(r_t \mid \sigma_t, \boldsymbol{\theta})$ = conditional density of the asset return under the SV model.

Let's walk through the steps of the EMM estimation procedure.[19]

1. *Estimate, via maximum-likelihood (possibly numerically), the parameter vector, $\boldsymbol{\zeta}$, of the GARCH auxiliary model. Denote the MLE by $\widehat{\boldsymbol{\zeta}}$.* That is, $\widehat{\boldsymbol{\zeta}}$ satisfies the first-order condition (the first derivative (score) of the log-likelihood function evaluated at $\widehat{\rho}$ is zero),

$$S_T(\widehat{\boldsymbol{\zeta}},\boldsymbol{\theta}) \equiv \frac{1}{T}\sum_{t=1}^{T}\frac{\partial}{\partial\boldsymbol{\zeta}}\log g(r_t \mid \sigma_t,\widehat{\boldsymbol{\zeta}}) = 0, \tag{10.15}$$

for a sample of size T. The score, S_T, is a vector of the same dimension as $\boldsymbol{\zeta}$.
We suppose that, in some sense, $\boldsymbol{\zeta}$ and $\boldsymbol{\theta}$, are close—$\boldsymbol{\theta}$ is the "true" set of parameters that, we believe, generated the data (r_t, σ_t), while $\boldsymbol{\zeta}$ is the set of parameters of another credible data-generating model. That is, without claiming a functional correspondence between f and g, we can write

$$f(r_t \mid \sigma_t,\boldsymbol{\theta}) \sim g(r_t \mid \sigma_t,\boldsymbol{\zeta}).$$

2. *Guess a value for $\boldsymbol{\theta}$ and simulate a sample $(r^*_{(n)}, \sigma^*_{(n)})$ of size N ($n = 1, \ldots,$ N) from the "true" data-generating process, $f(r_t|\sigma_t, \boldsymbol{\theta})$.* Then, evoking the "closeness" of $\boldsymbol{\zeta}$ and $\boldsymbol{\theta}$, we could expect that[20]

$$S_N(\widehat{\zeta},\boldsymbol{\theta}) = \frac{1}{N}\sum_{n=1}^{N}\frac{\partial}{\partial\zeta}\log g(r^*_{(n)}|\sigma^*_{(n)},\widehat{\zeta}) \approx 0. \tag{10.16}$$

[19]We express gratitude to Doug Steigerwald from the Department of Economics at the University of California, Santa Barbara, for providing consulting assistance on the topic of EMM estimation.
[20]The expression in (10.16) is the empirical analog to the GMM moment equation

$$S(\widehat{\zeta},\boldsymbol{\theta}) = \int \frac{\partial}{\partial\boldsymbol{\zeta}}\log g(r_t \mid \sigma_t,\widehat{\zeta})f(r_t \mid \sigma_t,\boldsymbol{\theta})\,d\sigma_t.$$

Note that $\boldsymbol{\theta}$ is only implicitly present above (its value determined $r^*_{(n)}$ and $\sigma^*_{(n)}$).

3. *Compute the value of the criterion function, Δ, using the MLE, $\widehat{\boldsymbol{\zeta}}$, to assess the proximity of the score to 0:*

$$\Delta \equiv S_N(\widehat{\boldsymbol{\zeta}},\boldsymbol{\theta})'\widehat{I}_N^{-1}S_N(\widehat{\boldsymbol{\zeta}},\boldsymbol{\theta}). \tag{10.17}$$

The weighting matrix, $\widehat{I}_N$, is computed as the covariance matrix estimator

$$\widehat{I}_N = \frac{1}{N}\sum_{n=1}^{N}\left[\frac{\partial}{\partial\boldsymbol{\zeta}}\log g(r^*_{(n)} \mid \sigma^*_{(n)},\widehat{\boldsymbol{\zeta}})\right]\left[\frac{\partial}{\partial\boldsymbol{\zeta}}\log g(r^*_{(n)} \mid \sigma^*_{(n)},\widehat{\boldsymbol{\zeta}})\right]'.$$

4. *Iterate the procedure a large number of times by guessing a different value for $\boldsymbol{\theta}$, simulating a sample $\left(r^*_{(n)},\sigma^*_{(n)}\right)$ and computing the criterion function in* (10.17).
5. *Select as the EMM estimator of $\boldsymbol{\theta}$ the parameter vector value for which the criterion function has minimal value; that is,*

$$\widehat{\boldsymbol{\theta}} = \arg\min_{\boldsymbol{\theta}} \Delta. \tag{10.18}$$

ILLUSTRATION: FORECASTING VALUE-AT-RISK

Value-at-risk (VaR) is a measure of the possible maximum loss that could be incurred (with a given probability) by an investment over a given period of time. VaR has become the standard tool used by risk managers thanks in part to its adoption in 1993 by the Basel Committee (at the Bank for International Settlements) as a technique for assessing capital requirements of banks.[21] We discuss the advantages and deficiencies of VaR as a risk measure in Chapter 13. Here, we focus on how volatility models could be used to assess VaR.

In statistical terms, the VaR at significance level α is simply the $1 - \alpha$ quantile of the return distribution. Volatility model predictions can be used to compute the VaR, since a distribution's quantile is a

[21]VaR models originated with the work of the RiskMetrics Group at JP Morgan (Risk-Metrics Technical Document (1986)). For more on VaR, see Jorion (2000), Khindanova and Rachev (2000), and Rachev, Khindanova, and Schwartz (2001).

function of the distribution variance. Consider the model for asset returns in (10.2) and suppose that the disturbances, ϵ_t, have a normal distribution. Then the asset return is distributed conditionally as $N\left(\mu_{t|t-1}, \sigma^2_{t|t-1}\right)$. (The unconditional distribution is nonnormal and fat-tailed.) The 5% quantile of the normal return distribution (that is, the return threshold such that there is 5% chance of occurrences below it) is given by the expression

$$\mu_{t|t-1} - 1.65\sigma_{t|t-1},$$

where −1.645 is the 5% quantile of the standard normal distribution. In Chapter 11, we consider a Student's t GARCH(1,1) model. The 5% quantile of the return distribution is computed from the expression

$$\mu_{t|t-1} - 1.81\frac{\nu}{\nu - 2}\sigma_{t|t-1},$$

where −1.81 is the 5% quantile of the Student's t-distribution (with mean zero and scale 1) with ν degrees of freedom. (While the conditional return distribution is Student's t, the unconditional distribution is not and has tails heavier than those of the Student's t-distribution.) As an illustration, consider Exhibit 10.1 in which daily MSCI Canadian (innovations of) returns, together with the corresponding VaR at the 95% confidence level, are plotted. (See Chapter 11 for details on that illustration.) While returns are expected to violate the VaR threshold at the 5% confidence level about 5% of the time, the violations in this particular illustration are only 3.4%.

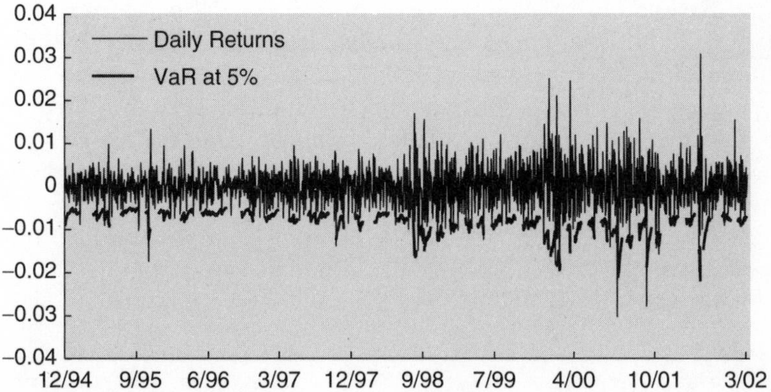

EXHIBIT 10.1 Daily MSCI canadian returns and value-at-risk

AN ARCH-TYPE MODEL OR A STOCHASTIC VOLATILITY MODEL?

The inevitable question arising in a discussion of volatility estimation is which type of models, ARCH-type or SV, is a better tool for modeling asset volatility. A definitive answer is not available. Nevertheless, casting aside the differences in the difficulty level of model estimation (favoring ARCH-type models), one could argue that evidence points to an advantage of the basic SV model over the basic GARCH(1,1) model. For example, Geweke (1995) performs a comparison of the two with the help of posterior odds ratios.[22] Although the two models, applied to exchange rates dynamics, fare similarly well in periods of low volatility and sustained volatility, the SV model provides a superior prediction record in periods of volatility jumps. In particular, empirically observed volatility jumps are more plausible under the SV model than under the GARCH model. We should note, however, that this conclusion is valid under normal distributional assumptions for both models. Asserting a heavy-tailed return distribution in the GARCH setting is likely to correct for that deficiency.

In a comparison of a different nature, Jacquier, Polson, and Rossi (1994) find that the SV model provides a better and more robust description of the autocorrelation pattern of squared stock returns than a GARCH model, while some investigations[23] have found that the GARCH-filtered residuals exhibit serial correlation, unlike the SV-filtered residuals.

WHERE DO BAYESIAN METHODS FIT?

In the previous chapters, we explained that the principal motivation for employing Bayesian methods in estimation of the model parameters is to account for the intrinsic uncertainty surrounding the estimation process. Since empirical finance modeling is often ultimately aimed at forecasting, clearly the plug-in approach where parameter estimates are substituted for the unknown parameters in the prediction formulas carries the risk of being the suboptimal approach. These arguments are valid with full force in the area of volatility estimation and prediction.

A different motivator for the use of Bayesian methods that we have not previously emphasized explicitly is the formidable power of the *Markov Chain Monte Carlo* (MCMC) *toolbox* in handling complicated models.

[22] We briefly described the posterior odds ratio in Chapter 3.
[23] For example, Hsieh (1991).

Even when an analytical expression for the likelihood function is available, incorporating the various inequality constraints that practical applications require is often not straightforward in a maximum-likelihood environment. Moreover, in situations where the likelihood function is nonlinear in the parameters (virtually all realistic models of financial phenomena), likelihood optimization could be a prohibitively arduous task, because of the existence of numerous local optimal points.

Although sometimes computationally complex, the MCMC framework provides a very flexible avenue for exploring the posterior distributions of not only the model parameters but functions of them, and to construct the predictive distribution, all in a single procedure.

In the next two chapters, we discuss the applications of Bayesian methods to, respectively, ARCH-type models and SV models and their extensions.

CHAPTER 11

Bayesian Estimation of ARCH-Type Volatility Models

In the previous chapter, we provided an overview of the two major groups of volatility models, the *autoregressive conditional heteroskedastic* (ARCH)-type models and the *stochastic volatility* (SV) models. The purpose of this chapter is to discuss in detail the Bayesian estimation of the first group of volatility models.

The Bayesian methodology offers a distinct advantage over the classical framework in estimating ARCH-type processes. For example, inequality restrictions, such as a stationarity restriction, are notoriously difficult to handle within the frequentist setting and straightforward to implement in the Bayesian one.[1] Moreover, in the Bayesian setting, one could easily obtain the distribution of the measure of stationarity and explore the extent to which stationarity is supported by the observed data.

Typically, the estimated sum of the parameters capturing the ARCH and *generalized autoregressive conditional heteroskedastic* (GARCH) effects[2] is very close to 1, suggesting that shocks to the conditional variance take a long time to dissipate. Engle and Bollerslev (1986) introduced the integrated GARCH (IGARCH) process to describe the process when the sum is equal to one. In that case, shocks to the variance have a permanent effect on future conditional variances, and the unconditional variance of returns does not exist. One possible explanation for the high persistence in volatility is that the ARCH and GARCH parameters vary through time, so that an increase in the estimated sum is actually an underlying change in the conditional variance parameters.[3]

---

[1]See, for example, Geweke (1989).

[2]These two parameters are α and β, respectively, in equation (11.2).

[3]See, for example, Lamoureux and Lastrapes (1990) and Diebold and Inoue (2001).

Changes in parameters can be divided into two broad categories: permanent and reversible. The first type of change takes the form of a permanent, deterministic shift in the parameter value and is caused by an exogenous factor, a structural break. Some examples of structural breaks are stock market crashes, changes in the data-collection and data-processing practices of data providers, and shifts in the economic paradigm.

It is possible that the time variation of model parameters is due to underlying transitions of the data generating process among different regimes (states of the world). Business cycle fluctuations are an example of such endogenous factors. The class of models usually employed to describe return and volatility dynamics in a regime-switching environment is the Markov (regime-) switching class of models.

In the first part of this chapter, we focus on the simple GARCH(1,1) model with Student's t-distributed disturbances. In the second part, in line with the growing interest among practitioners, we present a Markov regime-switching extension.

BAYESIAN ESTIMATION OF THE SIMPLE GARCH(1,1) MODEL

Most of the Bayesian empirical investigations of GARCH processes emphasize the computational aspects of the models, rather than the choice of prior distributions for the model parameters. One reason for this is that few, if any, restrictions exist on the choice of prior distributions since posterior inference is, without exception, performed numerically. As we discussed in the previous chapter, since the variance is modeled dynamically, the unconditional density of r_t is not available in closed form and the likelihood for the GARCH model parameters, $L(\theta \mid \mathbf{r}, \Im_0)$, is represented in terms of the product of the conditional densities of returns for each period (see (10.8) in Chapter 10).

In this chapter, in order to reflect the recent trend in the empirical finance literature, our focus is on the Student's t distributional assumption for the return disturbances. (Estimation based on the normal distribution is performed in a similar way.) This comes at the expense of only a marginal increase in complexity. Two sampling methods that were discussed in Chapter 5 are employed to simulate the posterior distribution of the vector of model parameters, θ, the Metropolis-Hastings algorithm and the Gibbs sampler.[4]

[4]See also Geweke (1989) for an application of importance sampling (discussed in Chapter 5) to the estimation of ARCH models.

The model we consider is described by the following expressions for the return and volatility dynamics,

$$r_t = \mathbf{X}_t\gamma + \sigma_{t|t-1}\epsilon_t, \tag{11.1}$$

for $t = 1, \ldots, T$, and

$$\sigma^2_{t|t-1} = \omega + \alpha u^2_{t-1} + \beta\sigma^2_{t-1|t-2}, \tag{11.2}$$

where $u_{t-1} = r_t - \mathbf{X}_t\boldsymbol{\gamma}$. The mean of returns in (11.1) is unconditional and modeled as a linear combination of $K - 1$ factor returns. If the variance of returns were constant, (11.1) would have defined a linear regression model for the return, r_t, $t = 1, \ldots, T$, of the type we discussed in Chapter 4.[5] The observations of the factor returns at time t are represented by the $1 \times K$ vector, $\mathbf{X}_t$, whose first element is 1. The $K \times 1$ vector, γ, is the vector of regression coefficients whose first element is the regression intercept.

Distributional Setup

Next, we outline the general setup we use in our presentation of the Bayesian estimation of the GARCH(1,1) model. We modify this setup in the second half of the chapter, where we discuss regime switching.

Likelihood Function Denote the observed return data by $r = (r_1, \ldots, r_T)$ and the model's parameter vector by $\theta = (\omega, \alpha, \beta, \nu, \gamma')$. Assuming that ϵ_t is distributed with a Student's t-distribution with ν degrees of freedom, we write the likelihood function for the model's parameters as

$$L(\theta \mid r, \Im_0) \propto \prod_{t=1}^{T}\left[\left(\sigma^2_{t|t-1}\right)^{-1}\left(1 + \frac{1}{\nu}\frac{\left(r_t - \mathbf{X}_t\gamma\right)^2}{\sigma^2_{t|t-1}}\right)^{-\frac{\nu+1}{2}}\right], \tag{11.3}$$

where σ_0^2, is considered as a known constant, for simplicity. Under the Student's t assumption for ϵ_t, the conditional volatility at time t is given by

$$\frac{\nu}{\nu - 2}\sigma_t^2,$$

for ν greater than 2.

[5] See also our discussion of modeling the conditional mean in Chapter 10. For simplicity, it is certainly possible to assume that $\mu_{t|t-1}$ is a constant (but unknown) parameter.

Prior Distributions For simplicity, assume that the conditional variance parameters have uninformative diffuse prior distributions over their respective ranges,[6]

$$\pi(\omega, \alpha, \beta) \propto 1 I_{\{\theta_G\}}, \tag{11.4}$$

where $I_{\{\theta_G\}}$ is an indicator function reflecting the constraints on the conditional variance parameters,

$$I_{\{\theta_G\}} = \begin{cases} 1 & \text{if } \omega > 0, \alpha > 0, \text{and } \beta > 0, \\ 0 & \text{otherwise.} \end{cases} \tag{11.5}$$

The choice of prior distribution for the degrees-of-freedom parameter, ν, requires more care. Bauwens and Lubrano (1998) show that if a diffuse prior for ν is asserted on the interval $[0, \infty)$, the posterior distribution of ν is not proper. (Its right tail does not decay quickly enough such that the posterior does not integrate to 1.) Therefore, the prior for ν needs to be proper. Geweke (1993a) advocates the use of an exponential prior distribution with density given by

$$\pi(\nu) = \lambda \exp(-\nu\lambda). \tag{11.6}$$

The mean of the exponential distribution is given by $1/\lambda$. The parameter λ can thus be uniquely determined from the prior intuition about ν's mean. Another prior option for ν is a uniform prior over an interval $[0, K]$, where K is some finite number. Empirical research indicates that the degrees-of-freedom parameter calibrated from financial returns data (especially of daily and higher frequency) is usually less than 20, so the upper bound, K, of ν's range could be fixed at 20, for instance. Bauwens and Lubrano propose a third prior for ν—the upper half of a Cauchy distribution centered around zero. In our discussion, we adopt the exponential prior distribution for ν in (11.6).

Finally, for reasons of convenience, we assume a normal prior for the regression parameters, γ,

$$\pi(\gamma) = \mathrm{N}(\mu_\gamma, \Sigma_\gamma). \tag{11.7}$$

---

[6]It is possible to assert a prior distribution for ω, α, and β defined on the whole real line, for example, a normal distribution. To respect the constraints on the values the parameters can take, that prior would have to be truncated at the lower bound of the parameters' range. In practice, the constraints are enforced during the posterior simulation as explained further below. Alternatively, one could transform ω, α, and β by taking the logarithm and assert such a prior on the log-parameters, with no truncation.

In this chapter, we are not bound by arguments of conjugacy (as in Chapter 4) and we assert a covariance for γ independent of the return variance, $\sigma^2_{t|t-1}$. (See Chapter 3 for our discussion of prior parameter elicitation.)

Posterior Distributions Given the distributional assumptions above, the posterior distribution of θ is written as

$$
\begin{aligned}
p(\theta \mid \mathbf{r}, \Im_0) \propto \prod_{t=1}^{T} & \left[(\sigma^2_{t|t-1})^{-1} \left(1 + \frac{1}{\nu} \frac{(r_t - \mathbf{X}_t\gamma)^2}{\sigma^2_{t|t-1}} \right)^{-\frac{\nu+1}{2}} \right] \\
& \times \exp\left(-\nu\lambda\right) \\
& \times \exp\left(-\frac{1}{2}(\gamma - \mu_\gamma)'\Sigma^{-1}(\gamma - \mu_\gamma) \right) \\
& \times I_{\{\theta_G\}}.
\end{aligned}
\tag{11.8}
$$

The restrictions on ω, α, and β are enforced during the sampling procedure by rejecting the draws that violate them. Stationarity can also be imposed and dealt with in the same way.

The joint posterior density clearly does not have a closed form. As it turns out, posterior simulations are facilitated if one employs the representation of the Student's t-distribution, which we discuss next, before moving on to sampling algorithms.

Mixture of Normals Representation of the Student's *t*-Distribution

Earlier, we assumed that the asset return has the Student's t-distribution,

$$
r_t \mid \gamma, \sigma^2_{t|t-1} \sim t_\nu\left(X_t\gamma, \sigma_{t|t-1}\right), \tag{11.9}
$$

where we use the notation for the Student's t-distribution established in Chapter 3. It can be shown that the distributional assumption in (11.9) is equivalent to the assumption that

$$
r_t \mid \gamma, \sigma^2_{t|t-1}, \eta_t \sim \mathrm{N}\left(\mathbf{X}_t\gamma, \frac{\sigma^2_{t|t-1}}{\eta_t} \right), \tag{11.10}
$$

where η_t, the so-called *mixing variables*, are independently and identically distributed with a gamma distribution,

$$
\eta_t \mid \nu \sim \text{Gamma}\left(\frac{\nu}{2}, \frac{\nu}{2} \right), \tag{11.11}
$$

for $t = 1, \ldots, T$. The expressions in (11.10) and (11.11) constitute the scale mixture of normal distributions (i.e., "normals") representation of the Student's t-distribution.[7] The benefit of employing this representation is increased tractability of the posterior distribution because the nonlinear expression for the model's likelihood in (11.3) is linearized. Sampling from the conditional distributions of the remaining parameters is thus greatly facilitated. This comes at the expense of T additional model parameters, $\eta = (\eta_1, \ldots, \eta_T)'$, whose conditional posterior distribution needs to be simulated as well.[8]

Under the new representation, the parameter vector, θ, is transformed to

$$\theta = \left(\omega, \alpha, \beta, \nu, \gamma', \eta'\right). \tag{11.12}$$

The log-likelihood function for θ is simply the normal log-likelihood,

$$\log\left(L(\theta \mid r, \Im_0)\right) = \text{const} - \frac{1}{2}\sum_{t=1}^{T}\left[\log\left(\sigma^2_{t|t-1}\right) - \log\left(\eta_t\right) + \frac{\eta_t(r_t - \mathbf{X}_t\gamma)^2}{\sigma^2_{t|t-1}}\right]. \tag{11.13}$$

The posterior distribution of θ has an additional term reflecting the mixing variables' distribution. The log-posterior is written as

$$\begin{aligned}\log\left(p(\theta \mid \mathbf{r}, \Im_0)\right) = {} & \text{const} - \frac{1}{2}\sum_{t=1}^{T}\left[\log\left(\sigma^2_{t|t-1}\right) - \log\left(\eta_t\right) + \frac{\eta_t(r_t - \mathbf{X}_t\gamma)^2}{\sigma^2_{t|t-1}}\right] \\ & - \frac{1}{2}(\gamma - \mu_\gamma)'\Sigma_\gamma^{-1}(\gamma - \mu_\gamma) \\ & + \frac{T\nu}{2}\log\left(\frac{\nu}{2}\right) - T\log\left(\Gamma\left(\frac{\nu}{2}\right)\right) + \left(\frac{\nu}{2} - 1\right)\sum_{t=1}^{T}\log\left(\eta_t\right)\end{aligned}$$

---

[7]Many heavy-tailed distributions can be represented as (mean-) scale mixtures of normal distributions. Such representations make estimation based on numerical, iterative procedures easier. See, for example, Fernandez and Steel (2000) for a discussion of the Bayesian treatment of regression analysis with mixtures of normals. In continuous time, the mean and scale mixture of normals models lead to the so-called subordinated processes, widely used in mathematical and empirical finance. Rachev and Mittnik (2000) offer an extensive treatment of subordinated processes. We provide a brief description of mixtures of normal distributions in Chapter 13.

[8]This is an example of the technique known as *data augmentation*. It consists of introducing latent (unobserved) variables to help construct efficient simulation algorithms. For a (technical) review of data augmentation, see van Dyk and Meng (2001).

$$-\frac{\nu}{2}\sum_{t=1}^{T}(\eta_t) - \nu\lambda,$$

$$\text{for} \quad \omega > 0, \quad \alpha \geq 0, \quad \text{and} \quad \beta \geq 0. \tag{11.14}$$

Next, we discuss some strategies for simulating the posterior in (11.14).

GARCH(1,1) Estimation Using the Metropolis-Hastings Algorithm

In Chapter 5, we explained that the Metropolis-Hastings (M-H) algorithm could be implemented in two ways. The first way is by sampling the whole parameter vector, θ, from a proposal distribution (usually a multivariate Student's t-distribution) centered on the posterior mode and scaled by the negative inverse Hessian (evaluated at the posterior mode). The second way is by employing a sampling scheme in which the parameter vector is updated component by component. Here, we focus on the latter M-H implementation.

Consider the decomposition of the parameter vector θ into four components, $\theta = (\theta_G, \nu, \gamma', \eta')$, where $\theta_G = (\omega, \alpha, \beta)$. We would like to employ a scheme of sampling consecutively from the conditional posterior distributions of the four components given, respectively, by

$$p\,(\theta_G \,|\, \gamma, \eta, \nu, \mathbf{r}, \Im_0),$$

$$p\,(\nu \,|\, \theta_G, \gamma, \eta, \mathbf{r}, \Im_0),$$

$$p\,(\gamma \,|\, \theta_G, \eta, \nu, \mathbf{r}, \Im_0),$$

and

$$p\,(\eta \,|\, \theta_G, \gamma, \nu, \mathbf{r}, \Im_0).$$

The scale mixture of normals representation of a Student's t-distribution allows us to recognize the conditional posterior distributions of the last two components, γ and η, as standard distributions. For the first two components, θ_G and ν, whose posterior distributions are not of standard form, we offer two posterior simulation approaches and mention alternatives that have been suggested in the literature.

Conditional Posterior Distribution for γ It can be shown that the full conditional posterior distribution of γ is a normal distribution,

$$p\,(\gamma \,|\, \theta_G, \eta, \nu, \mathbf{r}, \Im_0) = \mathrm{N}\,(\gamma^*, V). \tag{11.15}$$

The mean and covariance of that normal distribution are defined as

$$\gamma^* = V\left(X'D^{-1}X\widehat{\gamma} + \Sigma_\gamma^{-1}\mu_\gamma\right)$$

and

$$V = \left(X'D^{-1}X + \Sigma_\gamma^{-1}\right)^{-1},$$

where:

D in the diagonal matrix with diagonal elements $\sigma^2_{t|t-1}/\eta_t$ and off-diagonal elements equal to zero,

$$D = \begin{pmatrix} \frac{\sigma^2_{1|0}}{\eta_1} & 0 & 0 & \cdots & 0 \\ 0 & \frac{\sigma^2_{2|1}}{\eta_2} & 0 & \cdots & 0 \\ \cdots & \cdots & \cdots & \cdots & \cdots \\ 0 & 0 & \cdots & 0 & \frac{\sigma^2_{T|T-1}}{\eta_T} \end{pmatrix}, \tag{11.16}$$

where $\sigma^2_{1|0}$ is conditional on the initial variance, σ^2_0 (assumed known).

$\widehat{\gamma}$ = least-squares estimates of γ from running the regression $r_t = \mathbf{X}_t\boldsymbol{\gamma} + \sigma_{t|t-1}\epsilon_t, t = 1, \ldots, T$, for fixed values of the conditional variance parameters. The disturbance, ϵ_t, has a Student's t-distribution,

$X = T \times K$ matrix whose rows are the observations of the explanatory variables, X_t, for each time period, $t = 1, \ldots, T$.

Conditional Posterior Distribution for η The full conditional posterior distribution for the (independently distributed) mixing parameters, η_t, $t = 1, \ldots, T$, can be shown to be a gamma distribution,

$$p\left(\eta_t \mid \theta_G, \gamma, \nu, r, \Im_0\right) = \text{Gamma}\left(\frac{\nu+1}{2}, \frac{\left(r_t - \mathbf{X}_t\gamma\right)^2}{2\sigma^2_{t|t-1}} + \frac{\nu}{2}\right). \tag{11.17}$$

Conditional Posterior Distribution for ν It can be seen, from (11.14) that the conditional posterior distribution of the degrees-of-freedom parameter, ν, does not have a standard form. The kernel of the posterior distribution is given by the expression,

$$p\left(\nu \mid \theta_G, \gamma, \eta, \mathbf{r}, \Im_0\right) \propto \Gamma\left(\frac{\nu}{2}\right)^{-T}\left(\frac{\nu}{2}\right)^{\frac{T\nu}{2}} \exp\left[\nu\lambda^*\right], \tag{11.18}$$

where

$$\lambda^* = \frac{1}{2}\sum_{t=1}^{T}\left(\log(\eta_t) - \eta_t\right) - \lambda. \tag{11.19}$$

Geweke (1993b) describes a rejection sampling approach that could be employed to simulate draws from the conditional posterior distribution of ν in (11.18). In this chapter, we employ a sampling algorithm called the *griddy Gibbs sampler*. The appendix provides details on it.

Proposal Distribution for θ_G The kernel of θ_G's log-posterior distribution is given by the expression,

$$\log\left(p\left(\theta_G \mid \theta_{-\theta_G}, \mathbf{r}, \Im_0\right)\right) = \text{const} - \frac{1}{2}\sum_{t=1}^{T}\left[\log\left(\sigma^2_{t|t-1}\right) + \frac{\eta_t(r_t - \mathbf{X}_t\gamma)^2}{\sigma^2_{t|t-1}}\right],$$
$$\text{for} \quad \omega > 0, \quad \alpha \geq 0, \quad \text{and} \quad \beta \geq 0.$$

where $\sigma^2_{t|t-1}$, $t = 1, \ldots, T$, is a function of θ_G.

We specify a Student's t proposal distribution for θ_G, centered on the posterior mode of θ_G (the value that maximizes (11.20)) and scaled by the negative inverse Hessian of the posterior kernel, evaluated at the posterior mode, as explained in Chapter 5. Other approaches for posterior simulation, for example, the griddy Gibbs sampler, could be employed as well. (In this case, the components of θ_G would be sampled separately.)

Having determined the full conditional posterior distributions for γ and η, as well as a proposal distribution for θ_G and a sampling scheme for ν, implementing a hybrid M-H algorithm, as explained in Chapter 5, is straightforward. Its steps are as follows. At iteration m of the algorithm:

1. Draw an observation, $\boldsymbol{\theta}^*_G$, of the vector of conditional variance parameters, θ_G, from its proposal distribution.
2. Check whether the parameter restrictions on the components of $\theta_{G,i}$ are satisfied; if not, draw $\theta^*_{G,i}$ repeatedly until they are satisfied.
3. Compute the acceptance probability in (5.7) in Chapter 5 and accept or reject θ^*_G.
4. Draw an observation, $\gamma^{(m)}$, from the full conditional posterior distribution, $p\left(\gamma \mid \theta_G^{(m)}, \eta^{(m-1)}, \mathbf{r}, \Im_0\right)$, in (11.15).
5. Draw an observation, $\eta^{(m)}$, from the full conditional posterior distribution, $p\left(\eta_t \mid \theta_G^{(m)}, \gamma^{(m)}, \mathbf{r}, \Im_0\right)$, in (11.17).
6. Draw an observation, $\nu^{(m)}$, from its conditional posterior distribution with kernel in (11.18) using the griddy Gibbs sampler as explained in the appendix.

At each iteration of the sampling algorithm, the sampling strategy just described produces a large output consisting of the draws from the model parameters and the T mixing variables, η. However, since the role of the mixing parameters is only auxiliary and their conditional distribution is of no interest, at any iteration of the algorithm above the researcher needs to store only the latest draw of η.

Illustration: Student's *t* GARCH(1,1) Model

Next, we illustrate the GARCH(1,1) model with Student's t disturbances. Our data sample consists of the daily return data on the same eight MSCI World Index constituents we considered in Chapter 8. As dependent variable, we choose the Canada MSCI index return. We employ principal component analysis to extract the returns on the five factors with greatest explanatory power using the observed data of the eight indexes. We use these factor returns as the explanatory variables in $\mathbf{X}$. We estimate the GARCH(1,1) model using 1,901 return observations spanning December 1, 1994, to March 18, 2002. The prior parameters of the regression coefficients are determined using estimates from an earlier time period. (See Chapter 3 for our discussion on prior parameter elicitation.) We set the prior mean of the degrees-of-freedom parameter, ν, at 5, that is, $\lambda = 0.2$ in (11.6). The initial variance, σ_0^2, is treated as a known constant and set equal to the unconditional variance of $u = Y - X\boldsymbol{\gamma}$.

We let the MH algorithm run for 10,000 iterations and use only the latter 5,000 for posterior inference. Exhibit 11.1 presents histograms of the posterior draws of the three conditional variance parameters, ω, α, and β.

To explore whether the hypothesis of (covariance) stationarity is supported by the observed data, we compute the posterior distribution of the quantity $\alpha\nu/(\nu - 2) + \beta$ (see (10.8) in Chapter 10). The histogram of the draws from that posterior distribution is presented in part D of Exhibit 11.1. Only a small fraction of the posterior mass lies above 1, indicating that the hypothesis of stationarity is largely supported by the data. Further in the chapter, in our discussion on regime-switching models, we examine the extent to which that high degree of volatility persistence could be ascribed to the existence of regimes in the conditional volatility dynamics.

The posterior means and standard errors of all model coefficients are given in Exhibit 11.2. Notice that the posterior mean of ν is 9.24, suggesting that normality would have been an inadequate assumption for the distribution of MSCI Canadian daily returns.

Exhibit 11.3 plots the estimated time series of the (smoothed) volatility for the sample period, together with the time series of MSCI Canadian returns and squared return innovations.

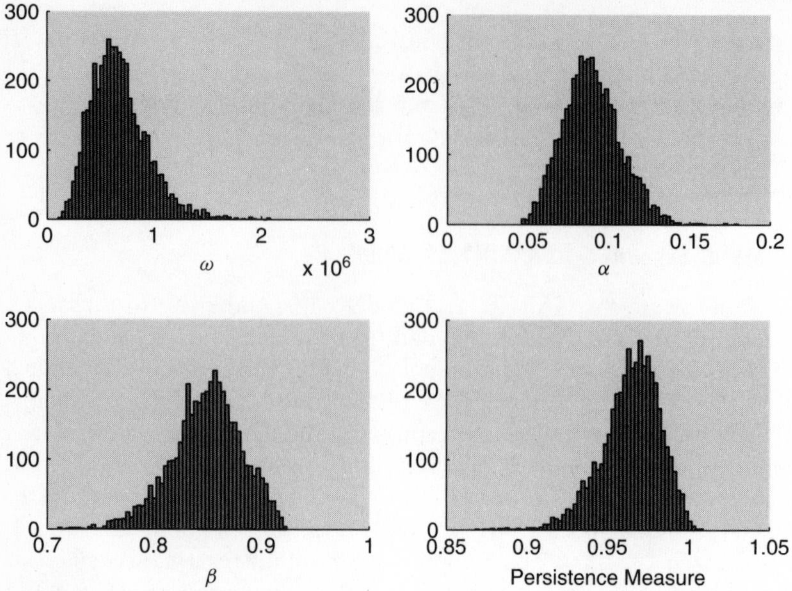

EXHIBIT 11.1 Histograms of posterior draws of the conditional variance parameters and persistence measure

ω	α	β	ν	Persistence Measure	
6.77e-7 (2.6e-7)	0.089 (0.018)	0.849 (0.033)	9.240 (1.496)	0.965 (0.017)	
γ^1	γ^2	γ^3	γ^4	γ^5	γ^6
−1.48e-4 (8.4e-5)	0.302 (0.004)	−0.083 (0.007)	−0.653 (0.008)	0.056 (0.009)	0.064 (0.012)

EXHIBIT 11.2 Posterior means of the parameters in the simple GARCH(1,1) model
Note: The posterior standard errors are in parentheses.

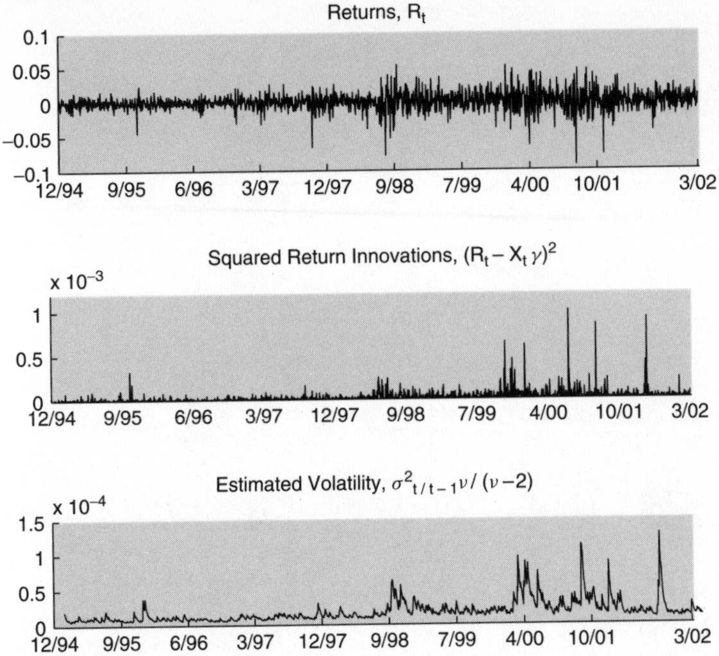

EXHIBIT 11.3 Estimated volatility

Finally, we consider the forecasting power of the simple GARCH(1,1) model and, in Exhibit 11.4, plot the time series of returns and squared return innovations for the period March 19, 2002, through December 31, 2003 (467 observations), together with the one-day-ahead volatility forecasts. We can see that the quality of the volatility forecast is generally very good. However, it does fail to capture accurately all shocks in the realized return data. For example, notice that the earlier spike in volatility around February 2003 is overpredicted, while the later spike around the same period is underpredicted. One could notice several more such prediction discrepancies.

The forecasting inaccuracy of the simple model could be ascribed to the possibility that the volatility dynamics themselves differ in different periods. Then, volatility forecasts produced by a simple (single-regime) model are likely to overestimate volatility during periods of low volatility and underestimate it during periods of high volatility. In the next section, we discuss a class of models extending the simple GARCH(1,1) model which could potentially provide more accurate volatility forecasting power. Regime-switching models incorporate the possibility that the dynamics of the volatility process evolves through different states of nature (regimes).

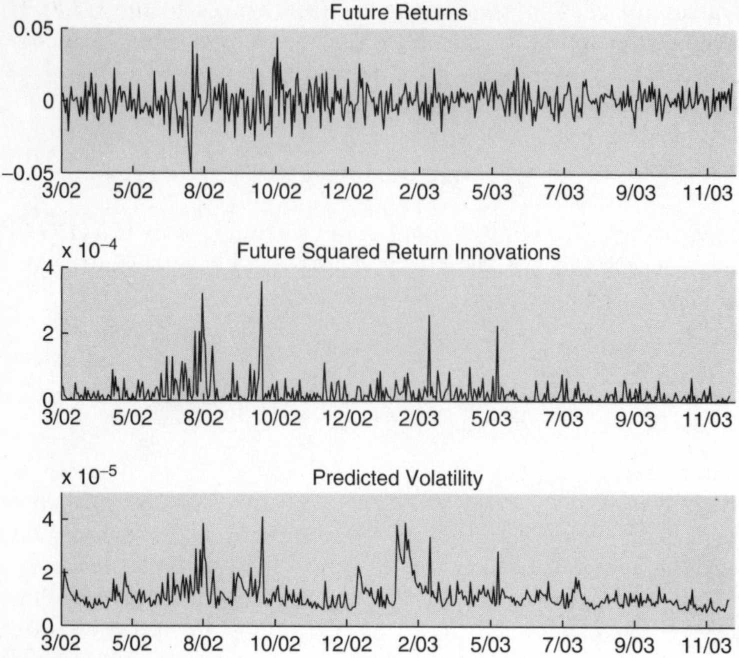

EXHIBIT 11.4 Volatility forecasts

MARKOV REGIME-SWITCHING GARCH MODELS

The *Markov switching* (MS) models, introduced by Hamilton (1989), provide maximal flexibility in modeling transitions of the volatility dynamics across regimes. They form the class of *endogenous regime-switching models* in which transitions between states of nature are governed by parameters estimated within the model; the number of transitions is not specified *a priori*, unlike the number of states. Each volatility state could be revisited multiple times.[9] In our discussion that follows, we use the terms *state* and *regime* interchangeably.

[9]It is certainly possible to introduce (test for) a deterministic permanent shift in a model parameter into the regime-switching model. For example, Kim and Nelson (1999) apply such a model to a Bayesian investigation of business cycle fluctuations. See also Carlin, Gelfand, and Smith (1992). Wang and Zivot (2000) consider Bayesian estimation of a heteroskedastic model with structural breaks only. The variance in that investigation, however, does not evolve according to an ARCH-type process.

Different approaches to introducing regime changes in the GARCH process have been proposed in the empirical finance literature. Hamilton and Susmel (1994) incorporate a regime-dependent parameter, g_{S_t}, into the standard deviation (scale) of the returns process in (11.2),

$$r_t = \mu_{t|t-1} + \sqrt{g_{S_t}}\sigma_{t|t-1}\epsilon_t,$$

where S_t denotes period t's regime. Another option, pursued by Cai (1994), is to include a regime-dependent parameter as part of the constant in the conditional variance equation (11.2),

$$\sigma^2_{t|t-1} = (\omega + g_{S_t}) + \sum_{p=1}^{P} \alpha_p u^2_{t-p}.$$

Both Hamilton and Susmel (1994) and Cai (1994) model the dynamics of the conditional variance with an ARCH process. The reason, as explained further on, is that when GARCH term(s) are present in the process, the regime-dependence makes the likelihood function analytically intractable.

The most flexible approach to introducing regime dependence is to allow all parameters of the conditional variance equation to vary across regimes. That approach is offered by Henneke, Rachev, and Fabozzi (2006), who model jointly the conditional mean as an ARMA(1,1) process in a Bayesian estimation setting.[10] The implication for the dynamics of the conditional variance is that the manner in which the variance responds to past return shocks and volatility levels changes across regimes. For example, high-volatility regimes could be characterized by hypersensitivity of asset returns to return shocks, and high volatility in one period could have a more lasting effect on future volatilities compared to low-volatility regimes. This would call for a different relationship between the parameters α and β in different regimes.

In this section, we discuss the estimation method of Henneke, Rachev, and Fabozzi (2006), with some modifications.

Preliminaries

Suppose that there are three states the conditional volatility can occupy, denoted by i, $i = 1, 2, 3$. We could assign economic interpretation to them by labeling them "a low-volatility state," "a normal-volatility state," and "a high-volatility state." Denote by π_{ij} the probability of a transition from

[10] See also Haas, Mittnik, and Paolella (2004), Klaassen (1998), Francq and Zakoian (2001), and Ghysels, McCulloch, and Tsay (1998), among others.

state i to state j. The transition probabilities, π_{ij}, could be arranged in the *transition probability matrix*, Π,

$$\Pi = \begin{pmatrix} \pi_{11} & \pi_{12} & \pi_{13} \\ \pi_{21} & \pi_{22} & \pi_{23} \\ \pi_{31} & \pi_{32} & \pi_{33} \end{pmatrix}, \tag{11.20}$$

such that the probabilities in each row sum up to 1. The Markov property (central to model estimation, as we will see below) that lends its name to the MS models concerns the memory of the process—which volatility regime the system visits in a given period depends only on the regime in the previous period. Analytically, the Markov property is expressed as

$$P\big(S_t \mid S_{t-1}, S_{t-2}, \ldots, S_1\big) = P\big(S_t \mid S_{t-1}\big). \tag{11.21}$$

Each row of Π in (11.20) represents the three-dimensional conditional probability distribution of S_t, conditional on the regime realization in the previous period, S_{t-1}. We say that $\{S_t\}_{t=1}^{T}$ is a three-dimensional (discrete-time) Markov chain with transition matrix, Π.

In the regime-switching setting of Henneke, Rachev, and Fabozzi, the expression for the conditional variance dynamics becomes

$$\sigma^2_{t|t-1} = \omega(S_t) + \alpha(S_t)u^2_{t-1} + \beta(S_t)\sigma^2_{t-1|t-2}. \tag{11.22}$$

For each period t,

$$(\omega(S_t), \alpha(S_t), \beta(S_t)) = \begin{cases} (\omega_1, \alpha_1, \beta_1) & \text{if } S_t = 1, \\ (\omega_2, \alpha_2, \beta_2) & \text{if } S_t = 2, \\ (\omega_3, \alpha_3, \beta_3) & \text{if } S_t = 3. \end{cases}$$

The presence of the GARCH component in (11.22) complicates the model estimation substantially. To see this, notice that, via $\sigma^2_{t-1|t-2}$, the current conditional variance depends on the conditional variances from all preceding periods and, therefore, on the whole unobservable sequence of regimes up to time t. A great number of regime paths could lead to the particular conditional variance at time t (the number of possible regime combinations grows exponentially with the number of time periods), rendering classical estimation very complicated. For that reason, the early treatments of MS models include only an ARCH component in the conditional variance equation. The MCMC methodology, however, copes easily with the specification in (11.22), as we will see below.

We adopt the same return decomposition as in (11.1) and note that, given the regime path, (11.22) represents the same conditional variance dynamics as (11.2). We return to this point again further below when we discuss estimation of that MS GARCH(1,1) model.

Next, we outline the prior assumptions for the MS GARCH(1,1) model.

Prior Distributional Assumptions

The parameter vector of the MS GARCH(1,1) model, specified by (11.1), (11.22), and the Markov chain $\{S_t\}_{t=1}^{T}$, is given by

$$\boldsymbol{\theta} = \left(\boldsymbol{\gamma}', \boldsymbol{\eta}', \nu, \boldsymbol{\theta}_{G,1}, \boldsymbol{\theta}_{G,2}, \boldsymbol{\theta}_{G,3}, \boldsymbol{\pi}_1, \boldsymbol{\pi}_2, \boldsymbol{\pi}_3, \boldsymbol{S}\right), \tag{11.23}$$

where, for $i = 1, 2, 3$,

$$\theta_{G,i} = (\omega_i, \alpha_i, \beta_i)$$

and

$$\boldsymbol{\pi}_i = (\pi_{i1}, \pi_{i2}, \pi_{i3}),$$

and S is the regime path for all periods,

$$\boldsymbol{S} = (S_1, \ldots, S_T).$$

Our prior specifications for γ, η, and ν remain unchanged from our earlier discussion: The regression coefficients, γ, the scale mixture of normals mixing parameters, η, and the degrees-of-freedom parameter, ν, are not affected by the regime specification in the MS GARCH(1,1) model. We assert prior distributions for the vector of conditional variance parameters, $\theta_{G,i}$, under each regime, i, and a prior distribution for each triple of transition probabilities π_i, $i = 1, 2, 3$.

Prior Distributions for $\theta_{G,i}$, i = 1, 2, 3 To reflect our prior intuition about the effect the three regimes have on the conditional variance parameters, we assert proper normal priors for $\theta_{G,i}$, $i = 1, 2, 3$.

$$\theta_{G,i} \sim \mathrm{N}(\mu_i, \Sigma_i)\, I_{\{\theta_{G,i}\}}, \tag{11.24}$$

where the indicator function, $I_{\{\theta_{G,i}\}}$, is given in (11.5). As explained earlier in the chapter, the parameter constraints are imposed during the implementation of the sampling algorithm.

Prior Distribution for π_i, i = 1, 2, 3 In Chapter 2, we explained that a convenient prior for the probability parameter in a binomial experiment is the beta distribution. The analogue of the beta distribution in the multivariate case is the so-called *Dirichlet distribution*.[11] Therefore, we specify a Dirichlet prior distribution for each triple of transition probabilities, $i = 1, 2, 3$,

$$\pi_i \sim \text{Dirichlet}\left(a_{i1}, a_{i2}, a_{i3}\right) \tag{11.25}$$

To elicit the prior parameters, a_{ij}, $i, j = 1, 2, 3$, it is sufficient that one express prior intuition about the expected value of each of the transition probabilities in a triple, then solve the system equations for a_{ij}.

Estimation of the MS GARCH(1,1) Model

The evolution of volatility in the MS GARCH model is governed by the realizations of the unobservable (latent) regime variable, $S_t, t = 1, \ldots, T$. Hence, the discrete-time Markov chain, $\{S_t\}_{t=1}^T$ is also called a *hidden Markov process*. Earlier, we briefly discussed that the presence of the hidden Markov process creates a major estimation difficulty in the classical setting. The Bayesian methodology, in contrast, deals with the latent-variable characteristic in an easy and natural way: The latent variable is simulated together with the model parameters. In other words, the parameter space is *augmented* with S_t, $t = 1, \ldots, T$, in much the same way as the vector of mixing variables, η, was added to the parameter space in estimating the Student's t GARCH(1,1) model. The distribution of S is a multinomial distribution,

$$\begin{aligned} p\left(\mathrm{S} \mid \pi\right) &= \prod_{t=1}^{T-1} p\left(S_{t+1} \mid S_t, \pi\right) \\ &= \pi_{11}^{n_{11}} \pi_{12}^{n_{12}} \ldots \pi_{32}^{n_{32}} \pi_{33}^{n_{33}} \\ &= \pi_{11}^{n_{11}} \pi_{12}^{n_{12}} \left(1 - \pi_{11} - \pi_{12}\right)^{n_{13}} \ldots \pi_{32}^{n_{32}} \left(1 - \pi_{31} - \pi_{32}\right)^{n_{33}}, \end{aligned} \tag{11.26}$$

[11] A K-dimensional random variable $p = (p_1, p_2, \ldots, p_K)$, where $p_k \geq 0$ and $\sum_{k=1}^K p_k = 1$, distributed with a Dirichlet distribution with parameters $\mathbf{a} = (a_1, a_2, \ldots, a_K)$, $a_i > 0$, $i = 1, \ldots, K$, has a density function

$$f(p \mid a) = \frac{\Gamma(\sum_{k=1}^K a_k)}{\prod_{k=1}^K \Gamma(a_k)} \prod_{k=1}^K p_k^{a_k - 1},$$

where Γ is the gamma function. The mean and the variance of the Dirichlet distribution are given, respectively, by $E(p_k) = \frac{a_k}{a_0}$ and $\text{var}(p_k) = \frac{a_k(a_0 - a_k)}{a_0^2(a_0+1)}$, where $a_0 = \sum_{j=1}^K a_j$. The Dirichlet distribution is the conjugate prior distribution for the parameters of the multinomial distribution. As we see in our discussion on the MS GARCH estimation, the distribution of the Markov chain, $\{S_t\}_{t=1}^T$, is, in fact, a multinomial distribution.

where n_{ij} denotes the number of times the chain transitions from state i to state j during the span of period 1 through period T. The first equality in (11.26) follows from the Markov property of $\{S_t\}_{t=1}^{T}$.

Based on our discussion of the Student's t GARCH(1,1) model and the hidden Markov process, as well as the prior distributional assumptions for π_i and $\theta_{G,i}$, $i = 1, 2, 3$, the joint log-posterior distribution of the MS GARCH(1,1) model's parameter vector θ is given by

$$
\begin{aligned}
\log\left(p\ (\theta \mid \mathbf{r}, \Im_0)\right) = \text{const} &- \frac{1}{2}\sum_{t=1}^{T}\left[\log\left(\sigma_{t|t-1}^2\right) + \log\left(\eta_t\right) + \frac{\eta_t(r_t - \mathbf{X}_t\gamma)^2}{\sigma_{t|t-1}^2}\right] \\
&- \frac{1}{2}(\gamma - \mu_\gamma)'\Sigma_\gamma^{-1}(\gamma - \mu_\gamma) \\
&- \frac{1}{2}\sum_{i=1}^{3}\left(\theta_{G,i} - \mu_i\right)'\ \Sigma_i^{-1}\left(\theta_{G,i} - \mu_i\right) I_{\{S(t)=i\}} \\
&+ \frac{T\nu}{2}\log\left(\frac{\nu}{2}\right) - T\log\left(\Gamma\left(\frac{\nu}{2}\right)\right) + \left(\frac{\nu}{2} - 1\right)\sum_{t=1}^{T}\log\left(\eta_t\right) \\
&- \frac{\nu}{2}\sum_{t=1}^{T}\eta_t - \nu\lambda \\
&+ \sum_{i=1}^{3}\sum_{j=1}^{3}(a_{ij} + n_{ij} - 1)\log\left(\pi_{ij}\right),
\end{aligned}
\tag{11.27}
$$

for $\omega_i > 0$, $\alpha_i \geq 0$, and $\beta_i \geq 0$.

Although (11.27) looks very similar to the joint log-posterior in (11.14), there is a crucial difference. The model's log-likelihood (given by the right-hand-side term in the first line of (11.27)) depends on the whole sequence of regimes, S. Conditional on $\mathbf{S}$, however, it is the same log-likelihood as in (11.13). We exploit this fact in constructing the posterior simulation algorithm as an extension of the algorithm for the Student's t GARCH(1,1) model estimation.

We now outline the posterior results for π_i, S, and $\theta_{G,i}$. The posterior results for the regression coefficients, γ, the degrees-of-freedom parameter, ν, and the mixing variables, $\boldsymbol{\eta}$, remain unchanged from our earlier discussion.

Conditional Posterior Distribution of π_i, i = 1, 2, 3 The conditional log-posterior distribution of the vector of transition probabilities, π_i, $i = 1, 2, 3$, is given by

$$\log\left(p\left(\pi_i \mid \mathbf{r}, \theta_{-\pi_i}\right)\right) = \text{const} + \sum_{j=1}^{3}\left(a_{ij} + n_{ij} - 1\right)\log\left(\pi_{ij}\right), \tag{11.28}$$

for $i = 1, 2, 3$, where $\theta_{-\pi_i}$ denotes the vector of all parameters except $\boldsymbol{\pi}_i$. The expression in (11.28) is readily recognized as the logarithm of the kernel of a Dirichlet distribution with parameters $\left(a_{i1} + n_{i1}, a_{i2} + n_{i2}, a_{i3} + n_{i3}\right)$. The parameters a_{ij} are specified a priori, while the parameters n_{ij} can be determined by simply counting the number of times the Markov chain, $\{S_t\}_{t=1}^{T}$, transitions from i to j.

Sampling from the Dirichlet distribution in (11.28) is accomplished easily in the following way.[12]

1. For each i, $i = 1, 2, 3$, sample three independent observations,

$$y_{i1} \sim \chi^2_{2\left(a_{i1}+n_{i1}\right)}, \quad y_{i2} \sim \chi^2_{2\left(a_{i2}+n_{i2}\right)}, \quad y_{i3} \sim \chi^2_{2\left(a_{i3}+n_{i3}\right)},$$

2. set

$$\pi_{i1} = \frac{y_{i1}}{\sum_{k=1}^{3} y_{ik}}, \quad \pi_{i2} = \frac{y_{i2}}{\sum_{k=1}^{3} y_{ik}}, \quad \pi_{i3} = \frac{y_{i3}}{\sum_{k=1}^{3} y_{ik}}.$$

Conditional Posterior Distribution of S In the three-regime switching setup of this chapter, the number of regime paths that could have potentially generated S_T, the regime in the final period, is 3^T. The level of complexity makes it impossible to obtain a draw of the whole $1 \times T$ vector, S, at once. Instead, its components can be drawn one at a time, in a T-step procedure. In other words, at each step, we sample from the full conditional posterior density of S_t given by

$$p\left(S_t = i \mid \mathbf{r}, \theta_{-S}, \mathbf{S}_{-t}\right), \tag{11.29}$$

where θ_{-S} is the parameter vector in (11.23) excluding S and $\mathbf{S}_{-t}$ is the regime path excluding the regime at time t. Applying the rules of conditional probability, $p\left(S_t = i \mid \mathbf{r}, \theta_{-S_t}\right)$ is written as

$$\begin{aligned} p\left(S_t = i \mid \mathbf{r}, \theta_{-S}, \mathbf{S}_{-t}\right) &= \frac{p\left(S_t = i, \mathbf{S}_{-t}, \mathbf{r} \mid \theta_{-S}\right)}{p\left(\mathbf{S}_{-t}, \mathbf{r} \mid \theta_{-S}\right)} \\ &= \frac{p\left(\mathbf{r} \mid \theta_{-S}, \mathbf{S}_{-t}, S_t = i\right) p\left(S_t = i, \mathbf{S}_{-t} \mid \theta_{-S}\right)}{p\left(\mathbf{S}_{-t}, \mathbf{r} \mid \theta_{-S}\right)}. \end{aligned} \tag{11.30}$$

[12] See Anderson (2003).

The first term in the numerator, $p\ (\mathbf{r}\,|\,\theta_{-S}, \mathbf{S}_{-t}, S_t = i)$, is simply the model's likelihood evaluated at a given regime path, in which $S_t = i$. The second term in the numerator, $p\ (S_t = i, \mathbf{S}_{-t})$, is given, by the Markov property, by

$$p\ (S_t = i, S_{-t}\,|\,\theta_{-S}) = p\ \left(S_t = i, S_{t-1} = j, S_{t+1} = k\,|\,\theta_{-S}\right) \\ = \pi_{j,i}\pi_{i,k}, \tag{11.31}$$

while the denominator in (11.30) is expressed as

$$p\ (S_{-t}, \mathbf{r}\,|\,\theta_{-S}) = \sum_{s=1}^{3} p\ (S_t = s, S_{-t}, \mathbf{r}\,|\,\theta_{-S})\,. \tag{11.32}$$

Using (11.30), (11.31), and (11.32), we obtain the conditional posterior distribution of S_t as

$$p\ (S_t = i\,|\,\mathbf{r}, \theta_{-S}, \mathbf{S}_{-t}) = \frac{p\ (\mathbf{r}\,|\,\theta_{-S}, \mathbf{S}_{-t}, S_t = i)\,\pi_{j,i}\,\pi_{i,k}}{\sum_{s=1}^{3} p\ (\mathbf{r}\,|\,\theta_{-S}, \mathbf{S}_{-t}, S_t = s)\,\pi_{j,s}\,\pi_{s,k}}, \tag{11.33}$$

for $i = 1, 2, 3$. An observation, S_t^*, from the conditional density in (11.33) is obtained in the following way:

1. Compute the probability in (11.33) for $i = 1, 2, 3$.
2. Split the interval (0, 1) into three intervals of lengths proportional to the probabilities in step (1).
3. Draw an observation, u, from the uniform distribution $U[0, 1]$.
4. Depending on which interval u falls into, set $S_t^* = i$.

To draw the regime path, $\mathbf{S}^{(m)}$, at the mth iteration of the posterior simulation algorithm:

1. Draw $S_1^{(m)}$ from $p\left(S_1\,|\,\mathbf{r}, \theta_{-S_1}\right)$ in (11.33). Update $\mathbf{S}^{(m)}$ with $S_1^{(m)}$.
2. For $t = 2, \ldots, T$, draw $S_t^{(m)}$ from $p\left(S_t\,|\,\mathbf{r}, \theta_{-S_t}\right)$ in (11.33). Update $\mathbf{S}^{(m)}$ with $S_t^{(m)}$.

Proposal Distribution for $\theta_{G,i}$, $i = 1, 2, 3$ The posterior distribution of the vector of conditional variance parameters is not available in closed form because of the regime dependence of the conditional variance. Since, in the regime-switching setting, we adopted informative prior distributions for

$\theta_{G,i}$, $i = 1, 2, 3$, the kernel of the conditional log-posterior distribution is a bit different from the one in (11.20) and is given by

$$\log\left(p\left(\theta_{G,i}\,|\,\theta_{-\theta_{G,i}}, \mathbf{r}, \Im_0\right)\right) = \text{const} - \frac{1}{2}\sum_{t=1}^{T}\left[\log\left(\sigma^2_{t|t-1}\right) + \log\left(\eta_t\right) + \frac{\eta_t(r_t - \mathbf{X}_t\gamma)^2}{\sigma^2_{t|t-1}}\right] - \frac{1}{2}\sum_{i=1}^{3}\left(\theta_{G,i} - \mu_i\right)'\,\Sigma_i^{-1}\left(\theta_{G,i} - \mu_i\right) I_{\{S_t=i\}},$$

for $\omega > 0$, $\alpha \geq 0$, $\beta \geq 0$, and $i = 1, 2, 3$.

For a given regime path, $\mathbf{S}$, the only difference between the posterior kernels in (11.20) and (11.34) is the term reflecting the informative prior of $\theta_{G,i}$. Therefore, specifying a proposal distribution for $\theta_{G,i}$ is in no way different from the approach in the single-regime Student's t GARCH(1,1) setting.

Sampling Algorithm for the Parameters of the MS GARCH(1,1) Model

The sampling algorithm for the MS GARCH(1,1) model parameters consists of the following steps. At iteration m:

1. Draw $\pi_i^{(m)}$ from its posterior density in (11.28), for $i = 1, 2, 3$.
2. Draw $\mathbf{S}^{(m)}$ from (11.33).
3. Draw $\eta^{(m)}$ from (11.17).
4. Draw $\nu^{(m)}$ from (11.18).
5. Draw $\gamma^{(m)}$ from (11.15).
6. Draw $\theta^*_{G,i}$, $i = 1, 2, 3$, from the proposal distribution, as explained earlier.
7. Check whether the parameter restrictions on the components of $\theta_{G,i}$ are satisfied; if not, draw $\theta^*_{G,i}$ repeatedly, until they are satisfied.
8. Compute the acceptance probability in (5.7) in Chapter 5 and accept of reject $\theta^*_{G,i}$, for $i = 1, 2, 3$.

The parameter vector, θ, is updated as new components are drawn. The steps above are repeated a large number of times until convergence of the algorithm.

Illustration: Student's *t* MS GARCH(1,1) Model

We continue with our earlier illustration in this chapter and this time estimate the GARCH(1,1) model in the regime-switching setting. We assert a Dirichlet prior with parameters $a_{ij} = 1, i, j = 1, 2, 3$, which implies uniform prior beliefs about the transition probabilities, $\pi_{i,j}$. We elicit the following prior means for the conditional variance parameter vector, $\theta_{G,i}$, $i = 1, 2, 3$,

$$\mu_1 = \begin{pmatrix} 0.0002 \\ 0.1 \\ 0.6 \end{pmatrix},$$

$$\mu_2 = \begin{pmatrix} 0.2 \\ 0.3 \\ 0.4 \end{pmatrix},$$

and

$$\mu_3 = \begin{pmatrix} 2 \\ 0.6 \\ 0.1 \end{pmatrix}.$$

Our prior choices are based on the following reasoning: The values of ω_i's prior means reflect our earlier designation of state 1 as the low-volatility state, of state 2 as the medium-volatility state, and of state 3 as the high-volatility state. (Recall the expression for the unconditional variance in (10.9).) We keep the sum of the prior means of α_i and β_i fixed but assert different trade-offs between those two parameters (for each i, $i = 1, 2, 3$). One could hypothesize that in periods of high volatility, investors tend to overreact to unexpected information arrivals and in general, to shocks in returns, compared to periods of low volatility. Then, the value of α could be expected to be higher than the value of β in high-volatility states. For simplicity, we set the prior covariance matrix of $\theta_{G,i}$ to be equal to the identity matrix for $i = 1, 2, 3$. We note that this choice implies somewhat strong beliefs for the prior means of ω_3 and of α_i and $\beta_i, i = 1, 2, 3$.

We keep the prior distributional assumptions for the rest of the model parameters.

The posterior parameter estimates for the Student's t MS GARCH(1,1) model are provided in Exhibit 11.5. We observe that the posterior means of the conditional variance parameters roughly comply with our prior intuition. The persistence of volatility in states 1 and 2 is substantially lower than that in the simple GARCH(1,1) model considered earlier in the chapter. There is clear evidence of nonstationarity in state 3. (Its measure of persistence has a posterior mean of 1.386.)

Exhibit 11.6 presents the posterior probabilities of regimes 1, 2, and 3, as well as the squared return innovations. We could conclude from it that state 1 is indeed the low-volatility state, state 2 is a medium-to-high

	ω_1	α_1	β_1	Persistence Measure
Regime 1	1.41e-5	0.031	0.048	0.053
	(4.7e-6)	(0.011)	(0.013)	(0.034)
	ω_2	α_2	β_2	
Regime 2	8.6e-5	0.074	0.301	0.377
	(2.1e-5)	(0.039)	(0.073)	(0.079)
	ω_3	α_3	β_3	
Regime 3	0.531	0.751	0.575	1.386
	(0.203)	(0.227)	(0.261)	(0.335)

	$\pi_{j,1}$	$\pi_{j,2}$	$\pi_{j,3}$
$\pi_{1,k}$	0.988	0.007	0.005
	(0.002)	(0.003)	(0.004)
$\pi_{2,k}$	0.030	0.938	0.032
	(0.008)	(0.022)	(0.024)
$\pi_{3,k}$	0.454	0.365	0.181
	(0.098)	(0.111)	(0.096)

ν	γ^1	γ^2	γ^3	γ^4	γ^5	γ^6
30.07	–9.2e-5	0.297	–0.078	–0.641	0.056	0.066
(4.61)	(9.8e-5)	(0.005)	(0.007)	(0.009)	(0.014)	(0.015)

EXHIBIT 11.5 Posterior means of the parameters in the MS GARCH(1,1) model
Note: The posterior standard errors are in parentheses.

volatility state, while state 3 is a transient state, which "switches on" when innovation shocks occur. This observations is supported by the posterior means of the transitional probabilities (see Exhibit 11.5). The volatility process only rarely visits state 3 and, when it does, it tends to transition to one of the other two states fairly quickly. Notice, in contrast, the tendency of state 1 and state 2 to last (the posterior means of $\pi_{1,1}$ and $\pi_{2,2}$ are, respectively, 0.988 and 0.938).

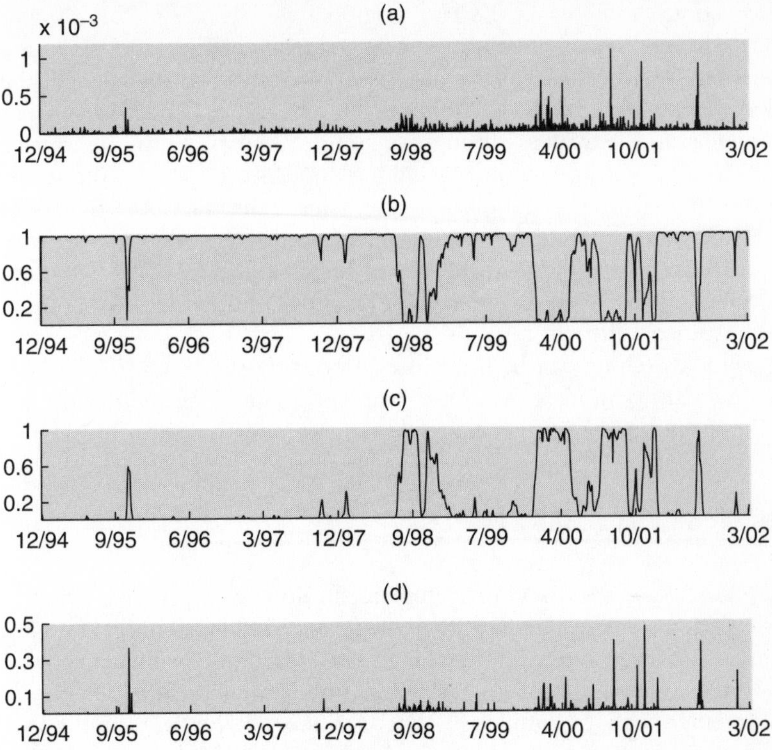

EXHIBIT 11.6 Posterior regime probabilities in the MS GARCH(1,1) model
Note: Panel (A) shows the plot of the squared return innovations. Panels (B), (C), and (D) contain the plots of the posterior probabilities of regimes 1, 2, and 3, respectively.

SUMMARY

In this chapter, we discussed the GARCH(1,1) model with Student's *t*-distributed disturbances and the Markov regime-switching GARCH(1,1) model. Estimation of both is easily handled in the Bayesian setting with the help of the numerical methods discussed in Chapter 5. Markov regime-switching models are governed by an unobserved latent variable (assumed to evolve according to a Markov process). Where a classical statistician would deal with the regime variable by integrating it out of the likelihood, the Bayesian practitioner simply simulates it along with the remaining model parameters.

The regime-switching GARCH(1,1) model we covered in this chapter provides a bridge to our presentation of stochastic volatility models in the next chapter. Stochastic volatility models are members of the class of the so-called *state-space models*. Volatility is the (unobserved) state variable in those models and it evolves through time according to an autoregressive process. Unlike Markov regime-switching models, in which transitions between regimes (states) occur in a discrete fashion, the volatility's dynamics in stochastic volatility models has a source of randomness that may or may not be correlated with the disturbances of the asset returns. The dynamics of the transitions between regime switches is time-continuous and driven by the stochastic volatility process.

Markov switching can be introduced into state-space models, such as stochastic volatility models. See, for example, Kim and Nelson (1999) for a detailed exposition.

APPENDIX: GRIDDY GIBBS SAMPLER

In Chapter 5, we discussed that implementation of the Gibbs sampler requires that parameters' conditional posterior distributions be known. Sometimes, however, the conditional posterior distributions have no closed forms. In these cases, a special form of the Gibbs sampler, called *the griddy Gibbs sampler*, can be employed whereby the (univariate) conditional posterior densities are evaluated on grids of parameter values. The griddy Gibbs sampler, developed by Ritter and Tanner (1992), is a combination of the ordinary Gibbs sampler and a numerical routine. In this appendix, we illustrate the griddy Gibbs sampler with the posterior distribution of the degrees-of-freedom parameter, ν.

Recall the expression for the kernel of ν's conditional log-posterior distribution,

$$\log\left(p\left(\nu \mid \theta_{-\nu}, \mathbf{r}, \Im_0\right)\right) = \text{const} + \frac{T\nu}{2}\log\left(\frac{\nu}{2}\right) - T\log\left(\Gamma\left(\frac{\nu}{2}\right)\right) + \left(\frac{\nu}{2} - 1\right)\sum_{t=1}^{T}\log\left(\eta_t\right) - \frac{\nu}{2}\sum_{t=1}^{T}\eta_t - \nu\lambda. \tag{11.34}$$

The griddy Gibbs sampler approach to drawing from the conditional posterior distribution of ν is to recognize that at iteration m we can treat the latest draws of the remaining parameters as the known parameter values. Therefore, we can evaluate numerically the conditional posterior density of ν on a grid of its admissible values. The support of ν is the positive part of the real line. However, a reasonable range for the values of ν in an application to asset returns could be (2, 30).[13]

Drawing from the Conditional Posterior Distribution of ν

Denote the equally spaced grid of values for ν by $(\nu_1, \nu_2, \ldots, \nu_J)$. We outline the steps for drawing from ν's conditional posterior distribution at iteration m of the sampling algorithm. Denote the most recent draws of the remaining model parameters by $\theta_{-\nu}^{(m-1)}$. (Note that this notation is not entirely precise since some of the parameters might have been updated last during the mth iteration of the sampler but before ν.)

1. Compute the value of ν's posterior kernel (the exponential of the expression in (11.34)) at each of the grid nodes and denote the resultant vector by

$$p(\nu) = \left(p(\nu_1), p(\nu_2), \ldots, p(\nu_J)\right). \qquad (11.35)$$

2. Normalize $p(\nu)$ by dividing each vector component in (11.35) by the quantity $\sum_{j=1}^{J} p(\nu_j)(\nu_2 - \nu_1)$.[14] For convenience of notation, let us redefine $p(\nu)$ to denote the vector of (normalized) posterior density values at each node of ν's grid.
3. Compute the empirical cumulative distribution function (CDF),

$$F(\nu) = \left(p(\nu_1), \sum_{j=1}^{2} p(\nu_j), \ldots, \sum_{j=1}^{J} p(\nu_j)\right). \qquad (11.36)$$

If the grid is adequate, the first element of $F(\nu)$ should be nearly 0, while the last element of $F(\nu)$ nearly 1.

1. Draw an observation from the uniform distribution ($U[0, 1]$) and denote it by u.
2. Find the element of $F(\nu)$ closest to u without exceeding it.

---

[13]This is the typical range of the degrees-of-freedom parameter of a Student's t-distribution fitted to return data. The higher the data frequency is, the more heavy-tailed returns are and the lower the value of the degrees-of-freedom parameter.
[14]Recall that the posterior kernel is the posterior density up to a constant of proportionality. The normalizing constant is the denominator in the Bayes formula (see Chapter 2) and given by $\int L(\theta | \mathbf{r}, \Im_0) p(\nu | \theta_{-\nu}, \mathbf{r}, \Im_0) d\nu$. This integral is approximated by the weighted sum $\sum_{j=1}^{J} p(\nu_j)(\nu_2 - \nu_1)$. The weight, $\nu_2 - \nu_1$, is constant, since the grid of ν values is equally spaced.

3. The grid node corresponding to the value of $F(\nu)$ in the previous step is the draw of ν from its posterior distribution.

The method above of obtaining a draw from ν's distribution using its CDF is called the *CDF inversion method*.

Constructing an adequate grid is the key to efficient sampling from ν's posterior. Since the griddy Gibbs sampling procedure relies on multiple evaluations of the posterior kernel, two desired characteristics of an adequate grid are short length and coverage of the parameter support where the posterior distribution has positive probability mass. A simple example illustrates this point. Suppose that for a given sample of observed data, the likely values of ν are in the interval (2, 15). Suppose further that we construct an equally spaced grid of length 30, with nodes on each integer from 2 to 30. The value of the posterior kernel at the nodes corresponding to ν equal to 16 and above would be only marginally different from zero. The posterior kernel evaluations at those nodes should be avoided, if possible.

If no prior intuition exists about what the likely parameter values are, one could employ a variable grid instead of a fixed grid. At each iteration of the sampling algorithm one must analyze the distribution of posterior mass and adjust the grid, so that the majority of the grid nodes are placed in the interval of greatest probability mass. Automating this process could involve some computational effort.

CHAPTER 12

Bayesian Estimation of Stochastic Volatility Models

In this chapter, we maintain our focus on volatility modeling and discuss Bayesian estimation of the second large class of volatility models, *stochastic volatility* (SV) models. Continuous SV models have enjoyed a lot of attention in the literature as a way to generalize the constant-volatility assumption of the Black-Scholes option pricing formula.[1] In empirical work, the discrete-time SV model of Taylor (1982, 1986) is their natural counterpart.

The characteristic distinguishing SV models from GARCH models is the presence of an unobservable shock component in the volatility dynamics process. Volatility is thus itself latent—its exact value at time t cannot be known even if all past information is employed to determine it. As more information becomes available, the volatility in a given past period could be better evaluated. Both contemporaneous and future information thus contribute to learning about volatility. In contrast, in the deterministic setting of the simple GARCH volatility process, the volatility in a certain time period is known, given the information from the previous period.

Together with ARCH-type models, SV models attempt to explain empirically-observed return characteristics such as time-varying variance (heteroskedasticity), heavy-tailedness, and volatility clustering. In an ARCH-type model, the heavy-tailedness of returns is tied solely to their heteroskedasticity because the source of volatility variability is volatility dependence on past volatility (and past return shocks). This is not the

[1]See Hull and White (1987), Chesney and Scott (1989), and Harvey, Ruiz, and Shephard (1994), among others.

case in SV models. Even if the volatility at time t did not depend on the volatility in the previous time period, the random component (innovation) in the SV process itself would induce heavy tails in the unconditional return distribution.

In this chapter, we present step-by-step the estimation of SV models within the Bayesian context. Our focus is on two *Markov Chain Monte Carlo* (MCMC) approaches. The first approach is the so-called "single-move sampler," examples of which we have seen already in Chapter 11. It consists of updating the parameter vector a single parameter at a time.

Some researchers have argued that when parameters are correlated, particularly in time-series models, that single-move procedure results in a slower speed of convergence of the Markov chain. Algorithms, called *multimove samplers,* updating several variables at a time, could then be a more efficient sampling alternative.

We conclude the chapter with a description of a jump extension to the SV model.

PRELIMINARIES OF SV MODEL ESTIMATION

From a practical perspective, the primary goal of a SV model is to provide inference for (estimate) the sequence of unobserved volatilities and to predict their values a certain number of periods ahead. MCMC methods offer a framework both for estimating the parameters of the SV models and for assessing the latent volatilities. The design of the MCMC procedure is crucial for the chain's speed of convergence. Estimation of latent variable models (SV models, in particular) highlights the importance of the design because the number of unknown parameters is of the same order as the sample of data.

Carlin, Polson, and Stoffer (1992) first presented a Bayesian treatment of state-space models, while Jacquier, Polson, and Rossi (JPR) (1994) offered the first Bayesian SV model analysis. Since then, the literature of Bayesian SV estimation has been prolific.

The basic SV model assumes that the dynamics of the logarithm of volatility is governed by a stationary stochastic process in the form of an autoregressive process of order 1 (AR(1)). The following two equations specify the SV model,

$$r_t = \exp(h_t/2)\epsilon_t \tag{12.1}$$

and

$$h_t = \rho_0 + \rho_1 h_{t-1} + \tau\eta_t, \tag{12.2}$$

where:[2] $h_t = \log(\sigma_t^2)$.
r_t = asset return observed in period t, $t = 1, \ldots, T$.
ϵ_t = disturbance of the return process distributed independently and identically with a standard normal distribution, $t = 1, \ldots, T$.
η_t = disturbance of the volatility process distributed independently and identically with a standard normal distribution, $t = 1, \ldots, T$.
ρ_0 and ρ_1 = parameters of the volatility process.
τ = scale parameter of the volatility disturbance.

For simplicity, we do not model the conditional mean of returns and assume it is zero in our discussion. The disturbances, ϵ_t and η_t, are assumed independent in the basic SV model. It is, however, possible to introduce correlation between them and thus model the empirically observed asymmetric response of volatility to return shocks.[3] The volatility process is stationary if the parameter ρ_1 takes values in the open interval $(-1, 1)$.

Likelihood Function

Let us denote the vector of model parameters by $\boldsymbol{\theta}$,

$$\boldsymbol{\theta} = \left(\rho_0, \rho_1, \tau^2\right).$$

---

[2]The model defined by (12.1) and (12.2) is an example of a (nonlinear) state-space model. A simple Gaussian linear state-space model is defined by the following set of equations:

$$y_t = a_t + \epsilon_t$$

$$a_t = a_{t-1} + \eta_t$$

for $t = 1, \ldots, T$, where the disturbances are independently distributed as $\epsilon_t \sim \mathrm{N}(0, \sigma_\epsilon^2)$ and $\eta_t \sim \mathrm{N}(0, \sigma_\eta^2)$. The variable a_t is unobserved and called the *state variable*. Inference about it is usually of interest in state-space models, as it provides knowledge about the system's evolution through time. Inference is based on the values of the observed variable, y_t, $t = 1, \ldots, T$. The first equation above is referred to as the *observation equation* and the second equation as the *state equation*. A widely employed tool in the estimation of state-space models is the Kalman filter, and later in the chapter we discuss how it can be integrated into an MCMC algorithm. The Bayesian framework alone can also be employed to deal with state space models, as we describe in the section on the single-move MCMC algorithm.

[3]See, for example, Jacquier, Polson, and Rossi (2004) for the Bayesian treatment of this model extension.

Since the volatility is unobservable, the likelihood function for $\boldsymbol{\theta}$ is not available in a closed form as we explained in Chapter 10. Instead, it is expressed as an analytically intractable T-dimensional integral with respect to the T latent volatilities,

$$L(\boldsymbol{\theta} \mid r) = \prod_{t=1}^{T} \int f\left(r_t \mid \sigma_1^2, \ldots, \sigma_T^2\right) f\left(\sigma_1^2, \ldots, \sigma_T^2 \mid \boldsymbol{\theta}\right) \mathrm{d}\sigma_1^2 \ldots \mathrm{d}\sigma_T^2, \qquad (12.3)$$

where we use the notation established earlier in this chapter and in Chapter 10. The reason for the likelihood intractability above is the same as in the case of regime-switching models. It is no surprise then that the approach to deal with the problem is data augmentation, as in the regime-switching setting. The latent volatilities are simulated together with the rest of the model parameters from their conditional distribution. A single algorithm thus helps obtain the Bayesian parameter estimates and evaluate the volatilities.

Next, we discuss the single-move MCMC approach to SV model estimation of JPR.

THE SINGLE-MOVE MCMC ALGORITHM FOR SV MODEL ESTIMATION

The single-move MCMC approach to SV model estimation is characterized by simulating the path of unobserved volatility element by element in the same way the regime path was simulated in Chapter 11.

Prior and Posterior Distributions

Were the variable h_t in (12.2) known, that expression would have defined a simple linear regression model. Within an MCMC sampling environment, at each iteration of the algorithm, h_t can indeed be treated as known when sampling the remaining parameters. One can, therefore, assert conjugate priors for the three parameters ρ_0, ρ_1, and τ in order to obtain standard-form posterior distributions for them. The conjugate priors in the normal linear model are a bivariate normal distribution and an inverted χ^2 distribution (see Chapter 4),

$$\begin{pmatrix} \rho_0 \\ \rho_1 \end{pmatrix} \equiv \beta \sim \mathrm{N}\left(\beta_0, \tau^2 A\right), \qquad (12.4)$$

and

$$\tau^2 \sim \text{Inv-}\chi^2\left(\nu_0, c_0^2\right). \qquad (12.5)$$

The posterior distributions are of the same form as the prior ones. Sampling from them is straightforward. (See Chapter 4.)

Conditional Distribution of the Unobserved Volatility

To simulate the unobserved volatility component by component, one needs to obtain the conditional density of the volatility in a given period, $\sigma_t^2, t = 1, \ldots, T$. Denote by $\boldsymbol{\sigma}_{-t}^2$ the vector of volatilities for all periods but period t. Using the Markov property, it can be shown that the conditional density is[4]

$$
\begin{aligned}
p\left(\sigma_t^2 \mid \boldsymbol{\sigma}_{-t}^2, \boldsymbol{\theta}, r\right) &\propto p\left(\sigma_t^2 \mid \sigma_{t-1}^2\right) p\left(\sigma_{t+1}^2 \mid \sigma_t^2\right) p\left(y_t \mid \sigma_t^2\right) \\
&\propto \frac{1}{\sigma_t} \exp\left(-\frac{r_t^2}{2\sigma_t^2}\right) \frac{1}{\sigma_t^2} \exp\left(-\frac{\left(\log\left(\sigma_t^2\right) - a_t\right)^2}{2b^2}\right), \qquad (12.6)
\end{aligned}
$$

where

$$
a_t = \frac{\rho_0(1-\rho_1) + \rho_1\left(\log\left(\sigma_{t-1}^2\right) + \log\left(\sigma_{t+1}^2\right)\right)}{1+\rho_1^2}
$$

and

$$
b^2 = \frac{\tau^2}{1+\rho_1^2}.
$$

The beginning log-volatility value, $h_1 = \log(\sigma_1^2)$, can be specified outside of the model for convenience and considered constant. As an alternative, JPR suggest that one could use the time-reversibility of the autoregressive process of order 1 for the log-volatility in (12.2), so that h_0 is obtained as a two-step backward prediction,

$$
h_0 = \rho_0 + \rho_1\left(\rho_0 + \rho_1 h_2\right). \qquad (12.7)
$$

The log-volatility value at time $T+1$, $h_{T+1} = \log(\sigma_{T+1}^2)$, could also be obtained from the autoregressive dynamics in (12.2); for example, by using a two-step forward prediction,

$$
h_{T+1} = \rho_0 + \rho_1\left(\rho_0 + \rho_1 h_{T-1}\right).
$$

The volatilities σ_1^2 and σ_T^2 can then be simulated according to (12.6).[5]

[4]The term $1/\sigma_t^2$ is the Jacobian of the transformation of σ_t^2 to $\log(\sigma_t^2)$ in the density of σ_t^2 in (12.6).

[5]Yet a third option for specifying the beginning log-volatility value, h_1, is to assume that it is randomly distributed according to the stationary volatility distribution,

$$
h_1 \sim \mathrm{N}\left(\frac{\rho_0}{1-\rho_1}, \frac{\tau^2}{1-\rho_1^2}\right).
$$

Since the conditional density in (12.6) is not of standard form, numerical methods are employed to simulate the unobserved volatility path. Various sampling approaches could be employed. Now, we discuss one based on the Metropolis-Hastings (MH) algorithm. The griddy Gibbs sampler explained in Chapter 11 can also be employed for component-by-component simulation.

Simulation of the Unobserved Volatility

As we discussed in earlier chapters, an adequate proposal density ensures efficient density simulation. Consider the full conditional density in (12.6). One could notice that it is made up of the kernels of two distributions. The first one,

$$\frac{1}{\sigma_t}\exp\left(-\frac{r_t^2}{2\sigma_t^2}\right)=\left(\frac{1}{\sigma_t^2}\right)^{-(1/2-1)}\exp\left(-\frac{1}{\sigma_t^2}\frac{r_t^2}{2}\right), \tag{12.8}$$

can be recognized as the kernel of an inverted gamma distribution with a shape parameter 1/2 and a scale parameter $r_t^2/2$. The second kernel,

$$\frac{1}{\sigma_t^2}\exp\left(-\frac{\left(\log\left(\sigma_t^2\right)-a_t\right)^2}{2b^2}\right), \tag{12.9}$$

is the kernel of a log-normal distribution, with parameters a_t and b^2.[6]

The inverted gamma distribution and the log-normal distribution have the so-called multiplicative property: The product of two or more variables

---

[6]Consider a normally distributed random variable, Y, with mean μ and variance s^2. Suppose that Y is transformed as $X = \exp(Y)$. Then X is said to be distributed with the log-normal distribution. Its density is given by

$$f(x\mid\mu,s^2)=\frac{1}{xs\sqrt{2\pi}}\exp\left(-\frac{(\log(x)-\mu)^2}{2s^2}\right).$$

The mean and the variance of X are functions of μ and s^2 given, respectively, by

$$E(X)=\exp\left(\mu+\frac{s^2}{2}\right)$$

and

$$\mathrm{var}(X)=\left(\exp\left(s^2\right)-1\right)\exp\left(2\mu+s^2\right).$$

The log-normal distribution is a very popular distribution in finance. For example, the assumption that asset returns follow a normal distribution immediately implies that the underlying asset prices are log-normally distributed, because the asset return for a given period, Δ, and price at time t, P_t, is defined as $\log\left(P_{t+\Delta}/P(t)\right)$.

with either distribution preserves the distributional form. Since both distributions are skewed to the right, one could be approximated with the other, so that the product has either the form of an inverted gamma or a log-normal distribution.

JPR choose to approximate the log-normal distribution in (12.9) with an inverted gamma distribution by matching their means and variances. Denote the parameters of the approximating inverted gamma distribution by ϕ_1 and ϕ_2. Then

$$\frac{\phi_2}{\phi_1 - 1} = \exp\left(a_t + \frac{b^2}{2}\right)$$

and

$$\frac{\phi_2^2}{(\phi_1 - 1)^2(\phi_1 - 2)} = \left(\exp\left(b^2\right) - 1\right)\exp\left(2a_t + b^2\right).$$

From these two equations, the values of ϕ_1 and ϕ_2 can be determined as

$$\phi_1 = \frac{2\exp(b) - 1}{\exp(b) - 1}$$

and

$$\phi_2 = \frac{\exp\left(a_t + 3b^2/2\right)}{\exp\left(b^2\right) - 1}.$$

The product of the inverted gamma distribution in (12.8) and the approximating one is also an inverted gamma with parameters

$$\phi_1 - \frac{1}{2} + 1$$

and

$$\phi_2 + \frac{r_t^2}{2}. \tag{12.10}$$

That inverted gamma distribution with parameters in (12.10) constitutes the proposal distribution for the conditional density in (12.6). Component-by-component simulation of the unobserved volatilities, σ_t^2, $t = 1, \ldots, T$, consists of the following MH algorithm steps. To draw σ_t^2 from its conditional distribution,

1. Draw $\tilde{\sigma}_t^2$ from an inverted-gamma distribution with parameters given in (12.10).
2. Compute the acceptance probability by applying the formula in (5.7) in Chapter 5 and accept or reject $\tilde{\sigma}_t^2$, as explained in that chapter.

Illustration

Exhibit 12.1 presents JPR's estimation results for four series of weekly returns—a value-weighted index of NYSE stocks, and three portfolios of stocks sorted according to their market capitalization—for the period July 1962 through December 1991. Before estimation, JPR remove the autoregressive and monthly systematic component from weekly returns. That is, the autoregressive and monthly components are estimated with a linear regression and the SV model in (12.1) and (12.2) is fitted to the residuals from that regression.

The variable CV^2 in the exhibit is the squared coefficient of variation of the volatility process, which is a measure of the variability of volatility and is defined as

$$CV^2 = \frac{\text{var}(h)}{\text{E}(h)^2} = \exp\left(\frac{\tau}{1-\rho_1^2}\right) - 1.$$

	NYSE	P_1	P_5	P_{10}
$\rho 0$	–0.39 (0.11)	–0.56 (0.12)	–0.71 (0.36)	–0.56 (0.18)
$\rho 1$	–0.95 (0.013)	–0.93 (0.016)	–0.91 (0.046)	–0.93 (0.022)
τ	0.23 (0.026)	0.32 (0.032)	0.32 (0.095)	0.29 (0.056)
CV^2	0.8 (0.24)	1.1 (0.28)	0.92 (0.27)	0.93 (0.25)

EXHIBIT 12.1 Single-move SV model estimation: Posterior results
Source: Adapted from Table 1 in Jacquier, Polson, and Rossi (1994). The posterior standard deviation is in parentheses. P_1, P_5, and P_{10} are the portfolios composed of the NYSE stocks in the first, fifth, and tenth decile, respectively, according to their market capitalization.

The values of CV^2 in the exhibit are the posterior means of the simulations of the coefficient of variation, computed using the simulations of h_t and τ^2. We could observe that the smallest stocks (of which portfolio P_1 is composed) are more variable than the larger ones, as indicated by CV^2, and all weekly series exhibit a high degree of volatility persistence indicated by the posterior means of ρ_1.

The JPR's single-move approach is attractive with its conceptual simplicity and ease of implementation. Some researchers have argued, however, that the successive MCMC parameter draws based on JPR's algorithm exhibit high correlations. As we explained in Chapter 5, the correlations' magnitude affects the speed of convergence (although not the convergence itself) of the sampling algorithm.

Next, we review an efficient sampling scheme developed by Kim, Shephard, and Chib (1998).[7]

THE MULTIMOVE MCMC ALGORITHM FOR SV MODEL ESTIMATION

We consider the same simple SV model as in (12.1) and (12.2). As a motivation for the discussion of the multimove sampling algorithm, consider Exhibit 12.2. It contains the plots of the autocorrelations of the posterior simulations for ρ_1 and τ from the single-move sampler of JPR and the multimove sampler of Kim, Shephard, and Chib. Simulations using JPR's sampling scheme have a higher degree of autocorrelation, indicating that the MCMC algorithm might take longer to converge.

Prior and Posterior Distributions

As in the earlier discussion, the prior distribution for τ^2 is the conjugate prior for the variance of normal models, namely, an inverted χ^2 distribution with parameters α and β.[8] Kim, Shephard, and Chib (1998) assert a normal prior for the intercept, ρ_0, in the volatility dynamics equation. The choice of prior distribution for the persistence parameter, ρ_1, is dictated by the goal of imposing stationarity (i.e., restricting ρ_1 within the interval $(-1, 1)$). That prior is based on the beta distribution. To obtain the prior, define ϕ to be a random variable taking values between 0 and 1, distributed with a

[7] See also Chib, Nardari, and Shephard (2002), and Mahieu and Schotman (1998) among others.

[8] Chib, Nardari, and Shephard (2002) assert a log-normal distribution for τ.

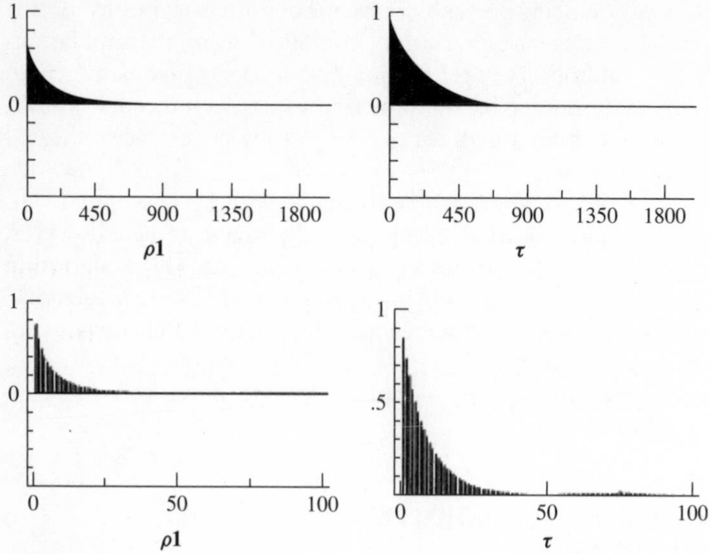

EXHIBIT 12.2 Comparison of the single-move algorithm and the multimove algorithm
Source: Adapted from Figure 2 and Figure 5 in Kim, Shephard, and Chib (1998). The plots in the upper row correspond to simulations obtained using the single-move sampler, while the plots in the lower row correspond to simulations obtained using the multimove sampler of Kim, Shephard, and Chib.

beta (ϕ_1, ϕ_2) distribution. Let $\rho_1 = 2\phi - 1$. Then, ρ_1's range is $(-1, 1)$, as required, and ρ_1 has the prior

$$\pi(\rho_1) = 0.5\,\frac{\Gamma(\phi_1 + \phi_2)}{\Gamma(\phi_1)\Gamma(\phi_2)}\,(0.5(1+\phi))^{\phi_1 - 1}\,(0.5(1-\phi))^{\phi_2 - 1}, \tag{12.11}$$

where Γ is the gamma function.

Since the prior distributions of τ^2 and ρ_0 are conjugate to the normal distribution, their posteriors preserve the prior distributional forms. The posterior distribution of ρ_1, however, is not of a standard form. To see that, observe that for a fixed sequence $h = (h_1, \ldots, h_T)$ the joint distribution of the unobserved volatilities represents a likelihood function for ρ_0, ρ_1, and τ^2. The log-likelihood function is written as

$$\log\left(L\left(\rho_0, \rho_1, \tau^2 \mid h\right)\right) \propto -\frac{T}{2}\log\tau^2 - \frac{\sum_{t=1}^{T-1}\left(h_{t+1} - \rho_0 - \rho_1 h_t\right)^2}{2\tau^2}. \tag{12.12}$$

Then the full conditional log-posterior distribution of ρ_1 is given by

$$\log\left(p\left(\rho_1 \mid h, r, \rho_0, \tau^2\right)\right) \propto (\phi_1 - 1)\log\left(\frac{1+\rho_1}{2}\right) + (\phi_2 - 1)\log\left(\frac{1-\rho_1}{2}\right) + \frac{\sum_{t=1}^{T-1}\left(h_{t+1} - \rho_0 - \rho_1 h_t\right)^2}{2\tau^2}. \tag{12.13}$$

Since the log-posterior density in (12.13) is not standard, one approach to posterior sampling is to use the MH algorithm. Kim, Shephard, and Chib use a normal proposal density centered on the least-squares estimate of ρ_1 from a regression of h_{t+1} on h_t and scaled according to the variance of that least-squares estimate. That is, the mean and variance of the normal proposal are given, respectively, by

$$\widehat{\rho_1} = \frac{\sum_{t=1}^{T-1} h_{t+1} h_t}{\sum_{t=1}^{T-1} h_t^2} \tag{12.14}$$

and

$$s_{\rho_1}^2 = \frac{\tau^2}{\sum_{t=1}^{T-1} h_t^2}. \tag{12.15}$$

Another approach to posterior simulation from (12.13) could be to apply the adaptive rejection algorithm of Gilks and Wild (1992). Next, we discuss the simulation of the unobserved volatilities, h.

Block Simulation of the Unobserved Volatility

The multimove algorithm approaches simulation of h as a block instead of component-by-component and is based on the methods for estimation of models in state-space form, to which the simple SV model defined by (12.1) and (12.2) belongs.[9] The Kalman filter is at the core of the methods for estimation and prediction in a state-space framework. Simulation algorithms associated with the Kalman filter can be integrated without effort into a general MCMC sampling setting. While a detailed discussion of filtering and smoothing are outside of the scope of the book, we present a brief overview of basic filtering and smoothing in the appendix to this chapter.[10]

[9]See West and Harrison (1997), Harvey (1991), and Durbin and Koopman (2001), among others, for discussion of state-space model estimation.

[10]For modifications and extensions of the basic Kalman filtering and smoothing algorithms targeted at achieving greater efficiency in the context of SV models, see, for example, Mahieu and Schotman (1998), Shephard (2005), Stroud, Muller, and Polson (2003), and Durbin and Koopman (2002), among others.

For the purpose of estimation, the expression (12.1) (the observation equation) needs to be transformed, so that the two SV model equations are linear with respect to the disturbances, ϵ_t and η_t, as well as the unobserved log-volatilities, h_t. Squaring and taking the natural logarithm of both sides, we obtain,

$$r_t^* \equiv \log\left(r_t^2\right) = h_t + \log \epsilon_t^*, \tag{12.16}$$

where $\epsilon_t^* = \epsilon_t^2$. Kim, Shephard, and Chib observe that the log-χ^2 distribution of $\log \epsilon_t^*$ can be adequately approximated with a discrete mixture of normal distributions with seven mixture components, so that[11]

$$\begin{aligned} \epsilon_t^* \mid \lambda_t = j &\approx \mathrm{N}\left(\mu_{\lambda_t}, v_{\lambda_t}^2\right) \\ P\left(\lambda_t = j\right) &= p_j, \end{aligned} \tag{12.17}$$

for $j = 1, 2, \ldots, 7$. The approximate density of ϵ_t^* is then

$$g\left(\epsilon_t^* \mid \lambda_t\right) = \sum_{j=1}^{7} p_j f_N\left(\epsilon_t^* \mid \mu_{\lambda_t}, v_{\lambda_t}^2\right),$$

where f_N is the density function of the normal distribution. The seven mixture probabilities, p_j, as well as the seven pairs of normal means and variances, μ_{λ_t} and $v_{\lambda_t}^2$, are estimated in a separate (maximum likelihood or moment-matching) procedure and then considered constants.[12]

The mixing variable, λ_t, is treated as an additional (unobservable) parameter in the SV model and simulated along with the remaining parameters in the MCMC procedure. Its conditional distribution is given by

$$p\left(\lambda_t = j \mid r_t^*, h_t\right) \propto p_j \exp\left(-\frac{\left(\epsilon_t^* - \mu_{\lambda_t}\right)^2}{2 v_{\lambda_t}^2}\right), \tag{12.18}$$

where $\epsilon_t^* = r_t^* - h_t$.

Next, we outline the steps of the MCMC sampling algorithm.

---

[11]The number of mixture components is determined empirically. Omori, Chib, Shephard, and Nakajima (2006) find that a 10-component mixture provides an even better approximation to the log-χ^2 distribution. As explained in Chapter 13, where we briefly discuss mixtures of normal distributions, an appropriately chosen mixture of normals could adequately approximate any distribution.

[12]To correct for the error from employing the discrete mixture approximation in (12.16), Kim, Shephard, and Chib reweigh the posterior parameter and volatility draws.

Sampling Scheme

In the simple SV model of the current discussion, the augmented parameter vector consists of the following components:

- The volatility parameters, $\boldsymbol{\theta} = (\rho_0, \rho_1, \tau^2)$.
- The path of unobservable volatilities, $h = (h_1, \ldots, h_T)$.
- The mixing parameters, $\boldsymbol{\lambda} = (\lambda_1, \ldots, \lambda_T)$.

The parameter components are sampled according to the scheme below. At iteration m of the algorithm:

- Simulate h using the disturbance smoother algorithm outlined in the appendix to this chapter.
- Sample ρ_0, ρ_1, and τ^2 from their posterior distributions outlined earlier.
- Sample $\boldsymbol{\lambda}$ from its conditional distribution above.

Illustration

Kim, Shephard, and Chib examine the daily GBP/USD returns to estimate the SV model (with a minor modification). They employ extensions of the Kalman filter and the smoother we discuss in the appendix. Exhibit 12.3 presents the plot of the GBP/USD absolute returns, as well as the filtered and smoothed volatility estimates. The filtered estimates characteristically tend to reflect volatility "bumps" with a delay compared to the smoothed estimates.

JUMP EXTENSION OF THE SIMPLE SV MODEL

In the previous chapter, we discussed in detail the Bayesian estimation of models allowing for the unobserved volatility to transition through a number of regimes. Similar Markov switching extensions are certainly possible to incorporate within SV models as well. For example, So, Lam, and Li (1998) and Casarin (2003) include a state-dependent parameter in the intercept of the volatility dynamics process thus scaling up or down the unconditional volatility of the return series.

Here we briefly outline a jump extension to the simple SV model. Jumps could be incorporated either in the return dynamics (the observation equation) in (12.1) or in the volatility dynamics (the state transition equation) in (12.2). The two have different implications for the return behavior.

A jump in the return dynamics equation is completely transient in nature. Its effect is dissipated momentarily and has no impact on the

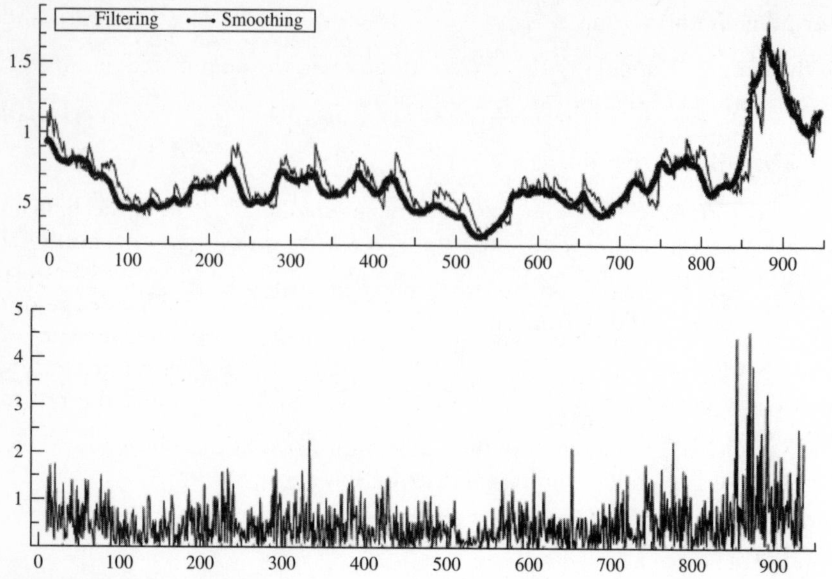

EXHIBIT 12.3 Filtered and smoothed volatility estimates in the multimove algorithm setting
Source: Figure 7 in Kim, Shephard, and Chib (1998).

distribution of returns in the future. Chib, Nardari, and Shephard (2002) consider such an extension to the simple SV model. The jump component is integrated into the return process in the following way:

$$r_t = j_t q_t + e^{h_t/2}\epsilon_t. \tag{12.19}$$

The variable q_t takes a value of 1 if a jump occurs at time t and a value of 0 if a jump does not occur. It is modeled as a Bernoulli-distributed random variable. The probability of a jump, $p \equiv P(q_t = 1)$, is, of course, unknown, and estimated along with the remaining SV model parameters. It has the meaning of the expectation of the number of jumps in a given period of time.[13] For instance, Andersen, Benzoni, and Lund (2002) estimate that, for daily S&P return data, the average number of jumps per day is 0.0137, corresponding to about 3 to 4 jumps per year (assuming 252 business days in a year). The prior distribution of p is assumed to be a (conjugate) beta distribution, with hyperparameters fixed to reflect our prior expectation of p.

[13]The expectation of a Bernoulli random variable is equal to p.

The size of a jump is represented by j_t in (12.19). Chib, Nardari, and Shephard (2002) model the distribution of j_t as

$$\log(1 + j_t) \sim \mathrm{N}\left(-0.5\delta^2, \delta^2\right). \tag{12.20}$$

A log-normal distribution is asserted for the parameter, δ.

Incorporating jumps in the volatility dynamics provide a mechanism to reflect the (persistent) impact of a jump today on the future conditional volatility. Eraker, Johannes, and Polson (2003) find that jumps in volatility complement jumps in returns. When both are included in the model, jumps in returns are less frequent and appear to explain crashlike movements of the stock market. Moreover, it has been argued that the return-generating process is modeled more effectively if the volatility jumps and the return jumps are correlated.

VOLATILITY FORECASTING AND RETURN PREDICTION

Of interest in volatility modeling is, naturally, the model's capacity to produce meaningful predictions for the volatility and the return. The simulations of the volatility path, h, in both the single-move and multimove simulation scenarios can be readily used for prediction.

Suppose there are a total of M draws of the augmented parameter vector, $(\rho_0, \rho_1, \tau^2, h)$. Then, for each period, t, we have available a sample, $h_t^{(m)}, m = 1, \ldots, M$, from the (smoothed) distribution, $p\left(h_t \mid r, \rho_0, \rho_1, \tau^2\right)$, of the unobserved volatilities.

Suppose that we would like to predict the volatility at time $T + 1$. For each draw $\left(\rho_0^{(m)}, \rho_1^{(m)}, \tau^{2(m)}, h^{(m)}\right), m = 1, \ldots, M$, we generate an observation using the equation for the volatility dynamics in (12.2),

$$h_{T+1}^{(m)} = \rho_0^{(m)} + \rho_1^{(m)} h_T^{(m)} + \tau^{(m)} \eta_T,$$

where $\eta_T \sim N\,(0, 1)$. Thus, we obtain a sample from the distribution of predicted volatilities, $p\left(h_{T+1} \mid h_T, \rho_0, \rho_1, \tau^2\right)$. This is an out-of-sample forecast, since both $\left(\rho_0, \rho_1, \tau^2\right)$ and h_T are based on information available up to time T only.

If we want to predict the return at time $T + 1$, we can obtain a sample from the predictive return density by computing

$$r_{T+1}^{(m)} = \exp\left(h_{T+1}^{(m)}/2\right) \epsilon_T,$$

for $m = 1, \ldots, M$.

SUMMARY

In this chapter, we discussed Bayesian estimation of the simple SV model. Two alternative approaches to estimation have been employed in the literature—a single-move sampling scheme and a multimove sampling scheme. The first one relies on traditional MCMC techniques to simulate the unobserved volatilities component-by-component. The second one uses the Kalman filter and smoother, state-space model estimation methods.

Recent research efforts have focused on extending and generalizing the Kalman filter and smoothing algorithms to increase simulation efficiency.

APPENDIX: KALMAN FILTERING AND SMOOTHING

Consider the observation and transition equations of the SV model, given respectively by (12.1) and (12.2). We want to obtain estimates of the unobserved volatility, h_t, $t = 1, \ldots, T$, given the observed sample of return data. At time t, one can distinguish between two types of volatility estimates:

1. A *filtered volatility estimate* at time t is obtained using only return data observed up to and including time t. Denote the estimate by $h_{t|t}$.
2. A *smoothed volatility estimate* at time t is based on information that became available after time t. Denote it by $h_{t|s}$, $s > t$.

The smoothed estimate has a smaller estimation error than the filtered estimate, since a larger amount of information is used in computing it.

Now, we briefly review the basic filtering and smoothing algorithms in the context of the SV model estimation.

The Kalman Filter Algorithm

The Kalman filter is a recursive procedure to obtain filtered estimates of $h_t = \log(\sigma_t^2)$. When applied to a linear model with normal disturbances the filter produces an optimal estimator (in the sense of having minimal mean squared error[14]).

We use the notation established in our discussion on the multimove algorithm. The Kalman filter process consists of two stages.

[14]The mean squared error (MSE) of an estimator, $\hat{\theta}$, is the expected value of the square of the error from the parameter, θ, $E\left[(\theta - \theta)^2\right]$. The MSE can be decomposed as

$$\text{MSE} = \text{var}\left(\hat{\theta}\right) + \left(\text{Bias}\left(\hat{\theta}\right)\right)^2,$$

Prediction Stage Based on the information available up to time $t - 1$, the log-volatility at time t is predicted and its variance computed, as follows:

$$h_{t|t-1} = \rho_0 + \rho_1 h_{t-1|t-1}$$
$$p_{t|t-1} \equiv var(h_{t|t-1}) = \rho_1^2 p_{t-1|t-1} + \tau^2. \tag{12.21}$$

The variance of $h_{t|t-1}$, $p_{t|t-1}$, is conditional on r_t and quantifies the uncertainty associated with the prediction, $h_{t|t-1}$.

Notice that we could use $h_{t|t-1}$ to obtain a prediction for the transformed return, r_t^*, in (12.15),

$$r_t^* = h_{t|t-1} + \mu_{\lambda_{t-1}}, \tag{12.22}$$

where $\mu_{\lambda_{t-1}}$ is the mean of the seven-component normal mixture in (12.16) at time $t - 1$. Since we actually observe the return at time t, we can compute the prediction error and its variance, respectively, as

$$E_t = r_t^* - h_{t|t-1} - \mu_{\lambda_{t-1}}$$
$$O_t = p_{t|t-1} + v_{\lambda_t}^2. \tag{12.23}$$

Both quantities, E_t and O_t, serve to update the log-volatility prediction and its variance in the updating stage below.

Updating Stage The predictions made at time $t - 1$ are updated with the new information made available at time t to obtain the filtered log-volatility estimate,

$$h_{t|t} = h_{t|t-1} + K_t\left(r_t^* - h_{t|t-1} - \mu_{\lambda_{t-1}}\right). \tag{12.24}$$

The expression in (12.24) is based on the reasoning that the error made in predicting the transformed return, r_t^*, provides an indication of the error that might be made in estimating h_t. The quantity K_t is called the "Kalman gain" and is defined as

$$K_t = \frac{\rho_1 p_{t|t-1}}{O_t}. \tag{12.25}$$

The higher the variance of the predicted log-volatility, $p_{t|t-1}$, relative to the variance of the predicted transformed return error, O_t, the greater the correction of $h_{t|t-1}$ at the updating stage. The direction of the correction depends on the sign of the prediction return error—overprediction of r_t^* at

where the bias of an estimator is the difference between its expected value and the parameter value.

time $t-1$ means that $h_{t|t-1}$ is likely lower than the unobserved h_t; therefore, at time t, $h_{t|t-1}$ is updated upward, and vice versa.

The updated variance of $h_{t|t}$ is given by

$$p_{t\,|\,t} = p_{t\,|\,t-1} - K_t \rho_1 p_{t\,|\,t-1}. \tag{12.26}$$

To summarize, for each time step, $t = 1, \ldots, T$, we compute the quantities in (12.21), (12.25), (12.24), and (12.26) and obtain the series of filtered log-volatilities, $h_{t|t}$.

The Smoothing Algorithm

The smoothing algorithm builds on the filtering one and produces smoothed estimates of the unobserved volatility with smaller variance than the filtered estimates. The basic smoothing procedure is very similar to the filtering one, only going in the opposite direction in time, backward. To obtain $h_{t|T}$, we compute the following recursive estimates, for $t = T-1, \ldots, 1$,

$$\begin{aligned}
D_t &= \frac{\rho_1 p_{t\,|\,t}}{p_{t+1\,|\,t}} \\
p_{t\,|\,T} &= p_{t\,|\,t} + D_t^2 \left(p_{t+1\,|\,T} - p_{t+1\,|\,t}\right) \\
h_{t\,|\,T} &= h_{t\,|\,t} + D_t \left(h_{t+1\,|\,T} - h_{t+1\,|\,t}\right).
\end{aligned}$$

The initial values of the recursion, $p_{T|T}$ and $h_{T|T}$, are the filtered estimates computed using (12.26) and (12.24), respectively.

In the context of SV models, Kim, Shephard and Chib (1998) and Chib, Nardari, and Shephard (2002), among others, apply extensions of the basic smoothing algorithm to improve computational efficiency. See De Jong and Shephard (1995), Koopman (1993), and Durbin and Koopman (2002) for more details on these smoother extensions.

SsfPack is a free-of-charge software for state-space models estimation using the Kalman filter. Koopman, Shephard, and Doornik (1999) provide documentation for using that software.

CHAPTER 13

Advanced Techniques for Bayesian Portfolio Selection

On October 19, 1987, the value of the Dow Jones Industrial Average plummeted by 22%, while the value of the S&P 500 index dropped by 20%. In the history of financial markets that day is referred to as "Black Monday." A daily change of that order of magnitude is a nearly impossible event if one assumes that stock returns are normally distributed. The frequency of returns exceeding three standard deviations from the mean is greater than the normal distribution suggests. Moreover, positive and negative returns do not occur with comparable frequency. These characteristics of asset returns—heavy-tailedness and asymmetry, respectively—are well-recognized by academic researchers and making their ways through to quantitative models employed for practical portfolio construction and risk management.[1]

The lack of normality in returns implies that the concept of risk has a richer content than the standard deviation (the traditionally employed risk measure) can reflect. The risk of appreciation of the value of one's investment is certainly welcome, while any rational investor attempts to avoid taking or seeks to minimize the risk of losses. The standard deviation fails to account for this sort of asymmetric investor preference.

Similarly, the covariance matrix does not necessarily contain all information about dependencies across asset returns. To evaluate portfolio risk, one needs to account, for example, for the stronger dependence across

[1]Some of the first academic papers focusing on the heavy-tailed characteristics of returns were published in the 1960s. Among them were Mandelbrot (1963) and Fama (1965). Some risk analytics providers who incorporate heavy-tailed return features in their risk-management platforms are FinAnalytica and Advanced Portfolio Technologies (APT).

returns when the market is down than when it is up and for the tendency of extreme returns to occur simultaneously.

The portfolio paradigm set forth by Markowitz (1952) of minimizing portfolio risk through assessing the contribution to risk of individual securities is as insightful today as it was more than half a century ago. However, the definition of risk has undergone changes and, accordingly, has led to a modification of the portfolio construction problem. Recent research has shown that portfolios derived within the classical mean-variance framework might come short of optimality since failing to recognize the components of risk related to the nonnormality of returns.[2]

In this chapter, we present a general setting for portfolio selection in the presence of atypical (relative to the classical framework) statistical properties of stock returns.[3] Both the frequentist and the Bayesian approaches can be employed for model estimation. However, since in the absence of normality analytical results may not be readily available, the Bayesian framework does offer purely practical advantages (apart from the ones already discussed in Chapter 6). In the first part of the chapter, we discuss one way to incorporate higher moments into portfolio selection based on utility maximization. In the second part, we present an extension of the Black-Litterman model that, in particular, employs minimization of a risk measure superior to the standard deviation (in the nonnormal setting).

We start with a brief overview of some distributional alternatives to normality.

DISTRIBUTIONAL RETURN ASSUMPTIONS ALTERNATIVE TO NORMALITY

A desirable characteristic of the return distribution is that it is flexible enough to accommodate varying degrees of tail thickness and asymmetry. The degree of tail thickness (kurtosis) is considered relative to the tail thickness of the normal distribution, whose kurtosis has a value of 3. A distribution with a value for kurtosis that exceeds 3 is considered heavy-tailed (leptokurtic), whereas kurtosis less than 3 indicates tails thinner than the normal ones (the distribution is then called *platykurtic*). The symmetry of a distribution could

[2]See Rachev, Ortobelli, and Schwartz (2004), Ortobelli, Rachev, Stoyanov, Fabozzi, and Biglova (2005), and Bertocchi, Giacometti, Ortobelli, and Rachev (2005).

[3]The empirical features of returns, such as heavy-tailedness, asymmetry, volatility clustering, and so on are not unique to stock returns, although we focus on them in our discussion. Instead, they are characteristic of the weekly, daily, and higher-frequency returns in most major asset classes.

be captured by various parameters and their particular definition determines the way asymmetry is measured.

Some groups of distributions that have been proposed to deal with heavy-tailedness and asymmetry are:

- Mixtures of normal distributions.
- Student's *t*-distributions (multiple versions and representations exist).
- Stable (non-Gaussian) distributions.
- Extreme value distributions.
- Other distributions, such as skew-normal and generalized hyperbolic.

Below we review some representatives of each of these groups.

Mixtures of Normal Distributions

A mixture of normal distributions ("mixture of normals") is obtained by varying the variance (and/or mean) of a normally distributed random variable. For example, suppose that the variance of a normally distributed random variable is σ_1^2 with probability π and σ_2^2 with probability $1-\pi$. The resulting normal distribution is a discrete scale mixture of normal distributions,

$$X \sim \begin{cases} \mathrm{N}\left(\mu, \sigma_1^2\right), & \text{with probability } \pi \\ \\ \mathrm{N}\left(\mu, \sigma_2^2\right), & \text{with probability } 1-\pi. \end{cases} \tag{13.1}$$

The density of X is then given by

$$f\left(x \mid \mu, \sigma_1^2, \sigma_2^2\right) = \pi f_{\mathrm{N}}\left(\mu, \sigma_1^2\right) + (1-\pi) f_{\mathrm{N}}\left(\mu, \sigma_2^2\right), \tag{13.2}$$

where $f_{\mathrm{N}}\left(\mu,\ \sigma^2\right)$ denotes the normal density with mean μ and variance σ^2.

Continuous mixtures of normals are usually employed to model asset returns. The variation of the normal parameter(s) is introduced in two ways. It is either governed by the realizations of a (unobservable) mixing continuous variable or some stochastic process is assumed for the dynamics of the normal mean/variance. When only the normal variance is varied, the resulting distribution is called a *scale mixture of normals*, whereas when both the mean and the variance are varied, the result is a *location-scale mixture of normals*.

We have come across mixtures of normals several times in the previous chapters. For example, as explained in Chapter 10, the distribution of the asset return in the simple GARCH and SV models is a mixture of normals, when the return disturbances are normal. Furthermore, in Chapter 11 we discussed that some heavy-tailed distributions can be represented as mean-scale mixtures of normals and we used that representation of the Student's t-distribution for facilitating the Markov Chain Monte Carlo simulation algorithm.

In general, an appropriately chosen (discrete) mixture of normals could provide an adequate approximation to most distributions. In Chapter 12, for example, we discussed that Kim, Shephard, and Chib (1998) use a seven-component mixture of normals to approximate a chi-square (χ^2) random variable in their treatment of the SV model.

Asymmetric Student's *t*-Distributions

The popularity of the Student's t-distribution as a heavy-tailed alternative to the normal distribution has led to the development of asymmetric versions of it.[4] Here we outline the Fernandez and Steel (1998)'s version.

Suppose that a random variable, X, has a symmetric (around zero) Student's t-distribution. Denote the Student's t-density function by $t(x)$. Then, by introducing a parameter, γ, $\gamma > 0$, we can transform $t(x)$ into an asymmetric Student's t density in the following way:[5]

$$t(x|\gamma) = \begin{cases} \frac{2}{\gamma+\frac{1}{\gamma}} t\left(\frac{x}{\gamma}\right) & \text{if } X \geq 0 \\ \\ \frac{2}{\gamma+\frac{1}{\gamma}} t(x\gamma) & \text{if } X < 0. \end{cases} \tag{13.4}$$

The parameter γ determines the probability mass on each side of the mode (equal to 0) and, therefore, the degree of skewness. The symmetric case corresponds to $\gamma = 1$.

---

[4]Asymmetric Student's t models have been proposed by Jones and Faddy (2003), Fernandez and Steel (1998), Hansen (1994), Azzalini and Capitanio (2003), and Rachev and Rüschendorf (1994) (in the framework of general subordinated (mixing) model), among others. See also Demarta and McNeil (2004) and Rachev, Mittnik, Fabozzi, Foccardi, and Jasi′c (2007) for the location-scale mixture of normals representation of the multivariate skew Student's t-distribution (a particular case of the generalized hyperbolic distribution, in which the mixing variable has the inverse Gaussian distribution).

[5]This density can be expressed in a more compact way using an indicator function:

$$t(x|\gamma) = \frac{2}{\gamma + \frac{1}{\gamma}} \left[t\left(\frac{x}{\gamma}\right) I_{\{X \geq 0\}} + t(x\gamma) I_{\{X<0\}} \right], \tag{13.3}$$

where $I_{X \geq 0}$ is 1 if $X \geq 0$ and 0 if $X < 0$.

The method above can be used to introduce skewness to any symmetric density.

Stable Distributions

Stable distributions are a class of distributions with very flexible features, which nests as a special case the normal (Gaussian) distribution.[6] The criticism of stable distributions that has prevented them from becoming a mainstream distributional choice is the lack of a closed-form density function (with the exception of the three special cases mentioned below). While this criticism was valid at one time, the advances in computer power make their application increasingly accessible today.

The stable distribution of a random variable, X, is defined through its characteristic function, $\varphi(t)$.[7]

$$\log(\varphi(t)) = \begin{cases} -\sigma^{\alpha}|t|^{\alpha}\left(1 - i\beta \operatorname{sign}(t)\tan\frac{\pi\alpha}{2}\right) + i\mu t, & \text{for } \alpha \neq 1 \\ -\sigma|t|\left(1 - i\beta \operatorname{sign}(t)\log(t)\right) + i\mu t, & \text{for } \alpha = 1 \end{cases} . \tag{13.6}$$

The stable distribution above is denoted by $S_{\alpha}(\beta, \sigma, \mu)$ and its four parameters are defined as follows:

1. α = *index of stability* or *tail parameter*. Regulates the thickness of the tails and takes values between 0 and 2; the lower α is, the heavier the tails of the distribution.
2. β = *skewness parameter*. Regulates the degree of asymmetry and takes values between -1 and 1; the symmetric case is obtained for $\beta = 0$.
3. σ = *scale parameter*.
4. μ = *location parameter*.

The density function of the stable distribution is available in closed form in only three special cases. These are

---

[6]Stable distributions (both Gaussian and non-Gaussian) possess the property of stability (sums of stable random variables are themselves stable), which is clearly appropriate for modeling returns. Moreover, a version of the Central Limit Theorem governs the asymptotic behavior of sums of stable random variables. Therefore, the financial modeling framework built around the normal distribution can be extended to the more general class of stable distributions.

[7]The characteristic function of a random variable, X, with density $f(x)$ is defined as

$$\varphi(t) = E\left(e^{itX}\right) = \int e^{itX} f(x)\,dx. \tag{13.5}$$

1. The Gaussian distribution, $N(\mu, \tau^2)$, for which $\alpha = 2$, $\beta = 0$, and $\tau = \sqrt{2\sigma^2}$.
2. The Cauchy distribution for which $\alpha = 1$ and $\beta = 0$.
3. The completely skewed to the left (right) Lévy distribution for which $\alpha = 1/2$, $\beta = -1$ ($\alpha = 1/2$ and $\beta = 1$).

The symmetric stable distribution ($S_{\alpha(0,\, \sigma,\, \mu)}$) can be represented as a mixture of normals. In the next chapter, we employ the asymmetric stable distribution in the Bayesian estimation of a multifactor model.

Extreme Value Distributions

Extreme value distributions are used to model the far tails of a distribution, i.e., extreme values (minima or maxima) of large sets of independent identically distributed (i.i.d.) random variables.[8] Suppose that a random variable, X, has a distribution function $F(x)$. Depending on the behavior of $F(x)$ for very large values of X (the far right tail of the distribution), three types of extreme value distributions can be defined for the greatest value of X (the distribution of the least value can be obtained by replacing X with $-X$):

Type 1. $F(x)$ behaves approximately like a normal distribution in the tails (the tails decay exponentially fast),

$$F(x) = \exp\left(-e^{-\frac{x-\eta}{\theta}}\right). \tag{13.7}$$

Type 2. $F(x)$ behaves approximately like a Student's t- or Cauchy distribution in the tails (the tails decay at the rate of a polynomial),

$$F(x) = \begin{cases} 0 & \text{for } x < \eta, \\ \exp\left(-\left(\frac{x-\eta}{\theta}\right)^{-k}\right) & \text{for } x \geq \eta. \end{cases} \tag{13.8}$$

Type 3. $F(x)$'s right tail is bounded, that is, the range of X is restricted from above,

$$F(x) = \begin{cases} \exp\left(-\left(\frac{\eta-x}{\theta}\right)^{k}\right) & \text{for } x \leq \eta \\ 0 & \text{for } x > \eta, \end{cases} \tag{13.9}$$

where η, θ, and k are parameters, $\theta > 0$ and $\eta > 0$.

---

[8]In fact, the extreme value distributions are the limiting distributions (as $N \to \infty$) of the extreme value among N i.i.d. random variables.

Skew-Normal Distributions

A number of researchers have extended the normal distribution by introducing skewness to it.[9] Sahu, Dey, and Branco (2003) define a skew-normal random variable, R, as the sum of two normal random variables, one of them restricted to be positive:

$$R = X + \delta Z, \tag{13.10}$$

where: X = normal random variable with mean μ and variance σ^2, $X \sim N(\mu, \sigma^2)$.

Z = standard normal random variable, restricted to take positive values only, $Z \sim N(0, 1)I_{\{Z>0\}}$; that is, its pdf is given by

$$f(Z) = \frac{2}{\sqrt{2\pi\sigma^2}}\exp\left(-\frac{Z^2}{2\sigma^2}\right)I_{\{Z\rangle 0\}}.$$

δ = skewness parameter, which can take any real value; $\delta = 0$ corresponds to the symmetric case and retrieves the original normal distribution.

Harvey, Liechty, Liechty, and Müller (HLLM) (2004) employ the multivariate skew-normal distribution in their investigation of portfolio selection with higher moments. The definition above is generalized to the multivariate case in the following way. Denote by $\mathbf{R}_t$ the vector of returns on the N stocks in a portfolio at time t. Then, assuming that stock returns follow a skew-normal distribution, we write

$$\mathbf{R}_t = \mathbf{X} + \Delta\mathbf{Z}, \tag{13.11}$$

where the $N \times 1$ vector $\mathbf{X}$ is distributed as $\mathrm{N}(\mu, \Sigma)$ and the $N \times 1$ vector $\mathbf{Z}$ is distributed as $\mathrm{N}(0, I_N)$ with density given by

$$f(\mathbf{Z}) = \left(\frac{2}{\pi}\right)^{N/2} |\Sigma|^{-1/2}\exp\left(-\frac{1}{2}\mathbf{Z}'\mathbf{Z}\right)\prod_{j=1}^{N} I_{\{Z_j>0\}}.$$

[9]See Azzalini and Dalla Valle (1996) and Azzalini and Capitanio (1999) for the original discussions of the skew-normal distribution (skew-elliptical distributions in general). Various extensions have been offered by Sahu, Dey, and Branco (2003), Branco and Dey (2001), and Adcock and Schutes (2005), among others.

The diagonal and off-diagonal elements of the $(N \times N)$ matrix Δ in (13.11) indicate the degree of skewness in the returns of the individual stocks and coskewness of stocks, respectively. Coskewness is discussed below.[10] We denote the skew-normal distribution above as $SN(\mu, \Sigma, \Delta)$.

The Joint Modeling of Returns

At the end of our overview of some heavy-tailed distributions, we briefly discuss the two conceptual paths extending the univariate modeling setting to a multivariate one. The first option is to consider the realized returns in each time period as the realization from a multivariate distribution. An alternative is to model the return on each asset separately, as following some univariate distribution, and then impose a dependence structure on returns using the copula framework.

Traditionally, multivariate distributions extend the univariate concepts to the class of the so-called "elliptical distributions" suitable to describe symmetric, unimodal multivariate relationships.[11] The most well-known representatives of the class of elliptical distributions are the multivariate normal distribution and the multivariate Student's *t*-distribution.

Multivariate theory, as applied to risk management, has concentrated primarily on elliptical distributions because of their analytical tractability. Moreover, in the elliptical case, the joint distribution of returns is determined uniquely by the marginal (univariate) distributions and their correlation matrix, so extending univariate modeling to the multivariate case is accomplished in a single step. The definition of elliptical distributions, however, imposes the restriction of symmetry and efforts have been devoted to developing asymmetric extensions.

Multivariate relationships could also be modeled through the use of copulas. The empirical evidence indicates that sometimes the normal

[10]In the skew-normal distribution formulated by Sahu, Dey, and Branco (2003), Δ is diagonal; that is, its off-diagonal elements are zero, thus ignoring coskewness.
[11]The density function of an N-dimensional random variable, $\mathbf{X}$, belonging to the class of elliptical distributions has the form

$$f(\mathbf{x}, \eta, \Omega) = C|\Omega|^{-1/2} g\left((\mathbf{x} - \eta)' \Omega^{-1} (\mathbf{x} - \eta)\right),$$

where η is a location parameter, Ω is a scale matrix, C is a normalizing constant, and g is a generator function which determines the particular distribution of $\mathbf{X}$ (in particular, the heaviness of its tails). For example, the generator function is $g(\mathbf{x}) = \exp(-\mathbf{x}/2)$ in the case of the normal distribution. See Lamantia, Ortobelli, and Rachev, (2006a) and Lamantia, Ortobelli, and Rachev (2006b) for discussions of some applications of elliptical and nonelliptical distributions to investment management.

distribution might describe adequately the behavior of a single asset's returns. However, when two or more assets are jointly modeled, their relationship is not described well by a multivariate (elliptical) normal distribution—there is, for example, a tendency for assets to exhibit coskewness and cokurtosis (concepts explained later in the chapter). The complexity of the dependence structure between stocks requires tools/measures other than the covariance to describe it. The use of copulas allows one to assert any assumptions for the univariate (marginal) distributions of stocks and then superimpose a dependence structure taking into account the empirical features of the multivariate data. Copulas are simply functions linking the univariate distributions with the multivariate one. (We briefly describe copulas in Appendix C.) Intensive research effort is underway to develop estimation methods (in the nonelliptical setting) able to handle dimensions (numbers of securities) of the order encountered in practice. Later in the chapter, we consider an extension of the Black-Litterman framework, which employs a copula to model the dependence between returns.

The two approaches for multivariate modeling are not in conflict. In fact, it can be shown that any multivariate distribution with continuous marginal distributions has a unique copula representation.

PORTFOLIO SELECTION IN THE SETTING OF NONNORMALITY: PRELIMINARIES

In Chapter 6, we discussed that there are three ways to select the optimal portfolio in the mean-variance setting. The corresponding portfolio optimization problems (accompanied by constraints on portfolio weights) are:

- Minimize portfolio's risk, $\omega'\Sigma\omega$, for a given minimal (required) return.
- Maximize portfolio's expected return, $\omega' E(\mathbf{R})$, for a given maximal risk.
- Maximize investor's expected utility function, generally taken to be a quadratic utility function of the type $E\left[U(\omega)\right] = \omega' E(\mathbf{R}) - \lambda\omega'\Sigma\omega$,

where we employ our usual notation:

$\boldsymbol{\omega}$ = vector of portfolio weights.
$E(\mathbf{R})$ = vector of expected returns.
Σ = covariance matrix of returns.
λ = risk aversion parameter.

These three representations of the portfolio problem are equivalent and lead to the same mean-variance efficient frontier.[12] The efficient frontier is

[12] See Rockafellar and Uryasev (2002) and Rachev, Ortobelli, and Schwartz (2004).

obtained by computing the optimal portfolios for varying required return, varying maximal risk, and varying risk-aversion parameter, respectively, in the three cases above.

The choice of modeling returns with a distribution other than the normal implies that the traditional definition of risk, the standard deviation of returns, must be foregone. In general, rational investors perceive as undesired the possibility of a downside occurrence in returns, unlike the potential for a return appreciation of equal size. Consequently, investors would like to minimize the risk from an investment but not necessarily restrict all of the uncertainty associated with its outcome. We say that they have a preference for positive skewness and a dislike for negative skewness. This observation sets the stage for a discussion on the choice of the most appropriate measure of risk.

For example, Markowitz suggested the use of the semistandard deviation as a measure of risk in order to capture the intrinsic preference for "good" volatility (Markowitz, 1959).[13] While we discuss some risk measures employed in portfolio risk management in Appendix A of this chapter, here we only note that in the setting of nonnormality, the optimal portfolio is obtained by modifying the problems above in either of the following ways:

- Maximize a utility function that includes higher moments in order to capture the richness of investors' risk preferences.
- Minimize directly an appropriate risk measure.

Next, we discuss the first approach to portfolio selection in which we follow HLLM (2004).

MAXIMIZATION OF UTILITY WITH HIGHER MOMENTS

As discussed earlier, properties of the return distribution other than the mean and the variance (the first two statistical moments) might be important to

[13]The semistandard deviation measures only the downside potential of returns and is defined as

$$\sqrt{\frac{1}{T}\sum_{t=1}^{n}\min\{0, r_t - \mu\}^2},$$

where r_t is the asset return at time t, μ is the expected return, and T is the number of return observations.

describe better the behavior of returns and, consequently, the risks that investors assume by investing in stocks. Of interest in portfolio construction are not only the higher moments of individual stock returns, but the dependence between higher return moments across stocks, especially the dependence between the third moments, the coskewness.

Coskewness

Coskewness describes the tendency of stocks to have same-sign returns (either positive or negative). The coskewness between the returns on assets i and j is defined as

$$\gamma_{i,j} = E\left[(R_i - \mu_i)\left(R_j - \mu_j\right)^2\right]. \tag{13.12}$$

Clearly, this measure is one-sided (not symmetric). It can be symmetrized as follows:[14]

$$\gamma_{i,j} = E\left[(R_i - \mu_i)\left(R_j - \mu_j\right)^2\right] + E\left[(R_j - \mu_j)(R_i - \mu_i)^2\right]. \tag{13.13}$$

As we can see, a stock with a positive coskewness is a desirable addition to a portfolio because it reduces the portfolio's likelihood of extreme negative outcomes.[15]

---

[14] Alternatively, coskewness can be defined as

$$\gamma_{i,j} = \max\left\{E\left[(R_i - \mu_i)\left(R_j - \mu_j\right)^2\right], E\left[\left(R_j - \mu_j\right)(R_i - \mu_i)^2\right]\right\}.$$

[15] By analogy with the beta of a stock (reflecting the systematic variation component of a stock's return), we can define systematic skewness as

$$\gamma_{i,M} = \frac{E\left[(R_i - \mu_i)(R_M - \mu_M)^2\right]}{\sqrt{\text{var}(R_i)\text{var}(R_M)}},$$

where R_M and μ_M are the market return and expected return, respectively. Harvey and Siddique (2000) replace $R_i - \mu_i$ by ϵ_i, the residual from a regression of stock i's returns on the contemporaneous market return, and $\text{var}(R_i)$ by $E(\epsilon_i^2)$ in their extension of the CAPM.

A number of researchers consider the implications of coskewness for asset pricing. Assets with negative coskewness must have higher expected returns, equivalently lower prices, than identical assets with positive coskewness in order to be attractive

By analogy with the covariance matrix, we can define the skewness matrix, S, for the returns on N stocks as the symmetric matrix

$$S = \begin{pmatrix} \gamma_{1,1} & \gamma_{1,2} & \cdots & \gamma_{1,N} \\ \cdots & \cdots & \cdots & \cdots \\ \gamma_{N,1} & \gamma_{N,2} & \cdots & \gamma_{N,N} \end{pmatrix}, \tag{13.14}$$

where $\gamma_{i,i}$ is the skewness of the return on stock i and $\gamma_{i,j}$ is the coskewness of the returns on stocks i and j as defined in (13.13).

Utility with Higher Moments

Consider a portfolio made up of N stocks with a portfolio weight vector ω and skewness matrix, S. The portfolio skewness is defined as

$$S_p = \omega' S \omega \otimes \omega, \tag{13.15}$$

where $\otimes$ denotes the Kronecker product.

To incorporate investors' preferences for (positive) skewness in the portfolio problem, we modify the expression for the expected quadratic utility in (6.4) in Chapter 6 as follows:

$$E\left[U(\omega'\mathbf{R}_{T+1})\right] = \mu_p - \lambda\sigma_p^2 + \gamma S_p, \tag{13.16}$$

where the portfolio mean and variance, μ_p and σ_p^2, are as defined in Chapter 6, λ is the "classical" risk aversion parameter, and $\mathbf{R}_{T+1}$ is the vector of next-period returns. The parameter γ measures the investor's propensity for skewness.

Recall from our discussion in Chapter 6 that simply plugging in the sample estimates of μ_p, σ_p^2, and S_p into the utility function above and maximizing it results in suboptimal solutions. Instead, portfolio optimization within the Bayesian framework recognizes and takes into account the uncertainty about the estimates of the three distributional moments. The "right ingredients" when maximizing the expected utility function in (13.16) are the moments of the future returns' distribution—the predictive expected returns, the predictive covariance, and the predictive (co)skewness of returns.

---

to investors. Cokurtosis, interpreted as the common sensitivity of returns to extreme movements, has also been considered. See Rubinstein (1973), Kraus and Litzenberger (1976), Barone-Adesi (1985), Dittmar (2002), and Ang, Chen, and Xing (2006) among others.

Distributional Assumptions and Moments

Denote by **R** the returns on the N stocks candidates for the optimal portfolio observed for T periods. Assume that returns follow the skew-normal distribution in (13.11). Then, **R** is a $(T \times N)$ matrix. Each row of **R**, $\mathbf{R}_t = \left(R_{1,t}, \ldots, R_{N,t}\right)'$, $t = 1, \ldots, T$, is an i.i.d. realization of $SN(\mu, \Sigma, \Delta)$.

The parameters of the skew-normal distribution, $\boldsymbol{\mu}$, Σ, and Δ are not the mean, the covariance matrix, and the skewness matrix of **R**. In fact, once we depart from the normality assumption, the distribution parameters rarely carry the interpretation of the statistical moments.[16]

HLLM provide the mean, covariance, and skewness of the multivariate skew-normal distribution as functions of the parameters of the skew-normal distribution, respectively,

$$\mathbf{m}(\mu, \Delta) = \mu + \left(\frac{2}{\pi}\right)^{1/2} \Delta \mathbf{1} \tag{13.17}$$

$$V(\Delta, \Sigma) = \Sigma + \left(1 - \frac{2}{\pi}\right)\Delta\Delta' \tag{13.18}$$

$$\begin{aligned} S(\mu, \Delta, \Sigma, \mathbf{Z}) = {} & \Delta E_3[\mathbf{Z}]\,\Delta' \otimes \Delta' + 3\mu' \otimes \left[\Delta\Delta'\left(1 - \frac{2}{\pi}\right) + \frac{2}{\pi}\Delta\mathbf{1}(\Delta\mathbf{1})'\right] \\ & + 3\left[\left(\frac{2}{\pi}\right)^{1/2} (\Delta\mathbf{1})' \otimes \left(\Sigma + \mu\mu'\right)\right] + 3\mu' \otimes \Sigma \\ & + \mu\mu' \otimes \mu' - 3\mu' \otimes V - \mathbf{m}\mathbf{m}' \otimes \mathbf{m}', \end{aligned} \tag{13.19}$$

where **1** is a compatible vector of ones and $E_3[\mathbf{Z}]$ is the $(N \times N^2)$ matrix of third moments of **Z**.[17]

Likelihood, Prior Assumptions, and Posterior Distributions

The unconditional (with respect to **Z**) likelihood for the model parameters does not have a closed form because of the presence of the unobserved mixing variable **Z**. The unconditional likelihood is given by the N-dimensional

[16] See Chapter 13 of Rachev, Menn, and Fabozzi (2005) for a general description of portfolio optimization with constraints on the skewness and kurtosis.

[17] Let **Z** be a zero-mean $N \times 1$ vector. The matrix of third moments of **Z** is defined as the $N \times N^2$ matrix, $E\left(\mathbf{Z}' \otimes \mathbf{Z}\mathbf{Z}'\right)$.

integral,

$$L(\mu, \Sigma, \Delta \mid \mathbf{R}_t) \propto |\Sigma|^{-T/2} \int_0^\infty \exp\left(-\frac{1}{2}\sum_{t=1}^{T}(\mathbf{R}_t - \mu - \Delta\mathbf{Z}_t)'\Sigma^{-1} \times (\mathbf{R}_t - \mu - \Delta\mathbf{Z}_t)\right)\exp\left(-\frac{1}{2}\mathbf{Z}_t'\mathbf{Z}_t\right)d\mathbf{Z}_t, \qquad (13.20)$$

where $\mathbf{Z}_t$ is an $(N \times 1)$ vector, the realization of the unobserved, mixing variable, $\mathbf{Z}$, at time t. We estimate the three model parameters, μ, Δ, and Σ, within the Bayesian framework and, in addition, simulate $\mathbf{Z}$, along with them. By simulating $\mathbf{Z}$, we avoid performing the multidimensional integration in (13.20).

The likelihood, conditional on $\mathbf{Z}$, is a multivariate normal likelihood. Then, evoking the property of conjugacy, we employ a normal and an inverted Wishart prior distributions and obtain posterior distributions of the same distributional forms. To reflect lack of particular prior intuition about the returns' means, skewness, and covariance, and uncertainty about the prior parameters, HLLM assert,

$$\mu \sim \mathrm{N}(0, 100I_N) \qquad (13.21)$$

$$\mathrm{vec}(\Delta) \sim \mathrm{N}(0, 100I_{N^2}) \qquad (13.22)$$

$$\Sigma \sim \mathrm{IW}(NI_N, N), \qquad (13.23)$$

where IW denotes the inverted Wishart distribution (see the appendix to Chapter 3 for its definition), I_n denotes the $n \times n$ identity matrix, and vec is an operator which stacks the columns of a matrix into a column vector, so that vec(Δ) is a $N^2 \times 1$ vector. For convenience, we combine μ and vec(Δ) into a single vector and define the $(N + N^2) \times 1$ vector

$$\eta = \begin{pmatrix} \mu \\ \mathrm{vec}(\Delta) \end{pmatrix}, \qquad (13.24)$$

with prior distribution $\mathrm{N}(0, 100I_{N+N^2})$.

HLLM (2004) provide the posterior distributions for η and Σ, which are easy to obtain with some straightforward (but tedious) multivariate algebra,

$$\eta \mid \mathbf{R}, \Sigma, \mathbf{Z} \sim \mathrm{N}\left(\mathbf{E}^{-1}\mathbf{e}, \mathbf{E}^{-1}\right)$$

$$\Sigma \mid \mathbf{R}, \mu, \Delta, \mathbf{Z} \sim \mathrm{IW}(\Xi, N + T), \qquad (13.25)$$

where: $E = \mathbf{E} = \sum_{t=1}^{T} \mathbf{s}_t' \Sigma^{-1} \mathbf{s}_t + \frac{1}{100} I_{N+N^2}$.
$e = \mathbf{e} = \sum_{t=1}^{T} \mathbf{s}_t' \Sigma^{-1} \mathbf{R}_t$.
$\Xi = \Xi = \sum_{t=1}^{T} (\mathbf{R}_t - \mu - \Delta \mathbf{Z}_t)(\mathbf{R}_t - \mu - \Delta \mathbf{Z}_i)' + N I_N$.
$\mathbf{s}_t = [I_N, \mathbf{Z}_t{}' \otimes I_N]$.

The conditional distribution of the latent variable, $\mathbf{Z}$, is given by

$$\mathbf{Z}_t \mid \mathbf{R}, \mu, \Sigma, \Delta \sim \mathrm{N}\left(A^{-1}a, A^{-1}\right) I_{\{Z_{it}>0\}}, \tag{13.26}$$

for $i = 1, \ldots, N$ and $t = 1, \ldots, T$, where

$$A = I_N + \Delta' \Sigma^{-1} \Delta$$

$$\mathbf{a} = \sum_{t=1}^{T} \Delta' \Sigma^{-1} (\mathbf{R}_t - \mu).$$

Notice that the posterior distribution of η in (13.25) is the full conditional distribution and thus depends on Σ. (We came across a similar situation in Chapter 5, in our discussion of the semiconjugate linear regression model.) Therefore, direct sampling from the posteriors is not possible. Instead, employing the Gibbs sampler is straightforward.

Sampling from the Conditional Distribution of Z Sampling $\mathbf{Z}$ as a vector from its normal conditional distribution is inefficient because the distribution is truncated at zero. Within the Gibbs sampler one would need to sample repeatedly from the normal distribution, $\mathrm{N}\left(A^{-1}a,\ A^{-1}\right)$, and reject the draw each time one of the N components is negative or zero. The rejection rate of such an algorithm will be high in multidimensional settings.

An alternative sampling approach is to draw $\mathbf{Z}$ component by component. The full conditional distribution of each component, z, of $\mathbf{Z}$ is given by $\mathrm{N}(\mu_z,\ V_z)\, I_{z>0}$, where μ_z and V_z are the corresponding elements of $\mathbf{Z}$'s posterior mean and covariance. This (univariate) normal density is sampled repeatedly until a nonnegative value for z is obtained.[18]

[18]HLLM (2004) employ the so-called "slice sampler" to sample from the distribution of z. This algorithm has a zero-rejection rate and is clearly advantageous when sampling efficiency is crucial. See also Damien, Wakefield, and Walker (1999) for the general methodology and examples of using the slice sampler.

Posterior Moments To obtain samples from the posterior distributions of η and Σ, and the conditional distribution of $\mathbf{Z}$, we employ the Gibbs sampler. As explained in Chapter 5, samples from the posterior distributions of any functions of η, Σ, and $\mathbf{Z}$ are obtained by evaluating the functions at all posterior draws. In particular, we compute the posterior distributions of the mean, covariance, and skewness of the skew-normal distributions as follows:

$$\begin{aligned}
\mathbf{m}^{(j)} &= \mathbf{m}\left(\mu^{(j)},\ \Delta^{(j)}\right)\\
V^{(j)} &= V\left(\Delta^{(j)},\ \Sigma^{(j)}\right)\\
S^{(j)} &= S\left(\mu^{(j)},\ \Sigma^{(j)},\ \Delta^{(j)},\ \mathbf{Z}^{(j)}\right),
\end{aligned}$$

where the subscript, j, denotes the jth posterior draw of the respective parameter, and $\mu^{(j)}$ and $\Delta^{(j)}$ are the respective components of $\eta^{(j)}$.

Predictive Moments and Portfolio Selection

The predictive mean, covariance matrix, and skewness for next-period returns, as given in HLLM, are

$$\tilde{\mathbf{m}} = E\left[\mathbf{m} \mid \mathbf{R}\right]$$

$$\widetilde{V} = E\left[V \mid \mathbf{R}\right] + \operatorname{cov}\left[\mathbf{m} \mid \mathbf{R}\right] \tag{13.27}$$

$$\widetilde{S} = E\left[S \mid \mathbf{R}\right] + 3E\left[V \otimes \mathbf{m} \mid \mathbf{R}\right] - 3E\left[V \mid \mathbf{R}\right] \otimes \tilde{\mathbf{m}} \tag{13.28}$$

$$- E\left[(\mathbf{m} - \tilde{\mathbf{m}})'(\mathbf{m} - \tilde{\mathbf{m}}) \otimes (\mathbf{m} - \tilde{\mathbf{m}}) \mid \mathbf{R}\right], \tag{13.29}$$

where $E[\cdot \mid \mathbf{R}]$ denotes the posterior mean and $\operatorname{cov}[\cdot \mid \mathbf{R}]$ denotes the posterior covariance matrix, computed numerically, as the posterior sample estimates.

We use the predictive moments to compute the portfolio expected return, variance, and skewness. Maximization of the expected utility in (13.16) can then be performed numerically using an optimization software.[19]

[19]State-of-the-art algorithms, called *evolutionary algorithms*, have been and are being developed for optimization in multidimensional problems, where there are likely many local optima. We just mention two major groups of these algorithms—genetic algorithms and Bayesian optimization algorithms—and refer the interested reader to Goldberg (1989) for the former and Pelikan (2005) for the latter.

λ	γ	Expected Utility	Optimal Allocations			
			GE	**Lucent**	**Cisco**	**Sun**
0	0	0.123	0.9e-3	0.1e-3	0.5e-3	0.99
0	0.5	0.109	0.405	0.409	0.186	0
0.5	0	−1.745	0.784	0.125	0.054	0.037
0.5	0.5	−1.731	0.785	0.129	0.065	0.021

EXHIBIT 13.1 Expected utility maximization and optimal allocations
Source: Adapted from Tables 4 and 6 in Harvey, Liechty, Liechty, and Müller (2004).

Illustration: HLLM's Approach

HLLM consider the daily returns on four stocks, General Electric (GE), Lucent Technologies (Lucent), Cisco Systems (Cisco), and Sun Microsystems (Sun) for the period from April 1996 to March 2002. Exhibit 13.1 presents their expected utility and optimal allocation results for different values of the risk aversion parameter, λ, and the propensity to skewness parameter, γ.

Next, we present an extension of the Black-Litterman (BL) approach, developed by Meucci (2006a), which takes into account the nonnormality of asset returns and employs a flexible approach to combining market information and portfolio manager's intuition. Admittedly, Meucci's framework cannot be categorized strictly as a Bayesian one. However, it does fit the Bayesian paradigm conceptually, since it provides the setting for pooling together information originating from different sources.

EXTENDING THE BLACK-LITTERMAN APPROACH: COPULA OPINION POOLING

The principal advantage of Meucci's approach is that it allows a portfolio manager to express subjective views on quantities he is intimately familiar with, such as term spreads, implied volatilities, risk factors, prices, and returns—in general, sources of randomness in the market—instead of on the distribution parameters. The distribution parameters rarely have intuitive interpretations, once the normality assumption is replaced, as we mentioned earlier in this chapter.

Meucci emphasizes that the extended framework is amenable to nonnormality assumptions for the distribution of the sources of randomness. Of course, the BL model could also be modified to account for nonnormality. Any resulting lack of analytical tractability can be handled with the MCMC methods.

One aspect of Meucci's model facilitates greatly its application in practice—the straightforward way of expressing (and incorporating) view confidence. Recall that in the original BL framework the view confidence is quantified by the corresponding diagonal element of Ω, the view covariance matrix. There is no agreement, however, as to the most appropriate way of translating view confidence into view variance. (We presented a backtesting procedure to do that in Chapter 8.) Meucci's approach combines the subjective and objective (market-implied) distributions of each view by simply taking their weighted average; the weight is the view confidence.

Finally, Meucci's extension of the BL model boasts a feature providing additional modeling flexibility: The dependence between views is specified by means of a copula function.

We review Meucci's framework next. For the source of randomness in the market we use stock returns, although, as mentioned already, a different market random quantity could be employed.

Market-Implied and Subjective Information

Suppose that return data are available on N stocks for T periods; denote the $(T \times N)$ data matrix by $\boldsymbol{R}$. We assume that each row of $\boldsymbol{R}$, $\boldsymbol{R}_t$, is a realization from a certain multivariate distribution. In the BL model, this distribution is multivariate normal with mean, μ, and covariance matrix Σ. To reflect the evidence for nonnormality in $\boldsymbol{R}$, Meucci (2006a) assumes that returns follow a multivariate asymmetric Student's t-distribution.[20]

As in the BL model, one might want to use market equilibrium as a center of gravity. Reflecting this equilibrium market information in the distribution parameters is not always straightforward in a nonnormal setting. The reasons for that are practical and conceptual. In the BL model, μ has the interpretation of the vector of expected returns. Its distribution is then naturally centered on the equilibrium risk premiums, Π. (See (8.4) in Chapter 8.) The location parameter in an asymmetric Student's t-distribution (or any other heavy-tailed distribution), however, is generally not the mean (unless the skew parameter is zero). Instead, the mean is a function of a few

[20]Meucci uses the multivariate asymmetric Student's t version of Azzalini and Capitanio (2003) and Azzalini (2005).

model parameters. It is then not immediately clear how to specify a prior reflecting the equilibrium information.

The conceptual difficulty originates from the fact that the CAPM model used to derive the equilibrium risk premiums in the BL framework assumes that returns are elliptically distributed. This contradicts the motivation for asserting an asymmetric, heavy-tailed distribution for returns and makes the expression defining Π in (8.2) in Chapter 8 inappropriate to use.

Meucci's framework is general enough and does not require that equilibrium arguments be employed.

Views and View Distributions

Suppose that a portfolio manager expresses K views on expected returns. The views are collected in the $K \times N$ view matrix, $\boldsymbol{P}$, as in Chapter 8. Recall that a row in $\boldsymbol{P}$ represents a view portfolio—a linear combination of the assets involved in the particular view.

Using the observed returns in $\boldsymbol{R}$, we could obtain the returns on the view portfolios that would have been realized if the view portfolios were held during the T periods of the sample. That is, the market-implied view returns are given by the $T \times K$ matrix, $\boldsymbol{W}$,

$$\mathbf{W} = \mathbf{R}\,\mathbf{P}'. \tag{13.30}$$

From a statistical and financial point of view, the collection of market-implied returns in $\boldsymbol{W}$ can be analyzed row-wise and column-wise. Traditionally, $\boldsymbol{W}$ is analyzed row-wise: each row, $\boldsymbol{W}_t$, $t = 1, \ldots, T$, represents the market-implied returns on the K views in period t. In the BL framework, $\boldsymbol{W}_t$ has a multivariate normal distribution.

Alternatively, one can consider the columns of $\boldsymbol{W}$. The kth column, $\boldsymbol{W}_k$, is interpreted as a sample of market-implied returns from the kth view's marginal distribution.[21]

Most multivariate distributions that would be used to describe the joint behavior of returns have marginal distributions of the same form. For example, the multivariate normal and asymmetric Student's t-distributions have, respectively, normal and asymmetric Student's t-margins. Therefore, the marginal view distribution is uniquely identified.[22]

---

[21]This dichotomy reflects the two approaches to the joint modeling of returns on multiple assets we mentioned earlier in the chapter.

[22]Meucci (2006b) extends the framework by considering a nonparametric, numerical approach. In it, there is no need to assume specific forms for the multivariate, nor marginal distributions.

Let us denote the market-implied distribution of the returns on the kth view by

$$\pi^{R}_{W_k}. \tag{13.31}$$

Portfolio managers' views need not be expressed as forecasts for the parameters of a distribution. Instead, managers can, for instance, simply specify a range for the expected return on a view portfolio. Such prior information can then be translated into a uniform distribution for the particular view over the given range. We denote the subjective distribution of returns on the kth view by

$$\pi_{W_k}. \tag{13.32}$$

Combining the Market and the Views: The Marginal Posterior View Distributions

The BL model combines the objective and subjective distributions of expected returns by means of Bayes' theorem to obtain their posterior distribution. A more general framework for combining probability distributions (and in particular, aggregating information from different sources) is the so-called opinion pooling framework.[23]

One of the simplest opinion pool methods is the linear opinion pool, in which probability distributions are aggregated as linear combinations. Weights are used to represent the quality of forecasts (sources of information). In our problem of combining market-implied and subjective view distributions opinion pooling is an attractive alternative to a full-blown Bayesian analysis, since the portfolio manager's confidence in views can naturally be employed as a weight.

Denote the cumulative distribution functions corresponding to the market-implied and subjective view densities, $\pi^{R}_{W_k}$ and π_{W_k}, by $F^{R}_{W_k}$ and F_{W_k}, respectively. Suppose that the manager's confidence in the kth view is c_k (expressed as a proportion). The posterior distribution of returns on the kth view is then given by

$$p_{W_k} = c_k \pi_{W_k} + (1 - c_k)\, \pi^{R}_{W_k}, \tag{13.33}$$

for $k = 1, \ldots, K$. As in the BL model, when confidence in a view is zero, the posterior view distribution coincides with the market-implied prior view distribution. Conversely, certainty in a view results in the posterior distribution being the same as the manager's subjective prior one.

[23]See, for example, Genest and Zidek (1986) and Cooke (1991) for a review of opinion pooling approaches and methods.

Views Dependence Structure: The Joint Posterior View Distribution

In the BL model, views are *a priori* assumed to be independent (the off-diagonal elements of the views' prior covariance matrix, Ω, in (8.4) in Chapter 8 are usually set to zero).[24] However, *a posteriori*, after blending together views and market, the dependence among stock returns is mapped onto the views. The mechanism of this mapping is implicit in the Bayesian updating procedure.

In this section's framework, we make it explicit. What allows us to do this is our bottom-up approach—market and views are combined at the univariate level. We extract the pattern of association contained in the collection of market-implied view returns in $\mathbf{W}$ and superimpose it on the K univariate posterior view distributions in the following way. (We provide an overview of copulas in Appendix C of this chapter.)

1. Fit a copula to the return data in $\mathbf{W}$, using the market-induced view distributions in (13.31) as the marginal distributions.
2. Obtain the joint posterior view distribution through mapping the copula onto the set of subjective marginal view distributions in (13.32) to derive the joint posterior distribution of the K views. Denote the sample from this joint posterior distribution by $\widetilde{\mathbf{W}}$.

Posterior Distribution of the Market Realizations

Finally, notice that our analysis until now has only centered on the returns of the K assets involved in the manager's views. One expects that "twisting" (via the views) of some of the stock returns would affect the remaining returns as well, since all returns are mutually dependent. Below we show how to reflect this feed-through effect. (In the BL model estimation, this view propagation is implicit; see Chapter 8.)

We express the market realizations, $\mathbf{R}$, in view coordinates in the following way:

$$\mathbf{R} \Rightarrow \begin{pmatrix} \mathbf{RP}' \\ \mathbf{RP}_n' \end{pmatrix}. \tag{13.34}$$

The first block matrix above, $\mathbf{RP}'$, is $\mathbf{W}$, as defined in (13.30). While $\mathbf{W}$ contains the market realizations of the K view portfolios, we can think of

[24]Recall from statistical theory that if the random variables X and Y have a bivariate normal distribution and their covariance is zero, $\text{cov}(X, Y) = 0$, X and Y are necessarily independent. The result is easily extended to any dimension. (In general, however, zero correlation does not imply independence.)

the lower block matrix, $\mathbf{RP}_n'$, as the market realizations of the "non-view" portfolios. There are, clearly, a large number of linear combinations of the $N - K$ market realizations not involved in the views and, accordingly, no single way to construct the lower block matrix. Meucci assumes that its row vectors are orthogonal.[25]

In (13.34) we substitute $\mathbf{RP}'$ with the sample from the joint posterior view distribution, $\widetilde{\mathbf{W}}$, and obtain a sample of the posterior distribution of the market realizations by reverting to the original market coordinates,

$$\widetilde{\mathbf{R}} \stackrel{d}{=} \begin{pmatrix} \widetilde{\mathbf{W}} \\ \mathbf{RP}_n' \end{pmatrix} \begin{pmatrix} \mathbf{P}' \\ \mathbf{P}_n' \end{pmatrix}^{-1}, \tag{13.35}$$

All elements of $\widetilde{\mathbf{R}}$ are now adjusted according to the views and their dependence structure. Notice that no analytical expression for the density of $\widetilde{\mathbf{R}}$ is available. This fact, however, does not obstruct portfolio construction.

In the presence of nonnormality, portfolio construction can be performed by minimization of a risk measure other than the portfolio standard deviation. (In appendix A of this chapter, we present a brief overview of some alternative risk measures.)

Portfolio Construction

In Appendix A of this chapter, we explain that the *conditional value-at-risk* (CVaR) is a risk measure with a number of desirable properties and can be used to formulate the portfolio selection problem as follows:

$$\min_{\omega} \mathrm{CVaR}_p,$$

subject to constraints.

This minimization problem is solved numerically. When only a large number of return scenarios (samples) is available (no analytical expression for the return density, as in Meucci's framework), the minimization is scenario-based. We outline the approach of Rockafeller and Uryasev (2000) for CVaR minimization in Appendix B.

---

[25] More formally, the matrix $\mathbf{P}_n$ is a $(N - K \times N)$ matrix spanning the null space of $\mathbf{P}$.

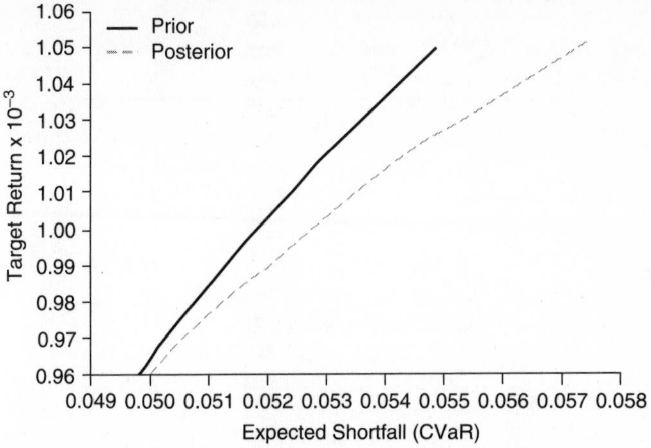

EXHIBIT 13.2 Mean-CVaR efficient frontiers
Source: Figure 4 in Meucci (2006a).

Illustration: Meucci's Approach

Meucci (2006a) adopts a pragmatic approach in his empirical illustration. Weekly return data on four international stock indexes are employed. The indexes are the S&P 500, the FTSE 100, the CAC 40, and the DAX. He asserts the asymmetric multivariate Student's t-distribution for the index returns and estimates its parameters by maximum likelihood by fitting it to the observed return data. (However, we emphasize that Bayesian estimation is also possible and even preferable if one would like to account for parameter uncertainty.)

A large number of simulations are then generated from the asymmetric Student's t-distribution (using the parameter estimates). The simulations make up the $T \times N$ matrix $\mathbf{R}$. A single view is expressed—the DAX is expected to realize between 0% and −2% in the following (one-week) period. The returns in $\mathbf{R}$ are updated according to our earlier discussion and CVaR minimization is employed to determine the optimal index allocations.

The mean-CVaR efficient frontiers before and after the view on the DAX index is reflected are plotted in Exhibit 13.2, while the corresponding prior and posterior optimal allocations are given in Exhibit 13.3. The pessimistic view on the DAX index worsens the expected return-risk trade-off and shifts the efficient frontier to the right. As in the BL framework, the view is

Index \ Target Return	0.96	0.99	1.02	1.05
Prior Allocations				
S&P 500	45	42	39	37
FTSE 100	43	37	32	26
CAC 40	5	8	11	13
DAX	7	13	18	24
Posterior Allocations				
S&P 500	47	45	39	35
FTSE 100	36	25	17	8
CAC 40	17	30	44	57
DAX	0	0	0	0

EXHIBIT 13.3 Prior and posterior optimal allocations
Source: Adapted from Tables A and B in Meucci (2006a).

propagated through the returns on the remaining indexes and their optimal allocations—adjusted accordingly.

EXTENDING THE BLACK-LITTERMAN APPROACH: STABLE DISTRIBUTION

In the previous section, we discussed that since the CAPM assumes that returns are elliptically distributed, using it to derive the equilibrium returns, π, in the presence of nonnormality lacks consistency. When more general (than normality) distributional assumptions are adopted, it is appropriate to consider also more general risk measures in obtaining π. Giacometti, Bertocchi, Rachev, and Fabozzi (2007) (GBRF, hereafter) investigate the choice of return distributions and risk measures in a normal, a Student's t, and a stable setting. We discuss their approach to equilibrium return estimation now.

Equilibrium Returns Under Nonnormality

The equilibrium returns, π, can be backed out from the portfolio selection problem, as mentioned in Chapter 8. Let us see how. Consider the utility maximization problem in (6.3) in Chapter 6. We rewrite it below for the case of a quadratic utility:

$$\max_{\omega}\left(\omega'\mu - \frac{A}{2}\omega'\Sigma\omega\right), \tag{13.36}$$

where ω, μ, Σ, and A are the usual notations for the portfolio weights, expected returns, return covariance matrix, and coefficient of relative risk aversion. To obtain the equilibrium returns, we assume the market is in equilibrium and the benchmark's market capitalization weights are the optimal weights, ω^*. The expression in (13.36) then takes the form

$$\max_{\omega}\left(\boldsymbol{\omega}\boldsymbol{\Pi} - \frac{A}{2}\boldsymbol{\omega}'\boldsymbol{\Sigma}\boldsymbol{\omega}\right), \tag{13.37}$$

so that Π is obtained as the vector of expected returns that would have produced ω^* in a procedure appropriately termed *reverse optimization.*

Under the assumption of return normality, Π is given by

$$\boldsymbol{\Pi} = A\boldsymbol{\Sigma}\boldsymbol{\omega}^*, \tag{13.38}$$

which is the same expression as the one in equation (8.2) in Chapter 8. In a general distributional setting, (13.37) is modified as follows:

$$\max_{\omega}\left(\boldsymbol{\omega}\boldsymbol{\Pi} - \frac{A}{2}\rho\left(\boldsymbol{\omega}'r\right)\right), \tag{13.39}$$

where $\rho\left(\boldsymbol{\omega}'\mathbf{r}\right)$ denotes an arbitrary measure of risk of the portfolio return, $\omega'\mathbf{r}$. GBRF investigate three possibilities for $\rho\left(\boldsymbol{\omega}'\mathbf{r}\right)$: the variance, the VaR, and the CVaR, and show that the equilibrium returns are given, respectively, by

$$\boldsymbol{\Pi} = \begin{cases} A\mathbf{V}\boldsymbol{\omega}^* & \text{when } \rho\left(\boldsymbol{\omega}'\mathbf{r}\right) = \text{variance} \\ \frac{A}{2}\left(\frac{\mathbf{V}\boldsymbol{\omega}^*}{\sqrt{\boldsymbol{\omega}^{*\prime}\mathbf{V}\boldsymbol{\omega}^*}}\text{CVaR}_\alpha - \boldsymbol{\mu}\right) & \text{when } \rho\left(\boldsymbol{\omega}'\mathbf{r}\right) = \text{CVaR} \\ \frac{A}{2}\left(\frac{\mathbf{V}\boldsymbol{\omega}^*}{\sqrt{\boldsymbol{\omega}^{*\prime}\mathbf{V}\boldsymbol{\omega}^*}}\text{VaR}_\alpha - \boldsymbol{\mu}\right) & \text{when } \rho\left(\boldsymbol{\omega}'\mathbf{r}\right) = \text{VaR,} \end{cases} \tag{13.40}$$

where: V = dispersion matrix equal to:
- Σ, the covariance matrix, under a normal distributional assumption.
- $S(\nu - 2)/\nu$, under a Student's t distributional assumption, where S is the scale matrix and ν is the degrees-of-freedom parameter of the Student's t-distribution.
- The dispersion matrix of the multivariate stable distribution.[26]

VaR_α = value-at-risk for the corresponding distribution.[27]
CVaR_α = conditional value-at-risk for the corresponding distribution.[28]

In an examination of the 50 largest constituents of the S&P 500 index, GBRF show that the combination of the stable distributional assumption and the covariance matrix as a risk measure yields the best estimates of the equilibrium returns, Π, while the stable distribution together with the CVaR as a measure of risk produce the second-best estimates of Π.

SUMMARY

The heavy-tailedness and asymmetry observed in asset returns could impact adversely portfolio choice based on the mean-variance framework. Apart from asserting a flexible nonnormal distribution for returns, one can employ two approaches for quantitative portfolio selection. The first approach involves specifying and maximizing an appropriate utility function. We presented HLLM's framework, in which the utility function includes explicitly the portfolio skewness.

The second approach consists of directly minimizing a risk measure, which implicitly accounts for the heavy-tailedness and asymmetry in the

[26]See Rachev and Mittnik (2000) for the definition of the multivariate stable distribution.

[27]The VaR_α for the Student's t-distribution can be obtained easily, as explained in Chapter 11. The VaR_α for the stable distribution can be computed numerically; see Rachev and Mittnik (2000) and Lamantia, Ortobelli, and Rachev (2006a).

[28]See GBRF for the closed-form expression for CVaR_α in the case of the Student's t-distribution and the integral representation of CVaR_α in the case of the stable distribution.

return distribution. The CVaR is such a risk measure, whose minimization can be performed using scenarios generated from the return distribution.

In the next chapter, we focus on multifactor models and present a unifying framework for portfolio selection and risk management.

APPENDIX A: SOME RISK MEASURES EMPLOYED IN PORTFOLIO CONSTRUCTION

The choice of risk measure employed in portfolio selection is not one to be taken lightly. Minimizing an unsuitable risk measure could produce suboptimal portfolio weights.[29]

Some risk measures capture the general uncertainty of returns and penalize both downside and upside deviations from the mean. Among them are the standard deviation and the mean absolute deviation. Since minimizing them limits the potential for growth of the portfolio value, even if returns have normal distribution (in general elliptical distribution, such that the first two moments are sufficient to describe it uniquely), these measures would produce optimal allocations that are not optimal for investors with preference for very high portfolio returns.

The so-called "safety risk measures," on the other hand, reflect only the downside potential of returns—what investors generally perceive as risk. We review some of them here.[30] Denote portfolio return by R_p. (To avoid some technical difficulties, we assume that R_p has a density.)

Lower Partial Moment The lower partial moment is a generalization of the semivariance proposed by Markowitz (1959). It only reflects return realizations below a certain target return level, R,

$$\mathrm{LPM}_q\left(R_p\right) = \left(E\left[\left(R_p - \overline{R}\right)^q\right] I_{R_p<\overline{R}}\right)^{1/q}, \tag{13.41}$$

where $q \geq 1$. The value of $q = 2$ corresponds to the semistandard deviation. Investor's risk aversion is directly related to the power, q, of the return deviation—the higher the risk aversion, the higher q.

---

[29]See, for example, Ortobelli, Rachev, Stoyanov, Fabozzi, and Biglova (2005).

[30]For more details on downside risk measures, see Sortino and Satchell (2001). Ortobelli, Rachev, Stoyanov, Fabozzi, and Biglova (2005) and Rockafellar, Uryasev, and Zabarankin (2003) discuss the properties of various risk measures applied to portfolio selection.

MiniMax The MiniMax of portfolio returns represents the worst outcome that could occur if the portfolio return falls below a certain threshold, L, and is defined as[31]

$$MM\left(R_p\right) = \inf\left\{L \mid P\left(R_p \le L\right) = 0\right\}. \tag{13.42}$$

Value-at-Risk (VaR) The value-at-risk at the $(1 - \alpha)$ confidence level ($\text{VaR}_{(1-\alpha)}$) of a portfolio is the maximum loss that could occur such that, with probability α, this loss is no greater than $\text{VaR}_{(1-\alpha)}$. Denote the portfolio loss by $L_p = -R_p$. Portfolio p's VaR is implicitly defined through the equation

$$P\left(L_p > \text{VaR}_{(1-\alpha)}(L_p)\right) = \alpha. \tag{13.43}$$

Equivalently, we can write that expression in terms of the portfolio's return distribution as

$$P\left(R_p < \text{VaR}_{\alpha}(R_p)\right) = \alpha. \tag{13.44}$$

That is, $VaR_{(1-\alpha)}(L_p)$ is the $(1 - \alpha)$ quantile of the loss distribution. (Equivalently, $\text{VaR}_{\alpha}(R_p)$ is the α quantile of the return distribution.) Some values of α used in practice are 0.1, 0.05, and 0.01. Under the assumption of normality, VaR is a multiple of the standard deviation. In that case, then, minimization of either risk measure results in the same optimal portfolio. The threshold, L, in (13.42) is often chosen to be the portfolio $VaR_{(1-\alpha)}(L_p)$.

Conditional Value-at-Risk (CVaR) The portfolio CVaR is the loss the portfolio is expected to realize if its loss exceeds $VaR_{(1-\alpha)}(L_p)$,

$$\text{CVaR}_{(1-\alpha)}\left(L_p\right) = E\left[L_p \mid L_p \ge \text{VaR}_{(1-\alpha)}\left(L_p\right)\right]. \tag{13.45}$$

Equivalently,

$$\text{CVaR}_{(\alpha)}\left(R_p\right) = E\left[R_p \mid R_p \le \text{VaR}_{(\alpha)}\left(R_p\right)\right]. \tag{13.46}$$

We now outline a few points of comparison between VaR and CVaR. These two measures are the focus of our attention because of the popularity of the first and the advantages of the second. Neither the lower partial moment nor the MiniMax provide information about the portfolio return in the left tail of the return distribution, which is of primary interest in portfolio risk analysis.

---

[31] MiniMax is proposed by Young (1998).

- VaR does not provide information for the distribution of portfolio losses beyond the α quantile.
- VaR is not subadditive; that is, the VaR of the portfolio return might be larger than the sum of the VaR's of the individual assets' returns (or sub-portfolio returns). This result is clearly very undesirable as it contradicts the intuition of portfolio diversification benefits.
- Portfolio optimization based on VaR is much more difficult than the one based on the CVaR. The reason is that when calculated using scenarios, the portfolio VaR is not smooth as a function of portfolio positions, is not convex, and has multiple local extremal points.

All of these shortcomings of VaR are overcome by CVaR. We discuss the approach to CVaR minimization due to Rockafellar and Uryasev (2000) in Appendix B.[32]

How does one compare the performance of portfolios generated through minimization of various risk measures? The generally accepted approach is to compare the portfolio return on a risk-adjusted basis by comparing various performance measures. Performance measures are then closely related to risk measures and could be discussed in parallel. The most commonly employed performance measure is the *Sharpe ratio*, defined as

$$\mathrm{SR}_p = \frac{E\left[R_p\right] - r_f}{\sigma_p}, \tag{13.47}$$

where r_f is the risk-free rate and σ_p is the portfolio standard deviation. The disadvantages of the Sharpe ratio are directly related to the deficiencies of the standard deviation as a measure of risk.[33]

Alternative performance measures corresponding to the risk measures discussed above have been defined. For example, Sortino (2000) and Sortino and Satchell (2001) propose the ratio between the portfolio's expected return and its lower partial moment. The performance measure using the MiniMax is suggested by Young (1998). Rachev, Ortobelli, and Schwartz (2004) propose using the $VaR_{99\%}$ (see also Favre and Galeano, 2002), whereas the STARR ratio uses the portfolio's $CVaR_\alpha(R_p)$ to adjust expected return for risk (Rachev, Martin, Racheva-Iotova, and Stoyanov, 2007).

---

[32] For more general constructions and detailed analysis, see Rachev, Stoyanov, and Fabozzi (2007).

[33] Moreover, in the case return distributions with infinite variance, such as the stable distribution, the Sharpe ratio is not defined.

APPENDIX B: CVAR OPTIMIZATION

CVaR has attractive properties as a risk measure compared to VaR—it is subadditive, a smooth function of portfolio positions, and its optimization is relatively straightforward. Rockafellar and Uryasev (2000) developed the CVaR optimization methodology, which we briefly outline here.[34]

Denote the returns on the N candidates for inclusion in the optimal portfolio by $\mathbf{R}$ and the $N \times 1$ vector of portfolio weights by ω. The portfolio optimization problem based on the portfolio CVaR is expressed as

$$\min_{\omega} \text{CVaR}_{\alpha}\left(R_p\right), \tag{13.48}$$

$$\text{subject to constraints}, \tag{13.49}$$

where $R_p = \omega'\mathbf{R}$. Institutional portfolio managers face at least the following two constraints,

$$\omega_j \geq 0, \quad j = 1, \ldots, N \tag{13.50}$$

$$\sum_{j=1}^{N} \omega_j = 1.$$

Consider the definition of CVaR in (13.46). The quantity $\text{CVaR}_{\alpha}\left(R_p\right)$ depends on $\text{VaR}_{\alpha}\left(R_p\right)$, which poses difficulties if no analytical expression for $\text{VaR}_{\alpha}\left(R_p\right)$ is available.

The insight of Rockafellar and Uryasev is that $\text{CVaR}_{\alpha}\left(R_p\right)$ can be substituted by the following simpler function,

$$F_{\alpha}\left(\boldsymbol{\omega}, C\right) = C + \frac{1}{1-\alpha} \int \left(-R_p - C\right)^{+} f\left(\mathbf{R}\right) \, d\mathbf{R}, \tag{13.51}$$

where $[v]^{+} = v$, when $v > 0$, and $[v]^{+} = 0$, when $v \leq 0$, $f\left(\mathbf{R}\right)$ is the density function of $\mathbf{R}$, and C is the VaR defined in (13.43).

Rockafellar and Uryasev show that $F_{\alpha}\left(\boldsymbol{\omega}, C\right)$ is convex with respect to C and

$$\min_{C} F_{\alpha}\left(\boldsymbol{\omega}, C\right) = \text{CVaR}_{\alpha}\left(R_p\right). \tag{13.52}$$

[34]For more advanced portfolio risk analysis and optimization techniques, see Rachev, Ortobelli, Stoyanov, and Fabozzi (2007).

The implication of (13.52) is that $\text{CVaR}_\alpha(R_p)$ can be minimized without knowledge of $\text{VaR}_\alpha(R_p)$. Most importantly, minimizing $F_\alpha(\boldsymbol{\omega}, C)$ with respect to all pairs (ω, C) is equivalent to minimizing $CVaR_\alpha(R_p)$,

$$\min_{\boldsymbol{\omega}, C} F_\alpha(\boldsymbol{\omega}, C) = \min_{\boldsymbol{\omega}} \text{CVaR}_\alpha(R_p). \tag{13.53}$$

Let (ω^*, C^*) be the pair, solution to the minimization in (13.53). The first component, ω^* are the portfolio weights that minimize $\text{CVaR}_\alpha(R_p)$. The second component, C^*, is generally the corresponding $\text{VaR}_\alpha(R_p)$.

Consider the case when no analytical expression for the density of returns, $f(\mathbf{R})$, exists. Instead, we have available a large number (M) of scenarios generated from it. Denote the scenarios with superscripts, $\mathbf{R}^m = (R_1^m, R_2^m, \ldots, R_N^m)$, for $m = 1, \ldots, M$. Then, the function, $F_\alpha(\boldsymbol{\omega}, C)$, can be approximated as

$$F_\alpha(\boldsymbol{\omega}, C) = C + \frac{1}{M(1-\alpha)} \sum_{m=1}^{M} \left(-\boldsymbol{\omega}' R^m - C\right)^+. \tag{13.54}$$

Rockafellar and Uryasev show that the problem of minimizing $F_\alpha(\boldsymbol{\omega}, C)$ can be reduced to a linear programming (LP) problem. To do that, we introduce auxiliary variables u^m such that

$$u^m \geq -\boldsymbol{\omega}' \mathbf{R}^m - C \tag{13.55}$$

and

$$u^m \geq 0, \tag{13.56}$$

for $m = 1, \ldots, M$. The minimization problem then becomes

$$\min_{\omega} \left(C + \frac{1}{M(1-\alpha)} \sum_{m=1}^{M} u^m \right), \tag{13.57}$$

subject to constraints (for example, those in (13.50)).

APPENDIX C: A BRIEF OVERVIEW OF COPULAS

Suppose that there are N risk factors, $R_1, R_2, \ldots, R_N$, available. The information about their codependence is contained in the collection of all conditional probabilities of the type

$$P(R_i < r_i \mid R_1 < r_1, \ldots, R_{i-1} < r_{i-1}, R_{i+1} < r_{i+1}, \ldots, R_N < r_N). \tag{13.58}$$

Notice that in order to compute these conditional probabilities, we need to know the marginal distributions of the risk factors. The question is how we can separate out the pure dependence structure information from the information about the marginal behavior.

Suppose that the risk factors' marginal distributions are given by the N CDFs,

$$F_1(R_1), F_2(R_2), \ldots, F_N(R_N). \tag{13.59}$$

Since a distribution function takes values only on the range [0, 1], computing the CDF in effect transforms each risk factor into a uniform random variable.

The copula function is a multivariate uniform distribution with margins the univariate uniforms in (13.59),

$$C(F_1(R_1), F_2(R_2), \ldots, F_N(R_N)). \tag{13.60}$$

Since the copula function contains the pure dependence structure of the sample of data, we have a mechanism at hand for generating scenarios—realizations of variables with certain codependence characteristics—from any distribution. We now demonstrate the procedure to generate scenarios, using a Student's t-copula (the Student's t-distribution is standardized, i.e., it has a mode of zero and a scale of 1).

Suppose that the N risk factors are stock returns and we have observations from T periods. Denote the $T \times N$ data matrix by $\mathbf{R}$.

Copula Estimation

1. Fit a univariate Student's t-distribution to each asset's returns (each column of $\boldsymbol{R}$). The distributions are fitted independently from each other. Denote the degrees-of-freedom estimates by $\widehat{\nu}_1, \ldots, \widehat{\nu}_1$.
2. Compute the marginal CDFs, using the degrees-of-freedom estimates,

$$\begin{pmatrix} F_1(R_{11,\hat{\nu}_1}) & \ldots & F_N(R_{1N,\hat{\nu}_N}) \\ F_1(R_{21,\hat{\nu}_1}) & \ldots & F_N(R_{2N,\hat{\nu}_N}) \\ & \ldots & \\ F_1(R_{T1,\hat{\nu}_1}) & \ldots & F_N(R_{TN,\hat{\nu}_N}) \end{pmatrix}. \tag{13.61}$$

3. Compute the observations of the copula, C_i, $i = 1, \ldots, T$,

$$C_i = \left(F_1\left(R_{i1,\hat{\nu}_1}\right) \ \ldots \ F_N\left(R_{iN,\hat{\nu}_N}\right) \right). \tag{13.62}$$

4. Assuming that C_i has a N-dimensional Student's t-distribution, estimate its parameter, ν^C.

Scenario Generation

1. Simulate N-dimensional vectors from the copula

$$\begin{pmatrix} V_1^1 & \ldots & V_N^1 \\ V_1^2 & \ldots & V_N^2 \\ & \ldots & \\ V_1^M & \ldots & V_N^M \end{pmatrix}, \tag{13.63}$$

where M is the number of scenarios (usually of the order of 10, 000 in practical applications).

2. Translate the copula scenarios to scenarios of a random variable with a N-dimensional Student's t-distribution, using the inverse-fitted univariate CDFs:

$$\begin{pmatrix} T_1^1 & \ldots & T_N^1 \\ T_1^2 & \ldots & T_N^2 \\ & \ldots & \\ T_1^M & \ldots & T_N^M \end{pmatrix} = \begin{pmatrix} F_1^{-1}(V_1^1, \hat{\nu}_1) & \ldots & F_N^{-1}(V_N^1, \hat{\nu}_N) \\ F_1^{-1}(V_1^2, \hat{\nu}_1) & \ldots & F_N^{-1}(V_N^2, \hat{\nu}_N) \\ & \ldots & \\ F_1^{-1}(V_1^M, \hat{\nu}_1) & \ldots & F_N^{-1}(V_N^M, \hat{\nu}_N) \end{pmatrix}. \tag{13.64}$$

The flexibility of modeling with copulas is clearly seen in the procedure above. Various copula functions can be used to capture observed patterns of dependence in the data. Some of the copulas most widely used in portfolio risk management are Student's t-copulas (skewed t-copula, grouped t-copula, etc.).[35]

[35] For copula modeling with applications to finance, see McNeil, Frey, and Embrechts (2005). See Demarta and McNeil (2005) for a discussion of Student's t-copulas.

CHAPTER 14

Multifactor Equity Risk Models

Multifactor models of equity returns evolved to address a key deficiency of the capital asset pricing model (CAPM), namely, the implicit assumption that the comovement of securities' returns can be explained by their covariance with the market and, therefore, the bearing of nonmarket risk is not rewarded. There are pervasive common factors in addition to the market that drive returns. Investors thus need to be compensated for bearing this nondiversifiable risk via additional risk premia. Different sets of factors have been proposed in the asset-pricing literature on this topic. For example, Fama and French (1992) examine the roles of the market beta, size, earnings-to-price, leverage and book-to-market equity, while Chen, Roll and Ross (1986) focus on macroeconomic predictors such as the spread between long and short interest rates, unexpected inflation, and industrial production.

Multifactor models play key roles in most stages of the investment management process. They could be used for security selection, portfolio construction, assessment of the potential performance of a portfolio, risk control relative to a benchmark, as well as performance attribution analysis.[1]

In this chapter, we use the multifactor setting to attempt to unify the topics of the previous chapters—mean-variance portfolio optimization, volatility modeling, advanced methods for portfolio construction, and Bayesian estimation—and present a simple version for what an integrated approach to portfolio risk modeling could look like in practice. We review the three types of multifactor models and then discuss in detail the estimation of a fundamental factor model, focusing on risk estimation and risk component analysis. We emphasize the application of multifactor models to returns scenario generation and show how to attribute risk when the conditional value-at-risk (CVaR) is employed as a risk measure. Then, we present

[1]For details on these applications of multifactor models, see Fabozzi, Jones, and Vardharaj (2002).

the Bayesian perspective to multifactor equity modeling and conclude with an illustration of a heavy-tailed multifactor model.

PRELIMINARIES

The multifactor equity risk model is a purely empirical construction. It does not involve any assumptions regarding investor behavior or market efficiency, as do equilibrium models such as the CAPM and the arbitrage pricing theory (APT) model. Multifactor models are simply tools to aid the investment management process. They offer a parsimonious structure to model equity returns, through the dynamics of a small number of variables.

In a multifactor equity model, the return on a stock is decomposed into return linearly related to the factors and a stock-specific return. The linear relationship between a stock's excess return and the risk factors estimated by any multifactor model is written as

$$R_i - R_f = \alpha_i + \beta_{i,1} f_1 + \beta_{i,2} f_2 + \cdots + \beta_{i,K} f_K + \epsilon_i, \tag{14.1}$$

where: R_i = rate of return on stock i.
R_f = risk-free rate of return.
f_j = rate of return on risk factor j.
$\beta_{i,j}$ = sensitivity of stock i to risk factor j.
α_i = residual return of stock i.
ϵ_i = specific return on stock i.

Neither the number nor the identity of the factors—pervasive sources of risk driving stock returns—are specified by theory. Numerous empirical studies, however, have uncovered factors with explanatory power. Multifactor models can be categorized into three groups based on the nature of the factors employed—statistical factor models, macroeconomic factor models, and fundamental factor models.[2]

Statistical Factor Models

Statistical factor models do not require *a priori* factor identification. On the contrary, factors (the time series of factor returns) are extracted from the

[2] Among the risk model vendors using the fundamental model approach are MSCI Barra and Northfield Information Services. FinAnalytica and Advanced Portfolio Technology (APT) provide risk models based on all three approaches.

sample of historical return data with the help of statistical techniques—most often, principal component analysis. The idea is to obtain, in order of decreasing importance, the factors that best explain the variability of returns. Each consecutive factor best explains the variation left unexplained by the previous factor.[3] The stronger the dependence (correlation) between the return series, the smaller the number of factors needed to explain a large proportion of variability. Generally, three to five factors are found to account for about 90% of return variability. After the factor returns are extracted, time-series regressions, as in (14.1), are run to estimate the sensitivities (exposures) of stocks to the risk factors.

Macroeconomic Factor Models

Macroeconomic factor models use macroeconomic time series, exogenous to stock returns, such as inflation, interest rates, industrial production, and default premiums to represent the common factors governing stock returns.[4] The stocks' sensitivities to the macroeconomic factors are estimated with time-series regressions as in the case of statistical factor models.

Fundamental Factor Models

Fundamental factor models attempt to explain a large proportion of return variability with company-specific variables—company attributes based on accounting data, such as dividend yield, company size, book-to-market ratio, as well as industrial and geographical classification. The factor sensitivities are determined from these observed firm attributes, while factor returns are estimated via cross-sectional regressions. A fundamental risk factor can be in fact a combination of several descriptors that capture aspects of the same company attribute. For example, the risk factor referred to as *value* might be designed to combine the book-to-price ratio, the earnings-to-price ratio, and the price-to-earnings-to-growth ratio, while "profit" might combine return on equity and cash flow return on equity.[5]

---

[3]More formally, denote the matrix of historical returns by R (each row corresponds to an observation of returns in a particular period). The matrix of cross products, $R'R$, is decomposed into orthogonal factors, whose contribution to the overall variability of returns is quantified by the matrix's eigenvalues. The magnitudes of eigenvalues help determine the number of factors to include in the factor model.

[4]See Chen, Roll, and Ross (1986).

[5]In a study by Connor (1995), macroeconomic factor models are found to have less explanatory power than statistical and fundamental models, while, perhaps surprisingly, the fundamental model outperforms the statistical one.

RISK ANALYSIS USING A MULTIFACTOR EQUITY MODEL

A multifactor model facilitates greatly the estimation of the return covariance matrix. In a mean-variance setting, where portfolio risk is defined through the covariance matrix, employing a multifactor model means that portfolio risk estimation is made simple—instead of computing the covariances between all pairs of returns, we consider the covariances between factors, which are many times fewer than the stocks. Suppose that 1,000 stocks are candidates for acquisition. The return covariance matrix of the candidate stocks consists of 1,000 variances and 499,500 (distinct) covariances. Estimating that large a number of parameters is a daunting task. Let us see how a multifactor model would help reduce the dimensionality of the problem.

Covariance Matrix Estimation

Suppose that our historical data sample consists of the returns on N stocks that are candidates for inclusion in the portfolio recorded over T periods of time. Stacking the returns for all stocks at time t, we rewrite (14.1) as

$$\mathbf{R}_t = \mathbf{B}\,\mathbf{f}_t + \boldsymbol{\epsilon}_t, \tag{14.2}$$

where: $\mathrm{R}_t = N \times 1$ vector of stock returns at time t.
$\mathrm{B} = N \times K + 1$ matrix of risk factor sensitivities.
$\mathrm{f}_t = K + 1 \times 1$ vector of risk factor returns at time t.
$\epsilon_t = N \times 1$ vector of stock-specific returns at time t.

The first element of f_t is 1, while the first column of B consists of the intercepts α_i, $i = 1, \ldots, N$, in (14.1). The expression in (14.2) represents the cross-sectional regression we might use to estimate a fundamental multifactor model. Recall that the unknown parameters we estimate in it are the factor returns, f_t, while the risk factor sensitivities, B, are observed.

Simple matrix algebra allows us to express the covariance matrix of stock returns, Σ, using (14.2) as

$$\boldsymbol{\Sigma} = \boldsymbol{B}\boldsymbol{\Omega}_f\boldsymbol{B}' + \boldsymbol{D}, \tag{14.3}$$

where: $\Omega_f =$ covariance matrix of the factor returns.
$D =$ covariance matrix (assumed to be diagonal) of the specific returns.

In the case of 1,000 candidate stocks and a 13-factor model, computing $\widehat{\boldsymbol{\Sigma}}$ in (14.3) would mean estimating (only) 1,091 quantities (13 factor return variances, 78 (distinct) factor return covariances, and 1,000 specific return variances). Clearly, employing a multifactor model makes portfolio risk estimation a whole lot easier.

To estimate the covariance matrices, Ω_f and D, we use as inputs the estimated factor and specific returns obtained from the cross-sectional regression in (14.2):

- A $T \times K$ matrix of estimated factor returns, denoted by $\widehat{F}$, in which each row, $\widehat{f}_t$, corresponds to the estimated factor returns at a point in time.
- A $T \times N$ matrix of estimated specific stock returns, denoted by $\widehat{E}$, in which each row, $\widehat{e}_t$, corresponds to the estimated specific returns at a point in time Row t of $\widehat{E}$ is obtained as

$$\widehat{e}_t = R_t - B\widehat{f}_t. \tag{14.4}$$

Different methods are available to obtain the estimates of the factor covariance matrix, $\widehat{\boldsymbol{\Omega}}_f$, and the specific return covariance matrix, $\widehat{\boldsymbol{D}}$. For example, $\widehat{\boldsymbol{\Omega}}_f$ can be estimated using the exponentially weighted forecast procedure we discussed in Chapter 8 in our coverage of covariance matrix estimation. The diagonal elements of $\widehat{\boldsymbol{D}}$ could be estimated using exponential weighting as well.[6] An ARCH-type model or a *stochastic volatility* (SV) model (discussed, respectively, in Chapters 11 and 12) could also be employed to estimate the specific variances of the stock returns.

Let us assume that we have obtained $\widehat{\boldsymbol{\Omega}}_f$, $\widehat{\boldsymbol{D}}$, and $\widehat{\boldsymbol{\Sigma}}$. For the time being, we take it for granted that portfolio risk is measured by the variance of portfolio returns. (See the section on scenario generation later in this chapter for a different take on portfolio risk estimation.) The variance of returns of a portfolio p with weights ω is given by

$$\begin{aligned}\sigma_p^2 &= \boldsymbol{\omega}' \, \Sigma \, \boldsymbol{\omega} \\ &= \boldsymbol{b}_p' \, \Omega \, \boldsymbol{b}_p + \boldsymbol{\omega}' \, D \, \boldsymbol{\omega},\end{aligned} \tag{14.5}$$

where b_p is the $K \times 1$ vector of portfolio exposures to the factors in the model,

$$\begin{aligned}\boldsymbol{b}_p &= \boldsymbol{\omega}' \boldsymbol{B} \\ &= \left(\sum_{i=1}^{N} \omega_i B_{i,1} \, , \, \cdots , \, \sum_{i=1}^{N} \omega_K B_{i,K} \right),\end{aligned}$$

[6]Litterman (2003) suggest shrinking each variance estimate to the average (across all assets) variance estimate in order to bring extremely high specific variances closer to the majority of the specific variances.

and $B_{i,k}$ is exposure of stock i to factor k. While all the covariance matrices above are estimates, we suppress the "hats" signifying that for notational simplicity.

It is certainly of great value to a portfolio manager to be able to identify the sources of risk for the managed portfolio. We now look at several ways to decompose portfolio risk, as well as to analyze these sources.[7]

Risk Decomposition

The expression (14.5) immediately suggests the decomposition of portfolio risk into a common factor component (given by $b_p' \; \Omega \; b_p$) and a specific component (given by $\omega' \; D \; \omega$).

An active portfolio manager manages a portfolio against a benchmark attempting to produce return in excess of the benchmark (active return) and, accordingly, bears risk in excess of the benchmark risk (active risk). Active risk is also called *tracking error*. Denote the assets' weights in the benchmark portfolio by ω_b. We define assets' *active weights*, ω_a, by the difference between the weights of the manager's portfolio and the benchmark weights,

$$\omega_a = \omega - \omega_b. \tag{14.6}$$

The (squared) active risk of the manager's portfolio is expressed as

$$\sigma_{p,a}^2 = \omega_a' \, \Sigma \, \omega_a, \tag{14.7}$$

which can also be partitioned into common factor and specific components:

$$\sigma_{p,a}^2 = b_{p,a}' \, \Omega \, b_{p,a} + \omega_a' \, D \, \omega_a, \tag{14.8}$$

where $b_{p,a} = B' \; \omega_a$.

Detailed risk decomposition is a prerequisite for effective portfolio management. In a multifactor model framework, a portfolio manager can assess the contribution of individual stocks and the various factor exposures (exposures to industries, investment styles, and others) to total (active) risk. We discuss how to analyze the sources of portfolio total risk.

Denote by ω_i the portfolio weight of stock i, by $\omega_{i,a}$ the active weight of stock i, and by $b_{p,k}$ the portfolio exposure to factor k. To obtain the expressions for the sources of active risk (tracking error), one needs to just substitute $\omega_{i,a}$ for ω_i. The marginal contributions of stock i and factor k are given mathematically by the derivatives of total risk with respect to ω_i and $b_{p,k}$.

---

[7]In the discussion below we follow Grinold and Kahn (2000) and Litterman (2003).

Marginal Contribution of Stock *i* to Total Risk The marginal contribution of stock i to total risk (MCTR_i) is given by

$$\begin{aligned}\text{MCTR}_i &\equiv \frac{d\,\sigma_p}{d\,\omega_i} = \frac{1}{2}\left(\sigma_p^2\right)^{-1/2}(\boldsymbol{\omega}\boldsymbol{\Sigma})_i \\ &= \frac{(\boldsymbol{\omega}\boldsymbol{\Sigma})_i}{2\sigma_p}, \end{aligned} \tag{14.9}$$

where the subscript i denotes the ith element of the vector. MCTR_i is the amount of portfolio risk associated with the holding of stock i. The percentage marginal contribution of stock i to total risk (PCTR) is obtained as

$$\text{PCTR}_i = \frac{\omega_i}{\sigma_p}\text{MCTR}_i. \tag{14.10}$$

Marginal Contribution of Factor *k* to Total Risk The marginal contribution of factor k to total risk (MCFTR_k) is written as

$$\begin{aligned}\text{MCFTR}_k &\equiv \frac{d\,\sigma_p}{d\,b_{p,k}} = \frac{1}{2}\left(\sigma_p^2\right)^{-1/2}\left(b_p\Omega\right) \\ &= \frac{\left(b_p\Omega\right)_k}{2\sigma_p}. \end{aligned} \tag{14.11}$$

The percentage contribution of factor k to total risk (PCFTR_k) is

$$\text{PCFTR}_k = \frac{b_{p,k}}{\sigma_p}\text{MCFTR}_k. \tag{14.12}$$

If a manager wants to control the risk coming from the exposure to factor k, he needs to know how each stock contributes to forming this exposure's risk. PCFTR_k can be broken down even further into stock contributions to the risk coming from the kth factor exposure of the portfolio,

$$\text{PCFTR}_{k,i} = \frac{\omega_i B_{i,k}}{\sigma_p}\text{MCFTR}_k. \tag{14.13}$$

When we define portfolio risk as the CVaR of portfolio return, instead of the variance of portfolio return, we can perform the same kind of risk decomposition in order to assess the risk contributions of individual stocks and factor exposures. In this chapter, we focus on scenario-based (numerical) computation of CVaR. Next, we present return scenario generation in a multifactor setting and explain CVaR decomposition further below.

RETURN SCENARIO GENERATION

In Chapter 13, we discussed some of the new directions for risk management and portfolio construction, in particular, the use of risk measures designed to address the deficiencies of the traditional metric—the standard deviation—and to provide adequate description of the tails of the return distribution. We described the modification of the portfolio selection problem based on one of these risk measures, the CVaR. In nonnormal settings, where no analytical expressions for densities or risk measures exist, CVaR minimization takes on an additional point of attraction—it can be scenario-based, performed on the basis of a large number of simulations from the returns distribution.

Scenarios of returns can be generated from some multivariate distribution fitted to the observed data. The reason for employing a multifactor framework is to take advantage of the risk decomposition this framework makes possible. We are able to identify the sources of risk, as measured by CVaR, as a step in a comprehensive risk-management process.

The process of stock return scenario generation has two stages:

1. For each t, $t = 1, \ldots, T$, estimate the cross-sectional regression in (14.2) and obtain the time series of factor return estimates $\widehat{F}$, and specific return estimates $\widehat{E}$,

$$\widehat{F} = \begin{pmatrix} \widehat{f}_{1,1} & \widehat{f}_{1,2} & \cdots & \widehat{f}_{1,K} \\ \cdots & \cdots & \cdots & \cdots \\ \widehat{f}_{t,1} & \widehat{f}_{t,2} & \cdots & \widehat{f}_{t,K} \\ \cdots & \cdots & \cdots & \cdots \\ \widehat{f}_{T,1} & \widehat{f}_{T,2} & \cdots & \widehat{f}_{T,K} \end{pmatrix} \tag{14.14}$$

and

$$\widehat{E} = \begin{pmatrix} \widehat{e}_{1,1} & \widehat{e}_{1,2} & \cdots & \widehat{e}_{1,N} \\ \cdots & \cdots & \cdots & \cdots \\ \widehat{e}_{t,1} & \widehat{e}_{t,2} & \cdots & \widehat{e}_{t,N} \\ \cdots & \cdots & \cdots & \cdots \\ \widehat{e}_{T,1} & \widehat{e}_{T,2} & \cdots & \widehat{e}_{T,N} \end{pmatrix}. \tag{14.15}$$

respectively.

2. Predict (simulate) the factor returns and stock-specific returns and use them as drivers to compute scenarios of the stock returns from

$$\widetilde{R} = B\widetilde{f} + \widetilde{e}, \tag{14.16}$$

where $\widetilde{f}$ and $\widetilde{e}$ are the predicted (simulated) factor and stock-specific returns.

Predicting the Factor and Stock-Specific Returns

The factor returns are likely not independent. A small number of suprafactors may govern the behavior of the model's factors. Therefore, it may be appropriate to analyze factor returns in a multivariate setting.

Stock-specific returns may or may not be independent across stocks. If one is confident that the fundamental multifactor model is correctly specified and the factors adequately represent the common drivers of stock returns, one could assume that the stock-specific returns are independent. Then, the time series of each stock-specific return could be treated as a sample from a univariate distribution. In contrast, if there are one or more factors omitted from the model in (14.2), the residuals from the cross-sectional regressions (i.e., the estimated stock-specific returns) are not independent, and it might be preferable to treat them as coming from a multivariate distribution.[8]

Two approaches to generating $\tilde{f}$ and $\tilde{e}$ can be followed:

1. *Assume a time-invariant behavior of* $\widehat{\mathbf{F}}$ *and* $\widehat{\mathbf{E}}$. To simulate the factor returns, denote the distribution of factor returns by $p(f \mid \boldsymbol{\theta})$, where f is a $1 \times K$ vector and $\boldsymbol{\theta}$ is a parameter vector. Estimate $\boldsymbol{\theta}$ using the sample of factor returns, $\widehat{\mathbf{F}}$ and denote the estimate by $\widehat{\boldsymbol{\theta}}$. Generate a large number of samples from $p(f \mid \widehat{\boldsymbol{\theta}})$.
   To simulate the stock-specific returns, proceed in a similar way, either in a univariate or in a multivariate setting, as per our discussion thus far.
2. *Assume a time-varying behavior of* $\widehat{\mathbf{F}}$ *and* $\widehat{\mathbf{E}}$. The types of time series processes to be fit to $\widehat{\mathbf{F}}$ and $\widehat{\mathbf{E}}$ depend on the particular situation. In general, a volatility model would be required to model the dynamics of the stock-specific returns. Factor returns may be considered to have a more stable dynamics and are subject to fewer shocks than stock-specific returns. Therefore, a low-order *multivariate autoregressive* (AR) structure, such as a multivariate AR process or a multivariate *autoregressive moving average* (ARMA) process may be sufficient to describe their joint dynamics.
   Factor and stock-specific returns are simulated from the respective fitted time-series models.

Risk Analysis in a Scenario-Based Setting

In a scenario-based setting, the analytical convenience of the risk decompositions outlined earlier in the chapter is not available. However, portfolio risk can still be decomposed; in this instance, only numerically.

[8]The arguments about model specification and missing explanatory variables are, indeed, valid for any regression model.

Suppose that the M return scenarios generated as described above are used to obtain the optimal portfolio in a mean-CVaR setting (see Chapter 13). Denote the return scenarios by $\widetilde{R}^m$, $m = 1, \ldots, M$, and the optimal portfolio weights by ω^*. The optimal portfolio return corresponding to each scenario is

$$R_p^m = \omega^{*\prime}\widetilde{R}^m,$$

for $m = 1, \ldots, M$. We thus obtain a sample of size M from the distribution of the portfolio return and we use it to analyze numerically the risk of the optimal portfolio.

Recall the definitions of the *value-at-risk* (VaR) and the CVaR in (13.40) and (13.42) in Chapter 13, respectively. We next show how the CVaR_α could be computed numerically, for a tail probability $\alpha = 0.05$.

Step 1. Arrange R_p^m, $m = 1, \ldots, M$, in ascending order,

$$R_p^{(1)} < R_p^{(2)} < \cdots > R_p^{(M)},$$

where $R_p^{(j)}$ denotes the jth smallest portfolio return, $j = 1, \ldots, M$.

Step 2. Determine the portfolio return smaller than 95% of the portfolio returns. Denote it by[9]

$$R_p^{([0.05M])}.$$

That is, $\text{VaR}_{0.05}(R_p) = R_p^{([0.05M])}$.

Step 3. Compute $\text{CVaR}_{0.05}(R_p)$,

$$\text{CVaR}_{0.05}(R_p) = \frac{1}{[0.05M]} \sum_{j=1}^{[0.05M]} R_p^{(j)}.$$

Let us now see how portfolio risk, $\text{CVaR}_{0.05}(R_p)$, can be decomposed into its sources.

Conditional Value-at-Risk Decomposition

The quantity $\text{CVaR}_{0.05}(R_p)$ as defined above is a measure of total portfolio risk. It is straightforward, however, to calculate the portfolio active risk (the equivalent of tracking error, when the standard deviation is used as a risk measure)—we simply substitute ω^* with the vector of active weights, ω_a (see (14.6)), then compute the sample of portfolio active returns,

---

[9]The square brackets in the superscript of $R_p^{([0.05M])}$ mean that $[0.05M]$ is equal to $0.05M$ if that is an integer and to the integer part of $0.05M$, if it is not.

$R^m_{p,a}$, $m = 1, \ldots, M$, and finally obtain the portfolio active $\text{CVaR}_{0.05}(R_{p,a})$ following the three steps in the previous section.

The decomposition of $\text{CVaR}_{0.05}(R_p)$ is not difficult since, being an expectation, it is additive and depends in a linear fashion on the stock returns, weights, and factor exposures. Using the factor-model representation of stock returns, the portfolio CVaR can be represented as

$$\begin{aligned}
\text{CVaR}_{0.05}(R_p) &= E\left[R_p \mid R_p < \text{VaR}_{0.05}(R_p)\right] \\
&= E\left[(\omega' B\widehat{f}_t + \omega' e_t) \mid R_p > VaR_{0.05}(R_p)\right] \qquad (14.17) \\
&= \omega' E\left[B\widehat{f}_t \mid R_p < VaR_{0.05}(R_p)\right] + \omega' E\left[e_t \mid R_p < VaR_{0.05}(R_p)\right].
\end{aligned}$$

The two terms in the last line above can easily be evaluated numerically and give us the decomposition of total (active) portfolio risk into a common factor component and a stock-specific component.

The CVaR decomposition in the scenario-based setting parallels the one in the analytical setting. Let us see how we compute numerically the risk components of $\text{CVaR}_{0.05}(R_p)$ above. (Active CVaR ($\text{CVaR}_{0.05}(R_{p,a})$), as well as other values of the tail probability, α, are treated in a similar way). We use the following sets of simulated data:

- The simulated factor returns, $\widetilde{f}^m$, $m = 1, \ldots, M$.
- The simulated stock-specific returns, $\widetilde{e}^m$, $m = 1, \ldots, M$.
- The portfolio returns, computed for each scenario, R^m_p, $m = 1, \ldots, M$.

We are also mindful of the correspondence among the scenarios of factor returns, specific returns, stock returns, and portfolio returns.[10]

Common-Factor Risk Component To compute the common-factor risk component of CVaR, we can use the procedure outlined below:

Step 1. Identify the portfolio returns smaller than $\text{VaR}_{0.05}(R_p)$.

Step 2. Identify the simulated factor returns, drivers of the portfolio returns in step 1, that is, the portfolio returns smaller than $R_p^{([0.05M])}$. Denote these factor returns by $\widetilde{f}^{(j)}$, $j = 1, \ldots, [0.05M]$.

[10]The procedures for computing the common-factor component and specific component are inspired by Yamai and Yoshiba (2002). See also Zhang and Rachev (2006).

Step 3. Compute the $N \times 1$ vector,

$$q = \frac{1}{[0.05M]} \sum_{j=1}^{[0.05M]} \widetilde{Bf}^{(j)}. \tag{14.18}$$

Step 4. The *common factor risk component of total risk*, $\mathrm{CVaR}_{0.05}(R_p)$, is then given by

$$\text{Common factor risk component} = \boldsymbol{\omega}^{*\prime} q. \tag{14.19}$$

Stock-Specific Risk Component The stock-specific risk component of $\mathrm{CVaR}_{0.05}(R_p)$ is obtained in a manner analogous to the common-factor risk component.

Step 1. Identify the portfolio returns smaller than $\mathrm{VaR}_{0.05}(R_p)$.
Step 2. Identify the simulated stock-specific returns in step 1, that is, the portfolio returns smaller than $R_p^{([0.05M])}$. Denote these specific returns by $\widetilde{e}^{(j)}$, $j = 1, \ldots, [0.05M]$.
Step 3. Compute the $N \times 1$ vector,

$$p = \frac{1}{[0.05M]} \sum_{j=1}^{[0.05M]} \widetilde{e}^{(j)}. \tag{14.20}$$

Step 4. The *stock-specific risk component of total risk*, $\mathrm{CVaR}_{0.05}(R_p)$, is then given by

$$\text{Stock-specific risk component} = \boldsymbol{\omega}^{*\prime} p. \tag{14.21}$$

Contribution of Stock *i* to Portfolio Risk The marginal contribution of stock i to portfolio risk, $\mathrm{CVaR}_{0.05}(R_p)$, follows the same general idea in the previous section.[11]

Step 1. Identify the portfolio losses larger than $\mathrm{VaR}_{0.05}(R_p)$.
Step 2. Identify the scenarios of returns corresponding to the portfolio returns in step 1, that is, the portfolio returns smaller than $R_p^{([0.05M])}$. Denote those scenarios of returns by $\boldsymbol{R}^{(j)} = \left(R_1^{(j)}, R_2^{(j)}, \ldots, R_N^{(j)}\right)$, $j = 1, \ldots, [0.05M]$.

[11]See Yamai and Yoshiba (2002).

Step 3. Compute the *marginal contribution of stock i to total risk*, MCTR_i,

$$\text{MCTR}_i = \frac{\frac{1}{[0.05M]}\sum_{j=1}^{[0.05M]} R_i^{(j)}}{\text{CVaR}_{0.05}(R_p)}. \tag{14.22}$$

The percentage marginal contribution of stock i to total risk (PMCTR_i) is computed as

$$\text{PMCTR}_i = \frac{\omega_i}{CVaR_{0.05}(R_p)}\text{MCTR}_i. \tag{14.23}$$

To assess the impact on risk of a change in the portfolio weight of stock i, recompute portfolio returns, R_p^m, $m = 1, \ldots, M$, and total risk, $\text{CVaR}_{0.05}(R_p)$, and perform again the calculations in steps 1 through 3.

Contribution of Factor *k* to Portfolio Risk The marginal contribution of factor k to total portfolio risk, $\text{CVaR}_{0.05}(R_p)$, is the kth element of q in (14.18). The percentage marginal contribution of factor k is computed accordingly.

BAYESIAN METHODS FOR MULTIFACTOR MODELS

Casting the multifactor model estimation in a Bayesian setting enjoys the usual benefits of addressing parameter uncertainty and incorporating prior knowledge or intuition. The Bayesian setting is, in addition, particularly amenable to scenario generation—the outputs from the *Markov Chain Monte Carlo* (MCMC) computations allow one to simulate the whole distribution of the parameters. Admittedly, the Bayesian analogue of the model and risk estimation outlined above is more time consuming and, certainly, more computationally intensive. Continuous advances in computing power, however, act to mitigate these drawbacks. Nevertheless, managers who employ quantitative strategies based on the usual Gaussian assumption for returns and use the standard deviation as a measure of risk might be better off with the simpler estimation framework discussed earlier in the chapter. The Bayesian multifactor framework is for portfolio managers who would prefer to:

- Incorporate parameter uncertainty (at all stages of the estimation process).
- Assume non-Gaussian distributions for stock returns, as well as factor returns.
- Employ sophisticated methods for volatility estimation, for example, ARCH-type processes or SV processes and their extensions.

- Optimize portfolios using the advanced techniques discussed in Chapter 13.

Next we outline the strategy for tackling the multifactor Bayesian problem.

Cross-Sectional Regression Estimation

Estimation of the cross-sectional regression in (14.2) can, in general, be performed, as explained in Chapter 4. The parameters whose prior distributions one needs to specify are the factor returns, $f_{t,1}, \ldots, f_{t,K}$, $t = 1, \ldots, T$, and the parameters of the return distribution. If one assumes that returns follow a heavy-tailed distribution, it is not unreasonable to assert a heavy-tailed prior for the factor returns as well. In a nonconjugate setting, one would most certainly have to resort to Markov Chain Monte Carlo (MCMC) methods to simulate the posterior distributions.

Posterior Simulations

Denote the sample from the posterior parameter distribution from the cross-sectional regression at time t by the $P \times Q$ matrix, Ξ^t,

$$\Xi_t = (\mathbf{\Theta}_t, \boldsymbol{F}_t),$$

where: Θ_t = matrix of P posterior draws of the return distribution parameters.
F_t = matrix of P posterior draws of the factor returns.
P = number of posterior draws after the burn-in sample is discarded.
Q = total number of model parameters.

For each t, $t = 1, \ldots, T$, we compute the posterior mean and denote it by $\widehat{\Xi}_t$, a $1 \times Q$ vector,

$$\widehat{\Xi}_t = \left(\widehat{\theta}_t, \widehat{f}_t\right). \tag{14.24}$$

The estimated stock-specific returns at time t are given by

$$\widehat{e}_t = \boldsymbol{R}_t - \boldsymbol{B}\widehat{f}_t,$$

where we apply the expression in (14.4) and $\widehat{f}_t$ is the vector of posterior means in (14.24).

Stacking the posterior means of the factor returns and the estimated stock-specific returns for all time periods, we obtain the time series of Bayesian estimates:

$\widehat{F} = T \times K$ matrix of time series of estimated factor returns.
$\widehat{E} = T \times N$ matrix of time series of estimated stock-specific returns.

Return Scenario Generation

To generate scenarios of returns, we first predict (generate scenarios of) the factor returns and the stock-specific returns, by either fitting time-invariant distributions or time-series processes to $\widehat{F}$ and $\widehat{E}$. Either is performed in a Bayesian setting. Then, the stock return scenarios are generated, as explained earlier in the chapter.

The Bayesian procedure above is more robust than that in the frequentist case. The reason is that factor and stock-specific returns are predicted on the basis of the posterior distributions of the time-series model parameters instead of the maximum likelihood estimates of these parameters. That robustness is then passed on to the predicted returns.

Optimal portfolio construction and risk analysis can be carried out in the manner discussed earlier in this chapter and in Chapter 13.

ILLUSTRATION

We illustrate the estimation of a heavy-tailed, multifactor model. We gather daily return data for 229 companies from the S&P 500 index (selected on the basis of completeness of the return and fundamental data history), for the three-year period January 1, 2001, through December 31, 2003, a total of 751 return observations. We build the model with six risk factors—size, success, value, volatility, yield, and profit—and 10 industry factors.[12]

We assume a stable distribution for the stock returns in each period t, $t = 1, \ldots, T$. (A brief introduction to the stable distribution was given in Chapter 13.) Its four parameters (the tail parameter, α, the asymmetry parameter, β, the scale parameter σ, and the location parameter, μ) together with the returns to the 16 factors, $f_{t,1}, \ldots, f_{t,16}$, make up the parameter

[12]We use the Global Industry Classification Standard (GICS) and take as factors the following industry sectors: materials, information technology, consumer staples, health care, utilities, financials, energy, industrials, consumer discretionary, and telecommunication services.

vector we need to estimate

$$\boldsymbol{\theta}_t = \left(\alpha, \beta, \sigma, f_{t,1}, \ldots, f_{t,K}\right).$$

The location parameter μ is not a stand alone parameter here but equals Bf_t. The stable distribution does not have a closed-form density function—all estimation is performed numerically.[13] Since analytical tractability is not an issue here, our choice of prior distribution is only based on economic rationale. For example, empirical evidence suggests that stock returns have a tail parameter with a value between 1 and 2. That is, stock returns exhibit tails heavier than the Gaussian tails (corresponding to $\alpha = 2$) but not too heavy (hence, $\alpha > 1$). Therefore, we assert a uniform distribution on the interval (1, 2) for α.

The asymmetry parameter, β, takes values between −1 and 1. For lack of any other prior information, we assert a uniform distribution on [−1, 1] for it. For the scale parameter we assume a gamma distribution and for factor returns we assume a stable distribution. We use the griddy Gibbs sampler algorithm, outlined in Chapter 11, for sampling from the posterior densities.

Exhibit 14.1 presents typical plots of the posterior densities of the stable parameters, α, β, σ, corresponding to one of the cross-sectional regressions, while plots of the posterior means from all cross-sectional Bayesian regressions are in Exhibit 14.2. Return prediction and risk analysis can be performed as explained earlier.

SUMMARY

This chapter presented an overview of the multifactor model framework. We described the process of traditional portfolio risk (as measured by the standard deviation) estimation within the cross-sectional model framework. Risk attribution can be performed analytically when the standard deviation is employed as a risk measure. In a nonnormal setting, risk attribution is simulation based. The Bayesian framework facilitates estimation and provides the natural simulation environment.

[13] Shall I give an outline of the density approximation?

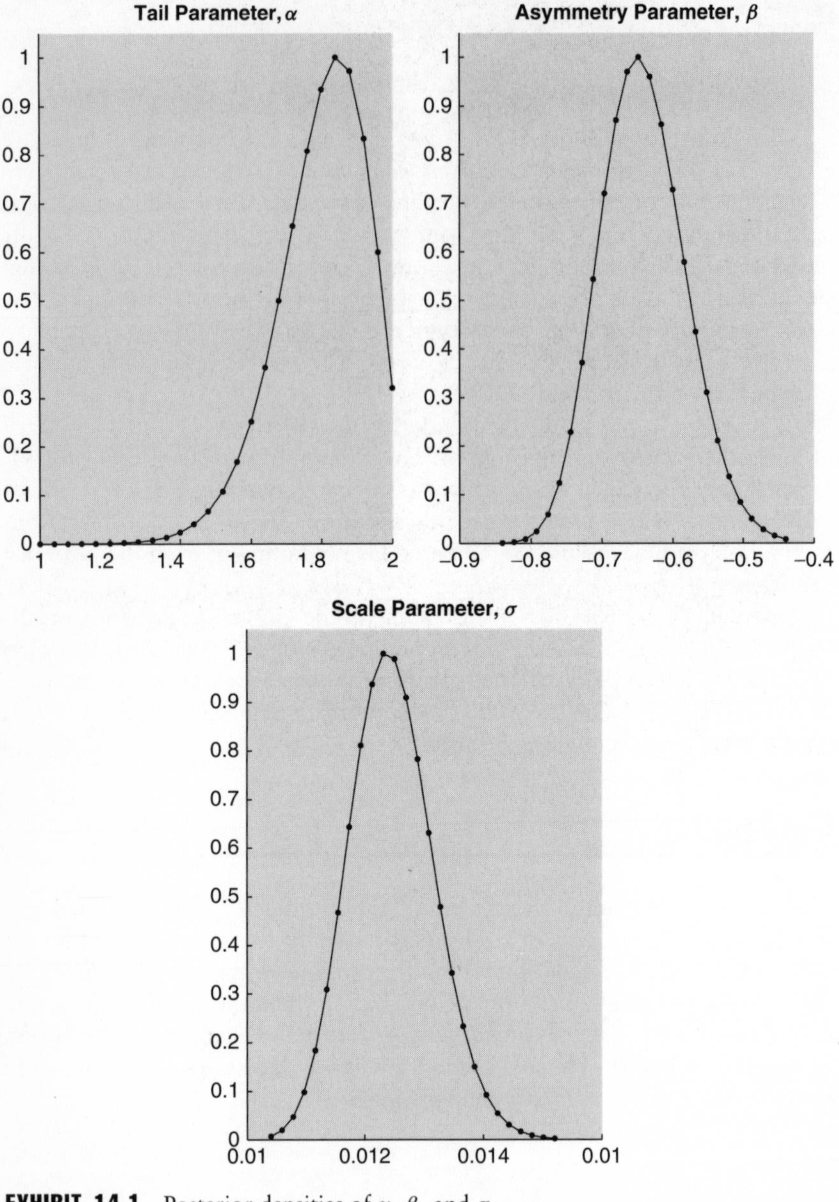

EXHIBIT 14.1 Posterior densities of α, β, and σ

Notes: The knots of the density curves correspond to the grid nodes on which posterior densities are evaluated.

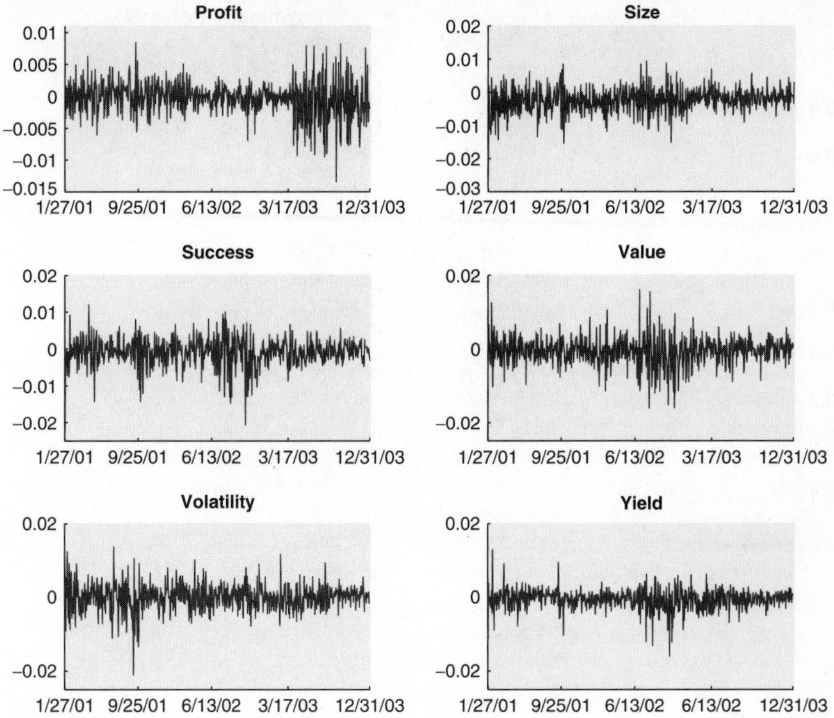

EXHIBIT 14.2 Posterior means of the factor daily returns in the stable distribution scenario

References

Adcock, C., and Shutes, K. 2005. An analysis of skewness and skewness persistence in three emerging markets. *Emerging Markets Review*, 6(4):396–418.

Barone Adesi, G. Arbitrage equilibrium with skewed asset returns. 1985. *Journal of Financial and Quantitative Analysis*, 20(4):299–313.

Aguilar, O. and West, M. 2000. Bayesian dynamic factor models and portfolio allocation. *Journal of Business & Economic Statistics*, 18(3):338–357.

Alexander, C. Bayesian methods for measuring operational risk. Discussion Papers in Finance 2000-02. ISMA Centre, The University of Reading, 2000.

Andersen, T. 1994. Stochastic autoregressive volatility: A framework for volatility modeling. 1994. *Mathematical Finance*, 4(2):75–102.

Andersen, T., Benzoni, L., and Lund, J. 2002. An empirical investigation of continuous-time equity return models. *Journal of Finance*, 57(3):1239–1284.

Andersen, T., Bollerslev, T., Christoffersen, P., and Diebold, F. Volatility forecasting. National Bureau of Economic Research. Working Paper Series, 2005.

Anderson, T. *An Introduction to Multivariate Statistical Analysis*. Hoboken, NJ: John Wiley & Sons, 2003.

Ang, A., Chen, J., and Xing, Y. Downside risk. 2006. *Review of Financial Studies*, 19(4):1191–1239.

Avramov, D. 2002. Stock return predictability and model uncertainty. *Journal of Financial Economics*, 64(3):423–458.

Azzalini, A. 2005. The skew-normal distribution and related multivariate families. *Scandinavian Journal of Statistics*, 32(2):159–188.

Azzalini, A., and Capitanio, A. 2003. Distributions generated by a perturbation of symmetry with emphasis on a multivariate skew *t*-distribution. *Journal of the Royal Statistical Society, Series B*, 65(2):367–389.

Azzalini, A., and Dalla Vale, A. 1996. The multivariate skew normal distribution. *Biometrika*, 83(4):715–726.

Baks, K., Metrick, A., and Wachter, J. 2001. Should investors avoid all actively managed mutual funds? A study in Bayesian performance evaluation. *Journal of Finance*, 56(1):45–85.

Barberis, N. 2000. Investing for the long run when returns are predictable. *Journal of Finance*, 55(1):225–264.

Bauwens, L., and Lubrano, M. 1998. Bayesian inference on GARCH models using the Gibbs sampler. *Econometrics Journal*, 1(2):C23–C46.

Bauwens, L., Lubrano, M., and Richard, J. *Bayesian Inference in Dynamic Econometric Models*. New York: Oxford University Press, 2000.

Ben-Tal, A., and Nemirovksi, A. Robust convex optimization. *Mathematics of Operations Research*, 23(4), 1998.

Ben-Tal, A., and Nemirovksi, A. 1999. Robust solutions of uncertain linear programs. *Operations Research Letters*, 25(1):1–13.

Berger, J. *Statistical Theory and Bayesian Analysis*. Berlin: Springer-Verlag, 1985.

Berger, J. 1990. Robust Bayesian analysis: Sensitivity to the prior. *Journal of statistical planning and inference*, 25(3):303–328.

Berger, J. 2006. The case for objective Bayesian analysis. *Bayesian Analysis*, 1(3):385–402.

Berger, J., and Bernardo, J. 1992. On the development of reference priors. In J. Bernardo, J. Berger, A. David, and A. Smith (eds.), *Bayesian Statistics*, Volume 4, Oxford, Clareton Press, pp. 35–60.

Bernardo, J. Noninformative priors do not exist: A discussion with José M. Bernardo. University of Valencia, 2006. Available at http://www.uv.es/~bernardo/Dialogue.pdf. 2006.

Bernardo, J., and Smith, A. *Bayesian Theory*. New York: John Wiley & Sons, 1994.

Bertocchi, M., Giacometti, R., Ortobelli, S., and Rachev, S. 2005. The impact of different distributional hypotheses on returns in asset allocation. *Finance Letters*, 3(1):17–27.

Best, M., and Grauer, R. 1991. Sensitivity analysis for mean-variance portfolio problems. *Management Science*, 37(8):980–989.

Best, M., and Grauer, R. 1992. The analytics of sensitivity analysis for mean-variance portfolio problems. *International Review of Financial Analysis*, 1(1): 17–37.

Black, F. 1976. Studies of stock market volatility changes. *Proceedings of the American Statistical Association, Business and Economic Statistics Section*, pp. 177–181.

Black, F., and Litterman, R. Global asset allocation with equities, bonds, and currencies. *Fixed Income Research*. Goldman Sachs, 1991.

Black, F., and Litterman, R. 1992. Global portfolio optimization. *Financial Analysts Journal*, 48(5):28–43.

Bollerslev, T. 1986. Generalized autoregressive conditional heteroskedasticity. *Journal of Econometrics*, 31:307–327.

Bollerslev, T., and Engle, R. 1986. Modelling the persistence of conditional variances. *Econometric Reviews*, 5:1–50; 81–87.

Branco, M., and Dey, D. 2001. A general class of multivariate skew elliptical distributions. *Journal of Multivariate Analysis*, 79:99–113.

Brockwell, P., and Davis, R. *Time Series: Theory and Methods*, 2nd ed. Berlin: Springer, 1998.

Buckle, D. 1995. Bayesian inference for stable distributions. *Journal of the American Statistical Association*, 90(2):605–613.

Busse, J., and Irvine, P. 2006. Bayesian alphas and mutual fund persistence. *Journal of Finance*, 61(5):2251–2288.

Cai, J. 1994. A Markov model of switching-regime ARCH. *Journal of Business and Economic Statistics*, 12(3):309–316.

Carlin, B., Gelfand, A., and Smith, A. 1992. Hierarchical Bayesian analysis of change point problems. *Applied Statistics*, 41(2):389–405.

Carlin, B., Polson, N., and Stoffer, D. 1992. A Monte Carlo approach to nonnormal and nonlinear state-space modeling. *Journal of the American Statistical Association*, 87(418):493–500.

Casarin, R. Bayesian inference for generalized Markov switching stochastic volatility models. Working Paper, 2004, CEREMADE. Available at http://www.citeseer.ist.psu.edu.

Chen, N., Roll, R., and Stephen, R. 1986. Economic forces and the stock market. *Journal of Business*, 59(3):383–403.

Chernov, M., Gallant, R., Ghysels, E., and Tauchen, G. 2003. Alternative models for stock price dynamics. *Journal of Econometrics*, 116(1–2):225–257.

Chesney, M., and Scott, L. 1989. Pricing European currency options: A comparison of the modified Black-Scholes model and a random variance model. *Journal of Financial and Quantitative Analysis*, 24(3):267–284.

Chib, S., and Greenberg, E. 1995. Understanding the Metropolis-Hastings algorithm. *American Statistician*, 49(4):327–335.

Chib, S., Nardari, F., and Shephard, N. 2002. Markov Chain Monte Carlo methods for stochastic stochastic volatility models. *Journal of Econometrics*, (108):281–316.

Chopra, V., and Ziemba, W. 1993. The effect of errors in means, variances, and covariances on optimal portfolio choice. *Journal of Portfolio Management*, 19(2):6–11.

Chung, K. *A Course in Probability Theory Revised*, 2nd ed. New York: Academic Press, 2000.

Clark, P. 1973. A subordinated stochastic process model with finite variance for speculative prices. *Econometrica*, 41(1):135–155.

Connor, G. 1995. The three types of factor models: A comparison of their explanatory power. *Financial Analysts Journal*, 51(3):42–46.

Cooke, R. *Experts in Uncertainty: Opinion and Subjective Probability in Science*. New York: Oxford University Press, 1991.

Cowles, M., and Carlin, B. 1996. Markov Chain Monte Carlo convergence diagnostics: A comparative review. *Journal of the American Statistical Association*, 91(3):883–904.

Cremers, M. 2002. Stock return predictability: A Bayesian model selection perspective. *Review of Financial Studies*, 15(4):1223–1249.

Damien, P., Wakefield, J., and Walker, S. 1999. Gibbs sampling for Bayesian nonconjugate and hierarchical models by using auxiliary variables. *Journal of the Royal Statistical Society, Series B*, 61:331–344.

de Jong, P., and Shephard, N. 1995. The simulation smoother for time series models. *Biometrika*, 82(2):339–350.

Demarta, S., and McNeil, A. 2005. The *t*-copula and related copulas. *International Statistical Review*, 73(1):111–129.

Diebold, F., and Inoue, A. 2001. Long memory and regime switching. *Journal of Econometrics*, 105(1):131–159.

Dittmar, R. 2002. Nonlinear pricing kernels, kurtosis preference, and evidence from the cross-section of equity returns. *Journal of Finance*, 57(1):368–403.

Durbin, J., and Koopman, S. *Time Series Analysis by State Space Methods*. New York: Oxford University Press, 2001.

Durbin, J., and Koopman, S. 2002. A simple and efficient simulation smoother for state space time series analysis. *Biometrika*, 89(3):603–615.

El Ghaoui, L., and Lebret, H. 1997. Robust solutions to least-squares problems with uncertain data. *SIAM Journal of Matrix Analysis Applications*, 18(4):1035–1064.

Engle, R. 1982. Autoregressive conditional heteroscedasticity with estimates of the variance of United Kingdom inflation. *Econometrica*, 50(4):987–1007.

Engle, R., Lilien, D., and Robins, R. 1987. Estimating time-varying risk premia in the term structure: The ARCH-M model. *Econometrica*, 55(2):391–407.

Eraker, B., Johannes, M., and Polson, N. 2003. The impact of jumps in equity index volatility and returns. *Journal of Finance*, 58(3):1269–1300.

Fabozzi, F., Focardi, S., and Kolm, P. *Financial Modeling of the Equity Market: From CAPM to Cointegration*. Hoboken, NJ: John Wiley & Sons, 2006.

Fabozzi, F., Focardi, S., and Kolm, P. 2001. Incorporating trading strategies into the Black-Litterman framework. *Journal of Trading*, 1(2):28–37.

Fabozzi, F., Jones, F., and Vardharaj, R. Multi-factor equity risk models. In F. Fabozzi and H. Markowitz (eds.), *The Theory and Practice of Investment Management*. Hoboken, NJ: John Wiley & Sons, 2002.

Fama, E. 1965. The behavior of stock market prices. *Journal of Business*, 38(1):34–105.

Fama, E. 1970. Efficient capital markets: A review of theory and empirical work. *Journal of Finance*, 25(2):383–417.

Fama, E. 1991. Efficient capital markets: II. *Journal of Finance*, 46(5):1575–1617.

Fama, E., and French, K. 1992. The cross-section of expected stock returns. *Journal of Finance*, 47(2):427–465.

Fama, E., and MacBeth, J. 1973. Risk, return, and equilibrium: Empirical tests. *Journal of Political Economy*, 81(3):607–636.

Favre, L., and Galeano, J. 2002. Mean-modified value-at-risk with hedge funds. *Journal of Alternative Investments*, 5(2):21–25.

Feller, W. *An Introduction to Probability Theory and Its Applications, vol 2,* 2nd ed New York: John Wiley & Sons, 1971.

Fernandez, C., and Steel, M. 1998. On Bayesian modeling of fat tails and skewness. *Journal of the American Statistical Association*, 93(441):359–371.

Fornari, F., and Mele, A. 1996. Modeling the changing asymmetry of conditional variances. *Economics Letters*, 50(2):197–203.

Francq, C., and Zakoïan, J.-M. 2001. Stationarity of multivariate Markov-switching ARMA models. *Journal of Econometrics*, 102:339–364.

Frost, P., and Savarino, J. 1986. An empirical Bayes approach to efficient portfolio selection. *Journal of Financial and Quantitative Analysis*, 21(3):293–305.

Gallant, R., and Tauchen, G. 1996. Which moments to match. *Econometric Theory*, 12(4):657–681.

Garthwaite, P., Kadane, J., and O'Hagan, A. 2005. Statistical methods for eliciting probability distributions. *Journal of the American Statistical Association*, 100(470):680–701.

Gelman, A., Roberts, G., and Gilks, W. Efficient Metropolis jumping rules. In J. Bernardo, J. Berger, A. Dawid, and A. Smith, editors, *Bayesian Statistics*, vol. 5, pp. 599–608, 1996.

Gelman, A., and Rubin, D. 1992. Inference from iterative simulation using multiple sequences. *Statistical Science*, 7(4):457–472.

Genest, C., and Zidek, J. 1986. Combining probability distributions: A critique and an annotated bibliography. *Statistical Science*, 1(1):114–148.

Geweke, J. Bayesian comparison of econometric models. Working Paper 532. Federal Reserve Bank of Minneapolis. 1994.

Geweke, J. Priors for macroeconomic time series and their application. Working Paper 64. Federal Reserve Bank of Minneapolis. 1993b.

Geweke, J. 1989. Bayesian inference in econometric models using Monte Carlo integration. *Econometrica*, 57(6):1317–1339.

Geweke, J. 1993a. Bayesian treatment of the independent Student's *t* linear model. Supplement: Special Issue on Econometric Inference Using Simulation Techniques. *Journal of Applied Econometrics*, 8:S19–S40.

Geweke, J. *Contemporary Bayesian Econometrics and Statistics*. Hoboken NJ: John Wiley & Sons, 2005.

Geyer, C. 1992. Practical Markov Chain Monte Carlo. *Statistical Science*, 7(4):473–481.

Ghysels, E., Harvey, A., and Renault, E. Stochastic volatility. In G. Maddala and C. Rao (eds.), *Statistical Methods in Finance*, Handbook of Statistics 14, pp. 119–191. Amsterdam: Elsevier Science, 1996.

Ghysels, E., McCulloch, R., and Tsay, R. 1998. Bayesian inference for periodic regime-switching models. *Journal of Applied Econometrics*, 13(2):129–143.

Giacometti, R., Bertocchi, M., Rachev, S., and Fabozzi, F. Stable distributions in the Black-Litterman approach to asset allocation. *Quantitative Finance*, forthcoming. 2007.

Gilks, W., Richardson, S., and Spiegelhalter, D. *Markov Chain Monte Carlo in Practice*. Boca Raton, FL: Chapman Hall/CRC, 1996.

Gilks, W. and Wild, P. 1992. Adaptive rejection sampling for Gibbs sampling. *Applied Statistics*, 41(2):337–348.

Glosten, L., Jagannathan, R., and Runkle, D. 1993. On the relation between the expected value and the volatility of the nominal excess return on stocks. *Journal of Finance*, 48(5):1779–1801.

Goldberg, D. *Genetic Algorithms in Search, Optimization, and Machine Learning*. Boston: Addison-Wesley, 1989.

Goldfarb, D., and Iyengar, G. 2003. Robust portfolio selection problems. *Mathematics of Operations Research*, 28(1):1–38.

Grinold, R. 1989. The fundamental law of active management. *Journal of Portfolio Management*, 15(3):30–37.

Grinold, R., and Kahn, R. *Active Portfolio Management: A Quantitative Approach for Producing Superior Returns and Controlling Risk*, 2nd ed. New York: McGraw-Hill, 2000.

Haas, M., Mittnik, S., and Paolella, M. 2004. A new approach to Markov-switching GARCH models. *Journal of Financial Econometrics*, 2(4):493–530.

Hamilton, J. 1989. A new approach to the economic analysis of nonstationary time series and the business cycle. *Econometrica*, 57:357–384.

Hamilton, J., and Susmel, R. 1994. Autoregresive conditional heteroskedasticity and changes in regime. *Journal of Econometrics*, 64:307–333.

Hansen, B. 1994. Autoregressive conditional density estimation. *International Economic Review*, 35(3):705-730.

Harvey, A. *Forecasting, Structural Time Series Models and the Kalman Filter* (reprint). Cambridge: Cambridge University Press, 1991.

Harvey, A., Ruiz, E., and Shephard, N. 1994. Multivariate stochastic variance models. *Review of Economic Studies*, 61(2):247–264.

Harvey, C., Liechty, J., Liechty, M., and Müller, P. Portfolio selection with higher moments. Social Science Research Network. Working Paper Series. 2004. Available at http://papers.ssrn.com.

Harvey, C., and Siddique, A. 2000. Conditional skewness in asset pricing tests. *Journal of Finance*, 55(3):1263–1295.

Harvey, C., and Zhou, G. 1990. Bayesian inference in asset pricing tests. *Journal of Financial Economics*, 26:221–254.

Hastings, W. 1970. Monte Carlo sampling methods using Markov chains and their applications. *Biometrika*, 57(1):97–109.

He, G., and Litterman, R. The intuition behind Black-Litterman model portfolios. Social Science Research Network. Working Paper Series, 1999. Available at http://papers.ssrn.com.

Henneke, J., Rachev, S., and Fabozzi, F. MCMC based estimation of Markov-switching ARMA-GARCH models. Technical Report. Department of Statistics and Applied Probability. University of California, Santa Barbara. 2007.

Herold, U. 2003. Portfolio construction with qualitative forecasts. *Journal of Portfolio Management*, 30(1):61–72.

Hoeting, J., Madigan, D., Raftery, A., and Volinsky, C. 1999. Bayesian model averaging: A tutorial. *Statistical Science*, 14(4):382–417.

Holton, G. 2004. Defining risk. *Financial Analysts Journal*, 60(6):19–25.

Hsieh, D. 1991. Chaos and nonlinear dynamics: Application to financial markets. *Journal of Finance*, 46(5):1839–1877.

Hsu, J. 1995. Generalized Laplacian approximations in Bayesian inference. *The Canadian Journal of Statistics*, 23(4):399–410.

Hull, J., and White, A. 1987. The pricing of options on assets with stochastic volatilities. *Journal of Finance*, 42:281–300.

Hull, J., and White, A. 1987. Pricing of options on assets with stochastic volatilities. *Journal of Finance*, 42(2):281–300.

Jacquier, E., Polson, N., and Rossi, P. 1994. Bayesian analysis of stochastic volatility models. *Journal of Business and Economic Statistics*, 12(4):371–389.

Jacquier, E., Polson, N., and Rossi, P. 2004. Bayesian analysis of stochastic volatility models with fat-tails and correlated errors. *Journal of Econometrics*, (122):185–212.

Jeffreys, H. *Theory of Probability*. New York: Oxford University Press, 1961.

Jegadeesh, N., and Titman, S. 1993. Returns to buying winners and selling losers: Implications for stock market efficiency. *Journal of Finance*, 48(1):65–91.

Jobson, J., and Korkie, B. 1980. Estimation for Markowitz efficient portfolios. *Journal of the American Statistical Association*, 75(371):544–554.

Jobson, J., Korkie, B., and Ratti, V. Improved estimation for Markowitz portfolios using James-Stein type estimators. *Proceedings of the American Statistical Association, Business and Economic Statistics Section*, 1979.

Johnson, N., Kotz, S., and Balakrishnan, N. *Continuous Univariate Distributions, Vol 1*. New York: John Wiley & Sons, 2nd ed, 1994.

Johnson, R., and Wichern, D. *Applied Multivariate Statistical Analysis*. Upper Saddle River, NJ: Prentice Hall, 2002.

Jones, M., and Faddy, M. 2003. A skew extension of the *t* distribution, with applications. *Journal of the Royal Statistical Society, Series B*, 65:159–174.

Jorion, P. 1986. Bayes-Stein estimation for portfolio analysis. *Journal of Financial and Quantitative Analysis*, 21(3):279–292.

Jorion, P. 1991. Bayesian and CAPM estimators of the means: Implications for portfolio selection. *Journal of Banking and Finance*, 15(3):717–727.

Jorion, P. 1992. Portfolio optimization in practice. *Financial Analysts Journal*, 48(1):68–75.

Kandel, S., McCulloch, R., and Stambaugh, R. 1987. Bayesian inference and portfolio efficiency. *Review of Financial Studies*, 8(1):1–53.

Kandel, S., and Stambaugh, R. 1996. On the predictability of stock returns: An asset-allocation perspective. *Journal of Finance*, 51(2):385–424.

Kass, R., Tierney, L., and Kadane, J. 1989. Approximate methods for assessing influence and sensitivity in Bayesian analysis. *Biometrika*, 76(4):663–674.

Kass, R., and Wasserman, L. 1996. The selection of prior distributions by formal rules. *Journal of the American Statistical Association*, 91(435):1343–1370.

Khindanova, I., and Rachev, S. Value-at-risk: Recent advances. In G. Anastassiou (ed.), *Handbook of Analytic-Computational Methods in Applied Mathematics*, pp. 801–858. Boca Raton, FL: Chapman & Hall/CRC, 2000.

Kim, C., and Nelson, C. 1999. Has the U.S. economy become more stable? A Bayesian approach based on a Markov-switching model of the business cycle. *The Review of Economics and Statistics*, 81(4):608–616.

Kim, S., Shephard, N., and Chib, S. 1998. Stochastic volatility: Likelihood inference and comparison with ARCH models. *Review of Economic Studies*, 65(3):361–393.

Klaassen, F. Improving GARCH volatility forecasts. Social Science Research Network. Working Paper Series, 1998. Available at http://papers.ssrn.com.

Koopman, S. 1993. Disturbance smoother for state space models. *Biometrika*, 80(1):117–126.

Koopman, S., Shephard, N., and Doornik, J. 1999. Statistical algorithms for models in state space using SsfPack 2.2. *Econometrics Journal*, 2:107–160.

Kotz, S., Balakrishnan, N., and Johnson, N. *Continuous Multivariate Distributions, Models and Applications, vol. 1*. New York: John Wiley & Sons, 2nd ed., 2000.

Kraus, A. and Litzenberger, R. 1976. Skewness preferences and the valuation of risk assets. *Journal of Finance*, 31(4):1085–1100.

Lamantia, F., Ortobelli, S., and Rachev, S. 2006. An empirical comparison among VaR models and time rules with elliptical and stable distributed returns. *Investment Management and Financial Innovations*, 3(1):8–29.

Lamantia, F., Ortobelli, S., and Rachev, S. 2006. VaR, CVaR, and time rules with elliptical and asymmetric stable distributed returns. *Investment Management and Financial Innovations*, 4(1):19–39.

Lamoureux, C., and Lastrapes, W. 1990. Persistence in variance, structural change, and the GARCH model. *Journal of Business and Economic Statistics*, 8(2):225–234.

Larsen, G., and Resnick, B. 2001. Parameter estimation techniques, optimization frequency, and portfolio return enhancement. *Journal of Portfolio Management*, 27(4):27–34.

Ledoit, O., and Wolf, M. 2003. Improved estimation of the covariance matrix of stock returns with an application to portfolio selection. *Journal of Empirical Finance*, 10(5):603–621.

Leonard, T. 1982. Comment on "A simple predictive density function." *Journal of the American Statistical Association*, 77:657–658.

Leonard, T., and Hsu, J. *Bayesian Methods: An Analysis for Statisticians and Interdisciplinary Researchers*. Cambridge: Cambridge University Press, 1999.

Leonard, T., Hsu, J., and Tsui, K. 1989. Bayesian marginal inference. *Journal of the American Statistical Association*, 84(408):1051–1058.

Litterman, R., and the Quantitative Resources Group. Goldman Sachs Asset Management. *Modern Investment Management: An Equilibrium Approach*. Hoboken, NJ: John Wiley & Sons, 2003.

Litterman, R., and Winkelmann, K. Estimating covariance matrices. *Risk Management Series*. Goldman Sachs, 1998.

Lo, A., and MacKinlay, A. 1990. Data-snooping biases in tests of financial asset pricing models. *Review of Financial Studies*, 3(3):431–468.

Madigan, D., and Raftery, A. 1994. Model selection and accounting for model uncertainty in graphical models using Occam's window. *Journal of the American Statistical Association*, 89(428):1335–1346.

Mahieu, R., and Schotman, P. 1998. An empirical application of stochastic volatility models. *Journal of Applied Econometrics*, 13(4):333–359.

Mandelbrot, B. 1963. The variation of certain speculative prices. *Journal of Business*, 36(4):394–419.

Markowitz, H. 1952. Portfolio selection. *Journal of Finance*, 7(1):77–91.

Markowitz, H. *Portfolio Selection: Efficient Diversification of Investments*. New York: Blackwell, 1959.

Markowitz, H. Autobiography. In Tore Frängsmyr (ed.), *Les Prix Nobel. The Nobel Prizes 1990*. Nobel Foundation, 1991.

Markowitz, H., and Usmen, N. 1996. The likelihood of various stock market return distributions, part I: Principles of inference. *Journal of Risk and Uncertainty*, 13:207–219.

McCullagh, P., and Nelder, J. *Generalized Linear Models*, 2nd ed. Boca Raton, FL: Chapman and Hall/CRC, 1989.

McCulloch, R., and Rossi, P. 1990. Posterior, predictive, and utility-based approaches to testing the Arbitrage Pricing Theory. *Journal of Financial Economics*, 28(1):7–38.

McNeil, A., Frey, R., and Embrechts, P. *Quantitative Risk Management: Concepts, Techniques and Tools*. Princeton, NJ: Princeton University Press, 2005.

Merton, R. 1980. An analytic derivation of the efficient portfolio frontier. *Journal of Financial and Quantitative Analysis*, 7(4):1851–1872.

Metropolis, N., Rosenbluth, A., Rosenbluth, M., Teller, A., and Teller, E. 1953. Equation of state calculations by fast computing machines. *Journal of Chemical Physics*, 21(6):1087–1092.

Meucci, A. Beyond Black-Litterman in practice: A five-step recipe to input views on non-normal markets. Working Paper. 2006b. Available at www.symmys.com.

Meucci, A. February 2006b. Beyond Black-Litterman: Views on non-normal markets. *Journal of Risk*.

Michaud, R. *Efficient Asset Management: A Practical Guide to Stock Portfolio Optimization*. New York: Oxford University Press, 1998.

Mittnik, S., and Paolella, M. 2000. Conditional density and value-at-risk prediction of Asian currency exchange rates. *Journal of Forecasting*, 19(4):313–333.

Neil, M., Fenton, N., and Tailor, M. 2005. Using Bayesian networks to model expected and unexpected operational losses. *Risk Analysis*, 25(4):963–972.

Nelson, D. 1991. Conditional heteroskedasticity in asset returns: A new approach. *Econometrica*, 59(2):347–370.

Nelson, D., and Foster, D. 1994. Asymptotic filtering theory for univariate ARCH models. *Econometrica*, 62(1):1–41.

Norris, J. *Markov Chains*. Cambridge: Cambridge University Press, 1998.

Omori, Y., Chib, S., Shephard, N., and Nakajima, J. Stochastic volatility with leverage: Fast and efficient likelihood inference. *Journal of Econometrics*, 2006. doi:10.1016/j.jeconom.2006.07.008.

Ortobelli, S., Rachev, S., Stoyanov, S., Fabozzi, F., and Biglova, A. 2005. The proper use of risk measures in portfolio theory. *International Journal of Theoretical and Applied Finance*, 8(8):1107–1133.

Palm, F. GARCH models of volatility. In G. Maddala and C. Rao (eds.), *Statistical Methods in Finance*: *Handbook of Statistics 14*, pp. 209–240. Amsterdam: Elsevier Science, 1996.

Pástor, L. 2000. Portfolio selection and asset pricing models. *Journal of Finance*, 55(1):179–223.

Pástor, L. and Stambaugh, R. 1999. Costs of equity capital and model mispricing. *Journal of Finance*, 54(1):67–121.

Pelikan, M. *Hierarchical Bayesian Optimization Algorithm: Toward a New Generation of Evolutionary Algorithm*. Berlin: Springer, 2005.

Rachev, S., Khindanova, I., and Schwartz, E. 2001. Stable modeling of value-at-risk. *Mathematical and Computer Modeling*, 34(9):1223–1259.

Rachev, S., Martin, D., Racheva-Iotova, B., and Stoyanov, S. Stable ETL optimal portfolios and extreme risk management. In *Decisions in Banking and Finance*. Berlin: Springer/Physika, 2007.

Rachev, S., Menn, C., and Fabozzi, F. *Fat-Tailed and Skewed Asset Return Distributions: Implications for Risk Management, Portfolio selection, and Option Pricing*. Hoboken, NJ: John Wiley & Sons, 2005.

Rachev, S., and Mittnik, S. *Stable Paretian Models in Finance*. New York: John Wiley & Sons, 2000.

Rachev, S., Mittnik, S., Fabozzi, F., Foccardi, S., and Jasić, T. *Financial Econometrics: From Basics to Advanced Modeling Techniques*. Hoboken, NJ: John Wiley & Sons, 2007.

Rachev, S., Ortobelli, S., and Schwartz, E. The problem of optimal asset allocation with stable distributed returns. In A. Krinik and R. Swift (eds.), *Stochastic Processes and Functional Analysis: A Volume of Recent Advances in Honor of M. M. Rao*, Lecture Notes in Pure and Applied Mathematics, pp. 295–347. New York: Marcel Dekker, 2004.

Rachev, S., Ortobelli, S., Stoyanov, S., and Fabozzi, F. Desirable properties of an ideal risk measure in portfolio theory. *International Journal of Theoretical and Applied Finance*, forthcoming (2007).

Rachev, S., and Rüschendorf, L. 1994. On the Cox, Ross, and Rubinstein model for option pricing. *Theory of Probability and its Applications*, 39(1):150–190.

Rachev, S., Stoyanov, S., Biglova, A., and Fabozzi, F. An empirical examination of daily stock return distributions for U.S. stocks. In D. Baier, R. Decker, and L. Schmidt-Thieme (eds.), *Data Analysis and Decision Support*, Studies in Classification, Data Analysis, and Knowledge Organization. Berlin: Springer, 2005.

Rachev, S., Stoyanov, S., and Fabozzi, F. *Advanced Stochastic Models, Risk Assessment, and Portfolio Optimization: The Ideal Risk, Uncertainty, and Performance Measures*. Hoboken, NJ: John Wiley & Sons, 2007.

Rockafellar, R., and Uryasev, S. 2000. Optimization of conditional value-at-risk. *Journal of Risk*, 2(3):21–41.

Rockafellar, R., and Uryasev, S. 2002. Conditional value-at-risk for general loss distributions. *Journal of Banking and Finance*, 26(7):1443–1471.

Rockafellar, T., Uryasev, S., and Zabarankin, M. Portfolio analysis with general deviation measures. Industrial and Systems Engineering Research Report No. 2003-8. University of Florida, 2003.

Roll, R. 1977. A critique of the Asset Pricing Theory's tests—Part I: On past and potential testability of the theory. *Journal of Financial Economics*, 4(1):129–176.

Rouwenhorst, G. 1998. International momentum strategies. *Journal of Finance*, 53:267–283.

Rubinstein, M. 1973. A comparative static analysis of risk premium. *Journal of Business*, 46(2):605–615.

Sahu, S., Dey, D., and Branco, M. 2003. A new class of multivariate skew distributions with applications to Bayesian regression models. *The Canadian Journal of Statistics*, 29(2):125–150.

Satchell, S., and Scowcroft, A. 2000. A demystification of the Black-Litterman model: Managing quantitative and traditional portfolio construction. *Journal of Asset Management*, 1(2):138–150.

Scherer, B. 2002. Portfolio resampling: Review and critique. *Financial Analysts Journal*, 58(6):98–109.

Sharpe, W. 1963. A simplified model for portfolio analysis. *Management Science*, 9:277–293.

Sharpe, W. 1994. The Sharpe ratio. *Journal of Portfolio Management*, 21(1):49–58.

Shephard, N., editor. *Stochastic Volatility: Selected Readings*. New York: Oxford University Press, 2005.

So, M., Lam, K., and Li, W. 1998. A stochastic volatility model with Markov switching. *Journal of Business and Economic Statistics*, 16(2):244–253.

Sortino, F. 2000. Upside-potential ratios vary by investment style. *Pensions and Investments*, 28:30–35.

Sortino, F., and Satchell, S. (eds). *Managing Downside Risk in Financial Markets*. Oxford: Butterworth-Heinemann, 2001.

Stambaugh, R. 1997. Analyzing investments whose histories differ in length. *Journal of Financial Economics*, 45(2):285–331.

Stambaugh, R. 1999. Predictive regressions. *Journal of Financial Economics*, 54(2):375–421.

Stein, J. Inadmissibility of the usual estimator for the mean of a multivariate distribution. *Proceedings of the Third Berkeley Symposium on Mathematics Statistics and Probability*, 1:197–206. University of California Press. 1956.

Stroud, J., Müller, P., and Polson, N. 2003. Nonlinear state-space models with state-dependent variances. *Journal of the American Statistical Association*, 98(462):377–386.

Tauchen, R., and Pitts, M. 1983. The price variability-volume relationship on speculative markets. *Econometrica*, 51(2):485–505.

Taylor, S. Financial returns modeled by the product of two stochastic processes—a study of daily sugar prices 1961-79. In O. Anderson (ed.), *Time Series Analysis: Theory and Practice I*, pp. 203–226. Amsterdam: Elsevier Science, 1982.

Taylor, S. *Modeling Financial Time Series*. New York: John Wiley & Sons, 1986.

Taylor, S. *Asset Price Dynamics, Volatility, and Prediction*. Princeton, NJ: Princeton University Press, 2005.

Tierney, L., and Kadane, J. 1986. Accurate approximations for posterior moments and marginal densities. *Journal of the American Statistical Association*, 81(393):82–86.

Treynor, J., and Black, F. 1973. How to use security analysis to improve portfolio selection. *Journal of Business*, 46(1):66–86.

van Dyk, D., and Meng, X. 2001. The art of data augmentation (with discussion). *Journal of Computational and Graphical Statistics*, 10(1):1–111.

Wang, J., and Zivot, E. 2000. A Bayesian time series model of multiple structural changes in level, trend, and variance. *Journal of Business and Economic Statistics*, 18(3):374–386.

Wang, Z. 1998. Efficiency loss and constraints on portfolio holdings. *Journal of Financial Economics*, 48(2):359–375.

West, M., and Harrison, J. *Bayesian Forecasting and Dynamic Models*, 2nd ed. Berlin: Springer, 1997.

Wild, P., and Gilks, W. 1992. Algorithm AS 287: Adaptive rejection sampling from log-concave density functions. *Applied Statistics*, 42(4):701–709.

Winkelmann, K. 2004. Improving portfolio efficiency. *Journal of Portfolio Management*, 30(2):23–38.

Yamai, Y., and Yoshiba, T. Comparative analyses of expected shortfall and value-at-risk: Their estimation, error, decomposition, and optimization. *Monetary and Economic Studies*, 87–121, January, 2002.

Young, M. 1998. A minimax portfolio selection rule with linear programming solution. *Management Science*, 44(5):673–683.

Yu, B., and Mykland, P. Looking at Markov samplers through cusum path plots: A simple diagnostic idea. Technical Report No. 413. Department of Statistics. University of California, Berkeley, 1994.

Zellner, A. *An Introduction to Bayesian Inference in Econometrics*. New York: John Wiley & Sons, 1971.

Zhang, Y., and Rachev, S. 2006. Risk attributions and portfolio performance measurements. *Journal of Applied Functional Analysis*, 4(1):373–402.

Index